Health, Heal the Amuse System

Humor as Survival Training*

Third Edition

Paul E. McGhee, Ph.D.

*Formerly known as How to Develop Your Sense of Humor:
An 8-Step Humor Development Training Program

KENDALL/HUNT PUBLISHING COMPANY
4050 Westmark Drive   Dubuque, Iowa 52002

CONTENTS

Contents

Part II: The Steps

Step 5: **Find Humor in Everyday Life 171**

Step 6: **Take Yourself Lightly Laugh at Yourself 195**

Contents

INTRODUCTION

> **"**Laughter is the most inexpensive and the most effective wonder drug. Laughter is a universal medicine.**"**
>
> (Bertrand Russell)

How do you make God laugh? Make Plans.

This book provides an 8-Step program for learning how to use your sense of humor to survive the ever-increasing levels of stress in our lives. It is the first training program designed to give you access to the many benefits your amuse system offers.

Research in recent years has pointed increasingly to key physical and mental health benefits that result from humor and laughter. As awareness of these benefits has grown, so has interest in developing one's own humor skills in order to obtain them. Stressed-out employees, patients coping with serious illnesses or recovering from serious injuries, people interested in personal growth, managers who want to communicate more effectively or boost employee productivity, parents trying to cope with raising kids, self-help and support groups—all want to learn to lighten up. Women have become especially interested in developing their sense of humor, because they've long felt relegated to the position of responding to men's humor.

Liz Carpenter worked in the White House during the Johnson administration. After she wrote a book about her experiences in the White House, Arthur Schlesinger, Jr. came up to her at a cocktail party and said, "I liked your book Liz, who wrote it for you?" Her immediate reaction was, "I'm glad you liked it Arthur, who read it to you?" Women who want to develop this kind of quick wit, but who have no experience generating their own humor, will find this book a valuable resource for creating the basic humor skills required to generate spontaneous witty remarks.

The 8-Step Humor Development Training Program is especially designed for the humor impaired, but you'll still benefit if you already have a good sense of humor. Consider yourself humor impaired if you've forgotten how—or never learned—to enjoy and produce humor. You're also humor impaired if you don't know how to lighten up and be playful. Your job and life experiences may have led you to suffer from the condition I call "Terminal Seriousness" (see Step 2). If this sounds like you, or someone you love, you need to know that TS can be a killer. It kills the quality of your life! It kills the sense of aliveness, joy, and fun in your life. It can even kill your effectiveness on the job, because it sets you up for extra stress—both on the job and in your personal life.

We generally assume that it's the serious employee who is most effective on the job. But if you take two equally competent employees doing the same job, the one with TS will be less effective in the long run, not more, because s/he will be more vulnerable to stress, experience more burnout, and suffer from lower morale and job satisfaction. S/he will be less resilient in the face of ever-growing job demands, unpredictable crises, and the uncertainty of permanent employment.

Acquired Amusement Deficiency Syndrome (AADS)

If you are someone who is serious all the time, you probably suffer from AADS—Acquired Amusement Deficiency Syndrome. In fact, Terminal Seriousness is the #1 symptom of AADS (see box below). AADS poses just as much of a threat to the quality of your life as AIDS does to the length of your life. Most people don't appreciate the quality of their life until it's taken away by an accident, disease, or other event which suddenly transforms their life. AADS gradually erodes your capacity to tap into the joyfulness of life, so that you don't even realize that you've lost it.

People suffering from AADS need an attitude adjustment. When your spine gets out of alignment, everything you do causes pain or discomfort. It interferes with every aspect of your daily life, and adds an extra obstacle to being effective on the job. A spinal adjustment by a good chiropractor, however, can eliminate the problem and re-establish a normal daily life.

Top 8 Symptoms of AADS

8. When in a restaurant with a group, gets out a calculator to divide up the bill.
7. Idea of fun is to spend a few extra hours on the weekend working to get ahead of competitors.
6. Preferred bed time reading is the annual report.
5. Prone to making mountains out of mole hills.
4. Emotional constipation.
3. Difficulty swallowing humor.
2. Persistent soreness about almost everything
1. Terminal Seriousness.

When you're serious all the time, your attitude gets out of adjustment, setting you up for persistent negative moods, with no counterbalancing positive ones. You need something which provides the attitudinal equivalent of going to a chiropractor. This Humor Development Training Program provides the needed adjustment. As you move through the eight steps, you will develop skills which give you greater control over the daily attitude you bring to your job, your relationships—your life. You will learn to generate a more positive and playful approach to life, and to prevent premature hardening of the attitudes.

Purpose of the 8-Step Program

The 8-Step Program is not designed to make you a comedy writer or stand-up comedian. Rather, it shows you how to build up the basic skills needed to use your sense of humor effectively on your job, and to cope with the stress in your life. You may eventually use these skills to pursue a career in comedy, but the program is geared toward those who have never made an effort to develop their sense of humor. It will improve fundamental skills at playing with language, finding humor in your own life, laughing at yourself, and most importantly, using humor to cope with stress. If you've joined the ranks of the humor impaired, your own natural sense of humor will re-emerge and be strengthened.

To fully benefit from the program, you need to **want** to develop your sense of humor. So ask yourself right now, "Am I suffering from AADS? Do I really want a better sense of humor? Do I want it enough to commit myself to a few months of fun while gradually building up my humor skills?"

These may seem like silly questions, since everyone knows it's important to have a good sense of humor. But improving your sense of humor involves developing some new intellectual, social, and emotional skills and habits; and like any other skill, it takes effort and persistence on your part to make real changes.

I often ask my audiences, "How many of you wish the people you work with had a better sense of humor?" Most of the hands go up. "How many of you wish your spouse had a better sense of humor?" Again, most of the hands go up—at least when spouses are not present. We all enjoy being around people who have a good sense of humor. And this is not restricted to those who are constantly telling jokes or funny stories. We just enjoy being around someone who knows how to be playful; someone who can lighten up and isn't deadly serious all the time. These people make day-to-day life more enjoyable, whether we're working with them, living with them, or buying something from them. If you're not now one of these people, you will be by the time you get to Step 8.

We want the other people in our lives to have a better sense of humor, but it doesn't occur to us that they would also like us to lighten up. As my audiences see most of the other hands go up, it gradually dawns on them that, "Wait a minute, they're talking about me! They want me to lighten up!" This is important for you to realize, since it will help sustain your commitment to go through all eight steps of the program.

Your Sense of Humor Is a Set of Skills

In going through the 8-Step Program, you will develop a new set of attitudinal, intellectual, social, emotional, and "expressive" skills.

Attitudinal

As noted above, the most important thing you'll obtain from the 8-Step Program is an attitude adjustment. You'll develop an attitude which allows you to appreciate the incongruous, absurd, ridiculous, and bizarre things which occur—both in the real world and in your own imagination. Most people want to immediately learn techniques they can use when under stress, but cultivating this general attitude in yourself is much more important than any specific techniques you might learn.

As children, we all had the seeds of this attitude, and our lives were filled with fun and laughter. It showed up as a love of play, including both physical play and play with ideas. You will see in Step 2 that the ability to adopt a playful frame of mind is the basic foundation for your sense of humor. But many adults lose their playfulness as they grow older and face the harsh challenges of life. In the process, they lose a powerful tool that would help them cope with those challenges.

Those who suffer from AADS fail to see that you can take your problems and commitments seriously without being a serious person all the time. They don't realize that taking yourself too seriously can actually interfere with your ability to handle your problems effectively. That's why the 8-Step Program starts by re-developing your basic sense of playfulness.

The goal is not to become someone who is playful all the time, but to have access to playfulness when you want to lighten up. Finding a way to respond playfully under conditions which normally make you feel angry, anxious, or depressed is a skill that can be developed; but it will not come easily—especially at first. Your effort will be rewarded, however, as it opens the doors to more joy, aliveness, and fun in your life.

This does not mean that you should deny either your feelings or the reality of the problems you face. We all know people who use their sense of humor to hide from problems; but if you are committed to dealing with yours, playfulness and humor will help maintain a frame of mind that enables you to cope with them more effectively.

Intellectual

Since humor is really a form of play with ideas (see Step 2), it is most essentially an intellectual skill. Steps 4, 5, and 6 will focus on specific techniques for honing the intellectual aspects of your sense of humor. Some of these techniques involve playing with language, while others involve sensitizing yourself to seeing humor in everyday life. Still others help you learn to poke fun at yourself.

With practice, you may approach the level of spontaneous verbal wit shown by Groucho Marx. Groucho had a popular television show called *You Bet Your Life* in the 1950s. One day a woman from Iowa was on the show, and she told Groucho she had eight kids. He said, "Eight kids! That's amazing. How come you have so many kids?"

"Well," she answered, "I guess my husband just likes me." Without hesitating, Groucho quipped, "Yeah, well I like my cigar too, but sometimes I take it out!"

Social

Humor is an important social skill. It helps you communicate more effectively, handle conflict situations, and persuade others to adopt your own point of view. It also makes you more likeable and has a major impact on the extent to which others see you as socially competent.

Being a good judge of when humor of any kind is and is not appropriate is another essential skill to develop. You also need to be sensitive to the kinds of humor that are and are not appropriate, depending on who is present, events that have occurred recently, and so forth. This means that you must be sensitive to social norms, stereotypes, and traditions associated with different groups.

Emotional

If you're like most people, your sense of humor disappears when you're under stress, or when you get angry, anxious, sad, or depressed. Embarrassment and other emotions also keep you from laughing at yourself. You develop emotional humor skills as you learn to find or create humor in the midst of these negative emotions. In the process, you gain greater control over them. Instead of being a victim of the emotion of the moment, you take charge and substitute a more positive emotional state—one which leaves you in a better frame of mind to deal effectively with the problem that produced the negative emotions to begin with. Making the effort to first use your sense of humor in the absence of any emotional turmoil (in Steps 1–6) gradually improves your ability to use it in more stressful circumstances.

Expressive

Finally, the expressive aspects of your sense of humor can be viewed as a skill. Some people are very good at expressing emotions, while others hold them in; and laughter is one form of emotional expression. Belly laughter isn't always appropriate, but the ability to express your amusement openly makes an important contribution to mental and physical health. Learning to laugh freely and heartily also opens you up to being more emotionally expressive in general.

Is It Too Late to Improve Your Sense of Humor?

Many people think that you're either born with a good sense of humor or you're not, and there's not much you can do about it. But humor skills can be learned, just as other skills are learned. We all had the same starting potential for a great sense of humor as kids. Some of us (and our parents) simply nurtured that potential in growing up, while others did not.

In one study of the development of humor skills, high school teachers attended 14 humor "training sessions" (with 20 hours total contact time).[1] The program was designed to first increase participants' understanding of the importance and benefits of humor in their life, and then to strengthen attitudes (such as a playful attitude), confront emotional barriers to using one's sense of humor (e.g., "I'm really not very funny"), and build specific skills for appreciating and producing humor. The study showed that teachers' overall attitude toward humor did not change, because their views of the importance of humor were already very high. They did, however, rate themselves at the end of the study as having learned the techniques required to produce humor. Other teachers also rated them after the sessions as having better skills at creating humor and making others laugh.

There is also evidence that adults can learn to use humor to cope better with life stress. Even a 5-session humor workshop was effective in improving adults' use of humor to cope with life stress.[2]

A recent study has examined the effectiveness of the 8-Step Humor Skills Program presented in this book in helping older adults improve their coping skills.[3] Using senior citizens living in a retirement community, one group spent 8 weeks going through the 8-Step Program in the manner described in this book, while a second group simply got together weekly to view comedy films. So the first group made an active effort to improve their humor skills, while the second group was passively engaged in humor without working on skill improvement.

While the two groups showed similar coping abilities at the beginning of the study, the group going through the Humor Skills Program scored significantly higher than the "passive" humor group on two different measures of coping at the end of the 8 weeks. The humor training group also scored higher at the end of the study on the "Humor under Stress" subscale presented at the back of this book (there were no group differences at the beginning of the study). Going through the 8-Step Program, then, not only helped these seniors cope better with the stress in their lives; they actually learned to use humor as a coping tool on high stress days.

So you're never to old to learn to use humor to cope with the stress in your own life. Whether you're 20, 50, or 70 years old, you can learn to lighten up! Remember, a good sense of humor helps prevent hardening of the attitudes.

If your goal is to become a comedy writer or a stand-up comedian, it may be too late for you. But it's never too late to rekindle the playfulness you once had or learn to play with language, find humor in your own life, and poke fun at yourself. It will, however, take some time and effort on your part. You don't become skilled at a sport, your job, driving a car, or any other activity without working at it—and without wanting to get better at it. But the great thing about working on your sense of humor is that it's not work at all. It's fun! If you're like most people who go through the 8-Step Program, you'll quickly decide that you'll never be without this source of joy in your life again.

Overview of the Book

Part I: The Work and Health Benefits of Your Amuse System

In order to stick with the 8-Step Program, you'll need to be convinced of the benefits you'll receive from doing so. Part I discusses the exciting research evidence demonstrating the benefits associated with humor and laughter, including their impact on the quality of your life. Chapter 1 documents the ways in which humor and fun boost productivity and quality of service. Chapter 2 focuses on the ways in which humor and laughter contribute to physical health, while Chapter 3 discusses the evidence demonstrating their ability to help you cope with stress. Be sure to read these chapters before beginning Step 1.

Part II: The Steps

Part II shows you what to do in order to build up the full range of skills needed to use your amuse system to cope with stress. Step 1 invites you to immerse yourself in humor in as many ways as you can in order to get a better sense of the kinds of humor you do and do not like. It also guides you toward an analysis of your present sense of humor, including both its strengths and weaknesses and early and current influences on its development.

Step 2 shows you how to overcome Terminal Seriousness and become more playful. Playfulness is shown to be the basic foundation for your sense of humor. As you become more comfortable with adopting a playful attitude in life, your own natural sense of humor emerges. This step is especially important for anyone now suffering from AADS.

Step 3 gives you the opportunity to work on being more expressive of your enjoyment of humor when you do find something funny. That is, it nurtures your ability to have a good belly laugh every day. It also eases you into using your sense of humor in an active manner by building up your skill at telling jokes. Step 4 further develops your verbal sense of humor by improving your ability to generate your own puns and other forms of verbal humor.

John and Lorena Bobbit have accepted new jobs. She's working with Chicago Cutlery, and he's with Snap On Tools.

Step 5 shows you how to find humor in your every day life—an essential skill for learning to use humor to cope with stress. You are asked to continue utilizing the skills already developed as you move on to succeeding steps.

Steps 6 and 7 focus on the most difficult parts of your sense of humor to develop. Step 6 demonstrates how to learn to laugh at yourself, including both qualities of yourself about which you are sensitive and embarrassing incidents or personal blunders. Step 7 invites you to use all the skills developed to this point and to apply them in stressful situations.

While memorized jokes and stories are considered here to be less important than spontaneous forms of humor, a good joke can sometimes help you poke fun at yourself or cope with annoying life circumstances. The following joke, for example, might be used to express your attitudes toward certain aspects of the present health care system.

A couple in their 70s goes to the doctor and says, "Doctor, we'd like you to check us out having sexual intercourse."

The doctor looks a bit puzzled, but agrees. After watching them, he says, "Well, I don't see anything wrong with the way you're having sex." So they pay him $40 and go on their way.

Two weeks later, the same couple comes in and again asks the doctor to watch them having sex. He gives the same evaluation, so they pay the $40 and go on their way.

This goes on for a several visits, and the doctor finally asks, "Why do you keep coming back here? You don't have any sexual problems."

The old man says, "Well, you see, I'm married, so we can't go to my place. And she's married, so we can't go to her place. And the Holiday Inn costs $75. So we come here, and it costs us $40. We bill it to Medicaid and get $37 back for a visit to the doctor's office."

The basic rationale behind the 8-Step Program is to first develop the basic humor skills required to use humor to cope when you're in a good mood and not under stress. Once you get better at adopting a playful attitude, generating your own jokes and other verbal humor, laughing heartily, and poking fun at yourself, it is easier to continue doing the same things in stressful situations. Most people want to move right to Step 7 and use humor to cope with stress, but those who do this generally aren't very successful. Remember that humor is a set of skills, and—as with all skills—you have to learn to walk before you can run.

Finally, Step 8 allows you to integrate everything you've learned in the first seven steps. By the time you get to this point, you may have let skills associated with some of the earlier steps slide. So Step 8 gives you the opportunity to consciously work at using each set of skills on a daily basis. Once you've done this for a couple of weeks or so, they'll become more firmly entrenched within you and will become a more permanent part of your coping style. Your survival training is then complete.

The Homeplay

The Homeplay is the most important feature of the 8-Step Program. It shows you the kinds of things you need to be doing from week to week in order to develop the skills associated with each step. In most cases, you probably won't be able to do all the things suggested in the Homeplay within a given week. However, I have seen many people go through the program, and it is clear that the amount of improvement you make is directly related to the time and effort you put into the Homeplay. Those who do most of the Homeplay each week are the ones who wind up being able to use humor to cope with stress.

As you move from one step to the next, you should focus your attention on the Homeplay for the new step. As the same time, try to sustain the habits you've adopted while working on the previous step. This will take less time than you think, since much of the Homeplay will become something you do automatically. You will learn to do it without thinking about it, and without taking time away from work or other activities you may be engaged in.

The Pre-Test and Post-Test

You will find at the back of this book a humor pre-test and post-test. The pre-test assesses your current sense of humor prior to beginning the 8-Step Program, along with key attitudes and moods which support the use of your sense of humor. Be sure to complete it before starting Step 1. Do not look at your answers to the pre-test until after you've completed the post-test. The post-test should be completed only after you have spent a week or two on Step 8, integrating all the skills you've learned in the Program.

An earlier version of this test has been shown to have good internal consistency, although both Americans and Germans have been shown to rate themselves higher than the mid-point of the scale.[4] This is consistent with the common observation that most people don't want to admit to having a poor sense of humor. In order to best determine how much you gain in going through this program, it is essential that you rate yourself honestly on both the pre- and post-test.

Completing the 8-Step Program as a Group

This book allows you to go through the program either alone or as part of a group. If you are doing this by yourself, make it a point to seek out someone to whom you can talk about things you're working on at the moment. This might be a friend, co-worker, or your spouse—anyone with whom you feel comfortable sharing your ideas, feelings, funny things you've noticed, successes, failures, etc. Ideally, you'll find a partner who can go through the steps with you. Those who have a partner generally make more progress—and make it more rapidly—than individuals who go through the program alone. A partner helps keep you focused on doing the Homeplay on a regular basis.

The 8-Step Program is ideally suited for use by groups of managers or other teams of employees within the work place. The "Group Session" section contains guidelines and suggestions for how to operate a group meeting in which all members of the group are completing the program as a unit. Ideally, you will have a special time designated for humor group meetings on a regular basis (weekly, bi-weekly, or monthly). The meetings have more impact if the focus is clearly on the humor skills program, and not on other company issues.

The meeting should be at least one hour long, and preferably two. You'll find that it takes this long to talk about all the things you're working on, and you'll get into interesting issues beyond the ones I've proposed for discussion. If yours is like most groups, you'll hate to stop at the end of two hours.

If you're unable to schedule a separate meeting for group sessions, try extending an already-existing departmental or unit meeting for an additional 30–60 minutes. This approach is generally less satisfactory, since the focus is only partly on the humor program per se. It is better than no meeting at all, however. Depending on the nature of your group, you can also try weekly meetings over lunch. This generally works better with smaller than with larger groups.

If you're going through the 8-Step Program within the context of a self-help group, patient support group, Alcoholics Anonymous group, or any other group that meets on a monthly or weekly basis, you may choose to select a sequence of eight meetings and devote all of the meetings to the 8-Step Program.

You will be asked in Step 1 to create telephone teams of three. Each person in the group will have two other people within the group whom they agree to talk to each week

Addictions / Dependencies

Alcohol
Co-Dependency
Debt / Overspending
Drug Abuse
Gambling
Overeating
Sex & Love Addiction
Smoking / Nicotine

Patient Groups: Physical Health

A.I.D.S.
Alzheimer's
Arthritis
Cancer
Chronic Fatigue Syndrome
Eating Disorders
Heart Disease
Multiple Sclerosis
Overweight
Pain, Chronic
Parkinson's

Bereavement

Disabilities

Amputation / Limb Deficiency
Blindness / Visual Impairment
Burn Survivors
Cerebral Palsy
Deaf / Hearing Impaired
Head Injury
Other Physical Disabilities

Patient Groups: Mental Health

Anxiety / Panic Attacks
Depression
Families of Mentally Ill
Obsessive-Compulsive

Others

Caregivers
Parents
Senior Citizens
Sexual Orientation
Singles

about how they are doing on the Homeplay. You can also talk about any other humor issues which come up for you during the week. This is an essential part of making the program work for you, since it assures that you'll keep humor on the "front burner." Remember, humor generally occurs in a social context; so you'll want to develop the habit of sharing your humor as you go along.

Who Will Benefit from the 8-Step Program?

Anyone who wants to improve their sense of humor, and learn how to use humor to cope with stress, will benefit from this humor training program. Even if you have Terminal Seriousness, and are suffering from AADS, you will learn to become more playful, create your own jokes and other verbal humor, find humor in everyday life situations, and laugh at yourself.

Management teams and other employees within corporations will benefit in two ways from improving their humor skills. They will receive the physical and mental health benefits resulting from humor themselves. These benefits will, in turn, improve their effectiveness on the job, thereby contributing to the corporation's health at the same time.

Support groups and self-help groups will also benefit from the 8-Step Program. People are generally very serious in these groups, and their meetings are often very heavy emotionally. This is not surprising, given the serious issues and life circumstances they are dealing with. But there is often a hunger for the ability to lighten up in these groups. I have provided seminars to many kinds of support groups, and the comments I generally hear afterwards are, "Boy, we needed that. We're all so damned serious all the time." I have heard this from members of Alcoholics Anonymous, Narcotics Anonymous, parent groups, senior citizens, head-injury, cancer, and Parkinson support groups, family members of patients with chronic diseases, and even teachers.

Developing your sense of humor will facilitate your progress within any of these groups. You can use the workbook and its guidelines for group discussion to integrate the development of humor coping skills into your ongoing regular meetings. The following groups may want to consider working collectively on developing their sense of humor. Family members of participants in these groups will also benefit from the 8-Step Program.

Nurturing Your Children's Sense of Humor

There is currently a tremendous amount of interest in the physical and mental health benefits resulting from humor. Many people want to improve their sense of humor and learn how to use it to cope. Ideally, there would be no need for a humor training program like the 8-Step Program. Nearly all children have the basic tools (playfulness, the ability to play with language, and a general love of humor) to learn to use humor as a coping skill, but these tools are rarely nurtured or reinforced by parents. In fact, parents may be annoyed by their children's riddles and other jokes and actively discourage them. Parents typically do not have good humor skills themselves, so they fail to model healthy and appropriate uses of humor. They especially fail to show their children that humor is an effective technique for adapting to difficult circumstances.

If you have children of your own, why not support their development of these skills right now, as they're growing up? After you finish the 8-Step Program yourself, you'll feel much more comfortable with having playful, humorous interchanges with your children. By supporting the development of your children's sense of humor now, you'll provide them with a valuable set of coping skills throughout their lives—and eliminate the need to later go through a humor training program like this one.

You'll want to establish limits on playfulness and humor, of course, just as you establish limits for other aspects of your children's behavior. In general, however, by engaging in playful and humorous interactions with your kids now, you'll provide an effective humor model which will give them an early jump on developing humor coping skills that will serve them throughout their lives. Actively reinforcing their early efforts at humor (within the limits of your own tolerance) is just as important as the humor modeling you provide.

A guy walks into a fancy bar, but they won't let him in without a tie. So he gets his jumper cables out of his car and ties them around his neck. He goes back to the bar and says, "Ok, can I get in now?" They answer, "Well, all right, but you'd better not start anything."

Part I

Why Improve Your Sense of Humor?

The Work and Health Benefits of Your Amuse System

Chapter 1
Humor in the Workplace:

Putting Fun to Work

> *"In general, a spirited environment is marked by laughter—enthusiasm for being on a team, and darn near anything to make the product or service better."* (Tom Peters)

A funny thing is happening in companies across America. A rapidly growing number of corporate leaders have come to view humor as an effective management tool that helps employees remain productive and provide quality service in an increasingly demanding work environment. They have learned that employees can maintain their professionalism and competence, while learning to lighten up on the job. They have seen that the payoff for putting humor and fun to work is lower stress, improved morale, better conflict management and communication skills, a stronger team identity, and better job performance.

Growing Job Dissatisfaction

As the 1990s progressed, more and more employees who used to love their jobs joined the ranks of the frustrated, angry, overworked, burned out, anxious or depressed. They adopted a mentality of just getting through the week, and lost their internalized concern about quality. Many turned down promotions or asked to leave management positions in order to reduce their job stress.

In the programs I provide to companies, I have seen the stress levels continue to mount with each passing year. Morale is down, and people just don't enjoy coming to work any more. They feel burned out, overloaded, short of time, and unable to keep up with the information explosion. They are tired of the demand to do everything faster, and anxious about losing their jobs. And they're afraid that they haven't yet seen the worst.

A New Kind of Leadership

Increasing employee dissatisfaction is just one sign of a growing need for a new kind of leadership. Other changes leave companies no choice but to rethink the demands of leadership. Most companies now have a horizontal rather than a vertical structure. Employees are more empowered to make decisions than ever before, but they also have heavier work loads, more time pressure, the demand for constant learning and a faster pace of change to deal with than ever before. Today's leaders must know how to motivate employees to sustain peak levels of performance, with a constant eye to sustaining quality. They must know how to bolster team spirit and nurture open communication. And they must do all this in the midst of growing job insecurity at all levels of the organization.

Leaders today must recognize the strong desire of an educated work force to have work that they enjoy doing. The resistance often encountered to the idea of making work enjoyable is surprising, since any corporate culture that enables people to feel good while they're doing their work increases the odds that employees will take pride in their work, be committed to quality, and do whatever it takes to help the team get the job done. Leaders must also know how to identify and develop resilient employees who can perform well in a demanding work environment. In the future, successful companies will increasingly be companies with resilient employees.

All of these considerations have supported the trend to put humor to work. To the great surprise of many CEOs, helping employees lighten up on the job has boosted productivity at the same time that it has provided an invaluable skill in coping with ever-increasing levels of job stress. While humor and fun are generally not mentioned in the context of Total Quality Management, they are essential to getting employees to "internalize" the commitment to quality. When the majority of employees love their jobs and have fun doing them, the motivation to provide quality comes from within.

At the top levels, of course, leadership involves the development and application of the basic values and philosophy of the company. This chapter includes numerous examples of CEOs who have become convinced of the value of humor and fun on the job, and their organizations reflect this value. The employees in these companies generally enjoy their work, and the CEOs believe this is crucial to maximizing productivity and quality.

According to the CEO of Rosenbluth International, Hal Rosenbluth, it is "almost inhumane if companies create a climate where people can't naturally have fun. . . . Our role and responsibility as leaders and associates is to create a place where people can enjoy themselves. I know our company is doing well when I walk around and hear people laughing."[1] (Note the sharp contrast between this and the memo forbidding smiling and laughter described in the next section.)

In the early 1960s, President Kennedy created a bold vision for people to work toward when he said that the United States would land a man on the moon and safely return him to Earth before the end of the decade. There was no technology available to do this at the time, but his commitment made it happen. My own belief is that companies today need to make the same kind of commitment to finding ways to make work enjoyable, if they want to survive and thrive in the 21st century.

The Importance of Making Work Fun

It wasn't very long ago that virtually all companies drew a sharp distinction between work and play. If you had fun, or were found joking, laughing, or showing a "playful attitude" on the job, you were considered to be goofing off, unprofessional, immature, and not taking your work seriously. Employees generally knew that humor and laughter were not welcome, even though there were no strict rules forbidding them.

I know of one major corporation, however, which did issue specific orders forbidding laughter on the job. The president of one division of the company was walking down the hall one day and heard some laughter coming out of two offices. The next day, the memo shown on the right was sent to everyone in the building. Over the past two decades, companies have abandoned many of their old assumptions about smiling, laughter and fun on the job.

John Naisbitt noted in his 1985 book, *Reinventing the Corporation,* that "Many business people have mourned the death of the work ethic in America. But few of us have applauded the logic of the new value taking its place: 'work should be fun.' That outrageous assertion is the value that fuels the most productive people and companies in this country."

In the decade and a half since this was written, a steadily increasing number of CEOs have become convinced that fun boosts the bottom line, and should take its proper place in corporate culture. According to Joel Slutzky, CEO of Odetics, Inc., a company that makes spacecraft flight recorders and robots, "every company should strive for this fun, loose environment. You can't get too uptight."[2] Slutzky is constantly on the lookout for ways to generate new forms of fun. He says that "(i)ntermixing fun in the environment has a very positive effect, because it causes a degree of [i.e., more] interaction that you wouldn't normally get."

> "Henceforth, there will be no laughing or smiling allowed in this building during working hours.
>
> Laughing distracts fellow employees. And if you're smiling, you are not thinking about your work."

Many companies now include fun among their core values, including AES Corporation, in Arlington, Virginia. At a recent conference on business ethics, AES CEO and president Dennis Bakke stated that "We regard our people as creative, thinking, capable, trustworthy, responsible, unique, and, yes, fallible. Building an organization that takes these assumptions seriously is extremely difficult and often leads to unorthodox and controversial approaches."[3] He provides a fun working environment to bring out these positive qualities in his employees.

Bill Dahlberg, CEO of Southern Company, an electric power company in Georgia, leaves no doubt in employees' minds about his commitment to the value of fun and humor. He works out of an office stocked with toys, which serve as a reminder to him and others to find ways to lighten up and make work fun.[4]

> **At the end of a job interview, the HR person asked the young MBA fresh out of MIT, "And what starting salary are you looking for?"**
>
> **The candidate said, "In the neighborhood of $125,000 a year, depending on the benefits package."**
>
> **The HR person said, "Well, what would you say to a package of 5 weeks vacation, 14 paid holidays, full medical and dental, company matching retirement fund to 50% of salary, and a company car leased every 2 years— say a red Corvette?"**
>
> **The MBA sat up straight and said, "Wow!! Are you kidding?"**
>
> **"Certainly," said the HR person, "but you started it."**

The growing trend toward making work fun is evident in an editorial written by John Brandt in *Industry Week* Magazine April 1, 1996. He expressed regret that in his own on-the-job training, he was advised to avoid humor and fun on the job. Years of work experience, however, had shown him just how wrong this advice had been. So he invited all employees to use April Fools' Day as a starting point to begin making work fun.

When people have fun on their jobs, they become energized and more productive. And yet, many organizations are afraid to try putting humor and fun to work, because they fear it will be taken as a message that it's OK to goof off. *The New York Times* reported in 1989 that the intentional wasting of time on the job costs American companies $170 billion a year.[5] I know of no company, however, that has found that encouraging a lighter attitude on the job leads to goofing off. In fact, the opposite is generally reported. Making work fun helps sustain quality and peak performance. Managers have seen that employees can lighten up on the job, and continue to be competent and professional. The key is taking your work seriously, while taking yourself lightly in doing that work.

Dick Kussman, vice president of one of AT&T's most successful sales departments, encouraged his staff (mainly telephone sales and service people) to find ways to make work fun. He has held team chili cook-offs and monthly unusual dress-up days, and sent fun video-taped messages to employees spread across the country. Kussman says, "I have yet to find anything worth accomplishing that you just can't have a good time doing."[6]

Royce Haines, president of Royce Medical, a company that makes orthopedic products, installed foosball and ping-pong tables for employees to use during breaks, and often holds trivia and team-sales contests to keep the spirit of fun alive. He finds that "(t)he better managers are at providing this kind of [fun-oriented] leadership, the better results they get."[7]

Some companies establish a fun work environment as a means of recruiting and retaining employees—a constant problem in the ultra competitive Silicon Valley. Remedy Corporation, a California company which produces computer products, has been extremely successful on both counts by maintaining a fun environment in which employees can enjoy their work. For example, it had managers wash the cars of all company employees to show appreciation for their efforts. Employees are hesitant to accept new jobs because they feel they simply wouldn't enjoy a job elsewhere as much.[8]

It is no surprise, then, that in *Fortune* magazine's list of "The 100 Best Companies to Work for in America," the top three (and many others) all place a major emphasis on finding ways to help employees make work fun.[9] These selections were made on the basis of such dimensions as "trust in management, pride in work/company, and camaraderie." The #1 company on the list, Southwest Airlines, is the most successful (financially) airline in the country, and is also best known for it's commitment to making work fun.

Thomas Edison knew the value of making work fun. Toward the end of his life, he said, "I never did a day's work in my life—it was all fun." While you may not be as creative and productive as Edison (he held over 1,000 patents), doing things to make your work fun will certainly help boost your creativity and effectiveness on the job.

What Makes a Job Fun?

Traditionally, we've thought of work as something we get paid to do, and play as something we can do when we're done working. In fact, the key distinction between work and play lies in the attitude we bring to what we're doing. If we enjoy doing it, it seems more like play—even though we're getting paid to do it. Tom Sawyer understood this distinction perfectly well when he got his friends to whitewash a fence for him by convincing them of how much fun it was, and that it wasn't work at all.

Experiencing work as fun doesn't have to come from organized fun activities of the type described later in this chapter. Research shows that many employees find their job fun if they are 1) doing mentally challenging work, 2) being creative, 3) doing what they're good at doing, 4) using their own initiative, or 5) simply enjoying their work. Everyone surveyed in this study agreed with the statement that their work needed to be more fun, but widespread individual differences were found in what they considered fun.[10] This suggests that a "fun committee" should be formed to find effective ways to add fun to work. The committee should consist of representatives from a wide range of departments, and committee membership should rotate.

David Abramis surveyed 930 employees from a range of work settings and interviewed 341 of them. He found that employees were aware of when managers were making efforts to make work fun, and these efforts were generally successful. Those who believed that their company made specific efforts to make work fun did experience more fun on the job. He also found that "people who believe that fun has positive effects in their lives are more likely to try to make their jobs fun."[11] And individuals who made conscious efforts to make their own work fun did have more fun on the job, regardless of the efforts made by their company.[12] "Fun people" were viewed by their colleagues as being intelligent, energetic, hardworking, outgoing, friendly, competent, not always serious, and able to laugh at themselves. It is precisely because of these qualities that so many companies now seek employees with a good sense of humor. Abramis noted that your own attitude toward your work and a determination to find ways to make it fun are crucial to enjoying your job.

Changing Corporate Perceptions of the Value of Humor

Humor is becoming widely accepted as a management strategy. "Increasingly, smart companies and executives are recognizing that humor is one of the most effective ways to deal with workplace challenges and the stress they cause."[13]

As early as the mid-1980s, a survey found that 84% of vice presidents and personnel directors in 100 of the largest corporations in the country felt that employees with a sense of humor are more effective on the job than people with little or no sense of humor. The organization conducting the survey concluded that "people with a sense of humor tend to be more creative, less rigid and more willing to consider and embrace new ideas and methods."[14] Another mid-1980s survey of 737 chief executives of major corporations showed that an amazing 98% of those completing the survey said they would hire a person with a good sense of humor over one who seemed to lack a sense of humor.[15] Tom Peters noted in his book, *In Search of Excellence* (1982), that humor can be used to "unleash excitement" on the job.

In a recent survey of business executives and deans of business schools, 62% of the deans responding to the survey said they felt that humor contributed to executive success; and nearly all the CEOs who responded felt that humor has an important role to play in the conduct of business, helping to keep business healthy.[16] Among 150 executives in the country's 1,000 largest companies, 90% said they believe a good sense of humor is important for advancement.[17]

Many executives have told me that they specifically look for evidence of a good sense of humor in prospective employees (especially for management positions), because they are convinced that humor helps them perform well under pressure without getting "bent out of shape" or overwhelmed.

Tom Peters has long had his finger on the pulse of American business. He is now convinced that every company can boost its creativity, team spirit and productivity by building more humor and a lighter style of interaction into the workplace.[18] Consistent with this view, an article in *HR Magazine* in 1994 specifically called for human resource managers to begin instituting programs that help employees learn to lighten up.[19] This book provides HR managers the tool they need to do so.

Herb Kelleher is probably the best known example of a CEO (Southwest Airlines) who insists on hiring employees with a good sense of humor. In filling any position, says Kelleher, "what we are looking for, first and foremost, is a sense of humor. . . . We don't care much about education and expertise, because we can train people. . . . We hire attitudes."[20] This approach has helped make Southwest Airlines the most successful airline in the country. Employees love working for Southwest, and do whatever it takes to sustain high levels of performance and quality service. And they have fun in the process!

Know When to Put Your Toys Away

One of the biggest causes of the negative view that many people have of fun on the job is the employee who either jokes or clowns around all the time, or makes poor judgments about when a lighter approach is and is not appropriate. With humor, it's just as important to know when to get serious as it is to know when to lighten up. If you're working on a serious or delicate issue with a client who doesn't know you well, humor of any kind may well be inappropriate. The client can easily view you as shallow or as not taking the problem seriously. So always establish your competence first. As you get to know the client better, you can try a "toe in the water" approach, and either continue in a lighter vein or stop, depending on how they react to you.

If your company is considering appropriate ways to create a lighter work atmosphere, you may want to have an initial meeting devoted to the importance of making good judgments about when to be serious and when to adopt a lighter approach. Make it a point to discuss issues related to amount of humor and fun on the job. Remember that humor and fun are ways of supporting your efforts to perform at high levels and provide quality. They are not your main goal. You should also discuss ways of retaining your professionalism on the job, while still supporting the spirit of fun (when that spirit is appropriate). The best way to avoid any problems which may result from employees going too far with humor and fun is to establish some general guidelines about limits in advance.

The Net Effect: Humor and Fun Increase Productivity

The surging interest in humor and fun on the job reflects the growing number of executives who have become convinced that humor boosts the bottom line. However, while many executives have seen humor and fun increase productivity in their own company, there remains surprisingly little research on the topic. In one study in which group members engaged in an anagrams task, groups which laughed more came up with more anagrams.[21] This suggests that work settings in which a team must put their heads together to come up with solutions to a problem will be more successful when they share humor and laughter. Humor in small groups creates an environment that supports employee accomplishment.[22] Consistent with this finding, women managers who use humor in the workplace are viewed as more effective by their staffs than those who don't use humor.[23] In the Abramis study described earlier, people who were able to find ways to make their job fun were more productive.

A good sense of humor makes good business cents.

In a survey of 750 major companies conducted by the Campbell Research Corporation in 1994, two-thirds of the companies had casual dress days (usually on Friday). Of that two-thirds, 81% felt that this improved morale, and 47% said it increased productivity.[24] Another group of researchers asked 322 employees at a large Canadian financial institution to rate their supervisors on leadership style and use of humor. A year later, the units that performed the best throughout the year had managers whose management style was geared toward raising employee performance through humor and other forms of intellectual stimulation.[25]

Impact of Humor

In the mid-1990s, The Bank of America challenged each employee to make a fellow employee laugh each day during April (national humor month). Those who did, received a book containing all the jokes and cartoons used by all employees during the month. When complaints were received that this wasted valuable employee time and paper in a frivolous, non-productive way, management defended its emphasis on fun by noting that "the highest percentage of workers' compensation payments was directly related to workplace stress. This wasn't just fun, it was good business."[26]

Matt Weinstein, who shows companies how to make work fun, has offered a great example of a manager who gradually came to see how fun boosts the bottom line. The story is about

> ". . . a line worker at an aircraft manufacturing company who approached his manager with a fun idea. The worker suggested that, on the first day of spring, the employees be allowed to go outside and stage a paper-airplane flying contest. The manager didn't see any point in this nonsense and called the idea insane.
>
> The intrepid employee, after talking with his coworkers, made a counterproposal: If the team met 150 percent of its production goal by 3 p.m. Friday, the manager would give the members an hour off for their contest. Sure enough, they met the quota, and the manger let them go out and play. Afterward the manager said, "If you could produce this well with an hour off, think of how much you could get done if you worked the whole day." [The guy completely missed the point, adds Weinstein.]
>
> The following week, the same courageous worker approached the manager with another proposal. If the team made 150 percent of quota by 3 p.m. Friday, they wanted to play volleyball in the middle of the factory floor. Again they made the quota and got their reward.
>
> The next week, the employee proposed the same deal—but this time, if the workers made the quota the manager would have to take them all out for ice cream. At this point, says Weinstein, the manager finally got the message: **Fun and productivity are not mutually exclusive but are in fact complementary** (emphasis added)."[27]

Karen Donnalley, who ran IBM's Inside Sales Center in 1996, had 75 telephone sales people working for her selling mid-sized computers to 17,000 customers in the southeast. She became convinced that people need to have fun on their jobs to be effective in sales. To bring out the spirit of fun, members of her team created an orchestra of inept musicians playing the tuba, drums, the accordion, and other odd instruments. They played a cacophonous 15-minute concert every morning. Also, "(s)alespeople smash a gong when they've made their first sale of the day and move a race horse bearing their picture out of a starting gate. In a year, her unit's sales rose 30%."[28] This approach was so successful that Japanese visitors began asking to tour her center.

Sports teams have long known that athletes perform better when they've loosened up—physically and mentally. Joking is often used for exactly this purpose. Prior to Game 6 of the 1992 World Series, the Toronto Blue Jays put a silly lineup on the wall, including non-star players and key players in the wrong positions. This was specifically designed to ease the tension of starting a do-or-die game.

If you have doubts about the capacity of humor and fun to boost productivity, try the approach of the former executive editor of the *Minneapolis Star Tribune*. After one of his reporters wrote a story describing how fun on the job improves the bottom line, he sent the following memo to all his staff: "Effective immediately, I would like to see a 25% increase in the amount of fun you have in the newsroom. . . . We'll review the situation at the end of six months, and if we haven't seen a reduction in absenteeism and an improvement in productivity, we'll try a different approach. To start things off, whoever writes me the funniest memo today wins a seat at Sunday night's World Series game. I judge."[29]

All of this evidence that humor and fun on the job support peak levels of job performance is supported by decades of research in psychology showing that while a moderate amount of tension, anxiety, or stress can boost performance, it progressively interferes with performance as tension gets higher than this moderate level. For many employees, a good part of every work day is now spent at tension levels that are worsening job performance and the quality of service provided. There is no more effective tool than humor to quickly reduce tension, and re-energize efforts to get the task completed.

In recent years, I have seen estimates that from 20 to 50% of the average worker's day is wasted due to stress, boredom or general malaise on the job. The cost to employers in increased health care costs and reduced productivity is enormous—somewhere between $200–$300 billion per year at the turn of the century. Making the work environment more enjoyable reduces this waste by improving morale, cutting stress-re-lated health problems, and boosting job performance and quality.

How Humor Boosts the Bottom Line

Increased Ability to Cope with Change

Every company in this country has had to adapt quickly in recent years in order to survive in a rapidly changing and increasingly competitive global marketplace. The success of any adaptive effort, however, depends wholly upon employees' ability to adjust to and support the change. The more skilled they are at adapting to change, the smoother the transition and the more successful the company.

One way to help assure a successful transition is to hire employees who already have such skills. Another is to provide existing employees with skills that help them adapt. Unfortunately, many companies have failed to anticipate the need to improve their employees' coping skills. Employees have had to learn to adapt on their own—to "sink or swim." Those who don't cope well become highly stressed, and their job performance and quality of service suffer as a result.

The average employee does not welcome change, because it generally means more work, learning a new way of doing things, etc. It's a natural tendency to resist change—especially change that causes you stress. If your company has made no effort to support your ability to adapt to change, you must take responsibility for building these skills on your own.

You must develop tools that provide personal and emotional resilience—the ability to bounce back from unexpected adversity that inevitably results from change. Learning to lighten up on the job helps give you the resilience you need to handle the rough days that always accompany change. In fact, your sense of humor is one of the most powerful tools you have to sustain this resilience on a day-to-day basis. As one of my favorite philosophers, Roseanne Roseanna Danna (Gilda Radner) of *Saturday Night Live* used to put it, "It's always something! If it's not one thing, it's another!" From the moment you walk into your office in the morning, you may not know exactly what kind of problem awaits you, but you know there'll always be something.

Remember that many of the specific skills you now use on your job will be obsolete a decade from now. The general skills (such as humor) you develop for coping with change will never be obsolete.

Reduced Stress

An artist, a psychologist, and a corporate manager are facing a firing squad. They are each allowed one last request. The artist says, "I'd love to have one last look at an impressionist painting." The psychologist asks to give a brief talk about coping with stress. The corporate manager then jumps up and says, "Shoot me first! I can't take another talk on stress management!"

There is now a great deal of research (discussed in Chapter 3) documenting humor's power as a stress management tool. For example, a study of 36 female executives showed that women who scored higher on a sense of humor test had higher self-esteem and suffered less burnout on the job than their low humor peers. Also, frequent daily hassles contributed more to burnout and low self-esteem among low sense of humor executives than highs. So these women's senses of humor helped protect them from both burnout and a loss of self-esteem.[30]

One overworked engineering group tried to lighten up the atmosphere by placing a note on the bulletin board announcing that John Roe and his wife had had a baby boy, and needed suggestions on what to call him. A playful "Name the Baby Contest" poster was put up to encourage fun names, and employees added suggestions for the next few days. The suggestions included names like Skid Roe, Tomor Roe, Golfp Roe, Zor Roe, Fidel Cast Roe and He Roe. Not surprisingly, the group noticed a sharp drop in stress as this was going on.[31]

Stress-Inducing Workplace Truisms

1. Two wrongs are only the beginning.
2. If at first you don't succeed, it's best to destroy all evidence that you tried.
3. Success always occurs in private, and failure in full view.
4. No one is listening until you make a mistake.
5. For every action, there is an equal and opposite criticism.

In order to thrive in the midst of growing global competition, companies must be resilient. And the resilience of any company depends on the resilience of its employees. As noted above, one of the most important benefits you receive from improving your sense of humor is increased resilience in the face of stress.

A Corporate Stress Epidemic

Over the past 20 years, job stress has continued to mount in the U.S. Every major company has learned that it has no choice but to provide some kind of stress management program for its employees. Billions of dollars are lost every year to absenteeism, stress-related loses in productivity, and work-related health problems. A 1995 report indicated that stress played a major factor in 70% of visits to the family doctor.[32] In the 1980s alone, stress-related claims in California increased 700%. And stress levels have continued to rise throughout the 1990s.

A frequently cited study commissioned by the Northwestern National Life Insurance Company in 1991 found that 34% of employees said they thought that stress on their job would cause them to burn out soon, and the same percentage said they had considered quitting their job in the previous year. Nearly half of those participating in the survey rated their jobs as "highly stressful." A recent *Newsweek* poll showed that 40% of employees felt that their employers ask too much of them.[33]

You Know You're Too Stressed When

1. You name all your pens, and insist that the meeting can't start until they're all present.
2. You notice an irresistible urge to bite the nose of your boss.
3. Your boss asks you to do something, and you say, "You want fries with that?"
4. You begin speaking in binary code.
5. You want to chew coffee beans.
6. You tell the drive-through attendant that your order is to go.
7. You begin discussing the vitamin content of antacid tablets.
8. Trees begin chasing you.
9. The sun is too loud.
10. You develop an unnatural fear of staplers.

Stress can have a profound effect upon workers. More and more managers are reporting staff coming in, closing the door and "unburdening." One hospital recently asked me to do a humor program because their nurses were so stressed out that they were developing serious physical symptoms themselves.

Other common effects of stress are burnout, reduced motivation to do the job, cynicism, negativism, a sense of hurt, frustration, feelings of rejection, failure, loss of self-esteem, a sense of hopelessness, and a generally reduced ability to function. Employees complain that they can't sleep, or don't feel well. They become more isolated, and work less and less as part of the team. There is a sense of having little control over key events in life. Energy level drops, and it's difficult to focus clearly on the task at hand. Not surprisingly, resistance to change often increases in the presence of these feelings. I have heard burned-out employees say they were simply disgusted with their jobs. The disillusionment even spills over into their personal lives, interfering with relationships with their spouse and children.

When we're stressed out, we make more mistakes, and don't see problems or solutions as clearly. We drop and spill things, and have trouble with mechanical tasks. We forget names or other information we've just heard, forget where we put our car keys, etc. If we were a car, we'd be operating on just half our cylinders. We'd lurch forward in the right direction, but with only half our usual speed or efficiency. A good laugh in this situation is like an engine tune-up. It gets us moving on all cylinders again. It recharges our batteries and keeps us going . . . and going . . . and going.

> **❝** *Gentlemen, why don't you laugh? With the fearful strain that is upon me day and night, if I did not laugh I should die, and you need this medicine as much as I do.***❞**
> (Abraham Lincoln, during the Civil War)

Causes of Job Stress

Each job, of course, has its own unique stressors. But many are common to all jobs. These include (threat of) being transferred to another state, moving to a new department, adapting to new procedures, losing an office window, dealing with different managers' ways of communicating/managing, paperwork, etc. The following, however, are consistent sources of stress at all corporations and hospitals.

1. Keeping up with change

   Many employees have come to hate change, because it never ends. As soon as you learn the latest technology or new procedures, a new version comes along, and you have to start all over again. It is the increasing pace of change that exacerbates this source of stress.

2. Doing more with less

   As downsizing has led companies to get leaner in recent years, two things have happened. First, those who remain are anxious that they will be the next to go. A 1997 survey by the International Survey Research Corporation found that 46% of workers say they are "frequently concerned" about losing their jobs. The same figure was 31% in 1992. Second, the reduced staff size means an increased work load for those who remain. In the midst of their job insecurity, they are asked to learn new skills and take on new responsibilities at the same time.

The light at the end of the tunnel has been turned off due to budget cuts.

Downsizing is designed to boost profits. Companies also realize that they must be lean in order to react quickly to the changing demands of the market-place. Company executives have been put in the difficult position of having to find ways to increase productivity and quality while raising the bar higher and higher for both management and non-management employees. From the employee's perspective, raising the bar higher under these conditions means only one thing—more stress!

A business writer for *Time* magazine noted in 1993 (at the peak of corporate downsizing) that the average manufacturing workweek at that point was 41.5 hours, the highest in 27 years. "The resulting increase in stress leads to discontent, lowers creativity and undermines corporate loyalty."[34]

Sometimes downsizing can have unexpectedly damaging effects on the downsizing company. Nynex, for example, let go thousands of workers in the first half of the 1990s. "Union rules protect senior workers, 'but our younger employees were the ones who had taken more time to educate themselves,' says a remaining technician. 'We have actually gotten rid of our best people.' This practice—of getting rid of the brightest workers—happens so often that it has its own term: brightsizing." (It has also been called dumbsizing.)[35]

After one of my programs at a major chemical company, an employee told me that the downsizing they went through created a lot of pressure to be perfect on the job. He said, "My feeling is that if I'm not perfect, I'll be the next to go, because part of the company's reputation is that we don't make mistakes."

A corporate consultant was speaking to a group of managers, and asked, "Is there anyone here who's a perfect manager? I've always wanted to meet a perfect manager."

No one raised their hand at first, but then he noticed a man in the back of the room waving his hand. "Ah," said the speaker. "I've finally found a perfect manager. Tell me sir, is it true that you're perfect?"

"No, no," said the man, "I'm raising my hand for my wife's first husband!"

3. Demand to do things faster

Customers in every domain of business now expect products and services faster than ever before. If your company can't provide something fast enough, they'll go to someone who can. This results in impossible deadlines that make employees feel that their back is against the wall every single day. As soon as one project is completed, there is another waiting in the wings that also has to be done immediately. Employees know that they have to work quickly and efficiently, but their working conditions are making it more and more difficult to do so. Anyone working under this kind of time pressure is desperate for anything that can give them a break from the constant tension. Laughter is one of the quickest and most effective ways you'll find to relieve such tension and get refocused on the task at hand.

Time: what keeps one damn thing after another from becoming everything at once.

4. Information overload

Once American businesses got on the information superhighway, there was an explosion of new information to be assimilated. Most employees now feel pushed to the limit to keep up with the latest information. And then there's e-mail and the Internet, which make us regret ever taking a day off—because of the mountain of messages we have to deal with when we return.

The Popularity of Dilbert Cartoons

When I have a chance to walk the hallways of companies a bit, I'm almost always struck by the number of Dilbert cartoons on doors, bulletin boards, etc. I've heard it over and over again: "That's exactly the way it is around here!" Scott Adams uses exaggeration and distortion to draw attention to the things that drive employees nuts. The comic relief provided by the cartoons eases some of the stress caused by the issues represented in the cartoons.

> **"***Knock knock. Who's there? Not you anymore.***"**
> (From a Dilbert cartoon)

In 1996 (August 12 issue), *Newsweek* published an article about the rising popularity of Dilbert among corporate employees. They provided the following test, called "Is it real . . . or is it 'Dilbert'?"

A. A software engineer, recently denied a promotion, is receiving his performance review. He asks his boss why he got passed over. "You're not a team player," says the boss. "What do you mean, I'm not a team player?" asks the stunned employee. The answer: "You didn't smile in the company photo."

B. A boss and a subordinate are traveling together on a business trip. At an airport layover, the subordinate goes to a pay phone to check the office for messages. The boss appears fascinated. "You mean," he says, "you can check voice mail while you're on the road?"

Amazingly enough, both happened in real life. Employees love Dilbert because the comic strip expresses their own frustrations and annoyances about the absurd things that happen on their job. According to Guy Kawasaki, a management expert with Apple Computer, "There are only two kinds of companies. Those that recognize that they're just like 'Dilbert,' and those that don't know it yet."[36]

Half the people you work with are below average.

Some of the common themes dealt with in Dilbert cartoons are downsizing, cost containment, heavy work loads, working in humiliating (and shrinking) cubicles, bosses tormenting their underlings, changes in technology, the latest management fads, and corporate double talk. Regardless of the theme, most people feel that the cartoon helps them deal with some of the tough parts of their job by helping them laugh at the absurdity of the things that happen.

An International Problem

The United States is not the only country coping with increased levels of job stress. The Japanese had such high levels of stress in the 1980's and 1990's that they coined a new word, "karoshi," to describe cases of death from overwork. Even Switzerland has in recent years been forced to deal with loss of employment, job insecurity, and increased work load among those who keep their jobs.

In the mid-1990's, a survey conducted by the Manufacturing, Science, and Finance Union of 412 workplaces (employing 140,000 workers) throughout the UK showed that job stress in the UK had reached "epidemic proportions." Seventy-one per cent said that stress levels were higher than five years ago. The increased occupational stress was attributed to ". . . growing workloads borne by fewer people, harder sales targets, performance-related pay, spiraling paperwork, fears about unemployment, and increasingly vicious management techniques." Additional stressors were insufficient time to do the job, poor relationships with bosses, little or no involvement in decision making, and lack of control over the job.[37] Sounds familiar, doesn't it?

47.2% of statistics are meaningless.

The survey showed that 64% of Scottish workers and 60% of English workers were suffering from stress. The organization conducting the survey concluded that this increased stress is leading to increased absenteeism and poorer job performance. One Manufacturing, Science and Finance officer argued that "Organizations are paying a high price for the stress epidemic in our workplaces. Employers should realize stress is bad for employees and bad for business. . . . The focus on stress must be shifted away from the sick individual and onto the sick organization."

At the end of the 1990s, European countries were just beginning to explore the usefulness of humor and fun on the job as a means of bolstering employee morale and productivity. I presented a keynote address at a conference in Basel, Switzerland in October of 1998 entitled "The New Leadership Paradigm: Successful Corporations are Putting Humor to Work." The interest among the media was very strong, since the idea of making work fun had never occurred to them. Corporate managers, however, were doubtful that this approach could work in Germany and Switzerland, since humor and fun are viewed as something you do after you finish your work, not during your work. After I assured them that a lighter approach led employees to be more productive—not less—they became more receptive to finding ways to build this idea into their own corporate cultures.

Improved Morale

One of the most consistent trends I have noticed in companies throughout the 1990s has been a drop in employee morale. People who used to love their jobs are burned out and just don't enjoy coming to work any more. A 1994 Roper poll found that employee morale and job satisfaction was at the lowest point it had ever been throughout the decades in which the poll has been taken.[38] Reduced workplace morale led the New Jersey Department of Labor in the mid-1990s to recommend that companies create a morale committee, whose purpose would be to come up with ways to boost employee morale.

One of the main causes of lowered morale has been the heavy downsizing that has been occurring for the past 10–15 years. A 1992 study by the American Management Association ". . . showed that of more than 500 firms surveyed that had cut jobs since 1987, more than 75% reported that employee morale had collapsed."[39]

There is strong interest now, among both employers and employees, in finding ways to improve the quality of the work environment and, in the process, boost morale. Educated employees want meaningful work, and want to enjoy their jobs. Since low morale generally translates into reduced productivity, it is clearly important for every company to make the effort to find ways to boost morale.

"The beatings will continue until morale improves!"

There is no more powerful tool for improving morale (with the possible exception of doubling one's salary) than making work fun. Fun, humor, and laughter are enjoyable in their own right, but they also make your work more enjoyable by reducing the stress your job generates—as well as the negative emotional state that goes with it. They help let go of frustrations and upsets that accumulate during the day. Jokes related to the source of the upset provide a means of airing complaints in a way that doesn't feed negativity in the office. This kind of venting is especially valuable in sustaining morale in situations where you simply have to learn to live with a negative situation for the time being.

The impact of occasional laughter on morale and productivity is very evident in the following letter sent to me by a corporate manager following her attendance at one of my programs. She said,

> *"Working with people on a daily basis can be so rewarding when there is laughter in the environment. In many of the crises I experience on the job—work stoppages, natural disasters and emergencies—laughter helps ease tensions, and the focus of getting tasks done becomes more enjoyable and less stressful. I've heard other managers and their employees comment on my employees' attitudes. I often hear, 'How do they make their sales and service objectives? That group laughs from the time they come in until the time they leave.' But the laughter is infectious, and the employees and myself enjoy coming to work with each other every day."*

During the Vietnam war, POWs were tortured and kept isolated in an effort to break their morale. Gerald Coffee, author of *Beyond Survival*, spent seven years in a Vietnamese

POW camp. He noted that one way he and fellow prisoners kept their morale up was by telling jokes to each other in Morse code through their prison walls.

In the film *Mary Poppins*, there is a scene (the one where she sings A Spoon Full of Sugar) in which Mary is trying to get the children to do some work they don't want to do. She gets them to do it by convincing them that whether it's work or fun depends on your point of view. She says, "In every job that must be done, there's an element of fun. Find the element of fun and it becomes a game." Bringing your sense of humor and a lighter attitude toward your work (while continuing to take your work seriously) assures that you'll always find that element of fun on your job.

Some companies use pranks to boost morale. Sun Microsystems Laboratories, Inc. encourages its engineers to come up with elaborate pranks on April Fools' Day. One day, the vice president of the company found a life-size replica of his office at the bottom of a shark tank in the San Francisco Aquarium. The management encourages these annual pranks, because they're convinced that they boost morale and stimulate teamwork.

While your company probably does not have humor and fun as a cornerstone in its basic philosophy, you still can receive the morale-boosting and productivity-enhancing benefits of humor and fun by taking personal responsibility for finding ways to make your job fun—at the same time that you maintain your usual competence and professionalism.

One of my favorite *Far Side* cartoons shows two devils in hell watching a funny looking guy smiling and whistling in the midst of the fire and brimstone. One devil says, "You know, we're just not reaching that guy." We've all seen people who somehow manage to stay in good spirits on the days they're dealing with the same deadlines and work overload the rest of us are struggling with. When you learn to improve your sense of humor, and to make your job fun, you take a big step toward becoming one of those people.

Energized Employees

If you're like most people, you feel physically and emotionally drained at the end of high stress days. A 1994 poll showed that 42% of American workers felt "used up by the end of the day."[40] It's no surprise that so many employees are burned out today. And this is precisely why leaders in many companies have made finding ways to revitalize their work force a top priority.

Most people use their weekends to revitalize themselves. They do things that are fun to regenerate the energy and aliveness that the work week steals from them. By building opportunities for fun and laughter into the workplace, you provide opportunities for this revitalization to occur every day.

> **❝*If you suppress laughter, it settles down and spreads around your hips.*❞**
> (Fred Allen)

In my humor programs, I do a laughter exercise in which everyone in the room does 20–30 seconds of side-splitting belly laughter. When the laughing stops, I ask what they notice about the difference in the way they feel as a result of the laughter. Someone usually says they feel more energized, more alive, or just "better." When I ask everyone to vote, 75–80% usually say they feel more energized by the laughter—even though they're perspiring, their heart rate is up, and they should be more tired. This energy boost is one of the keys to revitalizing yourself every day of your working life.

As job stress mounts, we wind up taking more and more of our work home with us. Even if we're not taking it home, we keep thinking and worrying about it. The anxiety, tension, frustration, and anger this produces disrupts the quality of home and family life and causes us to dislike our jobs even more.

Helen Gelinsky, president of the Families and Work Institute in New York, recently completed a 20-year study of work life balance. She found that in 1977, 38% of employees said their jobs were interfering with their family life. By 1998, the figure was up to 54%. Since there is every reason to believe that this trend will continue, it becomes imperative for individual employees to take personal responsibility for finding tools which help them leave the office behind at the end of the day.

As you improve your sense of humor, you'll find it easier and easier to let go of office upsets as you head home, allowing you to be totally present and have fun when you're with your family. And this, in turn, helps you return to work each morning refreshed and ready to tackle the day's problems.

Increased Creativity

One by-product of the rapid pace of change now occurring in all companies is that the old solutions to problems don't work anymore. In addition, there are new kinds of problems for which we have no prior experience in devising solutions. This means that to keep up with the competition, companies must nurture a corporate culture that supports innovative solutions to problems. They must create a work environment which nurtures the creative thinking skills of the employees they already have, and also hire more creative employees. It is no longer enough to have a few top managers who provide the creative force behind an organization. Creative problem solvers among empowered employees are needed at all levels.

> ***Creativity is like having sex in a wind tunnel.***
>
> (Robin Williams)

In recent years the *Wall Street Journal* columns by Hal Lancaster ("Managing Your Career") and Thomas Petzinger ("The Front Lines") have frequently drawn attention to the growing need for creativity in the workplace. You can assume that your company's competition is learning to work faster and smarter. So to get ahead of the competition, you have no choice but to be innovative. And a company becomes innovative only when it has innovative employees and provides a work environment that nurtures creativity.

Hal Rosenbluth, CEO of Rosenbluth International, has stated that "We know that the only way for us to continuously provide solutions to the needs of an ever-changing business world is to have the kind of environment where spontaneity thrives."[41] Making work fun, in his view, is essential to achieving this kind of environment.

There has been research since the 1950s documenting the close relationship between humor/fun and creativity. For example, simply listening to a humorous recording increases scores on a subsequently given creativity test.[42] People also perform more creatively on a task when it is framed as "play" than when it is framed as "work."[43] Simply watching comedy films is enough to improve creative problem solving, and the amount of improvement is greater than after watching a serious movie.[44]

The employees of Southwest Airlines consistently propose creative ideas which help the company increase profits. An important source of these innovative ideas is the fact that they have fun on the job. The company is committed to maintaining a work environment in which humor, laughter, fun and a playful attitude thrive, because it knows that this kind of work environment produces a frame of mind in which innovative solutions are most likely to occur. By tracking the money saved due to employees' creative suggestions, Southwest has determined that its employees' ideas save the company millions of dollars every year.

Even the memory of past funny situations is enough to trigger innovative ideas. During the Vietnam War, one soldier had the problem of being constantly covered with leeches while wading through swamps. He remembered a scene from *Monty Python's Flying Circus* about weird uses of panty hose and asked his mom to send him the biggest pair of panty hose she could find. It worked! The leeches were unable to penetrate the panty hose.

Because of the power of humor and a playful attitude to boost creative thinking, many companies have adopted the strategy of opening problem-solving meetings with a joke or other form of humor in order to loosen people up and get the creative juices flowing. Consider the impact of humor in the following meeting.

> **"Five managers sat nervously listening to the company president relaying a message from headquarters. 'As you know, the For Sale sign has been out on us for almost a year, and there have been no takers,' scolded the chief executive. 'If we don't get our act together soon, none of us will have a job by Christmas. . . .'**
>
> **The tension was felt by everyone. The boss wasn't kidding. The color of his face, the look in his eyes, and the perspiration beginning to show through his shirt removed any doubt about the seriousness of the situation. There was a silence for a minute that seemed like an eternity. Then the director of systems development turned to the head of engineering, who had just returned from vacation and was red from overexposure to the sun. 'Tell us Peg, did you use suntan lotion or barbecue sauce while you were at the beach?'"[45]**

The entire management team, including the president, broke up in laughter. This greatly relieved the tension, and enabled the group to move on to a frank and productive discussion of innovative steps that might be taken.

How does humor support creative thinking? One way is by emotionally distancing you from the problem for a while. How often have you heard people say that they had been working on a problem for days with no success? Finally, they gave up and went out and had some fun, and a solution just popped into their heads.

Most people think more creatively when they're not so seriously and intently focused on the task—when they're relaxed, and the pressure is off. The problem in most companies today is that the pressure is always on. So you need something that quickly and effectively reduces the pressure you feel as you look for a solution. Humor creates this more relaxed feeling automatically and naturally.

Humor also nurtures creativity by offering practice at stretching your thinking to make sense out of something. In jokes, for example, the punchline delivers the humor by obliging you to find some new unexpected meaning that is essential for the joke to make sense. It is not surprising, then, that going through a humor training program has been shown to increase scores on tests of creativity.[46] Both humor and other forms of creative thinking involve a shift away from the usual way of looking at things. More creative individuals see meaningful connections between ideas or events that others can see when they're pointed out, but have difficulty coming up with on their own. Humor primes the pump and gets the creative juices flowing.

As the premium placed on creative thinking and innovative problem solving continues to rise, companies in the future may well adopt the tactic of training their employees how to think. Boosting their humor skills and creating a lighter work environment provides training in creative thinking at the same time it makes work more enjoyable.

Team Building

Any professional race car driver will tell you that the race can be won or lost in the pits. Each member of the pit crew must coordinate their work with the efforts of others, and take the initiative to do whatever it takes to deal with unanticipated problems. Similarly, you need the full participation of everyone on your team for your company to come out ahead. This is especially the case in companies that have shifted in recent years to a more horizontal management structure.

Teamwork means never having to take all the blame yourself.

Humor is a powerful tool in building more cohesive groups. And this is important, because cohesive groups work together better in pursuing common goals—especially in situations where there are expectations for high performance. Managers in a variety of work settings who initiate humor have been shown to be more likely to become an integral part of a socially cohesive group.[47] Status differences with other team members are also minimized by humor. So joking or other forms of humor clearly provide an effective way of breaking down barriers if a manager wants to do so.

A successful team must be flexible, and know how to reduce the tension that results from conflicting ideas about how to deal with a problem. One plan will eventually be seen as being the best solution, and some may be upset that their approach was not adopted. Humor effectively eases this tension and upset and strengthens employee bonds that are threatened by failure of one's own pet solution.

❝*Teamwork is when other people do your work for you.*❞
(Dogbert)

A real test of pulling together as a team comes when facing a difficult deadline or other task that requires everyone to work overtime. Paul Malone, a business administration professor, has provided a great example of this in a non-business setting. He tells of an experience he had as a trainee in a U. S. Army Ranger course—a course designed to simulate combat situations.

> *"Our class . . . had just completed a 60-hour patrol. The patrol had gone poorly. The critiques . . . had been extremely harsh. We were all utterly exhausted and miserable, without sleep for almost three days, and caked with the mud of waste-deep swamps. Our only desire was to rest. To our collective disbelief and anguish, we received the order: 'Prepare immediately for another patrol.' Our sullen group moved slowly into the briefing area . . . [where the briefing ranger told a joke that was appropriate to the situation]. Something almost magical occurred. Slowly at first, the bedraggled group of trainees responded into what became a full minute of hilarious laughter. Suddenly, the environment changed; the Ranger became a fellow man, not a torturer;* **the men who had laughed together became a team** *(emphasis added) with a revitalized common cause. For at least a while, the exhaustion and discomfort of the group were forgotten."* [48]

Employees in many types of business often have to pull together and work as much overtime as necessary to get the job done—sometimes for weeks. Humor can be used to remotivate people and lift their spirits, helping produce a frame of mind in which people are willing to do whatever it takes to get the job done.

If you are a manager, sharing jokes or other humor with members of the team is a great way to break down barriers, but you must be sure that this joking relationship does not cause you to fail to use your authority in situations where you should. There is evidence that this erodes the respect members of the team have for you. [49]

Improved Communication

No matter what kind of job you have, communication is an important aspect of your work, whether it's in meetings, phone conversations with clients or discussions between managers and other employees. Many professional organizations (e.g., the American Institute of Certified Public Accountants) now give special emphasis to the development of good "people skills," and communication skills are generally at the top of the list. Unfortunately, good communication is often complicated by the fact that people are stressed out and overloaded with work. You have to earn attention and interest, both in your written and oral communications.

A recent poll reported by *Newsweek* indicated that the biggest work-related complaint that employees had was poor communication with management, with 64% claiming that this impeded their work. [50] Part of the value of humor on the job lies in its ability to lubricate the channels of communication, assuring that it occurs more smoothly and effectively.

Removal of Barriers between Management and Non-Management Staff

As long as distinctions are made between management and non-management employees, there will always be barriers to good communication. Some managers have a style which discourages open communication. When a manager uses humor (especially occasional self-directed humor), however, it says to everyone on the team that s/he's a regular person—s/he's one of us. To function as a team, you need openness and comfort in bringing up difficult issues, and shared positive humor is a powerful means of achieving that. Any organization that wants or needs the full commitment of its employees to work as a team needs to establish a relaxed and open work atmosphere. A manager who shows that s/he has a good sense of humor goes a long way in establishing this atmosphere.

> **❝***Have I reached the person to whom I am speaking?***❞**
> (Lily Tomlin, as Ernestine)

The Tennessee Valley Authority (a federal utility) improved communication within the company by having executives come to work in costumes, stage talk show sketches, and hold charity water balloon fights.[51]

In many organizations, people with opposing views don't express them, out of fear of reprisal. But it's essential that employees are comfortable expressing concerns and doubts about any decision that's made—especially in the midst of change. Humor creates an environment in which opposing views are more likely to be expressed.

Trust is important here. There's always an element of risk in proposing new ideas, which could either succeed or fail, if implemented. They also could be rejected or ridiculed. A history of shared positive humor helps create a sense of trust which enables employees to open up and express ideas freely without fear of ridicule or rejection.

Emotional Tone of Communication

Our daily communications on the job consist of much more than the information we give and receive. Their emotional tone is just as important. Think back to conversations you've had with people you've met in the past. Chances are you remember your emotional reaction to that person and the general feeling of the conversation much better than you remember what was said. Shared amusement and laughter help assure that both participants in the conversation will remember the good feeling they had long after the content is forgotten.

If you're talking, you're communicating.

This is especially important in situations where the initial mood of the conversation is hostile or confrontational. Research has shown that humor in this situation helps reduce hostile feelings among co-workers. The better mood that shared laughter provides puts you in a better position to resolve the conflict and get on with your job.[52] It is the fact that humor and laughter are incompatible with anger and other negative emotions that makes humor such a great tool for conflict management. Since conflict and stress are so common in the workplace these days, the savvy manager will cultivate appropriately-timed humor as a means of keeping tensions, frustration, and upset from escalating.

Awkward Communications

Humor helps ease employees into awkward communications. One woman who was promoted suddenly found herself as the boss of people who had previously been her peers. She knew this would be a sensitive issue, so she opened up her first meeting in her new position, by saying "Don't think of me as your boss. Think of me as a friend . . . a friend who's always right!" Everyone had a good laugh, and she was then able to proceed to a more relaxed discussion of how things would work from that point on.

If you're issuing some kind of criticism or bad news, people tend to stiffen up, react emotionally, and not hear what you want them to hear. Shared laughter helps take the sting out of these situations. It shows that you're not really upset at the employee, but that some changes do need to be made. This is especially effective when the manager confesses a similar mistake s/he him/herself has made in the past.

> **"** *If you're going to tell people the truth, you'd better make them laugh. Otherwise, they'll kill you.* **"**   (George Bernard Shaw)

A lighter approach is also an effective tool for easing into sensitive or awkward topics. Like sticking your toe in the water before jumping in, the reaction of the other person tells you whether it's safe to proceed with a more serious statement about the sensitive issue.

Humor can be used to get a negative message across in an inoffensive way. Instead of complaining about a less than full glass of orange juice you're served at a restaurant, you might say to the manager, "You know, I can help you sell 30% more orange juice than you're now selling." When the manger says, "Great, how?" you say, "Just fill up the glass." You will have made your point without attacking the manager—and you may even get more orange juice the next time!

Using Humor in Meetings

A young and an older mid-level corporate manager have offices right across from each other. Each one spends about half of his time each day in meetings. At the end of the day, the older manager always looks fresh and alert, while the young manager is always exhausted and emotionally drained. Finally, one day following four consecutive meetings, the young guy says to the older, "I don't get it. How do you manage to get through all these meetings and still look energetic at the end of the day? These meetings just wipe me out." The older manager says, "So who listens?"

An employee at a major photocopy company told me that 2/3 of the meetings he attends are ineffective. We've all been in meetings like this. They drain our energy, or bore us to tears. Using humor at appropriate times keeps people engaged and helps assure the success of the meeting.

It's no coincidence that Toastmasters International clubs always have humorous speech contests. They recognize that humor is one of the most important skills to master in delivering any kind of speech. But I remember seeing many speakers when I was a member of Toastmasters years ago delivering a fine speech in a style that looked perfectly natural—until the humor came. The jokes or funny stories seemed tacked on, because the speaker hadn't cultivated a humorous style of presentation. By going through the 8-Step program and becoming comfortable with humor in general, you'll discover your own style. Any joke, story or funny action that you insert into your talk will flow more naturally, because it will be a natural part of who you are.

Research examining the dynamics of humor in task-oriented meetings suggests that it can play the pivotal role in moving the group toward a consensual solution to a problem. One study examined 26 hours of videotaped meetings held by 6 different management groups.[53] The meetings generally opened up with "a stiff, serious tone and a communication process that was sometimes complaining and sometimes adversarial." Humor during this phase (whose average length was 30 minutes) was infrequent. When it did occur, it evoked laughter from only one or two participants, partly because it focused on discontent with others' point of view.

It was after this initial serious phase that—for a period of a few minutes—the pattern of joking changed into humor that caused the entire group to laugh. While the early joking emphasized the differences between people at the meeting (and was sometimes disparaging), this mid-meeting humor drew people together and led to smoother interactions as differences were discussed. This humor "appeared to allow them to continue by creating a more freely flowing pattern of communication, which led to the eventual resolution of their differences." It "seemed to facilitate a transition from a feeling of tension and defensiveness to a realization of relative safety and playfulness. . . . This apparently shared comic vision seemed to create a working bond, overcoming previous estrangement . . . it cultivated a climate in which creative, playful, unconventional problem-solving could mature." (p. 290–291) Following the laughter, the "groups seemed to progress much more rapidly through the remaining stages of the decision making process."

If you've been in many meetings, you've probably seen this impact of humor in action. You may want to plan ways of building positive humor into your meetings once differences of opinion have been clearly expressed, in order to speed up movement to a consensual solution. Anything you do to momentarily establish a playful atmosphere in the room helps create a non-judgmental frame of mind in dealing with differences of opinion. The shared laughter helps the meeting move more quickly toward the resolution phase, which means everyone can get back to their desks more quickly.

One manager was planning a meeting in which the team had to deal with a problem they had been putting off. Prior to the meeting he hung a sign on the wall containing a quote from W.C. Fields: "There comes a time in the affairs of men when we must take the bull by the tail and face the situation." This triggered laughter as people walked into the room, and made the point that the team had not committed themselves to coming to grips with the problem—which helped create a climate for doing so at the meeting.

The accelerating pace of business in recent years has created the need for rapid decisions. This increases the chances of making a mistake, since you may not be able to obtain all the information you need before making a decision. One manager who had made a mistake in judgment was preparing for a meeting designed to determine how to deal with the mistake, and move on. He walked in wearing a bull's eye on a T-shirt. The T-shirt playfully acknowledged that the blunder was his responsibility, and allowed other employees to vent their upset through laughter before the meeting even got started. This helped assure a more productive meeting.[54]

Another manager made a mistake, and knew he would have to justify his actions in the meeting that was about to take place. After presenting his defense as well as he could, he said, "That concludes my prepared evasion. I will now evade questions from the audience." This melted some of the negative feelings in the room, and allowed everyone to focus more clearly on how to best deal with the circumstances they were now in.

Once a mistake is made, managers need to acknowledge the error and move on. The ability to laugh at your mistake helps reduce the tension resulting from it and focus on moving forward.

If you're specifically interested in the use of jokes and stories in meetings, turn now to Step 3 in this book, and read the basic list of do's and don'ts in connection with joke/story telling. In addition to this list, make it a point to follow these two general rules in using humor in talks or meetings.

Basic Rules for Using Humor in Talks and Meetings

1. Be sure the humor is relevant to the point you need to make.
   We've all seen people in meetings tell jokes or anecdotes that have no bearing on the issue at hand. We're left trying to figure out the point of the joke, which assures we'll miss any important information provided during that time. Irrelevant humor is distracting, and may even be annoying.
2. Remember the sandwich approach.
   Make your point, then illustrate it with humor, and then remake the point again. The final reminder of the point is not always necessary, but helps assure that your audience doesn't go away remembering only the joke.

I once provided a program for a company which builds and operates large senior living communities. Residents paid a set fee for their meals, and were allowed to eat as much as they wanted—but were 'not allowed to take food from the dining room to their apartments. Despite the rules, food theft had become commonplace. In the context of encouraging employees to see the funny side of the extremes to which residents would go to sneak out fruit and other food for evening snacks, I walked onto the stage in a suit that had large inner pockets full of things like bananas, apples, carrot and celery sticks, rolls, a potato masher, a plastic turkey baster, and even a bottle of Pepsi. I went through 15–20 minutes of my talk before I got to the point where I was discussing this issue. As I encouraged the audience to find the funny side of the situation instead of getting angry at residents, I pulled these items out—one at a time—from my suit pockets, pants pockets, my socks, and even inside my shirt. (The big items were tucked in my shirt behind my back.) There were howls of laughter as I went on and on pulling items out. The audience left with an entirely different outlook on the theft problem.

If you're often in the position of leading meetings or speaking to groups, make a list of the key points or issues you generally discuss. Be on the lookout for cartoons, jokes, or personal incidents that illustrate or connect with these points in some way. When you find a joke or cartoon you think is funny, ask yourself, "What kind of point could this be used to illustrate?" Then simply put it in a file labeled by a key word. When your next meeting rolls around, you'll have quick access to humor that relates to the issues you'll be discussing. [Note: The Internet is a valuable source of jokes and stories.]

If you're looking for a funny way to start a meeting you know no one wants to attend, try opening it by saying, "After many requests, this staff meeting is being held anyway." At least part of the annoyance people feel in having to attend will melt away, increasing the chances of having a productive meeting.

Heightened Persuasiveness and Sales Skills

Any experienced sales person can tell you about the power of humor in sales. Humor helps break down any initial objections the potential buyer has by creating a positive emotional disposition toward both you and the product or idea. It also holds the buyer's attention even when s/he may prefer to direct attention elsewhere. This is why radio and television commercials now use humor so often. When you think of frogs and lizards, chances are a particular beer comes into mind (along with a mental grin) from the commercials of the mid-1990s.

While you may not sell a product, you're often in the position of selling ideas. Just as humor breaks down barriers to acceptance of a product, it will do the same for acceptance of an idea about which others may be skeptical at first. It relaxes your listeners and helps open their minds to the possibilities you're expressing. Once you've made the effort to improve your humor skills, you'll come to rely more and more on the persuasive boost that a good laugh offers.

> **"***Laughter is the shortest distance between two people.***"**
> (Victor Borge)

Humor can be just as persuasive in conflict situations. I grew up in Detroit, and at one point worked for Ford Motor Company. In the 1950s, Ford shut down several plants as a means of cutting costs. This was done on the advice of company accountants who were predicting continued reduced sales, and recommended yet another plant closing. Since the accountants held considerable power at the time, top management was afraid to disagree with them. Finally, someone said, "Why don't we close down all the plants, and then we'll really start to save money?" Once the tension-reducing uproarious laughter stopped, management felt confident enough to oppose the accountants and leave that plant open.[55]

Creative Marketing

A man is taking a tour of a factory that produces latex products. At the first stop, he's shown the machine that makes baby-bottle nipples. The machine makes a loud "hiss pop" noise. "The hiss is the rubber being injected into the mold," explains the guide. "The popping sound is a needle poking a hole in the end of the nipple."

He later comes to the area where condoms are produced. This machine makes a noise that goes "Hiss. Hiss. Hiss. Pop."

"Hey, wait a minute," he says. "I understand the 'Hiss. Hiss. Hiss.' But what's that 'pop' every so often?"

"Oh, it's the same as in the baby-bottle nipple machine. It pokes a hole in every fourth condom," says the guide.

"Well that can't be good for the condoms."

"No, but it's great for the baby-bottle nipple business."

Terry Paulsen provides a wonderful example of how a bank used humor to overcome its stodgy image.[56] They painted an outside wall with an image of a flying saucer crashing into the bank. Each of the four vans owned by the bank had one of the following images painted on its back door: a) masked robbers cracking a vault, b) counterfeiters inspecting their new bills, c) a washing machine laundering money, and d) two convicts playing cards (with one cheating). People became much more aware of the bank, and developed a likable positive image of it.

In sales, there's often a period of bargaining about the price of a product or service before the sale is completed. One study specifically looked at the value of humor in getting your client to pay a higher price. They found that when the seller used jokes and other verbal humor, the buyer was willing to pay a higher price. And this approach was effective for both male and female salespersons, and with both male and female buyers.[57]

President Reagen knew the power of humor in communication, and in bargaining. Prior to his first meeting with Michael Gorbachev in the SALT talks with the Soviet Union, there was a great deal of tension. There was considerable coolness in the initial stages of their meeting. This was no surprise, since Reagen had often referred to the Soviet Union as the "Evil Empire." Reagen melted the chilly atmosphere of the meeting by telling Gorbachev this joke:

Moscow has been having a terrible problem with people speeding, so the Moscow police were given strict orders to give anyone caught speeding a ticket. One day Gorbachev is late getting to the Kremlin, so he says to his driver, "You get in the back and let me drive. We'll get there faster."

They speed by a couple of motorcycle cops, and one of them takes off after the car. He comes back ten minutes later, and his buddy asks, "Well, did you give him a ticket?" "No, I didn't." "Why not? Who was it?" "I don't know, but his driver was Gorbachev."

Gorbachev loved the joke, and from that point on, tensions were eased and considerable progress was made in the bargaining. The shared laughter facilitated the bargaining process by creating a more positive climate for debate.

Customer Service

> **A middle-aged man dies, and soon finds himself with both St. Peter and the devil. St. Peter asks his name. And he says, "Bower, Johnny Bower." And St. Peter says, "Johnny Bower? Oh, I'm so sorry, you're not supposed to die for another 5 years. We'll have to send you back down."**
>
> **Mr. Bower is overjoyed, but he notices the two doors leading to Heaven and Hell, and hears what sounds like a party behind the door to Hell. He asks if he can go over and just look around. The devil says, "Of course, but just for a few minutes." So he goes over and finds an incredible party going on, with wonderful food and drinks, and everyone obviously having a great time. He says to himself, "If this is Hell, I want to be part of it!"**
>
> **So when he gets back to earth, he sins his brains out for the next 5 years, doing every immoral thing imaginable to be sure he winds up in Hell. And sure enough, 5 years to the day later, he's facing the devil again in front of the door to Hell. As the door opens, he hears no music, and there is no food or a party. There are just these flames leaping out from the door. In disbelief, he asks, "Where's the party? Where are all the people having fun?" The devil grins and says, "Oh, you fell for that? Well, 5 years ago you were a prospect. Now you're a customer."**

This story serves as a memorable reminder that we sometimes treat our customers differently once we've won them over—in spite of the fact that most successful companies today emphasize the importance of outrageous customer service. Companies that consistently provide excellent service have employees who take the initiative to do the little things, and employees are much more likely to do those little things when they enjoy their work. Also, a funny thing happens when your customers see that you love what you do. Since the spirit of fun is contagious, they are drawn toward you, and (other things being equal, such as prices of your competitors) want to do business with you. If your customers enjoy their contact with your company, they are more likely to want to develop a long-term relationship with you.

Having fun at your work helps assure that you'll leave your customers feeling better as you serve them. As Gene Webb, area supervisor for Quick Stop Food Mart Inc. notes, fun on the job makes your employees feel good, and ". . . if your employees feel good, they'll always make your customers feel good."[58] Just think about the difference in the reactions you've had speaking to people who answer the phone 1) with an upbeat and energetic voice that communicates they're having a great day and are eager to do whatever it takes to satisfy your needs, or 2) with a tone that suggests they are emotionally drained, are going through the motions, and hate their job. Who do you want to do business with?

An important part of service, then, is your attitude. A positive attitude is an essential "people skill" that many companies now try to cultivate in employees, since it is considered a cornerstone of quality customer service. Chances are your competitor is also committed to quality, so you need to go the next step and make customers' interaction with you enjoyable—even fun. This will help set you apart from others and bring your customers back, because your attitude will be remembered long after other details are forgotten. Cultivating your sense of humor helps assure that you bring a positive attitude to all of your customers, and boosts your chances of making the interaction fun. It also provides an effective tool for managing frustrations, upsets and tensions on the job. This is essential, because **stressed out employees do not provide quality service.**

If service is important in your business, you've probably heard statements like the following:

- 90% of customers who are dissatisfied with service don't complain.
- 80% of those dissatisfied customers will not come back.
- Each one will tell a minimum of 9 other people about his/her bad experience.

The opposite is also true. Satisfied customers come back, and also tell other people about their experience with you. This is especially the case when you do something that makes your customer's contact with you fun. It stands out so much from their experience with other companies that it's memorable. People can't resist saying to their friends, "You're not going to believe what happened to me today. . . ."

Stew Leonard's Dairy Store in Norwalk, Connecticut consistently applies this principle. One day, as shoppers came to the produce section, they found a band of mechanical farm animals playing country music. The store does something like this every day. People flock to the store for groceries, and can't help but tell their friends about that day's shenanigans. As one customer said, "The main reason I shop here is that it is fun."

The *Wall Street Journal* recently reported a study of Sears employees which found that a 5% increase in measured employee job satisfaction leads to a 2% increase in customer satisfaction. There is every reason to assume that as fun and humor on the job help boost employee satisfaction even more, customer satisfaction will show a corresponding increase.

A Quality Service Exercise

Try this as a fun exercise to get your employees more focused on quality and service. Break your team into groups of 3–5 people, and give each group the task of coming up with as many reasons as possible for "Why we should always provide poor quality and service." This will seem awkward at first, but the absurdity of it will soon be fun, and will help employees remember the positive reasons for commitment to quality. Some examples: a) The product they bought from us will break down, and they'll have to come to us for a new one; b) We'll be remembered because we're different; c) Our motto should be, "You're not worth it, and we don't care."

Humor as a Management Tool

I've often heard managers say that their job should be to model and motivate hard-working behavior toward common goals, not to run around having fun. These managers remain convinced that there's no place for fun on the job. And yet, given all the benefits to be derived from bringing humor and a lighter attitude to one's work, it's clear that managers should begin thinking of humor skills as a management tool.

In addition to helping employees cope with change, humor is the only management tool you'll ever find that will do all the following: Strengthen bonds between co-workers, create rapport with customers, get and hold attention, strengthen memory of the points you want to be remembered, persuade others to see (and perhaps adopt) your point of view, make communications less awkward, deflect criticism, reduce tension, frustration and anger, manage conflicts, reduce burnout, remove intimidating barriers between management and non-management employees, bolster eroding trust, boost morale and motivate employees, build resilience, stimulate creative problem solving, sustain a positive attitude on the job, and keep everyday hassles and problems in perspective

Following a systematic discussion of issues related to humor and corporate culture, Wilburn Clouse and Karen Spurgeon concluded that it is ". . . amazing that a well-developed sense of humor application is not a requirement for all leadership positions. Used appropriately, humor removes intimidation, stimulates creativity, encourages communication, and permits the employees to appreciate the work situation. . . . Part of the responsibility of effective leadership includes building a culture that supports a positive working environment to carry organizations successfully into the next century. Leadership that encourages self-esteem, cooperation, creative thinking, job satisfaction, and a place where people want to be is the emerging demand from the work force. Leadership that increases productivity and profit is the emerging demand from corporate owners and executives . . . **humor must be part of the solution** (emphasis added)."[59]

Leadership today is in turmoil as the transition from a hierarchical top-down structure to a flatter system continues. Each company must find its own path in dealing with all the issues discussed in this chapter. Because of the many benefits that result from learning to lighten up on the job, it is increasingly being viewed as essential to hire managers who have a good sense of humor themselves, and know how to sustain a lighter attitude on the job among those who work with and under them.

To be effective as a manager, you must be able to communicate your mission effectively, provide employees with the skills required to reach that mission, show that you're part of the team by being approachable and accessible, create a work environment that helps employees perform at peak levels and continue to provide quality service as the bar is raised higher and higher, nurture creativity, and adopt a "communication style" that makes employees feel comfortable in bringing new ideas to you. Good humor skills help assure that you'll succeed in each of these areas.

McGuffey's Restaurants have no doubts about the importance of making work fun. Managers are evaluated on how much fun they are to work with (this accounts for 20% of their raise). According to Keith Dunn, the president of the company, "We're in a service business with high turnover. It's part of a manager's job to bring fun to the workplace."[60] In recent years, Hewlett-Packard managers have also been evaluated on their ability to create enthusiasm among employees. Building fun and humor into the corporate culture insures that this enthusiasm exists.

If at first you don't succeed, try management.

Are managers who use humor more effective in achieving their goals than those who do not? A 1996 poll of 359 managers showed a higher overall effectiveness rating of both male and female supervisors who use humor on the job than those who do not. Professor Wayne Decker, who conducted the survey, noted the value of using humor in "expressing ideas, making light of a situation, assigning tasks, easing tensions, or even communicating work-related information."[61] The importance of humor in management was acknowledged by the editor-in-chief of *Industry Week* magazine in 1992:

> *"Why do we have to keep reminding ourselves about laughter's therapeutic and motivational power? And why do so many managements disdain laughter in favor of cold, sourpuss environments that perpetuate trouble and poison the very organizations they're supposed to nourish?*
>
> *By now,* **laughter and humor ought to be key ingredients of every managerial strategy** *(emphasis added). Successful firms . . . affirmed their value years ago. More recently, employee stress levels and the results of attitude surveys implore bosses to inject levity into their legions. . . . Organizations solve problems and prosper only when their people feel good about what they do and have an opportunity to smile when they do it. Managers who have to rely on fear, threats, gloom and doom are inept and utter failures. . . .*
>
> *Humor and laughter are signs of hope and promise. And what's most promising of all is that they still flicker among the staffs of every organization. If we know anything about managing and leading, we'll help turn the flickers into flames."*[62]

As a manager, you want to show self-confidence, and a good sense of humor helps you do that. According to Robert Orben, former Director of the White House Speech Writing Department, "A sense of humor implies a confident person. . . . If you can joke about a tough situation, you're saying, 'Yes, it's serious, but I'm in control.'" This is precisely the message President Reagen sent the nation after being shot in the early 1980s. As he was being wheeled into surgery, he looked at the cameras and said, "Honey, I forgot to duck" and said to his surgeons, "I sure hope you guys are Republicans." The joking remarks put the nation at ease, and let everyone know he had things under control. This is a valuable message for all managers to communicate on the tough days.

I am convinced that most employees would like to somehow make their work more fun. They certainly wish that those around them would learn to lighten up a bit. But many are afraid that letting the spirit of fun show up on the job would be viewed negatively by their superiors; or they simply don't know how to go about it. When managers provide a model for a lighter approach to work, while maintaining a high level of competence and professionalism in the process, this gives official permission for other employees to do the same—without fear of reprisal. Besides, you certainly can't expect employees to lighten up when their boss is always serious.

It is important for managers to be aware that there may be times that humor and fun on the job momentarily distract employees from doing their job. However, you need to fight the temptation to discourage the momentary fun—unless it goes too far or too long. Remember that this short break goes a long way in revitalizing employees and supporting your goals of high productivity and quality. Also remember that most employees want to do their job well, and may resent your comments. Sabotaging employee efforts to find ways to enjoy their job may actually reduce their performance and weaken their team commitment. The best approach is to simply ask each employee to use good judgment about when fun is and is not appropriate. If humor and fun activities are clearly interfering with work, however, a serious discussion of this issue is warranted.

If you decide to build humor into your management style, the first step is to better understand the nature of your own humor style. Step 1 of the Humor Skills Training Program helps you do that. Remember, you don't have to become a stand-up comedian to use humor in management. Your goal is to show that you have a sense of humor, and to nurture a work environment that invites others to do the same.

Motivating Employees

A great deal of attention is given in management seminars to motivating employees to do their jobs. When work contains an element of fun, this problem takes care of itself, because the process of doing one's job becomes intrinsically enjoyable. In David Abramis' employee survey, he found that people who described their jobs as fun felt more motivated by their work. When managers have fun at their jobs, this can motivate employees, as well. One employee at Merck, the pharmaceutical company, told me that her boss "is a joy to be around; he makes you want to come in to work."

A sales manager for one company justifies fun and laughter as follows: "We find that if we have five minutes of laughing and joking, we get down to work feeling more buoyed up. We do have fun, but it helps us to work harder."[63] While some may feel that TQM and a lighter work atmosphere are incompatible, it was a new commitment to TQM that caused this company to make even stronger efforts to sustain a lighter and more open atmosphere on the job.

For jobs that are boring or repetitive, humor or fun on the job is especially important in motivating employees. Monotonous jobs fail to provide sufficiently varied stimulation to keep the job interesting. They reduce alertness and interest, which leads to reduced efficiency. So anything which makes this work fun helps sustain attention, alertness, and peak levels of performance. Managers need to make special efforts to support humor and fun on such jobs.

It is important to remember that most employees with a college degree want to enjoy their work. They want meaningful and challenging jobs that they can look forward to on a day-to-day basis. But this is getting more and more difficult to achieve. The importance of these factors can be seen in the fact that a higher salary is often not the basis for choosing or staying at a job. As stress levels continue to mount, a growing number of employees are considering "quality of the work environment" in selecting a place of employment. Managers who learn to bring occasional fun and humor into the work setting go a long way toward assuring that top employees who want to enjoy their jobs will stay.

Bringing a lighter attitude to one's job doesn't change the fact that there will always be high stress days. But it does provide a positive counter-weight to the negative aspects of the work most employees do. Burnout comes when there are very few positive, fun experiences to counteract the negative ones. As word gets out that your company is a fun place to work, you'll not only keep the employees you have; you'll also attract qualified dissatisfied employees from other companies.

Continuing Education/Training

With the current rapid pace of change in knowledge and technology, companies must constantly retrain employees. At the turn of the century, American companies are spending over $200 billion a year to keep their employees at the cutting edge of new information and technology. Since many employees already feel overburdened by the demand of their jobs, trainers need every effective teaching tool they can find to 1) capture and hold interest/attention, and 2) maximize learning and retention. Humor has long been recognized as an invaluable tool in supporting learning—especially when it is used to illustrate the points being made.

Humor is also a powerful aide in learning from mistakes. In a series of training videos, John Cleese, one of the stars of Monty Python's Flying Circus, uses humor based on common mistakes to help employees learn to avoid these mistakes themselves. Exaggerating the mistake makes it memorable. It reminds us of similar blunders we've made ourselves, and makes us less likely to repeat them.

Managing Conflicts

Humor is an effective tool both for preventing conflicts and handling them when they do occur. In Chicago, one company had the problem of dealing with the sharply increased number of absent employees at the beginning of the baseball season. One innovative manager circulated a memo the week before opening day which said, "Any employee wanting to be present at the death or funeral of a relative, please notify management by 9 a.m. the day of the game." (Yes, absenteeism was down that spring.)

Conflict often occurs when people hold differences of opinion about an issue. When employees are entrenched in their own view, they're generally closed to considering other options. But a timely joke or funny incident reduces the tension surrounding the conflict and weakens the barrier to open communication about the issue. Shared laughter makes most people more willing to listen to opposing views.

The managers of two teams had an ongoing history of tension between them. Finally, one of them said to the other, "I'd love for my people to talk to your people, but right now my people aren't speaking to me." This statement made the other manager laugh, and helped open up a dialogue between the two of them.

Whining and negativity are problems that most managers have to deal with at some point. One manager handled this in a light way by putting up a few signs at key areas saying "You are entering a No Whining Zone." Another group of auditors and accountants has regular "Whine and cheese parties" to get the complaints out of their system in a fun way.

One source of conflict in most companies is the competition among team members for higher positions on the corporate ladder. According to Joan Kole, who runs Women and Work, a division of Kole & Company, "One way to alleviate competition-related stress between those vying for a promotion is to have the two come to work in running outfits and race to lunch or the break room."[64] This fun acknowledgment of the real competition keeps the tension surrounding the competition from getting too high.

Humor also can be used to handle conflicts with your clients. One company came up with a creative light way to get resistant customers to pay their bills. After a couple of "past due" letters, they would send the following: "I am a computer that handles billing. At this point, only you and I know that you haven't paid your bill. But if payment isn't received by March 22, I'll be forced to tell a human." Most of the time, the humorous approach got the bill paid.

Along the same lines, one sales representative used the following line to get clients to pay overdue accounts: "We appreciate your business, but give us a break. Your account is overdue 10 months. That means we've carried you longer than your mother did."[65]

Poking Fun at Yourself

Casey Stengel, the long-time skipper of the New York Yankees, once said that if you want to be a good manager, "the secret is to keep the five guys who hate you away from the four who are undecided." Quips like this showed his team that he didn't take himself too seriously, and it kept players focused on performing well, instead of on any differences they may have had with him.

As a manager, when you show fellow employees that you can laugh at your own expense, it makes you more likable and breaks down barriers between you and employees working under you. It also communicates maturity and self-confidence. Self-confidence "is the difference between a good manager and a mediocre one," according to Harry Quadracci, president of Quad/Graphics, Inc. He makes a special effort to build this quality into his managers by encouraging them to learn tap-dance and perform as a group at holiday parties.[66]

Remember that no matter how hard companies try to create a horizontal rather than vertical leadership structure, there will always be differences in power and authority in every organization. These differences create certain natural barriers to open (and honest) communication. But when a manager shows that s/he can laugh at his/her own expense, the barriers come down. A little self-effacing humor shows that, "Hey, s/he's just a regular person, and a real member of the team."

One word of caution should be noted here, however. Don't overdo putting yourself down in your humor. If you consistently poke fun at yourself, others may sense a lack of self-confidence. This undermines your ability to lead effectively. If you have reason to think that some members of your team feel you're not doing your job well, it may be best to avoid this kind of humor, since it will support their image of you.

If you do opt for self-effacing humor, be sure to always establish your competence first in the eyes of those under you. And restrict your humor to tangential areas of your job. One woman manager helped other women lighten up about themselves by offering a prize to the woman who had the greatest number of shoes under her desk. The winner had 40 pairs, and hadn't realized how funny this was until she won the prize.[67]

Destructive Humor

To this point, we have focused on the benefits of positive and constructive forms of humor. Unfortunately, negative humor can also be very common on the job. This may include ethnic, racial, or sexist jokes, or sarcastic humor. These forms of humor generally weaken team spirit and interfere with good communication and productivity. A barrier is immediately created between team members who must, nonetheless, continue working together. It is important, then, for managers to clearly communicate to employees the unacceptability of this form of humor.

Even if you find a joke very funny, and hold no hostile attitude toward the group being put down, someone else in your office may be offended by the joke. And remember, you don't have to be a member of the group put down in a joke to be offended by it. People may be offended by the general mind-set that they assume produces such humor. In that case, it won't help to say, "Come on, I was just kidding. It's only a joke. Lighten up!"

The problem, of course, is that the groups who are most commonly the butt of put-down jokes have often suffered real harassment and discrimination in other ways, and jokes which victimize them are reacted to as part of the bigger picture of their experience. And some people do use put-down jokes as a socially acceptable means of expressing their real attitudes toward the opposite sex or another racial/ethnic group. If you must tell jokes poking fun at others, try "rewriting" the jokes in such a way that the butt of the joke becomes a business competitor or another occupational group. The same joke can still be funny without feeling like a personal attack on anyone else in your office.

Managers also should remember that lawsuits have been brought against employees who tell jokes putting down racial or ethnic groups or the opposite sex—when such jokes are shown to be part of a broader package of discrimination or harassment against members of that group. Title VII of the Federal Civil Rights Act of 1974 makes the use of racial, ethnic or sexist humor illegal in the workplace, although the law does not specifically mention jokes. The section relating to ethnic humor states:

> *Ethnic slurs and other verbal or physical conduct relating to an individual's national origin constitute harassment when this conduct: 1) has the purpose or effect of creating an intimidating, hostile or offensive working environment; 2) has the purpose or effect of unreasonably interfering with an individual's employment opportunities.*

The section on sexist humor is similarly worded.

Apart from lawsuits, you lose a certain amount of credibility and authority in the eyes of your subordinates if you allow this kind of humor to occur in the workplace. Failure to prevent or stop destructive, negative forms of humor will be seen as indirect support of it. You also run the risk of neutralizing all the benefits humor and fun on the job have to offer. This humor divides and interferes with productivity. It is up to managers to be sure that employees are aware of the cultural diversity present in the company, and to sensitize them to the disruptive forces their negative humor sets in motion.

Sarcasm also puts people down, often in a more direct and personal way. If you exhibit or allow sarcasm on your team, the target of the sarcasm will rarely see the humor in your remarks. Quite the contrary, s/he will generally be upset. You've created an enemy of sorts, someone who will make less of a team contribution, and who may even try to sabotage the team. If you must use sarcasm, be sure that it's directed at a situation, and not at particular individuals. But even if you direct it toward your job, a constant pattern of such remarks creates a general climate of negativity which can deflate morale and team performance.

> **❝*It's only funny until someone gets hurt.*❞**   (Your mother)

Every company knows that it's hard to hang onto your best employees. They always have other offers and other options. One way to keep these employees is to do what you can to make their work enjoyable. But caution must always be exercised in opening the gates to humor, since many employees have not yet learned the distinction between positive and negative forms of humor. Negative or "excluding" forms of humor can actually drive good employees away. "One HR representative picked up a pattern when several departing employees, all excellent performers, said they had liked their jobs, but felt excluded from the camaraderie. One said he'd found the humor 'barbed.' Another said she'd never seen anything funny in jokes that seemed to convulse everyone else."[68]

In addition to racial, ethnic and sexist jokes, humor which challenges authority should also be avoided. Some employees find it fun and a challenge to find ways of using humor to show up their boss. "Consider the plight of the less technical boss who manages techies. Their jokes undermine his authority because they point out that he doesn't understand why they're funny. It is a deliberate challenge, because all the jokes he hears about portray him as a boob. It took the CFO of one Fortune 500 company weeks to figure out that his direct reports found it hilarious to watch his discomfort in meetings when they talked in bits and bytes."[69]

How can a manager deal with employees who consistently show negative humor? The best idea is generally a private conversation which focuses on the damaging effects such humor can cause. You can also try asking the person (in private) to explain why it's funny. This will be awkward and embarrassing, and will often cure this kind of humor on the spot.

As a manager, you must also guard against your own use of put-down humor. For example, you should avoid using humor to put down unproductive members of the team. Your superior position may allow you to get away with the joke, but it creates a barrier between you and your team.[70]

Finally, it is important to not overdo the amount of humor you model. While managers want to show that they have a sense of humor and cultivate its presence in the work environment, they must still be cautious to model a work style that keeps humor within limits. Obviously, constant joking and laughter will quickly begin interfering with work, rather than supporting it. The manager's own behavior must set an example of choosing the appropriate time, place, and amount of humor displayed on the job.

Pioneers in Putting Humor to Work: Southwest Airlines

There are many companies which have taken the initiative in recent years to transform the quality of the work environment by finding innovative ways to build opportunities for fun and humor into the normal everyday operations of their job. None has been more successful and innovative than Southwest Airlines. Southwest began operations in 1971 as a tiny carrier serving three Texas cities. Against all odds, and against the determined efforts of the major airline carriers to defeat it, Southwest has become an amazing success story.

There were many components that were crucial to Southwest's success, but one key has clearly been hiring people who are capable of having fun—people who take their work seriously without taking themselves too seriously. As noted earlier, Herb Kelleher, Southwest's CEO since 1978, has always adopted the strategy of "hiring for attitude." And the key element of that attitude is humor and fun. If a potential employee fails to show evidence of a sense of humor, he/she is not hired—regardless of prior experience and competence. The following questions are generally asked during an interview in order to obtain this information: "Tell me how you recently used your sense of humor in a work environment. Tell me how you have used humor to defuse a difficult situation."[71]

When you hire competent people who feel it's important to be able to laugh and have fun at your work, you have a winning combination, in Southwest's view. This is especially important when you have to constantly work leaner, harder, faster, and smarter in order to survive.

According to Kevin and Jackie Freiberg, who wrote a book which documents the history and philosophy behind Southwest's success, Kelleher has always said "I want flying to be a helluva lot of fun!" "Fun is taken very seriously at Southwest Airlines, and the company's recruiting and hiring practices are built on the idea that humor can help people thrive during change, remain creative under pressure, work more effectively, play more enthusiastically, and stay healthier in the process."[72]

A good example of the way Southwest has kept its sense of humor in the midst of adversity was its response a few years ago to a false claim by another airline. That airline had previously won an award as the number 1 on-time airline. On this particular year, however, Southwest had the best on-time record. The other airline continued to claim they were number 1, arguing that Southwest was just a regional airline and, therefore, in a different category. Southwest won a tremendous amount of positive public relations with their full page ad in USA Today which referred to the other airline's claim and said simply, "Liar! Liar! Pants on fire!"

To get passengers to listen to safety instructions, flight attendants often say things like, "Please put your seat backs into their most upright and most uncomfortable positions." On a flight I took from Los Angeles to San Francisco, the flight attendant said, "Please remain seated until the plane comes to a complete stop at the gate. If any of you violate this rule, we will be forced to turn around, go back to Los Angeles and start over again." I've heard of numerous occasions when the flight attendant said, "There may be 50 ways to leave your lover, but there are only 4 ways to leave this plane. . . ." Southwest's flight attendants have even been known to pop out of overhead luggage bins when passengers open them up to stow their bags.

A few other airlines have begun to apply the lesson taught by Southwest by bringing fun to flight numbers. Traditionally, even numbers are used to designate flights heading north or east, while odd numbers are used for flights heading south or west. In 1997, Northwest and United Airlines had a flight number 1492 going to Columbus, Ohio. There was also a flight number 1776 to Philadelphia by Northwest, and to Boston by United. Four different airlines had a flight 711 to Las Vegas, and TWA had a flight 777 to Las Vegas (in honor of slot machines). There was also Northwest's flight 500 to Indianapolis and TWA's flight 49 to San Francisco. According to Northwest Spokesman Jim Faulkner, the idea was to simply bring a little bit of lightheartedness to passengers when they hear the number at the boarding announcement. United's schedule manager Sheila Wiedemann went a step farther, adding, "It's something to keep you sane."

How to Build Humor and Fun into the Workplace

1. Hire competent employees who already value fun and have a sense of humor.

   If you begin with employees who already have humor and fun as part of their personality and style, they will automatically bring these qualities to their job. They will already have the skills you want to nurture throughout the organization. A core of people with strong humor skills is one of the most important keys to helping other employees build up these skills.

2. Be sure humor and fun are modeled by top management.

   No plan to change the corporate culture can work unless it is supported and modeled by top levels of management. Most employees assume that humor and fun on the job will be viewed negatively; so they need clear evidence that this is not the case. If they fail to see evidence of a lighter attitude in top management, they will be very cautious about using their sense of humor on the job—no matter how many fun activities are set up by the company. They will assume that their chances of getting ahead are better if they're always serious. Sean Greenwood, a full-time humor coordinator for Ben &

Jerry's Ice Cream in the mid-1990s, noted that "If your management doesn't support it, it's tough to go out and have fun at work."

A special meeting designed to emphasize this new organizational value generally handles any doubts employees have. This meeting should also offer guidelines for the limits of humor and fun; i.e., when and how much humor or fun is and is not appropriate. It may even be built into your company's philosophy or value statement.

We have seen the impact of commitment of top management in Herb Kelleher (Southwest Airlines) and other executives throughout this chapter. People like Tom Monaghan, founder of Domino's Pizza, made it clear to his employees and others that the way to build an excellent company was to allow employees to have fun in the process. Gary Rogers bought Dreyer's Ice Cream in 1977 and multiplied sales by a factor of 25, and profits by a factor of 30 in 10 years. How did he do it? By emphasizing quality, profits, and fun on the job.[73]

3. Establish a Fun Committee.

Every company has its own unique culture, and fun activities that work in one setting might not work in another. Establishing a fun committee not only helps assure that fun activities and events will actually be created; it assures that they will be appropriate for your company. This committee should rotate to keep ideas fresh and sustain ongoing commitment to fun on the job.

4. Provide challenging work.

Remember that fun on the job does not have to take the form of humor or silliness. Simply having challenging work is an important source of fun for many employees. While people often feel too overwhelmed by their workload to experience this form of fun, the drive for mastery of a challenging task remains a powerful source of fun for managers to tap into.

5. Plan structured fun activities at special events.

This may include special recognition dinners, fun contests, etc.

6. Encourage spontaneity on the job.

Spontaneity is central to play and fun. While a judgment must always be made about when any form of fun or humor is and is not appropriate, don't let this restraint kill your capacity for spontaneity. An employee once told me that he was traveling with his boss by car to another city for a meeting. They stopped mid-morning at a rest stop near a beautiful lake and pine trees and walked about and had a Coke from a machine. As they got back into the car, he noticed a day-planner opened up to that day. At 10 a.m., he saw "Stop and relax for 15 minutes."

Chances are that this man's boss had not internalized the notion of fun and enjoyment of his work. Fun and relaxation are simply one more item on a busy schedule. A similar approach is evident in the director of a large department of a company who actually stated in a meeting, "If you have anything funny to contribute, please save it until the end of the meeting." It wasn't that she thought it was inappropriate or disruptive; she just did everything by the book, and liked to keep to a tight schedule. If you want to improve your sense of humor, and get humor working for you on the job, you can't use a schedule for adopting a playful attitude. You need to be open to the spontaneity of the moment—even though you may not be able to act on your playful mood, because it is inappropriate at the moment.

7. Be aware of cultural differences.

With the growing levels of cultural diversity occurring in most work settings, it is essential for managers to raise the issue of cultural differences in fun and humor. What seems appropriate for one group may not be well-received by another.

8. Create a Humor Bulletin Board.

Encourage employees to contribute. Assign someone to monitor it for appropriateness of content. Make it a point to look for cartoons and jokes which poke fun at the circumstances that cause negativity or conflict in the office. Start with a blank board each Monday morning, but keep the old ones. Put them together in a book and give them to the employee who's had to deal with the most difficult customer that month, or was most effective in using humor to deal with a difficult problem on the job.

Another option is to place cartoons next to the serious messages you want people to read. They'll stop for the cartoons, but the other messages will get read, as well. In health care settings, make photocopies of the cartoons and create cartoon booklets for patients.

9. Create a Humor Break Room.

This room should contain cartoon and joke books, fun props, and VCRs and audio tape recorders (with several sets of ear phones) so that employees can take brief humor breaks. Put a suggestion box in the room so that the kinds of humor employees like can be made available. As a variation on this idea, have a tape recorder containing 1- to 2-minute samples of standup comedy routines set up in the coffee room (change the tape every day). This will allow employees to have a laugh while getting their coffee—without taking any extra time.

Marguerite Chandler, president of Edmar, Inc., in Bound Brook, New Jersey, stocked the employee lounge with comedy tapes, put up a humor bulletin board, and subscribed to a software service that provides a joke a day to employees.[74]

10. Create a Tension Release area.

Managing Office Technology magazine keeps a stuffed (toy) pig called "Babe" (named after the pig in the movie *Babe*) in the common area of the office. When deadlines or other problems get staff members too stressed out, they engage in a silly bout of kicking Babe—in full view of whomever happens to be passing by. It's a great stress-reliever, and creates the lighthearted spirit the company wants in the office.[75] The central office of one accounting firm has dart boards, hula hoops, decks of cards, and even a miniature golf course.

11. Have fun dress-up days.

Consider a day in which everyone is encouraged to wear a silly tie, shoes, shirt, etc. Many companies do this on Halloween or April Fools' Day. The chief technology officer of one company dressed up as a leprechaun on St. Patrick's Day, planted himself at the cafeteria cash register, and offered a free lunch to anyone who could stump him with a technical question. Steve Siegel, CEO at Lipschultz, Levin and Gray, an accounting firm, sometimes wears a gorilla mask at his desk. Employees often greet customers in chicken costumes.[76]

If you organize an ugly tie day, wear the ugliest tie you have, and would love to get rid of. Anyone at work that day can demand your tie in exchange for their own, and you have to then wear that tie the rest of the day until someone else demands a trade. (You can also demand a trade yourself.) Women can seize the opportunity to dispose of ties they've long wanted their husbands to get rid of.

12. Have cartoon caption contests.

This can be done using the bulletin board approach. Or send copies of a cartoon around before a meeting. Everyone who wants to do so submits a caption in advance. At the meeting, people vote on the funniest caption. Winner gets a fun prize.

Take photos of employees in unusual physical positions while interacting with each other. Put them on a bulletin board and invite funny captions below the photo. Give a prize to the caption judged funniest.

13. Put up on a bulletin board a list of funny basic truths you've observed about life. Encourage employees to add items.

Sample: "My 5-year-old discovered that no matter how hard you try, you cannot baptize a cat."

You can also have a sentence completion contest on a bulletin board. "You know it's a bad day when. . . ." Again, offer a prize for the funniest completion.

14. Promise someone an award (if they meet a quota or finish a task) that requires you to dress up in a fun costume.

15. Encourage employees to develop a skit in which they poke fun at themselves and their work.

16. Decorate the Board Room with funny posters.

17. Add pertinent cartoons or funny quotes to memos and meeting agendas.

18. Encourage employees to put funny signs on their office doors or in other appropriate places. Examples:

The buck doesn't even slow down here.
Oh no! Not another learning experience!
Stupidity does not qualify as a handicap. Park elsewhere!
Nothing's impossible for those who don't have to do it.
We do precision guesswork.
Incontinence Hot line . . . Can you hold please?
What happens if you get scared half to death twice?
All those who believe in psychokinesis, please raise my hand.
Oh Lord, give me the patience . . . and give it to me NOW!
You may know where you're going. God may know where you're going. Does your secretary know where you're going?

19. Use humor to promote upcoming events.

    Barbara Glanz provides a wonderful example in her book *Care Packages for the Workplace* of how a sense of fun and humor was used in one company to promote upcoming events. The manager of staff development "bought a mannequin that she lovingly named 'Sadie.' The first time Sadie appeared on the scene was after some downsizing had occurred in the organization. Dressed as a stressed-out woman, she made her debut in the lobby to advertise a workshop called 'Diminishing Stress Through Laughter.' She was missing a button, her slip was showing, her lunch bag was leaking, her shoes were untied, her nail polish was chipped, and it was definitely a bad hair day! . . . The employees immediately identified with her and began to make even more changes. They unzipped her skirt, turned her belt around, and simply used her as a catharsis for their stress. Sadie became a company legend!"[77] Sadie was such a hit that she continued to be used as a fun way to advertise subsequent events.

20. Put a "Food joke of the week" box in the front of the cafeteria. Invite employees to put in their favorite joke that relates to food or eating. Post the winner on a wall each week and offer a prize (free meal for two, antacid tablets, etc.).

21. Have a pizza "complaint party."

    Once your office has agreed to reduce complaining and negativity in the office, each person caught being negative or complaining puts a quarter into a pizza pot. At the end of the month the money is used to buy pizza and beer for everyone in the office.

22. Give a free bottle of champaign to the employee who has the toughest customer of the week.

23. Put up photos of the management team when they were children.

24. Keep a set of silly nose glasses in the men's and women's restrooms. People will not be able to resist checking themselves out in the mirror. (Attach it to a string—they'll want to take it with them.)

25. Be on the lookout for a motto to put over your desk that helps keep daily hassles in perspective.

    Consider checking out Dilbert for ideas. Samples: "I have seen the truth and it makes no sense." "Everything should be made as simple as possible, but no simpler." "Just when you manage to make ends meet, they move the ends." You can also be innovative and create a "Dilbert Committee," whose role would be to find aspects of office procedures which could be used in a Dilbert cartoon.

Building the Humor Skills of Your Employees

Even if your employer hasn't yet seen the importance of allowing a lighter attitude into the work place, you can still take personal control of your job stress and opportunities for fun on the job by developing humor skills on your own. This book provides all the training tools you'll need to start using your sense of humor to take control over the mounting stress in your life. In some cases, this will create a frame of mind in which you will be better equipped to take appropriate steps to eliminate the source of stress. In other cases, where you have no power to influence the source of stress itself, good humor skills will enable you to dramatically change the way you respond to the stressor. They will allow you to reframe the stressful situation in a way that sharply reduces the stress experienced.

By making the effort to improve your existing humor skills, you will maximize your chances of receiving all the humor benefits described throughout this chapter. These will boost your management skills, and enable you to continue remaining productive and providing quality service—even in the midst of the inevitable stress that goes with your job.

Chapter 2
Humor and
Physical Health

"Over the years, I have encountered a surprising number of instances in which, to all appearances, patients have laughed themselves back to health, or at least have used their sense of humor as a very positive and adaptive response to their illness."

(Raymond A. Moody, M.D.)

If you randomly select 100 people on the street and ask them if it's important to have a good sense of humor, most will say yes without hesitating. And yet the prevailing attitude toward humor was a negative one until the late 19th century.[1] Until that point, laughter was commonly considered detrimental to physical and spiritual well-being, as well as impolite and sinful by many.

A notable exception to this prevailing view was Henri de Mondeville, a 13th century surgeon, who argued that laughter facilitates recovery from surgery, while negative emotions slow recovery. Also, Immanuel Kant, in his *Critique of Reason,* suggested that laughter improves health by restoring equilibrium to the body.

These views, along with people's own experience, eventually forged the current view that humor makes an important contribution to physical and mental health. The familiar phrase, "Laughter is the best medicine," reflects this folk wisdom. The health-promoting and healing power of humor was given its biggest boost by Norman Cousins' book, *Anatomy of an Illness,* published in 1979. He came down with a serious illness called ankylosing spondylitis, and was given a 1 in 500 chance of surviving. Cousins was aware of the evidence from psychosomatic research showing that negative emotions were harmful to one's health, so he reasoned that the opposite must also be true. That is, positive emotions should promote health and healing. There was no evidence for this idea at the time, and many even laughed at it.

Cousins' bold move was to check himself out of the hospital (with the consent of his doctors) and into a nearby hotel. A nurse was present full time. He invited friends over

45

and spent a lot of time laughing while watching *Candid Camera* shows, Marx Brothers films and other comedy programs. Cousins beat the odds and recovered.

There is no way of knowing the extent to which laughter contributed to Cousins' recovery, but the widespread attention devoted to his story had a tremendous impact in boosting the public's belief that humor and laughter have the power to heal. His book also stimulated new research on humor and health. This chapter summarizes those research findings.

How Humor Contributes to Physical Health

The mere fact that you feel better after a good laugh is enough for many to conclude that humor must be good for you. But new evidence confirms what our grandparents knew all along. Your sense of humor not only enriches life; it also promotes physical, mental and spiritual health.

Muscle Relaxation

Stress management has become a multi-million dollar business in the United States and is rapidly growing in other countries. The Japanese, for example, are well acquainted the harmful effects of stress. They have created a new word, karoshi, which means "death from overwork."

Many stress management techniques have been developed, including physical exercise, progressive relaxation, biofeedback, deep breathing, meditation, massage, etc. The goal of these techniques is to produce muscle relaxation and the easing of psychological tensions that goes with it. You don't have to spend tremendous amounts of time, effort and money learning special relaxation techniques. You just have to find more humor in your life—and laugh more! Belly laughter produces relaxation automatically and naturally.[2]

This relaxation effect is easily noticeable when you have a good laugh. In my keynote addresses, I do a laughter exercise in which I get everyone in the room doing belly laughter for half a minute. Afterwards, I ask them what changes they notice in their bodies. The first comment is usually, "I feel a lot more relaxed." The next time you have a good long laugh, look for this feeling of relaxation and reduced tension.

Two separate mechanisms cause the relaxation you notice. Muscles not directly participating in the act of laughter tend to relax while you're laughing. That's why little kids fall down during fits of laughter. It's also why you seem to lose your strength when you're laughing (just try carrying a friend—or any other heavy object—across the room when you're laughing hard). When you stop laughing, the muscles that had been contracting relax. This is no different from what happens with any other physical activity. When you stop working muscles, their natural tendency is to relax. In combination, these two mechanisms produce a general pattern of muscle relaxation throughout your body.

> **"***There ain't much fun in medicine, but there's a heck of a lot of medicine in fun.***"**
> (Josh Billings)

One study showed that people using a biofeedback apparatus were able to relax muscles more quickly after watching funny cartoons than after looking at beautiful scenery.[3] The importance of this natural relaxation effect may be seen in the fact that relaxation not only helps reduce stress; it also helps alleviate heart disease,[4] headaches,[5] chronic anxiety,[6] and other problems. For patients with rheumatism, neuralgia, or other conditions characterized by a spasm-pain-spasm cycle, the reduced muscle tension that results from laughter disrupts this cycle and reduces the pain experienced.

Reduction of Stress Hormones

When you're under stress, your body undergoes a series of hormonal and other body changes which make up the "fight or flight" response. Even though there's no physical threat to your life, your body reacts as if there were. If you're under stress day after day, this preparation for a vigorous physical response (which never occurs) itself begins to pose a threat—to your health! Anything which reduces the level of stress hormones in the blood on a regular basis helps reduce this health threat.

The limited research on stress-related hormones and humor has shown that laughter reduces at least four neuroendocrine hormones associated with the stress response, including epinephrine, cortisol, dopac, and growth hormone.[7] This is consistent with research showing that various relaxation procedures reduce stress hormones.[8]

Immune System Enhancement

It has long been recognized that stress weakens the immune system, leaving you more vulnerable to illness.[9] Only in the mid 1980s, however, did researchers begin to study the impact of humor and laughter on the immune system. The best evidence that humor boosts the immune system comes from studies where immune system measures are taken before and after a particular humorous event—usually a comedy video. But research showing that individuals with a better sense of humor have stronger immune systems is also important, since it shows the importance (for your health) of making the effort to improve your sense of humor.

Immunoglobulin A

The greatest amount of research to date has focused on immunoglobulin A, a part of your immune system which serves to protect you against upper respiratory problems, like colds and the flu. Our saliva contains IgA, and this is often referred to as the body's first line of defense against upper respiratory viral and bacterial infections.

The studies show that watching as little as 30 or 60 minutes of a comedy video is enough to increase both salivary IgA[10] and blood levels of IgA.[11] This has been shown for both adults and children.[12]

Other Immunoglobulins

Immunoglobulins M and G have also been shown to be enhanced as a result of humor/laughter.[13] IgM is the antibody that arrives first as part of the humoral immune response. IgG antibodies are present in the greatest amount in the body, and are responsible for producing long-term immunity. When you are immunized for a particular illness, it is the IgG antibodies that are tested to see if the procedure has worked.

This same study showed that watching a comedy video produced increased levels of a substance called Complement 3, which helps antibodies pierce through defective or infected cells in order to destroy them.

B cells

Several different aspects of the cellular immune system have also been shown to be enhanced by watching a comedy video. B cells are produced in the bone marrow, and are responsible for making the immunoglobulins. If you count the number of these cells in the blood before and after a comedy video, you can demonstrate a significant increase in the number of B cells circulating throughout the body following humor.[14] This is not surprising, of course, since the increased levels of immunoglobulins following humor is now well documented.

Natural Killer Cells

Watching a one-hour humorous video also increases the activity—and number—of natural killer cells, although there is some evidence that this may be true only for individuals whose NK cell activity is lower than average.[15,16] Natural killer cells have the role of seeking out and destroying tumor cells in the body, as well as battling the latest cold- and flu-generating viruses and other foreign organisms. These cells destroy tumor cells and viruses by releasing a toxic substance. They are part of the body's first line of defense, and can attack foreign organisms even if they've never seen them before.

Among cancer patients, reduced natural killer cell activity is associated with an increased rate of spread of tumors.[17] So the significance of laughter's ability to increase the activity of these cells is clear. The previously-mentioned finding that humor's ability to boost NK cell activity is greatest among those with lower levels of NK cell activity is especially important for cancer patients. This is one reason oncology units of hospitals have become so interested in humor as a form of therapy.[18]

T-Cells

Another promising study has shown that humor may even have a place in the battle against AIDS. T-cells are another kind of immune cell produced by the thymus gland. The AIDS virus attacks "helper T-cells." Humor and laughter have been shown to increase both the number and level of activation of helper T-cells, and to increase the ratio of helper to suppressor T-cells.[19] This is an exciting finding, and suggests that a good sense of humor may contribute not only to a patient's ability to cope with the emotional impact of having the disease, but to the body's ability to battle it as well.

These data are supported by research showing that relaxation techniques increase levels of helper T-cells. For example, medical students' levels of helper T-cells have been shown to be reduced on the day of exams.[20] But when half the students were taught relaxation techniques, their level of helper T-cells increased. And the degree of increase was directly related to the extent to which they practiced the techniques learned. So the increased helper T-cell production found for laughter may have been due to the relaxation produced by laughter. Consistent with these findings, relaxation techniques have been shown to increase antibody production, natural killer cell activity, and the effectiveness of cytotoxic T-cells.[21]

> ❝*The art of medicine consists of keeping the patient amused while nature heals the disease.*❞ (Voltaire)

While we wait for researchers to settle this issue, I fully agree with the advice given by long-term AIDS survivor Michael Callen (who died in 1993): "It simply makes sense to try to mobilize whatever immune-system enhancing effects might flow from marshaling the mind. After all, even if your T-cells don't increase, how can having a cheerful, frisky, life-affirming attitude possibly hurt? . . . I highly recommend daily doses of laughter."[22]

Gamma Interferon

Humor has also been shown to increase levels of gamma interferon, a complex substance that plays an important role in the maturation of B cells, the growth of cytotoxic T cells, and the activation of NK cells.[23] It also tells different components of the immune system when to become more active, and regulates the level of cooperation between cells of the immune system. Given the specific types of immunoenhancement resulting from humor discussed above, this effect on gamma interferon is to be expected.

Taken as a whole, it's clear that there is something about humor and laughter that causes the immune system to "turn on" metabolically and do more effectively what it is designed to do—promote health and wellness in the face of internal or external threats. But your sense of humor is not a magic bullet which will cure cancer or other illnesses. Rather, it creates internal conditions which support the body's basic healing and health-maintaining mechanisms.

My guess is that future research will show that a major component of the power of humor to promote health and healing lies in its capacity to pull us out of the chronic negative mood we're left in by the constant stress in our lives, and to replace that mood with a more positive, optimistic outlook that lowers stress hormones and leaves the immune system operating on a higher level.

Duration of Humor-Induced Immunoenhancement

Only a few studies have examined the duration of the immunoenhancement effects of humor. This may be an artificial question, since emotional changes are known to cause fluctuations in the immune system, and your emotional state generally depends on whether or not you're dealing with anything stressful at the moment. If something happens to make you angry or anxious soon after watching a comedy video, this counteracts the immune benefits resulting from the video. This is where the strength of your own sense of humor comes in. If you are able to find a light side of the situation, you sustain the immunoenhancing benefits resulting from the humor you've been exposed to.

The limited research along these lines suggests that a strengthened immune system is sustained for 30 minutes for IgA, IgG, number of B cells, activation and number of T cells, activation and number of natural killer cells, and gamma-interferon. The immunoenhancement effect was still present 12 hours later for IgA, IgG, number of B cells, complement 3 and gamma-interferon.[24] No attempt has been made to study durations beyond 12 hours.

Sense of Humor and Immunity

Given all the evidence that watching a humorous video strengthens different components of the immune system, it makes sense that individuals who have a better developed sense of humor—meaning that they find more humor in their everyday life, seek out humor more often, laugh more, etc.—should have a stronger immune system, because they get more of the kinds of benefits offered by watching a comedy video by exercising their sense of humor more often. Consistent with this expectation, three studies have shown that individuals with higher scores on a sense of humor test have higher "baseline levels" of IgA.[25]

If people with a better sense of humor have a stronger immune system than their humor-impaired friends, you might expect that those with a less developed sense of humor would show more immunoenhancement from watching a comedy video. The available research, however, suggests that the opposite is true. Individuals with higher sense of humor scores show the greatest increase in IgA after watching a funny video.[26] This suggests that those with a better sense of humor may have appreciated the videos more, or laughed more.

> **"The simple truth is that happy people generally don't get sick."**
> (Bernie Siegel, M.D.)

Humor's ability to protect you against immunosuppression during stress was evident in a study which compared people with a well-developed sense of humor (they found a lot of humor in their everyday life or frequently used humor to cope with stress) to people with a poor sense of humor. Among those who rarely found humor in their own lives, especially when under stress, greater numbers of everyday hassles and negative life events were associated with greater suppression of their immune system (IgA). Among those with a well-developed sense of humor, on the other hand, everyday hassles and problems did not weaken the immune system.[27] Their sense of humor helped keep them from becoming more vulnerable to illness when under stress.

The Role of Mood

Your immune system is very sensitive to your mood, being stronger on your "up" days, and weaker on "down" days. This has been shown for both IgA and natural killer cell activity.[28] It appears to be the negative emotion or mood that accompanies stress that is responsible for the reduced level of antibody response when the immune system is asked to fight a virus or other antigen. This has been shown with reduced levels of natural killer cell activity,[29] lymphocyte proliferation,[30] serum antibody response to Hepatitis B vaccine,[31] and salivary IgA response to a novel antigen,[32] to name a few.

Part of the health-promoting power of your sense of humor lies in the fact that it helps keep the negative events that occur in your life from disturbing your mood.[33] It helps you keep an upbeat, optimistic outlook, even in the face of stress. Bernie Siegel has long emphasized the importance of a positive, optimistic mood in fighting cancer and sustaining wellness,[34] and your sense of humor is one of the best ways you have to maintain this mood on high-stress days.

Which Is More Important, Laughter or the Experience of Humor?

A key question with the immune system research concerns the relative importance of laughter versus the mental/emotional experience of humor. Only two studies have addressed this issue. In one, half the participants were encouraged to laugh at the comedy video, while the other half were asked to suppress laughter while watching. Comparable levels of increased salivary IgA were found for the two groups.[35] Since laughter did not boost the amount of IgA increase, this suggests that the experience of humor may be more important than how much you laugh. However, another study showed that how funny you find the video is not related to the amount of IgA increase shown.[36] The precise way in which one's own sense of humor provides immunoenhancement benefits is clearly complicated, and is not yet well understood.

Pain Reduction

I lived in Paris for three years in the 1980s. I spent a lot of time in a little neighborhood cafe, and almost every time I stopped by for an espresso, there was an old man at his corner table laughing with friends. He rarely went more than 10 minutes without laughing. I was amazed at this and asked him how he managed to stay in such a wonderful mood all the time. To my surprise, he said his laughter didn't always mean he was in a good mood. He laughed for two reasons. One was in order to get into a good mood. He lived alone and didn't like it. He knew that laughter would lift his spirits, so he forced himself to laugh until he really was feeling good.

The other reason was that he had arthritis and had a lot of aches and pains. One day he and his friends were doubling up with laughter about pranks they had played when they were kids. He noticed that his arthritis pain had disappeared during the laughter and didn't show up again until an hour later. From that day on, he was a laugher. It was his way of managing pain. He took control of his pain in a way that also improved the quality of his life. Recent research has supported his approach to pain management. When elderly residents of a long-term care facility watched funny movies, the level of pain they experienced was reduced.[37]

A man went to his doctor complaining of painful headaches. After concluding his tests, the doctor said, "There's only one solution, but it's extreme: castration." The patient said he could never resort to that, and he walked out.

As the weeks went on, his headaches got so painful that he couldn't take it any longer. Finally, he went back to the doctor and agreed to the castration.

The operation was a big success, and the patient couldn't believe that his headaches were finally gone. He felt like a new man. He was so excited about his new life that he went to a tailor and bought a whole new set of clothes— suits, shirts, socks, even underwear.

In jotting down all the appropriate information, the tailor finally asked, "What size underwear do you wear?"

"Forty," replied the man.

"Oh no," said the tailor. "You're a 44. If you wear underwear that tight, you'll get terrible headaches!"

Norman Cousins drew the attention of the medical community to this phenomenon in his book *Anatomy of an Illness,* as noted above. His spinal disease left him in almost constant pain. But he quickly discovered while watching comedy films that belly laughter eased his pain. In his last book, *Head First: The Biology of Hope,* he noted that 10 minutes of belly laughter (just counting the laughing time) would give him two hours of pain-free sleep.

Dr. James Walsh, an American physician, noted in his 1928 book *Laughter and Health,* that laughter often reduced the level of pain experienced following surgery and appeared to promote wound healing, but medical researchers seem to have been unaware of Walsh's observation. It was only after the publication of Cousins' book that researchers began to study laughter's ability to reduce pain.

Several studies have showed that watching or listening to humorous tapes increases the length of time individuals can endure having their hand in ice water before experiencing discomfort.[38] Amazingly, people who found the comedy material funnier were able to leave their hand in longer than those who found it less funny. Individuals who created humor more often themselves also showed reduced sensitivity to pain from the ice water, in comparison to those who created little humor.[39] The level of pain experienced during hydrotherapy (a very painful experience) by two young girls with burns was also found to be reduced by watching cartoons during hydrotherapy.[40]

Having a good sense of humor may yield the same pain-reducing benefits provided by watching a comedy video. Using a procedure called transcutaneous end nerve stimulation to induce pain, individuals who watched a humorous video reported less pain than those who watched a nonhumorous video.[41] But, those who watched the non-humorous video who scored high on a measure of sense of humor showed just as much resistance to discomfort and pain as did people who watched the funny video. So a good sense of humor does seem to help in managing pain.

      "*Humor is the instinct for taking pain playfully.***"** (Max Eastman)

A Japanese study showed that listening to an hour of traditional comic stories (Rakugo) reduced the level of pain experienced by rheumatoid arthritis patients.[42] This is an especially important finding, since the symptoms experienced by these patients (as well as patients with multiple sclerosis and numerous other medical conditions) generally worsen in the presence of negative emotional states. Finding something to laugh at when you're in pain can help reduce the pain at the same time that it substitutes a more positive for a negative mood and lifts your spirits. This may explain why rheumatoid arthritis patients who report more chronic pain also say they look for humor more often in everyday life.[43] They've learned that humor helps manage their pain.

Finally, a Swedish physician reported that six women suffering from painful muscle disorders got significant relief from pain through a 13-week course in humor therapy.[44] Throughout this period, they read funny books, listened to or watched funny tapes, and worked at "giving higher priority to humor in their everyday lives." They also attended lectures on humor research. Those patients who laughed the most in group sessions showed the greatest symptom reduction.

There is also widespread anecdotal evidence that laughter can help manage pain. Norman Cousins once described in a speech how he, Dr. Carl Simonton, and Jose Jimenez (a comedian from the old *Steve Allen Show*) went to talk to a group of patients at a VA Hospital. Jimenez had them falling off their chairs laughing. The doctors later told Cousins that 85% of the patients had been experiencing pain when they entered the room. But the laughter reduced or eliminated the pain for most of them.

In a study of 35 patients in a rehabilitation hospital, 74% agreed with the statement, "Sometimes laughing works as well as a pain pill."[45] The patients had such conditions as traumatic brain injury, spinal cord injury, arthritis, limb amputations, and a range of other neurological or musculoskeletal disorders. Given the power of humor and laughter to reduce pain, it is not surprising that humor has been applied as a "treatment" in managing pain associated with burns and dental work,[46] and as a component of general nursing care.[47]

Nurses often tell me they know a patient who tried Cousins' approach and found that it also reduced their pain. But not all who try it experience pain reduction. The reason for this inconsistency remains unclear.

> **"*A clown is like an aspirin, only he works twice as fast.*"**
> (Groucho Marx)

For those who do experience pain reduction following laughter, why does it occur? One possibility is distraction. Humor draws attention away from the source of discomfort—at least momentarily. The most commonly given explanation, however, is that laughter causes the production of endorphins, one of the body's natural pain killers. This explanation makes good sense, but as of 1998, no one has been able to demonstrate it with data. Investigators who have tried to show the endorphin-humor connection have failed to do so.[48]

Regardless of whether laughter does or does not cause the release of endorphins into the blood stream, its ability to reduce pain is undoubtedly partly due to its reduction of muscle tension. Even brief relaxation procedures have been shown to reduce pain—both in laboratory and clinical settings.[49] Many pain centers around the country now use meditation and other relaxation techniques to reduce the level of pain medication needed by patients. Laughter is just one additional technique for achieving the same effect.

This muscle relaxation effect has its practical side in hospitals. Some nurses tell patients jokes before giving them shots, because they know it keeps them from tightening up their muscles in anticipation of the shot.

To give you an idea of Cousins' sense of humor, one morning a nurse brought in a specimen bottle (to obtain a urine sample), and left it on his breakfast tray. There was also a bottle of apple juice on the tray, so Cousins poured some of it into the specimen bottle and finished his breakfast. When the nurse returned, she held the bottle up to the light and said, "Hmmm, it looks a little cloudy today." Cousins picked it up and said, "Well then, let's run it through again." And he drank it! Since this story is widely shared, other patients have been known to try the same trick. If you try it, be sure to keep track of which bottle is yours!

On another occasion, Cousins was about to take a bath in a tub filled with an oily substance designed to ease some of his joint problems. He described it as "a cross between stale oatmeal and used crankcase oil." When the nurse left for a moment, leaving the bottle containing the oily stuff near the tub, Cousins poured most of it down the drain. When the nurse returned, he held up the bottle and said, "I'm terribly sorry, but I can't get the rest of this down."

Cardiac Exercise

Have you managed to avoid getting caught up in the jogging, aerobics, and jazzercize crazes of recent years? If you hate to work out, laughter may be the exercise program you've been looking for. It's fun, requires no special training, shoes, or clothes. You don't even have to leave your couch or office to do it. And it takes no extra time from whatever you're already doing.

The next time you're having a good belly laugh, put your hand over your heart when you stop laughing. You'll see that your heart is racing, even after 15–20 seconds of laughter. It will remain elevated for 3–5 minutes. This has caused some to refer to laughter as "internal jogging." You can give your heart a good workout several times a day, just by laughing. One physician noted that his patients who say they laugh regularly have lower resting heart rates. While this is no substitute for real exercise, many seniors and bed-ridden patients don't have the option of other forms of physical exercise. For them, laughter is FUNdamental to good cardiac conditioning.

Other Benefits

Blood Pressure

Other physical health benefits may result from humor and laughter, but scientists have been very slow in looking for them. Laughter may turn out, for example, to help lower blood pressure. As your heart beats more rapidly during laughter, it pumps more blood through your system, producing the familiar flushed cheeks. Not surprisingly, blood pressure increases during laughter, with larger increases corresponding to more intense and longer-lasting laughs. If this were a lasting increase, it might point to a harmful effect of laughter. When laughter stops, however, blood pressure appears to drop below the level shown before the laughter started.[50] This drop below the pre-laughter baseline is short-lived, so it's not clear whether regular laughter helps keep blood pressure within manageable limits.

There is some evidence that the relationship between blood pressure and humor may be different for men and women.[51] Women who score higher on measures of sense of humor have been shown to have lower blood pressure than low sense of humor women, suggesting that a good sense of humor does help protect them against hypertension. A better sense of humor in this study, however, did not reduce the amount of blood pressure elevation among women during stressful situations. Men with higher humor scores did not show the generally lower blood pressure levels showed by women, but a better sense of humor did reduce the extent of their blood pressure increase under stress. More research will be required to sort these differences out, but these findings indicate that humor does offer some protection against the harmful effects of elevated blood pressure for both sexes.

In connection with job-related stress, individuals in higher-level occupations may want to make a special effort to improve their humor skills, since recent research has shown that the amount of stress-related elevation in blood pressure appears to be greater among those with higher-level jobs.[52] Among African Americans, hypertension was greater among higher-level occupations in general—regardless of the stress of the moment.[53]

Respiration

Laughter triggers a peculiar respiratory pattern which offers health benefits for certain individuals. In normal relaxed breathing, there is a balance between the amount of air you take in and breathe out. The problem is that when you are not breathing deeply, a considerable amount of residual air remains in the lungs. When you're under stress, breathing becomes even shallower and more rapid, reducing the amount of oxygen taken in and producing a still greater amount of residual air. This breathing also occurs more from the chest, instead of the diaphragm. (Relaxation techniques emphasize the importance of breathing from the diaphragm.) As this residual air stays in the lungs for longer periods of time, its oxygen content drops and the level of water vapor and carbon dioxide increases.[54] The health risk here arises for individuals prone to respiratory difficulties, since the increased water vapor creates a more favorable environment for bacterial growth and pulmonary infection.

Frequent belly laughter reduces this risk by emptying your lungs of more of the air that's taken in. When you laugh, you push air out of your lungs until you can't push out any more. Then you take a deep breath and start the same process all over again. Each time you laugh, you get rid of the excess carbon dioxide and water vapor that's building up and replace it with oxygen-rich air.

Hospitalized patients with respiratory problems are often encouraged to breathe deeply and exhale fully, but nurses have difficulty getting them to do so. Most patients enjoy a good laugh, though, so many nurses have learned to tell them a joke from time to time or give them a comedy tape to view.

Emphysema and other respiratory patients often have a build-up of phlegm or mucous in their respiratory tracts. Nurses try to get them to cough to loosen up and expel these substances, but they generally don't enjoy coughing, so the phlegm builds up. When they laugh, however, they inevitably start coughing, producing exactly the effect the nurses want—and the patients have a good time in the process.

Sedimentation Rate

One of the most interesting observations made by Norman Cousins' doctor following Cousins' use of humor and other positive emotions to fight his disease was that laughter reduced his sedimentation rate—an index of the degree of infection or inflammation in the body. Since Cousins' illness involved severe inflammation of the spine, his sedimentation rate was very high. His physician, Dr. William Hitzig, measured his sedimentation rate before and after rounds of hearty belly laughter while watching comedy films. He found that "just a few moments of robust laughter . . . knocked a significant number of units off the sedimentation rate. What to him was most interesting of all was that the reduction held and was cumulative."[55] Cousins noted that this reduced sedimentation rate was followed by increased mobility and reduced pain. Unfortunately, this is a single case, so there is no way of determining whether laughter really did cause the reduced inflammation. But Dr. Hitzig's observation is of such clear importance to medical research that it's surprising that investigators have not attempted to study it further.

Perceived Health

Another way to determine the relationship between humor and health is to simply ask people about their health. This generally is referred to as "perceived health." Both college students and older adults (55+) who report using humor more often as a coping style perceive themselves to be in better physical health.[56] A study of 36 executive women showed that those with higher scores on a measure of sense of humor reported fewer symptoms associated with physical health problems.[57] In the study of patients in a rehabilitation hospital described earlier, 94% of the patients indicated that when they laughed, they felt better.[58]

Psychoneuroimmunology and Humor

The exciting new work being done on humor and health is part of a broader research movement in the health sciences focusing on the impact of the mind on the body. In fact, an entirely new area of medical research has developed in the past decade, with the unwieldy name of "psychoneuroimmunology." Every year, more and more studies demonstrate that your thoughts, moods, emotions, and belief system have a fundamental impact on some of the body's basic health and healing mechanisms.[59] One expert in the area, Dr. Ron Anderson, noted in Bill Moyers' book *Healing and the Mind* that "There is no question that your body and mind tied together help you fight infection."

Whether or not you get sick depends on your body's ability to fight off infection and disease. In 1980 (prior to the discovery of the AIDS virus), the departing editor of the *New England Journal of Medicine,* Dr. Franz Ingelfinger, estimated that 85% of all human illnesses are curable by the body's own healing system. We've known for a long time that good nutrition, exercise, adequate sleep, avoidance of harmful drugs, and sanitary personal habits aide the body's ability to do this. We now know that building a positive focus in your life is equally important.

The body's healing system responds favorably to positive attitudes, thoughts, moods, and emotions (e.g., to love, hope, optimism, caring, intimacy, joy, laughter, and humor), and negatively to negative ones (hate, hopelessness, pessimism, indifference, anxiety, depression, loneliness, etc.). So you want to organize your life to maintain as positive a focus as possible.

This doesn't mean you should avoid negative emotions. You need to find ways to express whatever emotions you feel. Candace Pert, former Chief of the Section of Brain Biochemistry of the Clinical Neuroscience Branch at the National Institute of Mental Health, studies health influences at the neurochemical level. She noted recently that "repressing emotions can only be causative of disease."[60] Failure to find effective ways to express negative emotions causes you to "stew in your own juices" day after day, and this chronic immersion in negativity is what appears to produce harmful influences on health.

Surprisingly, negative emotions appear to have an enhancing effect on the immune system in the short run.[61] So short-term negative emotional states do not pose a health threat. The threat comes when you get caught up in negativity as a habitual style. You need techniques that keep you from wallowing in resistance-lowering negativity. The longer negative states persist in your mind/body, the greater the likelihood that they will lead to some negative influence on your health. Love is probably the most powerful tool for overcoming negativity. Humor, in my view, comes a close second.

The mechanisms by which your mind promotes health and healing aren't yet fully understood (see the following section), but your body certainly knows what to do. All you have to do is set up the right conditions for the mechanisms to operate.

While the focus here is on humor, any effective coping skill will help sustain health and well being. One study showed that people who cope less well with life's stresses were three times more likely to contract the flu during a flu epidemic.[62] This is not surprising, since poor copers have depressed levels of natural killer cell activity, while those judged to be coping well show higher levels of natural killer cell activity.[63]

It's tempting to think that good coping skills are essential only for the big stressors in life. However, the way you handle minor daily hassles has been shown to be a better predictor of illness than the way you respond to less frequent major stressors.[64]

Emotion: The Key to the Mind's Influence on Health

Candace Pert noted in Bill Moyers' *Healing and the Mind* television series that emotions—registered and stored in the body in the form of chemical messages—are the best candidates for the key to the health connection between mind and body. It is through the emotions you experience in connection with your thoughts and daily attitudes—actually, through the neurochemical changes that accompany these emotions—that your mind acquires the power to influence whether you get sick or remain well.

The key, according to Pert, is found in complex molecules called neuropeptides. "A peptide is made up of amino acids, which are the building blocks of protein. There are twenty-three different amino acids. Peptides are amino acids strung together very much like pearls strung along in a necklace."[65] Peptides are found throughout the body, including the brain and immune system. The brain contains about 60 different neuropeptides, including endorphins. These neuropeptides are the means by which all cells in the body communicate with each other. This includes brain-to-brain messages, brain-to-body messages, body-to-body messages, and body-to-brain messages.

Individual cells, including brain cells, immune cells, and other body cells, have receptor sites that receive neuropeptides. The kinds of neuropeptides available to cells are constantly changing, reflecting variations in your emotions throughout the day. The exact combinations of neuropeptides released during different emotional states has not yet been determined.

The kind and number of emotion-linked neuropeptides available at receptor sites of cells influence your probability of staying well or getting sick. "Viruses use these same receptors to enter into a cell, and depending on how much of the . . . natural peptide for that receptor is around, the virus will have an easier or harder time getting into the cell. **So our emotional state will affect whether we'll get sick from the same loading dose of a virus.**"[66]

This kind of conclusion from a researcher at the cutting edge of research on the mind/body connection should give you all the motivation you need to make the effort to improve your sense of humor. More humor and laughter in your life helps assure that these chemical messages are working for you, not against you.

> ❝ *The chemicals that are running our body and our brain are the same chemicals that are involved in emotion. And that says to me that . . . we'd better pay more attention to emotions with respect to health.* ❞
> (Candace Pert)

It was noted earlier that preliminary research suggests that humor/laughter stimulates the production of helper T-cells, the cells attacked by the AIDS virus. If humor were to help the body battle AIDS (there is presently no evidence that it does—or does not), it probably wouldn't be as a mere result of the production of more helper T-cells, since there would be every reason to expect these new cells to also be invaded by the virus. Rather, it would probably be due to the neuropeptides produced by the positive emotional state that goes along with humor and laughter.

Along these lines, Pert has noted that "The AIDS virus uses a receptor that is normally used by a neuropeptide. So whether an AIDS virus will be able to enter a cell or not depends on how much of this natural peptide is around, which . . . would be a function of what state of emotional expression the organism is in."[67]

> ❝ *This I believe to be the chemical function of humor: to change the character of our thought.* ❞
> (Lin Yutang)

Research on the immune system supports this view. For example, negative emotion has been found to be associated with reduced salivary IgA response to a novel antigen,[68] lower serum antibody responses to Hepatitis B vaccine,[69] reduced proliferation of lymphocytes,[70] and reduced natural killer cell activity.[71] Positive emotional states have similarly been linked to heightened immune response, both for IgA[72] and natural killer cell activity.[73]

The research on the effect of other emotions on health will not be exhaustively reviewed here, but some of the major studies will be presented to show you that there is no longer any doubt that your daily mood or frame of mind makes a significant contribution to your health—especially when it persists day after day, year after year. Anything you can do to sustain a more positive, upbeat frame of mind in dealing with the daily hassles and problems in your life contributes to your physical health at the same time that it helps you cope with stress and be more effective on the job. Your sense of humor is one of the most powerful tools you have to make certain that your daily mood and emotional state support good health.

Negative Health Influences

Survival

On the negative side, researchers have known for a long time that your emotional state influences your odds of survival—at least under certain conditions. Several studies have shown that, among older people, the death rate for both men and women increases sharply following the death of their spouse.[74] The greater the level of depression experienced, the greater the impact on the surviving spouse's health.

All of us have down days where we feel blue or depressed. The point at which this becomes a risk factor is when it persists. One study showed that among a group of adults given a test for depression, those who died of cancer 17 years later were twice as likely to have had high depression scores (17 years earlier) than those who developed no cancer at all.[75] Another study showed that patients with AIDS Related Complex who had weaker beliefs that they could do things to influence the course of the disease were less successful in fighting off AIDS.[76] These studies suggest that, at least in some circumstances, persistent negative emotion can put you at greater risk of death.

Among patients with heart disease, those with a pessimistic outlook about their ability to recover enough to eventually resume their daily routine were more than twice as likely as optimists to have died one year later, even when severity of condition was taken into account.[77] Another follow-up study of patients recovering from heart attacks showed that those who scored high on tests of sadness and depression were eight times as likely as more optimistic patients to die within the next 18 months.[78] Risk of death was tripled both among those who tended to hold in their anger and those judged to be very anxious.

The researcher who conducted the latter study sees the importance of helping heart patients reduce their pessimistic outlooks and negative emotions, but concluded that "we don't know how to change negative emotions." By the time you finish reading this book, you will know how to do so—by improving your skills at finding and creating humor, especially in the midst of negative life circumstances.

      ❝ *We're all in this together—by ourselves.* **❞**   (Lily Tomlin)

Symptoms

It is not surprising that the grief you feel after the death of a loved one can damage your own health. But even the commonplace bad moods and negative attitudes we all suffer can set us up for poorer health—if they occur day after day, month after month. This is difficult to document in research, but the herpes simplex virus (responsible for small ulcers, fever blisters, and cold sores around the mouth) provides a good way to demonstrate it. This virus, carried by about 1/3 of the U.S. population, normally remains latent, but persistent negative emotions can trigger an outbreak.[79] Pessimistic students, who can be expected to generally have more negative moods than optimistic students, have even been shown to develop more symptoms than optimistic students around exam time.[80] Pessimistic students also show more symptoms of illness over time than do optimistic students in the general population (i.e., regardless of their herpes simplex status), even when both groups start out equally healthy.[81]

In 1991, an article in the *New England Journal of Medicine* finally established that stress makes you more vulnerable to the common cold. However, your mood and coping skills also influence susceptibility to colds and the flu.[82] One study showed that those with low morale, and who cope less well with stress, are three times more likely to catch the flu during a flu epidemic.[83]

In the case of more severe illnesses, increased stress levels among coronary heart disease patients have been shown to increase the level of angina pectoris experienced.[84]

Multiple sclerosis is a good example of a disease known to incur exacerbations or worsening symptoms in the presence of negative emotional states. Anything MS patients can do to sustain a positive frame of mind on a day-to-day basis helps keep these exacerbations from occurring. One man who had difficulty controlling his shaking hand told me, "MS also has its good points; I never have to worry about stirring my coffee anymore."

In summarizing the entire field of research in this area, Blair Justice concluded in his book, *Who Gets Sick*, that while there are many exceptions, the general rule is that "Those who get sick the most seem to view the world and their lives as unmanageable."[85] What better reason could there be to learn to manage the stress in your own life more effectively? Your sense of humor makes life more manageable at the same time that it adds more joy and fun.

People who are chronically prone to depression, anger, or anxiety over the course of their lives have a greater risk of disease.[86] There is a growing conviction among many researchers that this increased susceptibility to disease is at least partly a result of the suppressive effects of negative emotions upon the immune system, although the disease that appears depends on specific vulnerabilities, health-related habits, and family history.

Generally speaking, you're most likely to become ill in response to stress if your immune system is already compromised. For example, since the immune system becomes weaker as you get older, senior citizens are more vulnerable to stress-related illness. Clearly, any tools which these individuals can acquire to help manage negative emotions should also help protect them against disease.

Finally, there is now ample evidence that mental factors influence the mechanisms which mediate pain. Many patients say that their pain is worsened when they feel depressed or when things seem hopeless. It is reduced, on the other hand, when they're distracted or doing something enjoyable. One researcher concluded that "thoughts and emotions can directly influence physiological responses—including muscle tension, blood flow, and levels of brain chemicals—that play important roles in the production of pain. . . . Psychological factors can also indirectly influence pain by affecting the way you cope with it."[87] New techniques for managing pain are designed to help reduce the occurrence of stress-increasing thoughts, emotions, and behaviors, because this serves to reduce the pain experienced. One of these techniques—the most enjoyable one—is humor and laughter.

Positive Health Influences

Survival

On the positive side, one important study showed that among a group of individuals 65 and older, those who were optimistic about their health, in spite of lab tests that showed them to be in poor health, had lower death rates over the next six years than those who were pessimistic about their health, in spite of health records which documented that they were in good health.[88] Optimism, in this case, became a self-fulfilling prophecy, leading individuals in relatively poor health to fare better than their healthier, but pessimistic peers.

The most dramatic evidence of the impact of a positive attitude on health comes from studies of survival rates of cancer patients. For example, among patients with metastatic (spreading) cancers, those who expressed greater hope at the time of their diagnosis survived longer.[89] In another study, over 400 reports of spontaneous remission of cancer were reviewed and analyzed. The patients themselves attributed their cure to a broad range of causes, but only one factor was common to all cases—a shift toward greater hope and a more positive attitude.[90]

One clinician traced unexpected tumor shrinkage to favorable changes in the psychosocial situation of the patient. Examples of such changes include "a sudden fortunate marriage; the experience of having one's entire order of clergy engage in an intercessory prayer; sudden, lasting reconciliation with a long-hated mother; unexpected and enthusiastic praise and encouragement from an expert in one's field; and the fortunate death of a decompensated alcoholic and addicted husband who stood in the way of a satisfying career."[91]

Norman Cousins described the preliminary findings of a national survey of oncologists, completed during his stay at the UCLA Medical School. Of the 649 who offered their opinions on the importance of various psychosocial factors in fighting cancer, "More than 90% of the physicians said they attached the highest value to the attitudes of hope and optimism."[92]

All of these findings are consistent with the findings of a recent study showing that method actors asked to generate the emotion of joy within themselves showed an increase in the number of natural killer cells circulating in the blood stream within 20 minutes.[93] Once they got themselves out of this positive state, their levels of natural killer cells quickly dropped again.

There have always been doctors who have emphasized the importance of a "will to live" in fighting serious diseases. Most recently, this banner has been carried nobly by Dr. Bernie Siegel, who emphasizes the importance of hope, determinism, optimism, and a "fighting spirit" among patients who are battling cancer. Research now supports this view, so it is important that doctors, nurses, and family members associated with people who are ill make an effort to support the development and maintenance of a positive outlook in the patient.

Evidence of the importance of a fighting spirit was obtained in another study of cancer survivors.[94] Cancer patients with a fighting spirit were most likely to be long-term survivors, and have no relapses. Short-term survivors were more likely to show a "stoic, stiff upper lip attitude," and to continue their lives either as if nothing were different, or with a sense of helplessness or hopelessness.

"If I'd known I was going to live this long, I'd have taken better care of myself."

AIDS patients with a more optimistic outlook have also been shown to survive longer,[95] as have men suffering heart attacks.[96] In describing preliminary findings from a study of AIDS survivors completed at the UCLA Medical School, Cousins reported that "the refusal to accept the verdict of grim inevitability" is one of the traits that characterizes AIDS patients who live long past the time predicted for them.[97] All of these findings clearly support the idea that positive beliefs, attitudes, and emotions contribute to your survival. And your sense of humor helps maintain this positive focus on a day-to-day basis.

Symptoms

A generally positive and optimistic attitude also reduces the severity and frequency of occurrence of symptoms. For example, college students with a more optimistic outlook on life were found to be in better physical health (as determined by their physicians) than their more pessimistic peers two decades later.[98] More optimistic students also had fewer sick days (e.g., due to colds and flu) in the month after optimism levels were determined and fewer visits to the doctor during the following year (even when initial health status and level of depression were controlled for).[99]

Attitudinal and emotional factors have even been linked to wound healing. For example, more optimistic patients showed the most rapid healing following an operation for a detached retina.[100] Consistent with this finding, one investigator concluded, following a thorough review of research in psychoneuroimmunology, that positive emotions facilitate the healing of wounds.[101] He felt that they did this by disrupting the production of neurotransmitters, hormones, and other substances which interfere with certain steps of the healing process.

Evidence is also emerging to show that hope, like optimism, contributes to improvement of symptoms. For example, among spinal injury patients with comparable injuries, those who expressed greater hope for improvement became more mobile and coped better emotionally than those who saw their situation as hopeless.[102]

In a study of men with HIV infection, meetings were arranged twice a week to practice relaxation methods and talk about coping with the problems confronting them. Early results showed that these procedures delayed the onset of more serious AIDS symptoms, strengthened the immune system, and boosted the men's emotional resilience.[103]

Apart from love, there is no better tool for maintaining a positive, optimistic frame of mind in the midst of serious illness than your sense of humor. That is one reason why many hospitals now make an effort to build humor into the health care setting (see discussion below). The problem, of course, is that it is impossible to have access to your sense of humor when you are ill if you haven't cultivated it when you're healthy and in good spirits. If you begin building your humor coping skills now, you'll have them when you really need them.

Do People with a Good Sense of Humor Get Sick Less Often?

We have seen that humor and laughter positively influence our body in ways that should sustain health, but little research has been done on whether a better sense of humor actually helps keep you from getting sick. However, since people with a better sense of humor have higher IgA levels, and those with higher levels of salivary IgA are less likely to get colds[104] or be infected with Streptococcus,[105] humor should reduce the frequency of colds.

The only study to directly examine this question found that the impact of one's sense of humor upon colds depends on the kind of sense of humor you have.[106] It was only individuals whose sense of humor took the form of seeking out and appreciating humor who had fewer and less severe colds/flu than their low humor counterparts. Surprisingly, those whose sense of humor took the form of initiating humor more often did not have fewer or less severe colds/flu. The researchers argued that being a person who likes to tell jokes or otherwise initiate humor takes them into more frequent contact with other people, which serves to expose them to infectious agents more often, robbing them of the advantage that a more active sense of humor otherwise offers. Obviously, more research is required to clear up this confusing picture.

The importance of active use of one's sense of humor in producing humor's health benefits was confirmed in another study in an unusual way. It found that among a group of mothers with newborn infants, those who actively used humor to cope with the stress in their lives had fewer upper respiratory infections—and their infants also had fewer infections.[107] This seemed to be because these mothers had higher levels of immunoglobulin A in their breast milk. Consistent with this finding, another study showed that mothers with low levels of IgA at the time of birth had babies who showed more illnesses in the first six weeks postpartum.[108] So breast-feeding mothers now have all the more reason to build plenty of laughter in their life every day.

Among adults, if we look at bodily symptoms alone, independent of any diagnosed illness, there is some evidence that individuals who have more negative reactions to humor (finding a lot of different types of humor aversive or objectionable) report more bodily symptoms and complaints.[109] Students complaining of cardiovascular symptoms and gastroenterological symptoms also have been shown to have this more negative reaction to humor.[110]

Coronary heart disease (CHD) has long been linked to the so-called Type A personality. One pair of researchers observed over 25 years ago that only type B individuals use humor as a coping tool in dealing with stress and hostile feelings.[111] Hostile humor has also been found to be the main kind of humor enjoyed by Type A patients, while Type B patients enjoy non-hostile as well as hostile humor.[112] This is consistent with the findings showing a close relationship between hostility and heart disease. While laughter at hostile humor must provide some of the benefits described above for CHD-prone individuals, those benefits are clearly not enough to offset the bodily effects caused by hostility to begin with. Developing non-hostile aspects of one's sense of humor to counteract this effect is essential for Type A individuals.

The Humor-in-Hospitals Movement

Chances are that you have never been in a hospital with a "humor program." The very idea of humor in hospitals may even strike you as an oxymoron (like "giant shrimp," "smart bombs," "military intelligence," etc.). If ever there were two things that don't go together, it's humor and hospitals. After all, hospitals are places for the very sick.

The last decade, however, has witnessed a (slowly building) revolution in health care, as more and more hospitals become convinced of the therapeutic power of humor. The humor-in-hospitals movement has also gained support because of the trend toward depersonalization in hospitals in recent years, as focus has shifted away from the person and toward application of the latest technology. Patients now want a more personalized relationship with caregivers, and humor helps establish it.

Patients generally arrive at hospitals in a state of stress and anxiety, are placed in a strange environment, submitted to degrading and embarrassing procedures by people they don't know, have their independence and sense of control removed, and don't always get the kind of explanations that they would like. Humor provides a means of establishing a more personal relationship with hospital staff, easing tensions and anxiety, and helping patients cope. The nurse who maintains a high level of competence, but also has a "light touch," has an extra means of saying, "I care."

Many nurses and hospital administrators are concerned that patients will perceive them as unprofessional, and as unconcerned about their health problems if they show a sense of humor while interacting with patients. There is evidence, however, that patients welcome the opportunity for humor and laughter during their hospital stay. The figures in brackets indicate the percentage of patients in one study who agreed with the following statements: 1) "Nurses should laugh more often with patients" [80%], 2) "Nurses should try to get their patients to laugh" [83%], 3) "Laughing helps me get through difficult times" [83%]. The following statements generated strong disagreement by the same patients: 1) "Nurses who laugh with patients are unprofessional" [94%], 2) "Nurses who laugh are insensitive to patients who are suffering" [91%], 3) "Laughter does not belong in a rehabilitation hospital" [89%].[113]

Types of Hospital Humor Programs

The best known approach to bringing humor and laughter to hospital settings is the use of clowns. Many hospitals now have volunteer clowns who visit patients in their rooms in order to boost their spirits and distract them from their anxieties and concerns. The Big Apple Circus Clown Care Unit was initiated in 1986, and has spawned many comparable clown units across the U.S. and around the world (e.g., the Fondation Theodora in France).

The power of clowns is evident in the following example provided by a clown from the Big Apple Circus. An 11-year-old boy had been doused with gasoline and set on fire by an older boy.

> *"He was conscious, but in terrible pain with major burns over more than half of his body. I went right into emergency with him. When the surgeons began cutting away dead flesh, I began telling funny stories and promising circus tickets and making scarves appear and disappear—anything to keep his mind off the agony. Pretty soon he was rolling his eyes in amazement and finally I got him laughing behind his medical mask. It was incredible. He was staring death in the face—and he was having fun!"*[114]

Another common approach to building a lighter touch into hospitals is to create a "humor cart." This is a cart which can be wheeled into patients' rooms, and which contains funny audio and video tapes, books of cartoons, games, funny props, etc. Several hundred hospitals around the country now have humor carts. Volunteers from the community often take responsibility for these programs.

A few hospitals have entire rooms devoted to fun and humor for ambulatory patients. These rooms are given such names as "The Lively Room," "The Living Room," or simply "The Humor Room." Sunnyview Rehabilitation Hospital, in Schenectady, New York even has a full-time humor coordinator, whose job is to be sure humor is made available to all of those patients who want it.

One of the first humor rooms was established at St. Joseph's Hospital in Houston. Representatives of this program have expressed their belief that the program leads to shorter hospital stays for many patients. The head nurse observed that some patients are able to reduce their pain and nausea medications following a visit to the humor room.

I know of one hospital which has a humor program built into its pediatrics department. The hospital recently was short of beds for adults, so a 70-year-old cancer patient was forced to stay in pediatrics for nearly a week. While he came in depressed, he had such a good time during his stay that when he was later re-admitted to the hospital, he specifically asked for a room in pediatrics.

One of the most effective means of making the therapeutic benefits of humor available to patients is through the daily interaction with hospital staff. Nurses and other staff members can have a powerful impact on patients' mood by bringing an occasional laugh to patients as they do their jobs. The Humor Skills Training Program provided in this book will help nurses find their own style of bringing humor to the bedside.

For a detailed discussion of guidelines for appropriate and inappropriate uses of humor in hospital settings, see a recent article in *RN Magazine*.[115]

SMILE: A New Approach to Personalizing Humor Intervention Programs

If humor does have the power to reduce patient tension and anxiety, help cope with the life circumstances that result from a serious illness, and even promote healing, these benefits should be maximized when the humor made available to patients is the kind of humor they especially enjoy. For example, evidence presented in the next section shows that the amount of reduction of pain medication requested following watching comedy films was greater when patients were able to choose the films watched (presumably, they chose films that were funnier to them). A software package has recently been developed in order to help hospitals and other organizations provide a personalized humor prescription to patients.

THE COMPUTER-BASED GUIDE
FOR CREATING
PERSONALIZED HUMOR PROGRAMS

Subjective Multidimensional Interactive Laughter Evaluation

The system is called SMILE, which stands for "Subjective Multidimensional Interactive Laughter Evaluation."[116] Patients complete a brief survey which touches on their recent emotional state, stress levels, support system, judgment of how well they're coping, attitudes toward humor, and more. The survey also obtains information on their favorite print cartoons, comedians, sit coms, etc. The computer provides a written summary of the information provided by the patient, including a specific recommendation of the kinds of humor and humorists preferred. This allows hospital personnel (usually volunteers) to provide comedy videos, cartoon books and other forms of humor which precisely match each patient's unique sense of humor.

One of the questions in SMILE asks whether the patient would welcome a more humorous style of interaction from nurses and other staff. If they say yes, a clown sticker (the image shown above) is placed on their chart (or on the door to the patient's room), so that staff can tell at a glance that it's ok to laugh and share humor with this patient.

Impact on Patient Outcomes

The main purpose behind the addition of therapeutic humor programs to hospitals is to provide a positive counter-weight to the negative circumstances that have brought patients to the hospital. But in the current climate of rising healthcare costs, it's also important to consider whether humor has any effect on recovery rate or other measures of improvement of one's condition. Since more work has been done on other mind-body approaches than upon humor, they will be discussed first.

Other Mind-Body Approaches

In one analysis of 191 different studies (involving 8600 patients), a wide range of mind/body interventions before and after surgery (e.g., guided imagery, hypnosis, relaxation procedures, biofeedback, and giving information) were found to be effective in improving surgery outcomes. "These interventions have been shown to work for virtually every imaginable kind of surgery—from back surgery to coronary-bypass operations to cancer resections."[117]

Since most health management systems are concerned about length of hospital stays, it is important to note that one analysis of 13 different studies showed that "psychosocial interventions reduced hospitalization by an average of 2.4 days. . . ."[118] A different analysis of 102 studies showed that 79% of them revealed a shorter length of hospital stay because of the mind-body procedure used.[119]

The most effective of the various procedures used over the past two decades involve what have been called "psychoeducational interventions." These involve providing patients health-related information about their condition and surgical procedure, as well as some kind of skill or exercise that helps them reduce pain or cope better.

In one analysis of 102 different studies, such interventions were found to have a significant positive impact on recovery rate, pain reduction, psychological well-being and satisfaction with care. This was found for abdominal, thoracic, orthopedic, gynecologic, cancer, and eye-ear-nose-throat patients.[120] An especially strong effect was found for the ability of these mind-body procedures to reduce medical complications and reduce the number of days after discharge before resuming normal activities. In a 1998 review of all

the research in this area, Henry Dreher concluded that in addition to providing prepara-
tory information about the upcoming surgery, the provision of coping and rehabilitation
skills plays a key role in the gains shown.[121] Relaxation techniques alone showed only
mixed success, in spite of the fact that they are one of the most popular approaches used
in many healthcare settings.

Hospital Humor Programs

In spite of the large number of hospitals around the world which have adopted clown
visits or other types of therapeutic humor programs for patients, there has been little
attempt to document their impact on such measures as speed of recovery, postoperative
pain, or wound healing. Hospitals have simply adopted humor programs because they
can see from their own experience that these programs work in helping patients cope.
If it saved the hospital money, that would simply be icing on the cake.

As indicated earlier, Dr. James Walsh noted 70 years ago that laughter appeared to
promote wound healing. Recent research in psychoneuroimmunology has confirmed this
finding for positive emotion in general. One researcher has suggested that it may not be
so much what positive emotion does that is the key, but what it prevents.[122] He feels
that the effect may be due to the disruption of production of neurotransmitters, hormones
and other substances (associated with stress and negative emotion) which interfere with
the healing process.

Humor's power to speed up wound healing may be due to its capacity to lower blood
levels of cortisol (see section on stress hormones), which can suppress natural killer cell
and lymphocyte activity and suppress the production of antibodies. This possibility is
supported by a study in which surgical patients were given training in guided imagery
and relaxation. It showed that these patients had more rapid wound healing than a control
group, and also had lower post-surgical levels of cortisol.[123]

Several studies (discussed above) have documented humor's ability to reduce pain in
many patients. In one study, patients were shown either comedy or serious movies (one
in the morning and one in the afternoon) on two consecutive days following orthopedic
surgery. In comparison with the serious movie, those who watched the comedies
requested 61% less "minor" pain medication (aspirin and mild tranquilizers) over the next
two days.[124]

Surprisingly, among those who watched the comedy films, the amount of major pain
medication requested depended on whether patients were able to choose the funny movie
they watched. Those who were able to choose movies that were funny to them requested
less major pain medication than those who were presented a movie to watch without
choosing. According to the researchers, "This unanticipated result is probably due to the
fact that humor preferences are idiosyncratic, and few things are as irritating as being
exposed to material that fails in its attempt to be funny. From an applied standpoint, our
results suggest that care should be taken to determine a patient's humor preferences
before humor is introduced into a hospital setting." The SMILE software described above
is ideally suited to do this.

Among a group of elderly residents who suffered chronic pain in a long-term care
facility, watching a 20-minute comedy program 3 days a week for 6 weeks significantly

reduced the amount of pain medication requested during this period.[125] This reduction was, not surprisingly, accompanied by a more positive mood.

The research on blood pressure suggests that humor will help many patients keep blood pressure down as they prepare for stressful medical procedures. It may even help reduce inflammation levels (see section on Sedimentation Rate).

Nurses have tremendous power to boost the spirits of their patients. And this, in turn, helps patients mobilize their own natural healing resources. If you are a nurse, you can use humor to help your patients cope. The catch is, of course, that you must first improve your own humor skills. Many nurses around the country are already transferring the benefits of the 8-Step Program to their patients. One nurse told me that her favorite line is, "I was going to tell you a joke, but I can see you're in stitches already."

Patients say that humor and shared laughter help raise their spirits, and take their minds off their illness and problems. In some cases, patients regularly exposed to hospital humor also leave the hospital earlier than they would normally be expected to. I know of a cancer center in Florida where the patients have such a good time while undergoing treatments that they often go back for visits long after their disease is in remission.

One physician observed that patients with spinal cord injuries who were able to laugh about their circumstances were much better at absorbing and dealing with the humiliation and frustration they often felt. They also had fewer complications than patients who were unable to find a light side of their condition. This doctor is convinced that humor and laughter play an important role in their recovery.

> **"Have you ever been treated by a doctor for this condition?"**
> **"No, they always make me pay."**
> **Sign in a doctor's office: "Amnesia patients must pay in advance."**

Many hospital staff are convinced that while humor helps both staff and patients relieve some of the tension that builds up, it also adds a more human touch to the hospital experience. The important point for you to consider is that if health care experts all over the country now see enough therapeutic value in humor to build it into hospital settings, it's certainly worthwhile to improve your sense of humor so that you can get this therapeutic effect into your own life every day. It will help you remain healthy, and support your recovery when you do get sick.

Chapter 3
Humor and Mental/ Emotional Health:
The Natural STRESS Remedy

> **"If it weren't for the brief respite we give the world with our foolishness, the world would see mass suicide in numbers that compare favorably with the death rate of the lemmings."**
>
> (Groucho Marx)

> **"A laugh can be very powerful. In fact, sometimes in life it's the only weapon we have."**
>
> (Roger Rabbit)

The last chapter showed how humor and laughter contribute to your physical health. The present chapter shows you the range of high stress situations in which people commonly use humor to cope. As Groucho Marx suggests, it helps you keep your sanity in the worst of conditions. It is a natural stress remedy that you'll soon be able to take full advantage of.

What Evidence Is There that Humor Helps You Cope?

Freud pointed out nearly a century ago that humor offers a healthy means of coping with life stress. Supporting evidence for this view has come from several sources. George Vaillant, in his book *Adaptation to Life*, reported that humor was a very effective coping mechanism used by many professional men under stress. Gail Sheehy, author of

Pathfinders, similarly found humor to be one way of overcoming crises and finding one's own path. These studies were based on in-depth interviews with people about their lives.

One of the most important questions relating to humor's ability to help you cope with stress is whether you can get any stress-reducing benefits by being a passive enjoyer of humor, or whether you need to be more actively involved in generating your own humor for it to become an effective coping tool. A study completed in Canada addressed this issue and found that even if you're someone who finds a lot of humor in everyday life, it doesn't help you cope with stress unless you also make an effort to actively use humor to deal with stress.[1]

So you may have a terrific sense of humor when everything is great, but if it abandons you when things go wrong, you'll be just as stressed out as the next person. That is why the Humor Development Training Program presented here begins by improving your humor skills when you're not under stress. As you get better at playing with language and finding humor in everyday life under the best of conditions, you'll gradually have access to these same skills under the worst of conditions.

Ideally, we all would have learned to use humor as a coping skill as children, since even elementary school children who are good at generating their own humor are more resilient or stress-resistant in growing up.[2] "Resilience" is a term that is increasingly being used in the business world to refer to people who can cope effectively with the rapidly increasing rate of change in our lives. It is resilient employees and resilient companies that thrive in the 1990s. Technological changes constantly put our coping skills to the test on the job—the greatest ongoing source of stress in most of our lives.

A good sense of humor is just one quality which helps you deal effectively with stress. Resilient or stress-resistant people have been found to have other qualities: 1) They view change as a challenge, even when it's unwanted change. It's seen as an opportunity for personal growth. 2) They feel a greater sense of control, believing that they are in charge—even when things don't go the way they want them to. They also see themselves as having greater control over their emotions. They know they can change their feelings by taking steps to deal with the problem. Poor copers tend to feel like victims, believing that life is not fair, and wondering, "Why should this happen to me?" This leads to feelings of helplessness, depression, and anxiety. 3) They maintain a more optimistic outlook in life. They feel that things will turn out for the best, not in a naive Polianna sense, but because of their confidence in their own abilities.[3]

> **❝***Tragedy and comedy are but two aspects of what is real, and whether we see the tragic or the humorous is a matter of perspective.***❞**
> (Dr. Arnold Beisser)

These qualities enable stress-resistant people to maintain their effectiveness in potentially stressful situations. Humor is an extraordinary tool which increases stress-resistance by supporting the development of each of these three qualities. It substitutes a frame of mind which enables you both to view the current problem as a challenge and to find innovative solutions to the problem. It helps you keep things in perspective, allowing you to take greater control over both the problem and your emotional reactions to it. And it nurtures an optimistic outlook.

The rest of this chapter focuses on several circumstances which test the limits of your ability to cope, and shows how humor helps you adapt. If it helps others cope in these extreme conditions, it can certainly help you cope with the stress in your own life.

Coping with Cancer

I have provided many seminars on humor and health to cancer patients. After virtually every program, someone comes up to me and says something like, "You know, what you said is so true. If it hadn't been for our sense of humor, my family and I would never have gotten through this." They often say that finding a light side of the situation was essential to keeping them going and that their sense of humor helped them maintain a sense of hope and determination to fight the disease. One woman who had had a double mastectomy told me that it wasn't that bad; for a short time after the surgery, it gave her more cleavage than she used to have (due to the resulting swelling). Bernie Siegel frequently talks about one of his patients who went through a mastectomy and a divorce at about the same time. She said she "gave up a tit and an ass."

It was noted in Chapter 2 that laughter increases the activity of natural killer cells, a part of your immune system whose role is to seek out and destroy tumor (cancer) cells. The fact that Gilda Radner, of *Saturday Night Live* fame, died of cancer shows that while humor may strengthen your immune system, it may not be enough to counter the force of the disease itself. But Gilda made it very clear that her sense of humor helped her cope with the disease and improved the quality of her life while she fought the battle. She knew that even though her body was losing it's fight against the disease, she was winning the battle to cope with it.

In her book, *It's Always Something,* she says, "The important thing is that the days you've had, you will have lived. What I can control is whether I'm going to live a day in fear and depression and panic, or whether I'm going to attack the day and make it as wonderful a day as I can." She knew that humor was her strongest ally in living her days fully. It also can be yours.

> **"***Live each day as if it were the last day of your life; some day you will be right.***"**
> (Anonymous)

Michael Landon, starring as Little Joe Cartwright in the long-running TV series *Bonanza,* was a model for us all during his bout with cancer. The media marveled at the way he kept up his spirits in the presence of poor odds of survival. His sense of humor played a crucial role in enabling him to do this. It was evident during his last television appearance, on *The Tonight Show.* While discussing his condition, he asked the studio audience if anyone had ever taken a coffee enema. When someone answered "yes," he said, "You must be fun to have breakfast with." At a news conference in which he discussed his health, he said he was especially helped in preparing for his death by a role he had played in *Highway to Heaven,* ". . . since I played a dead guy anyway." In the same interview, he added, "I think you have to have a sense of humor about everything," and that included his illness.

Michael Landon's ability to maintain a positive and fun attitude toward life helped sustain his family, friends and loved ones throughout his ordeal. There are many Michael

Landons across the country, and the reason they were all able to use humor to maintain a high quality life during their illness was that they had developed and used their sense of humor before they ever got a life-threatening illness. By committing yourself to completing the 8-Step Program, you too will learn to use your sense of humor in the most difficult of life conditions.

> **"***No matter what your heartache may be, laughing helps you forget it for a few seconds.***"** (Red Skelton)

Erma Bombeck reports in her book, *I Want to Grow Up, I want to Grow Hair, I Want to Go to Boise*, that when she visited a cancer camp for children and adolescents, she found that they often used humor. She was amazed at their vitality and ability to retain a playful attitude in life while battling their disease. One girl was waiting to see her doctor and noticed some plants on the window sill that had gone unwatered and were dying. She said, "Well, I certainly hope he's better at taking care of his patients than he is his plants."

A boy who had had a leg amputated developed the habit of draping his artificial leg over his shoulder when in the car, taking great delight in the reactions of people in other cars. A teenager was asked by her friend, "What's your sign?" She answered, "Cancer, of course!" Another teenager noticed two preschoolers staring at her wig (worn because of the chemotherapy-induced hair loss). She suddenly ripped off the wig and said to them, "See what happens when you don't eat your veggies!" The startled children ran off.

Do these remarks mean that these kids were not taking their disease seriously? Absolutely not. They indicate that they want to keep on living life every day, even though they have cancer. They have the built-in exuberance of childhood and youth, and this enables them to maintain a zest for life. Joking about cancer is not a form of denial in these kids. It's a reflection of their success in coping with the reality of the disease. They are refusing to lie down and become victims.

A friend of mine works in a pediatric oncology unit of a hospital, and often finds the children using humor to take control of their fears and anxieties. One 8-year-old wrote a letter to her nurse (who has long hair), opening with, "Dear hairy scary nurse, I love spinal taps . . ." In the same letter, she said that if the nurse ever got sick, she [the girl] would take care of her, assuring her that she would "take good care of her and give her lots of shots."

Many cancer patients who successfully fight off the disease later say that getting cancer was the best thing that ever happened to them; that they had been taking life for granted and had never really known how to live. When their survival was in doubt, they learned to live as if they had little time left and to enjoy one day at a time. They gained more aliveness in their everyday life and learned to be more present to their experiences. Rediscovering a sense of playfulness and humor will give you this same renewed zest for living and the ability to "be here now" (see Step 2). So why wait until you get cancer to learn to live life fully and fill each day with joy and fun?

Hospital Humor

Doctors and nurses confront life-threatening tragedy every day. So if humor does help cope with tragedy, we would expect it to show up in hospitals. And we should find the most humor in those areas of the hospital where the threat and actual occurrence of death is the greatest; namely, in the emergency room, operating room, and critical care units. Surely doctors and nurses would use humor here if it really helps you cope.

This is exactly what happens. While humor is common in all areas of the hospital, it is most common in the emergency room, operating room, and critical care unit. These also are the areas where humor is the crudest and most macabre. Humor has also been found to be the most common coping mechanism of staff members in a psychiatric emergency room.[4] In seminars I do for nurses, I generally ask the audience which areas of the hospital they think have the most macabre and raunchy humor. The unhesitating response is always ER, OR, and CCU. The following jokes would not be unusual in a hospital.

What's the difference between humor and aroma?
Humor is a shift of wit . . .

Do you know what happened to the nurse who swallowed a razor blade?
She performed a tonsillectomy, a hysterectomy, and circumcised an intern.

In decades past, when tuberculosis was a common health threat, the following jingle was popular in sanitoriums.[5]

T.B. or not T.B. That is congestion. Consumption be done about it? Of corpse! Of corpse!

Staff members who are initially put off by crude hospital humor gradually learn to enjoy it—or work elsewhere. They realize that this kind of humor helps them live with what they must confront every day, and helps them fight burnout and do their job effectively.

The following letter demonstrates doctors' and nurses' awareness of the importance that humor and laughter play in helping them cope with the constant stresses of their jobs. It was written by the nurse anesthetist present during the surgery on a man who died during the surgery.

> *"You saw me laugh after your father died.*
> *I was splashing water on my face at a sink midway between the emergency room lobby where you stood and the far green room where his body lay. Someone told a feeble joke and I brayed laughter like a jackass, decorum forgotten until I met your glance . . . your eyes streaming with tears . . .*
> *My laugh was inappropriate, and for that I apologize. But it was, nonetheless, a necessity.*
> *I laughed, nominally, at a corny joke. It's no secret that hospital people seem to enjoy warped humor . . . we're often too morbid: burned patients become crispy critters; Vietnam casualties were Jungle-Burgers. It's not pleasant. Neither is hospital work, at times . . .*
> *While we may appear emotionless behind our various masks, please understand: Much of the stress that health care workers suffer comes about because we **do** care. We cared about your father . . .*
> *That day you saw me laugh, I knew that another patient was waiting who needed my care and full attention in surgery. As I stood at that sink and washed sweat and*

vomitus from my face and arms, my laugh was no less cleansing for me than were your tears for you."[6]

If you're the next patient to go under the knife with this team after they've lost a patient, you want them to have a good laugh (at anything; it doesn't matter what) before they begin with you. The laughter relieves the tension and upset that could distract them and prevent them from giving you their best efforts during your surgery. Doctors and nurses laugh every day at things the rest of us would find morbid, cold, and unfeeling (if we knew about it). But this laughter is essential to fighting burnout on their jobs and keeping them prepared to deal with the next crisis situation—with a life on the line.

Hospital staff also laugh at more benign forms of humor, including what patients say. For example, after completing his examination of a young woman, a male gynecologist told her she had acute vaginitis. Her response was, "Why thank you." Another woman was concerned about the dangers of tampons. She asked her doctor if she was at risk for toxic waste syndrome.

Humor in Emergency and Disaster Situations

Emergency Workers

Other kinds of employment, of course, also involve daily contact with death, illness, injury, and suffering. And the same pattern of joking occurs. Paramedics and emergency medical technicians are frequently exposed to death and dying, often under physically and emotionally trying conditions. Humor has been shown to be one of the main tools for coping with their own emotional reactions to these situations.[7] Police officers also must learn to deal with frequent exposure to sudden death in traffic accidents, suicides, homicides, and the taking of lives themselves. They, too, commonly use humor as a means of coping with stress and relieving tension.[8]

These people laugh at things most of us would consider in bad taste. But they laugh because it helps them adapt to the terrible things they are exposed to. They need the release offered by laughter. It helps them counter the psychological gravity they experience every day on the job.

Firemen, EMS workers, ambulance drivers, and policemen often talk about "crispy critters" after fires, or "road pizza" after traffic accidents. Following major disasters, such as hurricane Andrew, the World Trade Center bombing, the California brush fires of 1993, and the Los Angeles earthquake of 1994, there is generally a critique among the emergency response team concerning how they handled the situation. There's often a great deal of humor in these discussions, as emergency workers let go of the incredible tension and strain that builds up throughout the response to the disaster.

The following lengthy joke was told to me by an emergency worker involved in handling the Mississippi flood in 1993. It is typical of the crude side of their sense of humor.

There were these two EMT (emergency medical technician) students who were pretty shaky. They were in real danger of not passing their training course. But they got through it. After their finals, everyone was saying, "I don't know how you did it, but you made it." And the two new graduates were saying, "All right! We did it! We're EMT's, and now we're going to save the world!"

So they all go out to celebrate. They're in this restaurant eating, and the guy at the next table suddenly stands up, grabs his throat, and starts turning blue. He's obviously choking. The two guys jump up and say, "Plan B! We're cool, we can handle this."

So the two of them get up take off their pants and start licking each others' butt. The guy who was choking starts laughing so hard that the lodged food comes flying out, and he's fine. At that point, one of the new EMTs says to the other, "Hey, that Hiney Lick manoeuver really works!"

There has been little systematic research on the use of humor in disaster situations, but one study of 79 emergency workers responding to an apartment building explosion found that 42% of them said they used humor to cope in such situations. And four out of every five who said they used humor during, or after responding to, emergencies said it did help them cope.[9] Another study showed that the humor initiated by emergency responders—generally spontaneous and related to the situation of the moment—plays a significant role in reducing their own stress.[10]

Since most members of emergency response teams learn through their own experience that humor is an important coping tool, and since some health care professionals suggested over a decade ago that emergency workers need to develop their sense of humor as an adaptive defense mechanism,[11] it is surprising that no program has been established to enable them to develop these skills. The 8-Step Program provided here is the first program to do so.

> **❝** *Life does not cease to be funny when people die any more than it ceases to be serious when people laugh.* **❞**
>
> (George Bernard Shaw)

Following a recent program I provided at the convention of the National Coordinating Council on Emergency Management, many came up to me afterwards and said that they often look for any excuse to laugh after the emergency is handled, or start laughing for no reason at all. They know that belly laughter is very therapeutic for them, and will help them reduce the emotional residue they carry around in the days and weeks following the disaster.

All emergency workers are thoroughly prepared to deal with the disaster itself, but they are generally not trained to cope with the emotional trauma they experience after the incident is handled. "Critical incident stress debriefing teams" are generally available to help them cope with the emotional aftermath of their own involvement with the disaster, but humor and laughter allow them to "let go" of much of the emotional burden even before the CISD team comes in. One fire fighter said that this laughter provides a much-needed "emotional delousing."

Newcomers to disaster relief teams are often put off by their colleagues' humor, because it seems inconsiderate and inappropriate. The longer they stay on the job, however, the more they change their view and see it as an essential part of staying effective on the job, and of maintaining good mental health. (See Step 7 for a discussion of how humor helps you cope with high stress situations.)

A woman teaching a class on emergency planning told me about her own initial shock at the "horrible" humor displayed by three Emergency Medical Service workers in her class. She found it totally inappropriate, because "they're supposed to be sympathetic and concerned about these people's well being." She communicated this to them, once she'd taken as much of their humor as she could. At that point, one of the guys who had been joking around all the time got real serious and said,

> *"You have to understand, it's our way of coping. It's our way of surviving the job we have. When I first started, the terrible things I saw really bothered me. I tried to act real macho, like it wasn't bothering me, but it really was. I wasn't aware of how much it was eating away at me until I responded to a hit-and-run incident, in which a mother and baby had been hit. The mother was killed outright, but the baby was still alive until just before we got there. I was trying to resuscitate the baby. I just kept going and kept going, trying to get the baby to breathe. My friend finally put his hand on my shoulder, saying, 'Enough is enough.'*
>
> *From that point on, I always found things to laugh at. Without humor as a means of stress release, I really couldn't handle it. As far as I was concerned, that child was my child. Losing that child made me realize I'd been shoving to the back of my mind all the upset I had experienced from the things I'd seen. I love my job, and I'd never change it, but I'd never survive it if I didn't find things to laugh at."*

I do many programs for disaster response groups and other emergency workers (e.g., in hospitals), and an important part of the program is confirming the value of the macabre humor they already know plays an important role in maintaining their effectiveness on the job. For the newcomers, it eases their discomfort about joining in with jokes and funny incidents that they had been considering inappropriate. As one emergency responder told me, humor is an "emotional condom."

Emergency workers' humor generally shows up after the emergency situation has been handled. In some cases, however, it shows up in the middle of their efforts to deal with a tragedy. One EMS worker was carrying a dismembered arm, following a suicide committed by jumping in front of a train. He said to his buddy, "Hey, give me a hand, will ya?" An ambulance driver explained to me that a woman he was about to take to the hospital kept saying that she'd had "brain farts." She repeated it over and over, as if she thought it was important. He restrained his laughter until they were safely in route to the hospital, and he realized that she meant brain "infarcts."

A colleague of this same ambulance driver described the wonderful laugh he had in thinking back to the reactions of onlookers as he began working with a woman who had been hit by a truck. She had just come from a deli carrying a large sandwich which she was clutching to her chest when she was hit. She was still clutching it when the EMS vehicle arrived. As he pulled away her coat and tugged at the tightly-gripped sandwich, pieces of ham, tomato, cheese, and bread were sent flying in all directions. He could hear the onlookers gasp, thinking that all this stuff was coming from her insides. Again, the belly laugh he had afterwards in describing this helped relieve the tension of the moment and left him in a better state of preparedness for the next emergency.

Another EMS worker told me how difficult it was for her to forget what she witnessed after responding to a call about a woman who had walked into a moving propeller at the airport. While this was an emotionally wrenching experience for her, she recognized that having a good laugh at something when she left the scene of the accident was essential for her to keep from becoming a victim of the tragedy herself. It took one of her colleagues to come up with a crude single-word joke that fit the situation: "Disaster." (Dis-assed her.)

Disaster Victims/Survivors

Sandy Ritz is a public health nurse who helped coordinate relief efforts following hurricane Iniki in Kauai (1992), and also assisted following the Oakland fires (1993) and the Los Angeles earthquake (1994). She notes that humor is very common among the survivors of such tragedies,[12] concluding that it helps them cope and gives them hope. It helps strengthen the feeling, "we're all in this together."

Ritz argues that the humor shown by survivors reflects the four emotional phases survivors generally go through following a disaster.[13] During the Heroic phase, humor is designed to relieve tension and ease fear and anxiety. The Honeymoon phase follows, and may last from a week to six months following the disaster. Humor is most likely to occur in this phase, according to Ritz, and generally reflects feelings of optimism about recovery. A period of disillusionment then follows, and may last from two months to two years. Feelings of anger, resentment, disappointment, and powerlessness tend to emerge here, and are reflected in gallows humor and other forms of humor aimed at putting down disaster workers and the agencies which are blamed for their problems. Finally, a Reconstruction phase is entered, characterized by acceptance and recovery. A greater general receptiveness to humor returns, and it again shifts toward a more positive focus.

Ritz has created many cartoons which reflect survivors' concerns and their phase of adjustment to the disaster. These cartoons were published in newspapers at the time of the disaster, and provided a valuable means of helping survivors find a light side of their difficult plight. She believes that cartoons and other sources of public humor provide a positive force of healing and empowerment in the communities affected by disasters.[14]

As a reflection of the need for humor, she noted that following hurricane Iniki, many families got together and watched funny videos together. What made this impressive is that the entire island of Kauai was without electricity for over two months. The only way they could do this was by finding someone who had a generator, someone else whose VCR had survived, and yet another family that had salvaged some comedy tapes. They obviously knew they needed a good laugh. A few of her cartoons are included here to give a sense of the humor circulating at the time.

T-shirts reflect another way in which survivors actively use humor to cope. Ritz notes that following Hurricane Iniki, one nurse was seen wearing a T-shirt with the words, "I suffer from PISS: Post-Iniki Stress Syndrome." Many wore T-shirts in Los Angeles following the earthquake saying, "Shift Happens!"

Consistent with Ritz's observations, a field study of the coping strategies adopted by survivors of Hurricane Hugo revealed that humor and joking were second only to "talking it out."[15] My own conversations with many disaster relief workers confirm these findings. The survivors who do best at using humor to cope, however, are those who already had the habit of finding and using humor in their everyday life. While you will hopefully never have a disaster to deal with in your own life, improving your sense of humor now will put you in a position to have humor as an additional coping skill if you do.

One of the best examples I ever saw of this followed a tornado in the midwest. A man whose house had been destroyed, and whose car was flattened by a fallen tree, put a sign on his car saying, "Compact car!" The sign did nothing to give him back his car or home, but served to say, "This is not going to destroy me; I can deal with this and go on." Another man coped by putting a sign in the place his home used to be saying, "Gone with the wind."

The General Public

Even the general public finds humor in natural and man-made disasters. It shows up in our laughter at the tasteless jokes that always sweep the country following any national tragedy. Who among us has not at least grinned at jokes like the following?

Did you know that Christa McAulif had "blue" eyes? One "blew" this way and one "blew" that way.

(Following the explosion of the Challenger space shuttle;
Christa McAulif was the teacher on board.)

Jeffrey Dahmer's mother visits him and has a meal at his apartment. She says, "You know Jeffrey, I really don't care much for your neighbors." Jeffrey says, "OK, then try the veggies."

(Dahmer was convicted of cannibalism in Milwaukee.)

Following the accident involving Cleveland Indians players Crews and Olin, the autopsy report revealed that the cause of death was "Pier pressure."

(The boat in which they were riding ran into a dock.)

How many Branch Davidians can you get in a Volkswagen? Two in the front, two in the back . . . and 181 in the ash tray.

(Following the fire at the Branch Davidian complex in Waco.)

What did the devil say when David Koresh arrived in hell? "Well done!"

(Koresh was the leader of the Branch Davidians.)

How do you pick up one of the Branch Davidian women? With a Dust Buster.

> **Before the fire, "WACO" stood for "We ain't comin' out." After the fire, it stood for "What a cook out."**
>
> **At one point John Bobbit considered dropping the charges against his wife, because he figured the evidence wouldn't stand up in court.**
>
> (His penis was cut off by his wife.)
>
> **Jeffrey Dahmer asks Lorena Bobbit, "Excuse me, are you going to finish what you have in your hand?"**

Why do we laugh at such jokes? Are we simply cruel and heartless, having no sympathy for the victims of these tragic events? Or does the laughter fill some positive psychological function? A newspaper reporter once told me that reporters covering these tragedies are responsible for getting many of these jokes going. They often see the tragedy first-hand, or are otherwise closely involved with it. This is very tough on them emotionally, even though they have no personal acquaintance with the victims. The humor helps them distance themselves from the situation enough to be able to get their story out without being victimized by their own emotions. It also provides a means of letting go of the feelings that build up as they cover the story.

The rest of the country needs the same release. We were all saddened by the destruction of Hurricanes Andrew and Iniki of 1992, the midwestern floods of 1993, and the Los Angeles earthquake of 1994. But finding a way to laugh at these tragedies help everyone put them behind them and get on with their lives. The more intimately you are involved with the tragedy, the greater the need for release, and the greater the power of humor to help you accept the harsh reality of the situation and get on with the business of coping. But even if you were only a distant observer of the floods and earthquakes, you probably chuckled at jokes like,

They changed the zip code for Des Moines, Iowa: 50H20.

What's the new area code for Los Angeles? 911.

Concentration/POW Camps

> **"***I would never have made it if I could not have laughed. Laughing lifted me momentarily . . . out of this horrible situation, just enough to make it livable . . . survivable.***"**
>
> (Victor Frankl)

Bill Cosby once said, "If you can find humor in anything, you can survive it." The ultimate test of this would have been the Nazi concentration camps of World War II. If ever there were a situation incompatible with humor, this was it. And yet the psychiatrist Victor Frankl, a prisoner in the camps himself, noted in his book, *Man's Search for Meaning*, that humor was one of the things that helped people survive in the camps. Finding things to laugh at helped maintain a sense of meaning and purpose in life—even in conditions as extreme as those in the camps.

Many hung on with the thought that they would one day see a loved one again. Others used their imaginations to create humor. Frankl states that he and another prisoner tried to invent at least one funny story or joke every day. For example, in one joke they created, a prisoner points toward a Capo (a prisoner who also acted as a guard) and said, "Imagine! I knew him when he was only the president of the bank!"

> *Humor, more than anything else in the human makeup, affords an aloofness and an ability to rise above any situation, even if only for a few seconds.*
>
> (Victor Frankl)

> *To become conscious of what is horrifying and to laugh at it is to become master of that which is horrifying.*
>
> (Eugene Ionesco)

In another frequently told story, a prisoner accidentally bumps into a Nazi guard. The guard turns and shouts, "Schwein!" (which means "pig" in German). The prisoner bows and says, "Cohen. Pleased to meet you." This joke clearly demonstrates how humor helps reverse who's in control and who seems to be the superior being. Even in the terrible conditions of the camp, the joke provided a means of momentarily overcoming adversity.

Captain Gerald Coffee, who spent seven years in a POW camp in Vietnam, has said that the POWs were kept isolated in an attempt to break their spirit. They managed to keep their spirits up, however, by tapping on the wall of fellow prisoners and telling jokes in morse code. Coffee feels that humor was essential to his survival as a POW.

When I interviewed him, Captain Coffee said that humor was the one thing that was almost constant throughout his stay in the camps, even if it was sometimes a grim humor. For example, the prisoners often were tortured with ropes. When a new POW would appear, they would always explain the daily routines and how they went about communicating with each other. Then they'd say, "It's not so bad once you get to know the ropes." They would look for humor wherever they could find it, including the way they and their captors lived, and even the brutality of the guards.

The POWs often got depressed about their aloneness and feared that they would never get back home. Anything that could break through this depression and anxiety was always welcome. In his book, *Beyond Survival*, Coffee describes an old cell that had been converted to a shower. Someone had scratched onto the wall "Smile, you're on Candid Camera." You can imagine the effect discovering this message had on a prisoner standing there with his head bent down, wondering if he'll ever get out alive. In Coffee's case, he said, "I laughed out loud, enjoying not only the pure humor and incongruity of the situation, but also appreciating the beautiful guy who had mustered the moxie to rise above his own dejection and frustration and pain and guilt to inscribe a line of encouragement to those who would come after him . . . he deserved a medal for it."[16]

> **"***Laughter sets the spirit free to move through even the most tragic circumstances. It helps us shake our heads clear, get our feet back under us and restore our sense of balance and purpose. Humor is integral to our peace of mind and ability to go beyond survival.***"**
>
> (Captain Gerald Coffee)

Coffee's stories remind me of an old Shel Silverstein cartoon showing two men being held prisoners in a dungeon. They are clamped to a wall with irons around their wrists and ankles. Below them is a pit containing alligators, and it's 30 straight up to the top of the dungeon. So they're against the wall like two insects on a pin. One looks at the other and says, "Now here's my plan."

Coffee believes that there was a constant awareness in the POW camps that humor helped keep things in perspective. In spite of how bad things got, it helped them distance themselves from it for a moment and see that things could be worse. If it helped keep their problems in perspective, it certainly will do the same with yours.

One of the most significant things to emerge from my conversation with Captain Coffee was his view that "having some humor skills before being confronted by the adversity played a very important role" in being able to use humor in the camps. And that is precisely why the 8-Step Program is designed as it is. If you want to have access to your sense of humor under high stress situations, you first need to develop your humor skills in non-stressful situations. That is why it is essential for you to spend the necessary time with each of the preliminary steps, instead of jumping right into Step 7.

Similar stories have been told by hostages held by terrorist groups in the 1980s. Terry Anderson, held captive in Lebanon for 2,454 days, describes in his book, *Den of Lions*, how a sense of humor helped him and his fellow prisoners cope.

> **"***Despite everything, it's amazing sometimes how much laughing we do. Irish hostage Brian Keenan's terrible shaggy-dog stories, John McCarthy's imitations, Tom's [Sutherland] awful puns and drinking songs, Frank's [Reed] tales of Boston. Even the idiotic and frustrating things the guards do set us off in giggles. There's often a bitter touch to it. But not always. Just as often, it's just a relief to be able to laugh at something.***"[17]**
>
> (Terry Anderson)

Alan Sharansky overcame his fear of a (threatened) firing squad in the former Soviet Union by joking about it. But he was not successful at it at first. The relief was initially very short-lived, if it occurred at all. But he gradually saw the power joking gave him. Real mastery over his fear took 15–20 tries. From that point on, he stopped being at the mercy of his fears.

Finding humor in the face of death was called "gallows" humor by Freud. His classic example was of a man who was about to be shot by a firing squad and was asked if he wanted a last cigarette. "No thanks," he said, "I'm trying to quit." Again, the joke helped the doomed man turn the tables and take a form of control in the situation.

A sociologist pointed out that over the centuries, many cultures have used humor as a means of dealing with death.[18] In India, those doomed to death by fire were expected to laugh while climbing up to their own pyre. Parents in ancient Phonecia often laughed if their children had been committed to death on the pyre. Elderly parents in Sardinia were expected to laugh when being immolated by their own children. All these practices clearly reflect the belief that laughter can help master even the fear of death itself.

You will never face the threat of a pyre or a firing squad in your life, and you will hopefully never wind up in anything comparable to a POW or concentration camp, but you may have other kinds of stress that feel just as threatening to you. If humor could help Frankl, Coffee, Anderson, and Sharansky deal with their problems, it can certainly help you deal with yours.

Humor and War

Few situations are more stress-inducing than war. It's hard to imagine the spirit of fun and playfulness emerging in the midst of war. And yet jokes and spontaneous humor proliferate during wartime. They generally ridicule the enemy and serve to reduce the terrible tensions, fears, and anger that accompany every war. They also momentarily reduce the perceived threat posed by the enemy and help generate a sense of control in situations where you're really quite powerless.

Citizens joked more than usual in London during the Nazi bombing attacks in WWII, as well as in Czechoslovakia throughout the period of Nazi occupation.[19] Some world leaders even got into the act. When Winston Churchill was told that Mussolini had decided to enter the war in 1939, he announced to the British people, "The Italians have announced that they will fight on the Nazis' side. I think it's only fair. We had to put up with them last time."

The Jewish people have a greater reputation than any other group for maintaining their sense of humor in the midst of adversity. During the 1991 war with Iraq, Israeli humor began to surface immediately as a means of coping with the threat. The Israelis were in an awkward position in this war, since they were resisting the temptation to be dragged into it—even though they were being attacked. They felt powerless, since their defense was in the hands of the Americans. But this is precisely the kind of situation where humor has real power to help you cope. They were stuck with a high-stress situation and simply had to deal with it one way or another. As Scud missiles began to fall, people feared for their lives, because they believed that Saddam Hussein would launch a gas attack, as he had against the Kurds in his own country.

The proof of the Israelis' understanding of the coping value of a playful attitude and humor came as the entire world watched the citizens of Jerusalem and Tel Aviv go to their sealed rooms. They sometimes spent hours in these rooms, fearing that a Scud might drop on them at any moment. People were terrified during the early days of the war, still carrying the residues of memories of gas chambers during the Holocaust. What you didn't know was that during the initial attacks, Israeli radio stations sponsored a nation-wide anagrams game to see who could come up with the greatest number of words from the letters composing the name "Saddam Hussein." Government leaders realized that providing the opportunity to have fun in a game would help relieve the tension and anxiety built up while waiting in the closed-off rooms.

> **"***In prehistoric times, mankind often had only two choices in crisis situations; fight or flee. In modern times, humor offers us a third alternative; fight, flee—or laugh.***"** (Robert Orben)

In a recently published study of Israeli humor during the Gulf War, the researchers pointed out that Israelis felt helpless during the war and that joking helped overcome this feeling.[20] They noted that humor was more prominent in this war than in any other Israeli war, precisely because of the "immense feelings of rage and helplessness and a profound wish to retaliate" that emerged. The Israelis needed to joke more in this war because they weren't in a position to directly retaliate by fighting. Laughing at Saddam helped reduce the feeling of danger.

The following jokes (all reported by the researchers) were typical of those that emerged as the war went on. People sometimes joked directly about the things they were afraid of.

> **How do you play Israeli roulette?**
> **Give 3 gas masks to 4 people in a sealed room.**

> **Why don't Shamir and Saddam meet?**
> **Because there's no chemistry between them.**

> **Tel Aviv residents are advised to eat plenty of beans during the alert. The reason? To fight gas with gas.**

> **One Tel Aviv resident was said by his neighbors to be immune to chemical missiles; he's such a big fart that he neutralizes them.**

Many of the jokes took advantage of the Jewish tradition of playing with language.

> **What's the new name of Tel Aviv?**
> **Til Aviv.**   ("Til" is the Hebrew word for missile.)

> **What's the new name of Israel?**
> **Scudinavia.**

> **What's the reverse of Saddam in English?**
> **Madd ass.**

The most common butt of the jokes was Saddam, as you would expect.

> **What's the difference between Saddam and the wicked Haman?**

Haman was hanged, and then we wore the masks. With Saddam, we wear the masks first.

What do Saddam and his father have in common?
Neither one pulled out in time.

Other jokes poked fun at the Iraqis in general.

Every Iraqi tank has five gears, four reverse and one forward. Why does it need the forward gear? In case it's attacked from the rear.

What went wrong with the Iraqi missiles?
They had Soviet bodies, French warheads, and German planning, but local assembly.

The best known example of this kind of humor, of course, was provided by *M.A.S.H.* This long running television series—whose reruns are still popular—captures in every episode the way humor helps Hawkeye and the others cope with the traumas of war, especially with the endless strings of wounded and dead sent to their primitive surgical tents.

A nurse who served in the Vietnam war recalled her experiences 24 years later, saying that nurses were exposed to things they had never been exposed to before because helicopters brought in wounded that would have died in the battlefield in the past.[21] Nurses were constantly faced with amputations, mutilations, and terrible wounds throughout the war, "And if you allowed yourself to feel, you could not have continued to do your job."

This nurse noted that it was years before many of her colleagues realized that the war had left them spiritually and emotionally dead. When one nurse returned home after the war, she discovered that her capacity to enjoy daily life had disappeared. This is one reason why so many who serve in the military during war time intuitively sense that finding something to laugh at is essential to their emotional survival. The book *Catch 22* shows how many succeed in laughing in the midst of war. It captures the humor of absurd situations that inevitably accompany any military conflict.

I know of only one study that has examined how humor helps cope with the stress of war-like conditions.[22] It focused on 19- and 20-year-old soldiers participating in a training course for combat NCOs in the Israeli Defense Forces. Participants rated each of their fellow members (5 people) on how frequently they initiated any kind of humor. Their commanders and peers also rated how well the soldiers coped under stress during the training. Soldiers who joked, told funny stories, or clowned around more were judged by both their peers and commanders to be coping better with the stressful conditions provided in the combat training. As in the case of the Gulf war study described above, the researchers in this study concluded that joking and funny stories helped the soldiers feel in control. This sense of being in control helped keep stress levels within reasonable bounds and helped them perform at a higher level.

This is precisely how humor will help you in your own life. It will help you take charge of the stress you're under at the moment by keeping your emotional reaction from getting out of hand. This leaves you in a much better position to take action to change the situation.

Humor and a Healthy Marriage

Satisfaction with one's marriage has been shown to make a stronger contribution to general life satisfaction than anything else—including one's work and career.[23] A good marriage fills our fundamental human need for intimacy. The emotional and social support provided by marriage is a key factor in helping partners cope with all kinds of stress in their lives.[24]

Every marriage or other long-term intimate relationship, however, has ongoing stress and strain built into it. While these problems may seem minor in comparison to the stressors discussed above, marital stress has a tremendous impact on our lives. And the high divorce rate attests to the extent of relationship stress in the country. If humor is an effective tool for handling conflict, couples who value humor and have a good sense of humor should have healthier, happier—and longer—marriages. They should be drawn closer together and have an extra strong foundation for battling any marital stresses that arise.

> **"***Laughter is the shortest distance between two people.***"**
> (Victor Borge)

> **"***The couple that plays together stays together.***"** (Paul McGhee)

A study of couples married 45 years or more showed that both husbands and wives believed that a good sense of humor plays an important role in the long-term success of a marriage.[25] Among Israeli married couples, enjoying and creating humor within the relationship makes an important contribution to marital satisfaction among both husbands and wives.[26] When a husband or wife indicates that they don't appreciate their spouse's sense of humor, this is often an indication of problems within the relationship.[27]

In one study, a distinction was made between positive and negative uses of humor within the relationship. Positive use was defined as humor which draws the couple toward closer intimacy and helps manage conflict. Negative use was defined as humor involving the expression of hostility and which increased distance between partners. Not surprisingly, couples showing positive forms of humor showed better marital adjustment than those using negative humor.[28] The difficulty here, of course, is that we have no way of knowing whether the positive or negative humor caused the good or poor marital adjustment or was a result of it.

There is some evidence that women may be better than men at using humor to reduce relationship conflicts. In a study of young married couples (married an average of eight years), wives' use of humor to soften conflict situations was associated with increased happiness and marital satisfaction. Among men, however, it was associated with decreased marital satisfaction and more destructive forms of behavior.[29] The reason for this difference is not yet clear, but the explanation may lie in the kind of humor women and men use in general. It may be that men are more prone to using sarcastic, belittling, or other negative forms of humor which increase distance from one's spouse, while women use more positive forms of humor that reduce distance and promote intimacy. Regardless of the reason, this gives men an extra incentive for learning to use humor more effectively.

Part II

The Steps

A. Surround Yourself with Humor You Enjoy
B. Determine the Nature of Your Sense of Humor

> "*A person reveals his character by nothing so clearly as the joke he resents.*"
> (G.C. Lichtenberg)

> "*You show your character in nothing more clearly than by what you think laughable.*"
> (Goethe)

Step 1 eases you into the 8-Step Humor Development Training Program by immersing you in humor and helping you better understand your own sense of humor. You will clarify the strong and weak parts of your sense of humor and understand better the influences that shaped it over the years. You will also establish a foundation for selecting certain steps of the program for special attention and effort.

Take the Sense of Humor Pre-Test

Before beginning the Program, complete the humor pre-test found at the end of the book. Be sure to answer as honestly as you can, instead of giving answers you would like to be true. This test assesses where you now stand in terms of key dimensions of your sense of humor—especially those related to each step of the program. Once you have completed the pre-test, put a paper clip on those pages and avoid looking at them again until after you have completed the entire Program. You will be asked to take the post-test after completing Step 8. By comparing your answers on the pre- and post-tests, you will be able to determine how much progress you've made.

Surround Yourself with Humor You Enjoy

If you have a poorly developed sense of humor, or a generally serious demeanor, humor probably hasn't played a very prominent role in your life. The best way to change that is simply to build more outside sources of humor into your life. Spend more time around friends who make you laugh. Seek out funny films, TV programs, and comedy tapes. Look at cartoons in magazines and other publications. Go to comedy clubs. Immerse yourself in humor wherever you can find it. This will not only be fun, but will also help you better understand your own sense of humor. It will add a more positive, playful focus to your everyday interactions with people and ease you into becoming more sensitive to humor in your own life. It will whet your appetite to start building up your humor skills.

You should also begin to think about the kinds of humor you like and don't like. If you don't have a clear notion of the humor you prefer, expose yourself to all kinds of comedy films, stand-up comedians, etc. To better understand your likes and dislikes, actively ask yourself, "What kind of humor is this? What do I like or dislike about it? Why is this funny?" This may reduce the mirth of the moment, but don't worry, it's only temporary. Make it your goal here to explore different types of humor, and to get a clear picture of your humor tastes. This will enable you to continue to surround yourself with humor you enjoy as you move through the program. For example, if you find that Richard Pryor or Steve Martin really breaks you up, you may want to see all of their films, or collect their stand-up comedy tapes.

As you expose yourself to more and more humor, you may begin to notice some of it "rubbing off" on you. You may find yourself remembering some of your favorite jokes or routines, without even trying to. (For a real kick, memorize the "Who's on first?" routine of Abbott and Costello.) You may even start to think along the lines of your favorite comedian. This will give you a tremendous boost as you move through the 8-Step Program.

"It is more important to have fun than it is to be funny."
(Laurence J. Peter)

To build more humor into each day, look at your daily routines and determine where you can make time for some kind of humor. I start many mornings by listening to a comedy tape during a brisk walk. A local county library has a stock of about 200 comedy cassettes, and I simply sign out five or six at a time and listen to a different tape each morning during my walk. If I find a tape that is especially funny, I may listen to it two or three times before returning it. This helps put me in a positive mood as I start the day.

If you have an audio tape deck in your car, cassettes are an ideal way to assure that you get a regular dose of humor twice a day. Be sure to try this, and take particular note of the effect it has on your mood, both when you're in traffic and when you arrive either at work in the morning or at home in the evening. Remember that part of the real power of humor lies in its ability to help manage your mood. Listening to comedy tapes in your car will leave you in a frame of mind that enables you to be more effective at work and more fun to be around at home.

This early exposure to humor is much more important than you might think. It will help you build a foundation for creating your own humor later on. So be sure to fight any tendency to skip over this part of Step 1.

Determine the Nature or Your Sense of Humor

Have you ever thought about the nature of your sense of humor, and how yours differs from that of your spouse, friends, or colleagues? Completing the exercises and activities provided for Step 1 will improve your understanding of your sense of humor as it now exists, providing you an additional basis for determining the progress you make as you complete each step. You will continue to have new insights about your sense of humor as you go through the program.

A reviewer from the *New York Times* asked me following the publication of my first book in 1972, *The Psychology of Humor,* "Doesn't doing research on humor wind up destroying your sense of humor?" I assumed he was kidding, but he wasn't. A common attitude expressed in AP or UPI write-ups about humor in the 1970s was that we would probably lose our sense of humor by studying it too much. If you are concerned about this, remember that many comedy writers and comedians become real students of humor, and become very analytical about what does and does not work in getting laughs. And it makes them better performers, not worse.

However, you may notice a short-term drop in your humor responsiveness as you work on certain steps. If you love photography, and take a camera with you on your vacation, what happens? If you're like me, the joy of the experience is reduced by the fact that you spend all your time looking for a picture worth remembering. This can also happen when you start thinking about your sense of humor. You will be asked several times during the 8-Step Program to be more analytical and to think more about humor. This is an important element in improving your humor skills, but it can also temporarily make you a bit less spontaneous and expressive of your enjoyment of the moment. This will disappear as you move through the program.

> **"***Humor can be dissected as a frog can, but the thing dies in the process . . .***"**
> (E.B. White)

I recently attended a performance of a friend who does stand-up comedy. He did a brilliant set in which he had the audience rolling with laughter. When the next comedian came up to do his thing, my friend hardly cracked a grin—even though the audience was laughing. He was watching the audience, looking for nuances of what did and did not work, and why. By the time he came back to chat with me, he was his usual playful, funny self. The point here is that if professional comedians find that giving an occasional thoughtful look at humor helps them be funnier, it will certainly help you.

Your Sense of Humor Is Unique

One of the most important things to know as you start developing your sense of humor is that, like your thumb print, it is unique. Certain parts will resemble others' sense of humor, but no one else will laugh at exactly the same things you do.

You also want to remember that it is not written down somewhere on tablets of stone that certain things are funny, while other things are not. There is no 11th Commandment, "Thou shalt laugh at X!" "Thou shalt not laugh at Y!" Different cultures laugh at different things. Men and women share enjoyment of some jokes, but not others. Democrats laughed more at jokes about Dan Quayle than did republicans. Your sense of humor will reflect your particular values, knowledge, sensitivities, and experience.

There will be times that you'll be falling on the floor with laughter, while others just don't get it. If this makes you uncomfortable, try thinking of yourself as the only person clever enough to see the funny side of the situation.

The reverse will also occur. Everyone else will be laughing, but you just don't get it. Think back to a time this happened. Do you remember the uncomfortableness—even panic—that set in as people looked at you through their laughter? "What's the matter, don't you get it? Hey, does anyone want to explain it to him/her?" It's implied that you're not very bright, or that you don't have much of a sense of humor. The key here is to remember that your sense of humor is just as valid as the next person's. It's just not funny to you.

As you move through this program, make it your goal to be just as much at ease when you fail to see what others are laughing at as you are when you're the one who get's it, while others do not. I used to have a cartoon on my office door which showed a crowd laughing in a movie theater. Everyone was laughing except one man in the center of the cartoon. Sweat was dripping from his brow. The caption read, "Wait a minute, is this satire?"

Analyze Your Past and Present Humor Tastes

The easiest way to start thinking about your sense of humor is to examine the kind of humor you now enjoy and that you have enjoyed in the past. Think about the TV sit coms, comedians, cartoonists, or films that do and do not strike you as funny. As a kid growing up in the 1950s, I was always in stitches over Sid Caesar, Imogine Coca, Carl Reiner, and Howard Morris in the *Show of Shows*. I never missed Jackie Gleason in *The Honeymooners* (although I thought Art Carney as "Norton" was funnier than Gleason). I loved Lucy in *I Love Lucy*. Later on, Jonathan Winters could make me laugh with the slightest facial expression. Monty Python showed me a part of my sense of humor I never knew I had—nonsense. I still enjoy the original cast of *Saturday Night Live*. And then there was Bob Newhart, George Carlin, David Steinberg, Lily Tomlin, Steve Martin . . .

In looking back at my favorite comedians, I realized that I was somehow drawn to an odd combination of types of humor. Part of me enjoyed primitive, physical forms of humor (slapstick). I hate to admit it, but I watched The Three Stooges—even in junior high school. Another part of me enjoyed clever ways of playing with language—especially when it was created on the spot. Although I memorized a lot of riddles as a kid, I've never been a joke-teller as an adult. My own style is spontaneous humor that just pops into my mind at the moment. And then there was my early enjoyment of everyday situations where every-thing seemed to go wrong. This was probably what drew me to *I love Lucy*.

Humor Log Exercises

Use the exercises provided below to map out your own humor profile. Record your responses in your own personal Humor Log.

1. What sitcoms on television did you enjoy the most during the 1950s, 1960s, 1970s, 1980s and 1990s? (Choose the decades which apply to you.)
2. What were your favorite comedy radio shows (if you're over 55) when you were growing up?
3. List the comedy films you enjoyed the most in the last decade (go back further if you can). Who made you laugh the most in these films?
4. List the stand-up comedians who you think are very funny. Put a star next to the three you like the most.
5. List the comedians who turn you off (because you find their humor distasteful, boring, sexist, or unoriginal).
6. What are your favorite cartoons in magazines and newspapers?
7. Among your friends and colleagues, whom do you find funny? Who always makes you laugh?
8. Among your friends and colleagues, whom do you rarely find funny?
9. What kinds of everyday situations do you laugh at most often?
10. In what everyday situations do you rarely laugh?
11. Record in your Humor Log the common threads you see in your humor preferences. Do this separately for TV sitcoms, early radio shows, films, stand-up comedians, friends, and everyday situations.
12. Based on all the above, describe your sense of humor.

Once you've answered these questions in as much detail as you can, become a detective and go back through your answers looking for common threads. Ask yourself, "OK, why did I like her? Why did I find her funny, but not him?" "What kind of humor shows up most often in the films I generally like?" "Why do I never laugh at John's jokes, even though others find him very funny?" You'll gain more insights from this exercise if you write your answers down. Once they're written down, it will be easy for you to go back and look for common threads.

In my case, I realized that *I Love Lucy* reminded me of people I knew. I was amazed at all the dumb things Lucy did, and the absurd situations she got into. My early enjoyment of slapstick humor probably also accounts for my secret desire to imitate Ed Norton in *The Honeymooners.* Physical mannerisms were always a part of Norton's humor. When I think of Jonathan Winters, I picture his wonderful facial expressions. Again, this is a physical form of humor. I have to ask myself, "OK, so I liked physical, slapstick, clowning types of humor as a kid. Do I still like it?" While it's not at the top of my list, I can see that it's still capable of making me laugh—especially if it's combined with other kinds of humor.

When I think back to such *Saturday Night Live* characters as Roseanne Roseanna Danna (Gilda Radner) and Ernestine the telephone operator (Lily Tomlin), I realize that I loved the way they exaggerated characteristics of people I'd seen in real life. I roared at *All in the Family,* and still enjoy the reruns today. How could a racist, sexist, opinionated Archie Bunker be so funny? How could Edith's naivety and odd way of running around the house still be funny to me today? I think part of it is because I know people just like the two of them, and Archie shows how narrow people can be. They also remind me of the absurd things that happen every day. So part of the essence of my sense of humor must be that I enjoy the odd and absurd things people do and say.

This is probably why I liked a TV show Art Linkletter had when I was growing up called *Kids Say the Darndest Things*. I liked the unpredictability of the kids. They say things that make sense to them but are interpreted differently by adults. Sometimes kids are funny just because of their honesty. For example, there was the woman who was trying to save a little money by getting her 5-year-old daughter on the bus without paying (fares were required for age five and up). As she hustled the girl by the driver, the driver said, "Just a minute little girl, how old are you?" "Four and a half," said the girl. "And when will you be five?" "Just as soon as I get off this bus."

> **❝**In matters of humor, what is appealing to one person is appalling to another.**❞**
> (Melvin Helitzer)

Thinking about how much I enjoyed *Candid Camera* made me realize that I like humor based on people's reactions to unusual situations. In the crazy scenes they created, different people had very different reactions to the same situation—and each person's reaction was funny in its own way. I realize now that there is a thread of spontaneity that goes through much of the humor I like. I've always been a people watcher—and their unpredictability is part of what makes them fun to watch.

Why do I like George Carlin? I like the way he and other comedians play with language. I like coming up with my own puns and enjoy hearing comedians come up with all kinds of creative language play. I like the cleverness of much of what Carlin has to say. I also liked this quality in David Steinberg.

During the first half of his career, I thought Rodney Dangerfield was very funny. He somehow created visual images that stayed with me, as he proved the many ways in which he gets "no respect." He complained, "My wife, she's cheatin' on me again. This time it's with a midget. But hey, at least she's cuttin' down." My all-time Dangerfield favorite deviated from his usual "no respect" theme. He said, "I got my wife a toy poodle. She almost killed it trying to get batteries in it!"

So, by putting all this together, I can see that I've retained some enjoyment of slapstick and clowning forms of humor from my childhood. But I like to see it combined with other more clever forms of humor. I like humor that plays with word meanings—especially when it's created on the spot. I enjoy jokes, but don't have a lot of interest in telling them. They lack spontaneity. I love the humor of real life situations that develop—both in real life and in sit coms. I don't like put-down humor, especially when it seems to thinly mask the person's real feelings.

How Do You Show You Have a Good Sense of Humor?

> **❝**A man will confess to treason, murder, arson, false teeth, or a wig. How many of them will own up to a lack of humor?**❞**
> (Frank Moore Colby)

In spite of the increasing attention now being given to the importance of humor in our lives, researchers who study humor do not agree on what it means to have a good sense of humor; nor do they agree on how to measure it. My own 20 years of conducting research on humor has led me to the conclusion that there are five basic ways in which you can show a good sense of humor. You may show yours in only one of these ways, or in any combination of the five. To maximize the health and coping benefits you receive from humor and laughter, you'll want to strengthen your weak areas as you move through the 8-Step Program.

Enjoyment of Others' Humor

You may rarely initiate humor, but still show a well-developed sense of humor in your appreciation of the humor of others. It may show up in your enjoyment of jokes, funny stories, sit coms, comedy films, or any other source of humor produced by someone else. If you're like me, you can't get enough of Gary Larsen's "Far Side" cartoons. I know people who are humor junkies. They have enormous collections of cartoon books, and spend a lot of time in comedy clubs or going to comedy films. Many of us fall into this category, and it's an excellent starting point for developing other aspects of your sense of humor.

Research has shown, however, that your sense of humor will be a more powerful ally in helping you cope with life's burdens when you take a more active role in initiating or creating your own humor. So if you are now mainly a humor appreciator, you will want to give special attention to becoming more of a humor initiator.

Initiating Humor

There are many ways to initiate or "do" humor. You may be great at remembering jokes and funny stories, and have one for every occasion. You can be known as a terrific humorist by relying completely on memorized jokes and stories. Some great joke tellers rarely show spontaneous wit. They have a great delivery and a well-developed sense of timing, and yet never learn to think like a humorist themselves. You will gain more of the rich benefits offered by humor, however, when you learn to create your own humor. By the time you finish the 8-Step Program, you will have moved beyond the limits of retelling canned jokes; you will have learned to think like a humorist.

> **“**My way of joking is to tell the truth. It's the funniest joke in the world.**”**
> (George Bernard Shaw)

Your way of initiating humor may lean toward clowning around and physical forms of humor. Chevy Chase was very good at this on *Saturday Night Live*. Other excellent examples from past eras include Charlie Chaplin, Buster Keaton, Red Skelton, Soupy Sales, and Jonathan Winters. Cultivating this aspect of your sense of humor is very valuable. I often begin my seminars on Humor and Stress by giving the audience an opportunity to do something silly—to be physically playful. This usually breaks down barriers to mental playfulness and spontaneity, crucial to the development of other aspects of their sense of humor.

Since young children often show slapstick and other physical kinds of humor, it is often viewed as immature or childish. Some people stiffen up when I ask them, for example, act out in as silly a manner as possible how they would react if a fish had fallen into their shirt or blouse and was flopping around. People who show that they can "go with the flow," and be physically playful in an uninhibited and spontaneous manner, tend to make more rapid progress in developing other aspects of their sense of humor.

Finding Humor in Everyday Life

You may rarely act funny, show spontaneous wit, or tell jokes or funny stories, but still demonstrate a finely honed sense of humor through an ability to see the funny side of everyday events. You see the absurdity of your office routine. You notice the ironies and incongruities of life. One woman told me that she was waiting in line at a New Jersey State Inspection station on a hot summer day, when a wasp flew into her car and landed on the front windshield, just below the rear view mirror. Since she was allergic to bee stings, she took her shoe off and gave it a good swat. The heel must have found a weak spot; she shattered the windshield! She was next in line for inspection, and just cracked up laughing at the looks she got from the inspectors as she drove through. She didn't let the circumstances interfere with her ability to find a light side of the situation. This is one of the most important skills you can develop.

> **❝***You've got to realize when all goes well, and everything is beautiful, you have no comedy. It's when somebody steps on the bride's train or belches during the ceremony, then you've got comedy.*❞
> (Phyllis Diller)

Laughing at Yourself

Finding humor in your own mistakes, or in characteristics of yourself that you don't particularly like, is one of the most difficult ways of showing a good sense of humor. When you make a blunder, you probably get embarrassed, and this embarrassment interferes with your ability to find a light side of the situation. Your ego gets in the way of your ability to enjoy what others see as funny—even though you may see it intellectually. If this is the strong suit of your sense of humor, you're lucky. For most, this will be one of the hardest humor skills to develop.

Women are generally better at this than men. So you men may choose to spend a little extra time on Step 6. Learning to laugh at yourself is well worth the effort you put into it. It's a tremendously liberating feeling to be able to just let go of the embarrassment of the moment, and not carry it around with you. The more emotional weight you carry as a result of embarrassment, the more likely your are to be left in a frame of mind in which nothing is ever funny.

Finding/Creating Humor in the Midst of Stress

This is the most difficult part of your sense of humor to develop. But it is the one skill people who attend my seminars want to develop the most. Your sense of humor abandons you when you're under stress—even though you may be known for your great sense of humor when all is well. Your anger, anxiety, or depression takes over in high stress situations, leaving you incapable of seeing anything funny. If you sometimes have access to your sense of humor in mildly stressful situations, this gives you a head start in learning to reap the full power of humor to help you manage life stress.

Use the rating scale shown below to indicate how typical each of the following ways of showing a good sense of humor is of you.

1 = Very typical of me
2 = Somewhat typical of me
3 = Not very typical of me
4 = Not at all typical of me

____ Enjoyment of the humor of others
____ Initiating my own humor (in general)
____ Jokes
____ Relating personal experiences
____ Spontaneous wit (including puns)
____ Clowning around (physical humor)
____ Finding humor in everyday life (when not under stress)
____ Laughing at myself
____ Finding humor in the midst of stress

Based on these ways of showing a good sense of humor, list the strong and weak areas of your sense of humor in your Humor Log. Also record the areas you would most like to improve.

Development of Your Sense of Humor

One of the best ways to understand your present sense of humor is to examine its development during your childhood and adolescence, including the impact of your parents and other significant figures.

Humor Log Exercises: Your Early Sense of Humor

1. Were you a funny kid? Were you generally playful or more serious?
2. Describe the way you remember your sense of humor as a child. Do this separately for the preschool and elementary school years. (If your parents are living, talk to them about what you were like as a kid. Specifically ask if you laughed more/less than other kids, told a lot of riddles and jokes, played practical jokes, etc. You may be surprised to find that their memory of this does not match your own.)

3. Were you a funny adolescent or young adult? Describe the way you remember your sense of humor during adolescence and early adulthood.
4. Use the 4-point scale presented in the previous section to rate the following five basic ways of showing a good sense of humor. Do so for A) the preschool years, B) the elementary school years, C) adolescence, and D) your early adult years.

	A	B	C	D
Enjoyment of humor	___	___	___	___
Initiation of humor	___	___	___	___
Finding humor	___	___	___	___
Laughing at self	___	___	___	___
Humor under stress	___	___	___	___

Based on these ratings, record in your Humor Log how your sense of humor has changed over time. Look for continuity or for points at which it took a sudden step forward or backward. If you're middle-aged or older, also look at your sense of humor throughout your adult years.

Humor Log Exercises: Early Influences

1. Who during your childhood, adolescence, and early adulthood had the greatest influence (positive and negative) on the development of your sense of humor?
2. Describe your mother's sense of humor.
3. Describe your father's sense of humor.
4. What similarities do you see between your parents' sense of humor and your own?
5. How did your mother influence your sense of humor?
6. How did your father influence your sense of humor?
7. How did other people in your life influence your sense of humor?

Did your parents show a sense of humor with each other? With you? In the way they handled everyday problems? How would you describe their sense of humor? Can you remember them having a generally playful style of interaction with you during your childhood? Were they humor initiators? Did they laugh out loud a lot? Could they laugh at themselves? Did they react positively when you made an effort to do something funny (e.g., by going along with your riddles)? Ask yourself the same questions about grandparents or other significant figures in your life.

I have had people tell me that they were physically punished by their parents for telling jokes and trying in other ways to be funny as they were growing up. Perhaps you remember your parents saying things like, "Oh yeah? You think that's funny? I'll show you funny!" or "Stop that cackling; people will think you're an idiot!" or "You'd better get serious, or you'll never amount to anything!"

> ❝ *When the first baby laughed for the first time, his laugh broke into a million pieces, and they all went skipping about. That was the beginning of fairies.* ❞
>
> (J.M. Barrie)

Also look for negative parental reactions to any aspect of your early attempts at humor. Many parents feel that humor and play are the "work of the devil," or that they will somehow interfere with the ability to get a good education, get a job, etc. They feel they're doing their children a favor by forcing them to get serious about life early. They think they're helping develop skills at adapting to future hardships. In fact, they're robbing their children of the opportunity to nurture a powerful coping skill for stress-prone lives. You may find that you're using the 8-Step Program to redevelop skills you once had, but lost because parents, teachers, bosses, or life experiences drilled them out of you.

> **❝** *The one serious conviction that a man should have is that nothing is to be taken too seriously.* **❞**   (Samuel Butler)

Humor Log Exercises: Current Influences

1. In what situations does your sense of humor now show up most often?
   Think about when and where you laugh the most and initiate the most humor. Is it at work? At home? What is it about these situations that brings out your sense of humor? Think about both the nature of the situation and the people who are there.
2. In what situations does your sense of humor now show up least often?
   Are there any situations (at work, home, or elsewhere) in which you are always serious? What is it about these situations that causes your sense of humor to abandon you? Think about both the people present and the situation itself.
3. Do you show more of a sense of humor with men or with women? Why?
   Think about this both in terms of whether (and how often) you initiate humor, and how you react to the humor of others. Are men threatened by women who initiate a lot of humor? Do women feel obliged to "hold back" their sense of humor when around men?
   Many adults go through a mid-life crisis, and emerge from it with a new set of values about what's important in life. A common feature of this shift is a belief that life is just too short and too important to be taken so seriously all the time. These individuals want a high quality life in the second half of their years, and a sense of humor is seen as an important way of achieving day-to-day happiness. Don't wait until your own mid-life crisis to start making humor a more integral part of your life.

GROUP SESSION

Use the first session to talk about participants' goals in completing the program, along with any other issues pertinent to your particular group. Also discuss as many of the exercises and questions presented in the "Humor Log Exercises" as time permits. Do this for all future meetings, as well.

The group leader should decide whether topics are to be discussed in pairs, groups of 3, 4, etc., or among the group as a whole. The most effective approach is often to first discuss a topic in pairs, allowing each person in the group a chance to talk, and then open it up to the group as a whole.

Introductions

If some members of the group do not know each other, find a playful way to allow everyone to introduce themselves. For example, each person can give their name and produce a silly sound or action that expresses how they felt when they walked into the room. Or they can briefly describe the silliest, funniest, or most embarrassing thing they ever did.

Goals You Want to Achieve

Each participant should pair up with another person and describe what s/he would like to gain from the program. For example, which aspects of their sense of humor would they especially like to improve? If the group is small, goals may be described to the whole group.

Opening Fun Activity

Start each meeting with some kind of fun activity to help put the group into a more playful mood. This should be a game which invites cooperation and draws people together in some form of playful—even silly—interaction, not a competitive game. The leader can have something prepared for the first session, but a volunteer should be asked to bring in a fun activity for each of the remaining sessions. Feel free to play your favorite games from childhood, since they are usually very effective in regenerating the playful mental attitude that nurtures your sense of humor.

What Is Humor?

You know when something is funny to you, but have you ever thought about how you would define humor? Ask for a few definitions from the group and see if there's a consensus. What does it mean to say that you have a sense of humor? What do you really mean when you say something is funny?

Humor Terms

If you have a pen and paper with you, break into small groups and generate as many words as you can which relate to humor and laughter in some way. This exercise will help you map out the distinctions we make about humor.

Describe Your Sense of Humor

Describe your sense of humor to a partner, using whatever terms come to mind. Or describe it using the "Five ways of showing a good sense of humor" described in Step 1.

If you have time, discuss the following:

1. What medium of humor do you prefer (films, stand-up comedy, cartoons in magazines or books, literature, sitcoms, etc.)?
2. What are your favorite sitcoms, comedy films, stand-up comedians, or (print) cartoons? Why do you like them?
3. What kind of humor do you dislike, or find distasteful? Why do you dislike it? Is it annoying to find others laughing at humor you find distasteful?

Analysis of Particular Examples of Humor

Use a few specific jokes or cartoons to generate a discussion of why group members do or do not find it funny. One of the jokes or cartoons should be put-down humor. Use this as a vehicle for discussing your views about put-down humor in general. Why is disparagement humor so popular? Why do most countries have a favorite victim in jokes? Is political humor generally of the put-down variety? Can you laugh at jokes disparaging others without really disparaging them?

Influences on Your Sense of Humor

Use specific questions from the Humor Log Exercises to discuss with a partner the most important influences on your sense of humor, including both past and present influences.

Sex Differences

What gender differences have you observed in humor? Make it a point to discuss stereotypes.

Visualization Exercise

Think back to a period of your childhood when you had a lot of joy and laughter. Relive in your mind's eye a specific instance when you were having fun and laughing. Recapture what led up to the situation, who was there, and how you felt. Be with the experience for a couple of minutes. Then think about whether you still have experiences like that today. Discuss the feelings you experienced during this exercise.

The Negative Side of Humor

The 8-Step Program focuses on the many positive benefits resulting from humor, but humor can also take negative forms and trigger negative outcomes. Discuss any of the negative aspects of humor that you can think of. Some possibilities include 1) perceptions that you're immature, unprofessional, incompetent, or not serious about your work, 2) people who are always joking when you're trying to have a serious conversation, 3) insensitivity to the appropriate time or place for humor, 4) offensive forms of humor, and 5) people who laugh indiscriminately at everything.

Is it Too Late to Improve Your Sense of Humor?

Are you too old to develop your sense of humor? Is it ever too late to learn to lighten up? Why do some people come out of their "mid-life crisis" with a lighter attitude toward their work, and toward life generally?

Choose Telephone Partners

You will make greater progress in improving your sense of humor if you have a regular opportunity to talk to someone else about your efforts at each step. Organize telephone teams (2 or 3 people per team). Agree to call each other at least once between sessions to discuss how you're doing. This will help sustain your motivation to keep doing the Homeplay, and add to the fun you'll have along the way.

HOME PLAY

1. Make it a point to seek out humor from some professional source each day. This might include sitcoms or other comedy programs on television, comedy films (in a theater or on your own VCR), books of cartoons, magazine and newspaper cartoons, audio tapes of stand-up comedians, etc.

2. As you listen to comedy tapes, or think about your favorite comedians, make it a point to think about their styles. Which aspects of each comedian's style seem to fit your personality and sense of humor? Consider copying these comedians in any way that makes sense as you work on developing your own sense of humor.

3. Find at least one cartoon each week that has some special significance for you, or which you find especially funny, and put it in a high visibility place at work (e.g., on your desk, or on a bulletin board) or at home (e.g., on the refrigerator). Be on the lookout for cartoons you like, and add regularly to your collection. If you find yourself with too many, put the old ones in a folder and save them as you replace them with new ones. You may want to create a booklet of your favorite cartoons that you can look at whenever you need a good laugh.

4. Read one funny novel. (*Catch 22* is a classic.)

5. Go to your local bookstore (or library) and look through several cartoon books. Buy the one you like the most.

6. Find a library that has comedy audio tapes, and sign out several. Listen to one every day. If you have a tape deck in your car, ideal times to do this are on the way to and from work. If you jog or take walks, listen to the tapes on your Walkman. When possible, find a time when you can listen without distraction. Notice the effect this has on your mood.

7. Go to one comedy film or watch a comedy video tape on your VCR.

8. Listen to several sitcoms, and decide which programs you like the best (if you are a TV viewer). Use these as a basis for thinking about your own sense of humor.

9. Get a joke book and read through it.

10. Think about the nature of your sense of humor, and about influences on the development of your sense of humor. Talk to people who know you well about how they view your sense of humor. Develop a clear view of the strong and weak aspects of your sense of humor.

STEP 2

Learn to Adopt a Playful Attitude
Overcome Terminal Seriousness

"The human need to play is a powerful one. When we ignore it, we feel there is something missing in our lives."

(Leo Buscaglia)

"So long as there's a bit of a laugh going, things are all right. As soon as this infernal seriousness, like a grassy sea, heaves up, everything is lost."

(D. H. Lawrence)

"Laughter removes the burden of seriousness from the problem, and oftentimes it's that very serious attitude that is the problem itself."

(Bob Basso)

If you have a disease that is considered incurable, doctors say that you have a terminal illness. The disease has progressed to the point that only a miracle could help you recover. Some people have been so serious and somber for so long that it seems hopeless for them to ever again show a sense of joy, aliveness, and fun in their life. They, too, are suffering from a disease. I call it "Terminal seriousness."

It is appropriate, of course, to be serious in many situations; I'm not suggesting that you should never be serious. The problem arises when you lose the capacity to be playful; when you are unable to lighten up even when the situation calls for it. You may feel that people who are sometimes light and playful are shallow and oblivious to the real problems of the world. After all, we have cancer, violent crime, unspeakable atrocities committed in the midst of war, chaos and hopelessness in our inner cities, racism, pollution, and more. You should take these conditions seriously. But if you want to improve the quality of your life, one key is learning to maintain your commitments to change these conditions, while taking yourself less seriously in the process. You'll find yourself less stressed out by them, and in a better frame of mind to make change happen.

If you are suffering from TS, and need extra incentive to learn to lighten up on the job and in your life generally, you might consider how you and your somber colleagues are perceived. In my seminars, I generally ask the audience what terms they would use to describe people who are very serious all the time. The list always includes such adjectives as cold, dull, boring, tiresome, sad, lonely, no fun, tight, rigid, and so forth. I've never seen an exception to this. People with TS are not enjoyable to be around, even though they may be very competent, professional, and effective on the job. So if you have TS, you need to know that this is how you're perceived. But if you decide that you want to defrost your refrigerator personality, a playful attitude is the most effective tool you'll find. Remember that when your inner child dies, your joy and aliveness and sense of fun die too. The trick is to continue to be competent, responsible, and professional in your work, but let a little kid live in your big body.

> **❝*Life is too serious to be taken seriously.*❞**   (Oscar Wilde)

> **❝*Anything worth taking seriously is worth making fun of.*❞**
> (Tom Lehrer)

A Playful Attitude: The Basic Foundation for Your Sense of Humor

The key to improving your sense of humor is the rediscovery of the playful outlook you had when you were a child. Children are, by nature, playful. They would spend all day playing, if you let them. The joyous laughter that accompanies their play leaves no doubt that they are happy. However, while all parents want their children to be happy, they also want them to become responsible adults and to make something of their lives. And many parents feel that the sooner they get their child to stop playing and get serious about life, the greater her chances of later becoming a successful adult. Teachers strengthen this idea, doing everything they can to teach children to look at life seriously, and start developing the knowledge and skills required to be successful.

Children do need to learn that there's more to life than play, but I am convinced that we go too far in shaping our kids to be less playful. We produce adolescents and adults who have lost the ability to lighten up and be playful—even when its appropriate. In my seminars and workshops, I always give the audience an opportunity to do something playful and silly. There are generally a few people who stiffen up and glare at me for putting them in such an awkward and embarrassing situation. Others are very comfortable and just have fun with any silly activity thrown their way.

Which camp do you fall into? Are you easily embarrassed when you do something that is at odds with your image of yourself as professional, competent, serious, and respectable? If you are, then you'll need to spend extra time on Step 2. If not, you're probably already comfortable being playful. But you should still complete Step 2 to further develop the playful essence of yourself. Use the opportunity to strengthen the "elf" within yourself.

Most people want a quick fix—techniques that will help them manage the stress in their lives right now. While some of these techniques are provided in Step 7, they're only marginally effective by themselves. The real power of humor to help you cope shows up when you first strengthen the basic foundation that causes your sense of humor to blossom. That foundation is the ability to be mentally playful.

When you become more playful, you automatically become more spontaneous and enjoy whatever you're doing more than you otherwise would. And in this frame of mind, things just naturally strike you as being funnier than they do when you're more serious. Other positive emotions and moods are also more likely to emerge when you're playful.

A woman at a singles dance keeps sneezing, and can't seem to stop. A guy walks up and asks if she's ok. She says, "Yeah, I've been sneezing for five minutes."

"God, that's terrible!" says the guy. And she sighs, "Well, it's not that bad, because each time I sneeze, I have an orgasm."

So he says, "Wow! Are you taking anything for it?"

"Yeah," she says, "pepper!"

I have been to many dances and other events for singles, and I'm always amazed at the serious, even somber, faces. Both men and women wander about, annoyed at the lack of interest shown toward them. They seem oblivious to the fact that a serious (often interpreted as angry, depressed) expression is a signal that you're probably not someone who is enjoyable to be around. An upbeat, playful attitude automatically produces a facial expression that is more inviting; it communicates that you're approachable, not caught up in your own problems, and probably fun to be around.

❝*Gaiety is the most outstanding feature of the Soviet Union.*❞
(Joseph Stalin)

Your goal should not be to become someone who's always playful and never serious. This isn't very adaptive, and is one of the things your parents and teachers worked so hard to overcome. If you generally are serious, your initial goal should initially be to recapture the ability to be playful in just a few situations. Once you have achieved that, you can focus on learning to shift from a serious to a playful style whenever you choose, or whenever the situation calls for it. You want to become more flexible in this sense—able to easily switch gears and create a playful mood.

The Meaning of a Playful Attitude

What does it mean to adopt a playful attitude? We all have a general idea of what play is and know when we are and are not being playful. But have you ever thought about the real nature of play? Are you, by definition, playful when you're playing? This may be true for young children, but it's often not true for adolescents and adults. We use the term "play" to refer to such activities as tag, hide-and-seek, baseball, cards, chess, football, playing the piano, etc. But are you always playful when engaged in those activities?

By the time you enter school, play becomes competitive and goal-oriented, and you're anything but playful. You're determined to win, or at least do well, when playing. This is not the kind of play that forms the core of your sense of humor.

The dictionary defines play as activities which are amusing, fun, or otherwise enjoyable in their own right, regardless of what follows. In other words, play is intrinsically enjoyable. There is no particular goal you're trying to achieve. Once the focus shifts to an outcome (pleasing someone, doing better than others, achieving a specific level of performance, etc.), it stops being fun. It may even become work!

> **"**You are led through your lifetime by the inner learning creature, the playful spiritual being that is your real self.**"**
>
> (Richard Bach)

I know of a child who used to love to draw. She would draw all day long, just for the fun of it. She would even draw while watching television. Then she started an art class in school, and the teacher asked her to bring in two new drawings each week. The teacher told her things she was doing well and where she needed to do better. Now she had specific goals to meet in her drawings. Her mother began paying her 25 cents for every drawing she did, in order to encourage her to do better. This combination of external demands and rewards took the fun out of drawing, and she started to draw only what she had to do for her classes. Drawing became work, instead of fun.

Since much of the stress in your life comes from the hassles and minor problems that are there every day, you're never really free from stress. Learning to be more playful, even in difficult situations, helps you lift yourself out of the stress of the moment, leaving you in a better position to roll with the punches life throws your way. It also reduces the accumulative effect of stress on your body, helping you protect your health. At the same time, it increases your effectiveness on the job and in your personal life.

Think of a playful attitude as a skill. The key is getting yourself to the point where you take control over when you are and are not playful, rather than having it hinge on whether good or bad things are happening in your life, or whether you are around positive or negative people. And remember, it's much more important to learn to have fun and be in the spirit of fun than to be funny.

Why Is a Playful Attitude the Foundation for Your Sense of Humor?

I argued in my 1979 book, *Humor: Its Origin and Development* (now out of print), that humor is a form of intellectual play—play with ideas. We inherit a basic disposition toward playfulness, and this shows up in different ways as we move through childhood and adolescence, reflecting the development of new intellectual and social skills.

Humor is experienced when you're mentally playful. Without this playful frame of mind, the same event will be seen as interesting, puzzling, annoying, frightening, depressing, etc., but it won't be funny! That's why some people who are very good at spotting the incongruities, absurdities, and ironies (qualities that every good humorist works with) of life never find any humor in them. They simply don't bring the right outlook or attitude to the things they see.

Learning to be mentally playful is the key to improving your sense of humor. As you become more comfortable with (and skilled at) being playful, your natural sense of humor emerges. You don't need to learn specific humor techniques to cope with the stress in your life. You simply need to unleash the playfulness you had when you were a kid, but which has been suppressed over the years. Once the child within you is let out, the rest will take care of itself.

Does Play Have an Important Biological Function?

When you think about it, playing is a very odd thing to do. It appears to serve no purpose. It seems like something you do when you don't have other important things to do. And yet most animals play. Since any behavior that is common to an entire species generally serves an important function, could it be that play also makes an important biological contribution to our lives?

> *If animals play, this is because play is useful in the struggle for survival; because play practices and so perfects the skills needed in adult life.*
> (Susanna Miller)

Animal Play

As you go up the phylogenetic scale from simpler to more complex animals, there is an increasing disposition to play when not hungry, sexually aroused, or under some immediate threat from the environment. The specific ways in which animals play are generally closely linked to the skills they need to adapt and survive. That's why many animals engage in play fighting. They take turns attacking and being attacked. They nip at each other's necks, chase each other, jump in the air, run in circles, buck and kick, spin, and practice other maneuvers that will be important later on. One of the oldest theories of play claims that play exists precisely because animals need to practice these skills in a safe context, so that when the time comes that they need them to get food or defend themselves, they'll be ready.

Recent research on animals has shown that play also makes a crucial contribution to brain development. Natalie Angier recently summarized this research as follows:

"An animal plays most vigorously at precisely the time when its brain cells are frenetically forming synaptic [the space at which one nerve cell communicates with another] connections, creating a dense array of neural connections that can pass an electrochemical message from one neighborhood of the brain to the next. As it turns out, the neurons sprouting especially high numbers of synapses during an animal's days of frivolity are located in the brain's cerebellum, a . . . region in charge of coordination, balance, and muscle control. Scientists believe that the intense sensory and physical stimulation that comes from playing is critical to the growth of these cerebral synapses, and thus to proper motor development."[1]

Higher primates, dolphins, and humans play for a longer period of their early development than animals lower on the phylogenetic scale. It is no coincidence that brain development in these species also extends over a longer period of time. The developing brain needs the stimulation provided by play for optimal development. This stimulation becomes even more significant, considering that while the brain undergoes its most rapid development during early in life, it doesn't stop developing when adulthood is reached. New connections between different neurons in the brain can continue throughout life. Play is not the only kind of stimulation that does this, of course, but it has all the right features to do it in a very effective way. That's one reason play evolved to be such an important part of our biological makeup.

Children's Play

In examining the play of different species, it's clear that those capacities that will be important to effective adaptation and survival as an adult are the strongest focus of play during the animal's youth. What happens if we apply this principle to humans? What capacities are crucial to our adaptation and survival? It's not our strength, speed, or agility. It's our intelligence. So it's no coincidence that the most prominent aspect of children's play involves play with the mind.

> **❝** *Play reaches the habits most needed for intellectual growth.* **❞**
> (Bruno Bettelheim)

This may surprise you, since, when you think of children's play, you probably think of rough and tumble play (at least among boys). There's no doubt that young children's play is very physical. But if you look closely, you'll see that there's usually a symbolic feature to the play as well. They're not just running, jumping, or hitting; they're chasing a bad guy, jumping over a pit full of snakes, playing Wonder Woman, or punching out Darth Vader. From the point at which children first become capable of symbolic thinking, late in the first year of life, their imagination becomes the central focus of their play. And it is out of this make-believe play that humor emerges. Humor is exactly what you'd expect in a species with advanced thinking abilities. Given the inherited tendency to play with whatever abilities we have, this symbolic thinking capacity has to produce some form of abstract play. That's precisely what humor is!

> **A father walks into a room and catches his son masturbating. He says, "You know son, if you keep that up, you're going to go blind." And the kid says, "I'm over here, dad."**

So you were meant to enjoy humor. If you're a parent, chances are that you've played the game of "Show me your eye . . . show me your nose . . ." with your toddler. Even if you always do this in a serious way, the day eventually comes when your child gets a funny expression in her eyes and shows a playful smile when you say, "Show me your ear." Does she point to her ear? No. She points to her nose, and laughs! All healthy children like to turn reality on its ear. They delight in calling things by the wrong name and trying to fool you. As the child gets older, what parent hasn't suffered through the riddle stage, in which 6- to 9-year-olds go on endlessly laughing at the same riddles?

If play serves to build up skills that are essential to effective adaptation as an adult, how does humor help you adapt? Why does humor exist? I think one of the main reasons it exists is to help you adapt to the stress in your life. It is precisely because of your superior intellectual capacities that you have such high stress in your life. You've probably heard the expression, "You create your own stress." This refers to the fact that it is your interpretation of events that causes you stress, not the events themselves. Your sense of humor helps you create difficult circumstances in a less stressful way.

> *When you're depressed, the whole body is depressed, and it translates to the cellular level. The first objective is to get your energy up, and you can do it through play. It's one of the most powerful ways of breaking up hopelessness and bringing energy into the situation.*
> (O. Carl Simonton, M.D.)

You rarely are confronted with life-threatening situations. Your stress is generally more psychological in nature. Your boss doesn't appreciate your work. You have too many demands on your time. You impose expectations on yourself that can't be met. You spend your entire life carrying around upsets about the past and anxieties about the future, and it all adds up to stress. Your sense of humor is one of nature's natural remedies. But while humor helps you cope, it's also fun. That is why kids spend so much time with riddles and other forms of humor.

So it's worth asking why nature has built in the intrinsic enjoyment we derive from humor during childhood. I'm convinced that it's, in part, designed to assure that we spend a lot of time practicing it as children, so we'll be able to use our sense of humor when we need it as adults. But the environment many adults grew up in not only failed to support the development of their sense of humor; it actively interfered with it ("Act your age!" "Grow up, will ya?" "Get serious!" "Stop goofing around all the time!" "Wipe that stupid grin off your face!"). This has led them to the point that they need something like the 8-Step Program to learn the skills they should have had all along.

If play stimulates brain development, and humor is a form of play, then how does humor contribute to brain development? Since humor utilizes higher cerebral centers that permit symbolic thinking, it follows that these are the areas stimulated by humor. So humor not only reflects your existing thinking capacities; it also helps expand them! Part of the brain development that occurs should be similar to that which occurs as a result of the stimulation that results from any form of interest, curiosity, and attention to new ideas. But humor offers something much more powerful, as well. It nurtures creative thinking abilities.

> *Necessity may be the mother of invention, but play is certainly the father.*
> (Roger von Oech)

We've known for a long time that a close relationship exists between humor and creativity. Arthur Koestler argued in *The Act of Creation* that original humor involves the same type of thinking that is involved in creative insights in the sciences and the arts. More creative individuals see bridges between ideas that others don't. They bring together ideas that don't seem to have any meaningful connection, and create their own link. So it's no surprise that a positive correlation has often been found between measures of creativity and both playfulness and the ability to create humor.[2] One study even showed that exposing high school students to a semester-long humor training program increases their creativity.[3]

To adapt well in today's world—especially the business world—you need to be creative. So improving your humor skills may improve your ability to come up with innovative solutions to problems at the same time that it increases your ability to deal with stress. Of course, becoming a more effective problem-solver can indirectly lower job stress by eliminating real problems before they become stressful.

Play and Work

One of the most important roles I play in the programs I do for corporations is to provide justification for the decision to let a playful attitude and fun into the work place. Managers and CEOs need to be convinced that humor and play skills really do help employees cope with job stress; that they increase morale, job satisfaction, a sense of team identity, communication, creativity, and productivity. Many managers assume that "If you're having fun, then you can't be working." They see any sign of playful behavior as a waste of time—taking time away from being productive. But once they see that fun on the job creates a work environment in which people enjoy their work more and work better, play is seen as the partner of work, not it's enemy.

To benefit from Step 2, you must be convinced that **fun is not a 4-letter word!** Give yourself permission to let go, be playful (when it's appropriate), and laugh more often. It's ok to have fun at what you do, as long as you maintain your usual high standards about the quality of your work. It's just as important to change your negative attitudes toward play and fun as it is to work on humor skills per se.

> **"** *The supreme accomplishment is to blur the line between work and play.* **"**
> (Arthur Toynbee)

> **"** *Play: Work that you enjoy doing for nothing.* **"**   (Evan Esar)

> **"** *The trouble with the rat race is that even if you win, you're still a rat.* **"**
> (Lily Tomlin)

You may be very capable of being playful, but rarely let this quality show. Many people have told me that they would love to lighten up and be more playful on the job, but are concerned about what people would think if they did. They're afraid they'll be viewed as unprofessional, incompetent, and irresponsible—a goof-off. In many companies, this is exactly what would happen. This is changing, however, as awareness of the positive contributions made by fun in the work place grows. Companies now realize that you can have fun on the job, and still be competent and maintain your professionalism. More importantly, when jobs become fun, people like their work more and do it more effectively.

A doctor's wife is unable to sleep because the toilet is dripping. So she has her husband call the plumber. The plumber listens, but then grumpily declares, "But it's 2 a.m.!" And the doctor says, "So what? If your child was sick, wouldn't you call me?" "You're right," says the plumber, "so I'll tell you what to do. Throw a couple of aspirins in the bowl, and if it's not better in the morning, call me."

Others say they can't take the time to have fun in life. One woman told me after a program, "I don't have time to slow down. I have too much to do. I can't afford to have fun!" I say that you can't afford **not** to have fun. You need to rediscover your sense of fun before it's too late! If you're committed to doing your job well, then building a playful outlook and fun into your daily attitude will help you be more effective on your job (and be more enjoyable to be around), because you'll be less vulnerable to stress. If it's hard for you to make room for fun in your life, try visiting a hospice. You rarely find residents of a hospice saying they wish they'd worked harder and achieved more. If they talk about work and play, they generally say they wish they'd played a little more and worked a little less. Don't wait until you're in a hospice to figure this out.

Play and Sports

Have you ever thought about how you engage in games and sports? The goal is to win, to compete effectively against the opponent. And you're anything but playful! When you're being playful, you are much more likely to enjoy the game or sport just for the fun of it. You may also enjoy winning, but it's not the most important part of playing the game.

Professional sports offer an excellent example of the lack of a playful attitude in games. Games at the professional level long ago became serious business, so few professional athletes have fun while playing the game. I am always delighted to watch the rare professional athlete who is able to show a playful side, while retaining an obvious commitment to excellence.

Yanick Noah, the French tennis star, always loved to have fun when playing tennis, and fans responded to his playful attitude all over the world. (Jimmy Connors also became more playful in his later playing years.) Yanick won the French Open in 1983, but his basic philosophy was to always enjoy himself, have fun, and retain a good sense of humor.

He frequently demonstrated these qualities during a match. I still have a vivid image of him chasing a ball that his opponent had put away at a very sharp angle to win the point. He had built up such speed in racing for the ball that he jumped over a barrier and kept running down the aisle leading away from the seating area (pretending to be still going for the ball). He finally stopped when he came to a door, where a fan was drinking a glass of wine. He took the glass and stormed back onto the court with it, exhibiting a look of, "OK, you're in big trouble now—you've gotten me angry!" The fans loved it.

In another match, the umpire (who sits on the high chair at the center of the court) got off his chair to go inspect the spot where a ball had hit near the line in Noah's opponent's court. While the umpire's back was turned, Noah ran over and climbed up on the chair, imitating the umpire with exaggerated gestures. When the umpire returned, Noah playfully pointed to the other side of the court, as if the umpire should pick up the racquet and resume play. Again, the fans howled.

> **❝We live in an ironic society where even play is turned into work. But the highest level of existence is not work; the highest level of existence is play.❞**
> (Conrad Hyers)

Noah says that he cannot play tennis any other way. He must have fun at what he does. He loves to win, but is not willing to sacrifice his playfulness just to win. In any case, he couldn't possibly leave it behind, because it is an integral part of who he is. In this sense, he is an ideal model for us all. His zest for living is obvious. He creates joy in living his life, and spreads it to those around him. This will happen to you too, once you release the child within you who still wants to be playful.

> **❝This is what it's all about. If you can't have fun at it, there's no sense hanging around.❞**
> (Joe Montana)

> **❝Most of the time, I don't have much fun. The rest of the time, I don't have any fun at all.❞**
> (Woody Allen)

The goal, then, is to learn to have fun and be in the spirit of fun. The game, and the sharing of the game with friends, simply provides the context for doing so. What would it be like to live every day as if one of your goals was to have fun every day?

Living Your Life as Play

According to an old saying, "The past is a canceled check, you can't spend it anymore. The future is a promissory note which might not be paid off. The present is cash, spend it wisely." What does it mean to spend the present wisely? There are many answers to this question, of course, but one is simply to be fully engaged in the experience of the moment. How often are you really present to your experiences? Would your life be enriched by being more present to the moment?

> **❝Having a wonderful time; wish I was here.❞** (Bumper sticker)

Plato once said, "Life must be lived as play." What do you think he meant by that? What bearing does it have on your life? I'm not sure what Plato meant, but I know what it means to me. Several philosophical and religious traditions (e.g., Zen) stress the value of learning to live more fully in the moment. Special programs have been developed to help people learn to "Be here now!" When you think about it, "now" is really all you have. Life is a series of "nows." And yet you spend most of your time caught up in upsets and disappointments about the past, on the one hand, and anxieties about the future, on the other. Or you go through your life half asleep, with no real joy or passion of any kind. In the film *Awakenings*, Leonard says at one point, "We don't know what it's like to live. We've forgotten how to experience joy." Rediscovering play wakes you up and makes you more present to life, giving you more joy in the process.

"What did the Zen Buddhist say to the hot dog vendor?"
"Make me one with everything."

Zen has been a dominant force in Japanese culture for centuries. Since the Japanese have long been a ritualistic people, concerned about protocol and doing things right, they need something like Zen to help them overcome the self-consciousness that automatically goes along with concern about "doing things right." A playful spirit has the same power to overcome self-consciousness, because it also helps you merge with the activity of the moment.

> **❝** *I still get wildly enthusiastic about little things . . . I play with leaves. I skip down the street and run against the wind.* **❞**
> (Leo Buscaglia)

When children and adults are engaged in playful play, and having fun, they are fully engaged in the "now." They aren't preoccupied with problems and daily concerns. They leave them behind. You don't want to hide from your problems, of course, but you also don't want them to weigh you down all the time. Dealing with them in the midst of a lighter attitude will help you cope with them more effectively. You'll also find it therapeutic.

Plato also suggested that we "practice dying;" that is, learn to live life as if we didn't have much time left. Patients with terminal illnesses often learn to fully appreciate every day given to them, knowing that their days are limited. But why wait until you have six months or a year to live before you learn to create joy and aliveness in your life? A playful attitude and your sense of humor help you create these qualities and reinstall them into your daily life.

Many adults go through a mid-life crisis in their 40s or 50s, during which they re-examine their life and values. Every such crisis is unique, but a common outcome is a determination to spend less time engulfed in work, and more time with the things one loves and enjoys—especially close relationships. There is a shift away from past achievements, and toward the time you have left.

Many also emerge from their crisis with the realization that they've lost the sense of joy and aliveness in their lives. They develop a renewed sense of the importance of lightening up about everyday problems. They realize that most of the things that have bent them out of shape during their life aren't that important. They learn to put things in perspective, and to stop taking everything so seriously. They learn to lighten up!

> **"** *People do not quit playing because they grow old. They grow old because they quit playing.* **"** (Oliver Wendell Holmes)

Some, however, never learn to lighten up, and enter their senior years in a continuing ebb of bitterness, anger, anxiety, or depression at the unfair path life has always laid before them. Others simply have a vague sense of regret or longing; a sense that they've somehow missed something important in life by being such a serious person decade after decade. This is demonstrated by an 85-year-old woman in the hills of Kentucky, who said:

> **"** *If I had my life to live over, I'd make more mistakes this time. I'd relax; I'd limber up. I'd be sillier than I've been this trip. I'd take fewer things seriously . . . You see, I'm one of those people who live sensibly, day after day . . . If I had it to do over again, I'd travel lighter than I have.* **"**

This woman clearly regrets the lack of playfulness in her life, but feels it's too late to change. If you recognize yourself in her, don't wait until you're 85 to realize that the quality of life improves when you become more playful. This book will help you avoid her fate.

My own grandmother was a serious woman most of her life, but found her sense of humor blossoming as she got older (she lived to be 98). She was a very religious person, so she was always aware of how much she had to be thankful for. "After all," she said, "Just think of where I'd be if wrinkles hurt."

Why Do We Become Less Playful During Adulthood?

George Burns, who recently died at the age of 100, once said, "You can't help getting older, but you can help getting old." Who better demonstrates the power of humor to prevent "hardening of the attitudes?" Many senior citizens live out their golden years with bitter resentment at how unfair life has been to them, and their sense of humor dies in the process. By improving your sense of humor now, you'll still find joy in aging, even if you do have health problems along the way. As anthropoligist Ashley Montagu put it, "Die young as late as possible. That way you'll live longer."

Think back to when you were a child. What was the one thing you wanted to do all day long? You wanted to play. I know that I did, because it's written on my second grade report card (twice), "Paul plays too much!" Everything else was a distraction from playing. When you were playing, you were having fun.

So what caused you to lose your playfulness? Or, as Joel Goodman (another speaker on humor) is fond of saying, "What made you lose the 'elf' in 'yourself'?" For some of us, it was our parents. Many parents see play as "the devil's workshop" and consider it their duty to stifle playful urges. They fear that play will cause their children to never amount to anything. I have had adults tell me that when they were kids, their parents physically punished them for being too playful, laughing, and telling jokes.

A boy came home with a report card that included four D's and three F's. He asked his father, "What do you think my problem is, heredity or environment?"

Most children are allowed to be as playful as they want until they go to school. Then the cruel reality of work hits them. "You can't play until your school work is done." Parents know the importance of doing well in school, so they give their children less and less time for play as they get older. Kids learn the importance of achievement, and the journey toward adult seriousness is begun.

> *It is paradoxical that many educators and parents still differentiate between a time for learning and a time for play without seeing the vital connection between them.* (Leo Buscaglia)

Teachers play a role in this too, of course. Most teachers consider play an enemy of learning—in spite of overwhelming evidence that children learn well when learning is fun. They fear that play and fun will take over the classroom, and no one will get any work done. In fact, students do sometimes justify this fear. In the ninth grade, one of my classmates' favorite pranks was to—at an agreed-upon time on the wall clock with the big second hand—all "accidentally" knock a book, pencil, or other object off our desk (we generally did this with substitute teachers). The most impressive reaction we ever got was from a biology teacher who was writing on the board at "zero minute." She just walked over to her desk, picked up a book of her own, and dropped it on the floor, saying, "Sorry I'm late." Needless to say, this teacher had a good sense of humor, and knew how to make playfulness work for effective instruction, not against it.

> *The true object of all human life is play. Earth is a task garden; heaven is a playground.* (G.K. Chesterton)

When "Teacher of the Year" honors are given out, the winning teacher is often described as having a "good sense of humor." So a playful attitude must be an important ingredient in effective teaching. And research has shown that humor does promote learning and retention.[4] Both preschool and school-aged children learn better when learning is fun. Teachers would do well, then, to help teach children how to control and manage their playfulness and humor, not extinguish it.

Employers eventually take over the role of "play killer" and make it clear that only a serious approach to the job will lead to promotions. Employees quickly learn to project seriousness and an image of professionalism as a means of demonstrating commitment to their work. By the time you finish Step 2, you will be able to maintain a high level of competence and professionalism on the job, and still adopt a lighter, more playful style (when appropriate).

> *It's never too late to have a happy childhood.*
> (Anonymous)

So we go too far in pushing both children and adults to abandon their initial playful approach to life. The trick is to learn when it's appropriate to be playful, and when it's not. Start viewing a playful attitude as a skill which you can utilize whenever it's adaptive to do so. Once companies realize that their employees are not going to be goofing off—taking time away from work—all day long, you can begin putting play and humor to work, both on the job and in your personal life.

Physical Versus Mental Play

All play comes from a playful frame of mind. Yet, we can distinguish between physical and mental play. When you allow yourself to loosen up and be physically playful, barriers to mental playfulness begin to disappear. You automatically loosen up mentally, and ease naturally into the spirit of humor. You begin to notice and do funny things. I have seen many stiff and humorless people transformed once they feel comfortable with being physically playful.

For some, this will be the most difficult step to work on. But once you break through and learn to genuinely enjoy being playful, you will be astounded at its impact on your life. You will rediscover a quality of aliveness, joy, and presence to your everyday life that you've long forgotten. Woody Allen once said, "Most of the time, I have very little fun in my life. The rest of the time, I have no fun at all." If this is you, rest assured that everything will change as you become more playful.

Using Props to Induce a Playful Attitude

If you've been a serious person most of your life, you'll need all the help you can get for Step 2. Silly toys and props will help you out. Make it a point to go out and buy several. They can be anything that brings out your sense of fun, silliness, or playfulness. One woman I know keeps a set of wind-up false teeth in her desk. When wound up, the teeth just sit on her desk going "clackety-clackety-clackety-clack." She says it always helps her lighten up when things get tough.

A corporate Vice President who I taught to juggle scarves says that when the tension gets too high, she closes her door, gets out the scarves and spends a few minutes juggling. It has helped her lighten up every time she's tried it. Maybe blowing bubbles will work for you, or a silly hat, or cartoons, or a silly buzzer. Silly nose glasses work well for me, partly because of the reaction I always get from other people (I have 30 different animal noses).

If you have a management position, try keeping a few silly props sitting on your desk, file cabinets, book case shelves, etc. People who've done this find that when employees come in, either to complain or just to talk, they generally go over and unconsciously pick up a toy or prop and start fiddling with it. You can see the tension ease as they play with it. Such brief playful respites elevate their mood and leave them leave them in a better frame of mind for effectively continuing their job.

Unexpected Rewards from Cultivating a Playful Attitude

Step 2 establishes the foundation on which you will extend your present humor skills. But you also will notice some immediate benefits as you become more comfortable with being playful. You will find that you enjoy your job than you used to. Your job hasn't changed, but you've changed. While work may not yet be fun, you can expect more job satisfaction and higher morale—just because you now spend a greater part of your day in a positive, playful mood.

You'll notice that you don't get caught up in as many conflicts as you used to. You won't be as emotionally drained by frustration, anger, anxiety, or depression as you used to. You'll be less rigid and more willing to let people have their own point of view. You also may become more effective in situations requiring bargaining. Politicians have long used humor to establish a playful, convivial atmosphere in situations where both sides have to make concessions. A recent example of this occurred in the signing of the accord between Israel and the Palestine Liberation Organization on September 13, 1993. Prior to the signing, secret negotiations took place for a year and a half in Norway at the home of Johan Jorgen Horst, the Norwegian Foreign Minister. These negotiations regularly lasted long into the night.

Horst discovered that by allowing his 4-year-old son to play on the living room floor with Israeli and PLO officials, he could create an environment more conducive to productive negotiations. Playing with the young boy helped them maintain a more convivial frame of mind, and kept decades of anger and distrust from exploding and killing the negotiations. Horst later said that the playful atmosphere was "at least as important as secrecy in this peace process." If a playful attitude can help resolve differences between people who have been deadly enemies for generations, it can certainly help you handle your daily conflicts.

❝*Are we having fun yet?*❞

(Carol Burnett)

Humor Log Exercises

Record your responses to the following questions in your Humor Log.

On Play and a Playful Attitude

1. What does it mean to be a playful person, or to adopt a playful attitude in life?
2. Does it make sense to distinguish between playful and non-playful forms of play? How do they differ?
3. Does it make sense to distinguish between physical and mental forms of play? How do they differ?
4. How will learning to become a more playful person help develop your sense of humor?
5. Why does society view playfulness so negatively?
6. Plato once said, "Life should be lived as play." How would you interpret this?

7. Think of people you know who are serious all the time. Write down as many words as you can which describe these people.

8. Think of people you know who have a playful attitude, but are still competent, responsible, etc. Write down as many words as you can which describe these people. Compare the qualities you listed for 4) and 5). Which kind of person would you rather a) work with? b) be married to? c) have as a close friend?

9. What qualities do you associate with young children when they're playing?

10. What stereotypical negative views do many have of playful adults?

11. When were you most playful in your life?

12. When did you stop being playful? What led you to stop?

13. A well-known saying states, "We do not stop playing because we grow old; we grow old because we stop playing." How can a loss of a playful outlook on life make us grow older?

14. Do middle-aged and elderly people who have retained a playful outlook seem younger than their more serious-minded peers?

15. Senior citizens often become increasingly negative and serious as they get older. Are you ever too old to learn to lighten up?

16. It's important to learn when a playful response is not appropriate. List a few examples of such situations.

17. List those friends, relatives, and coworkers who have the kind of playful attitude you would like to develop.

18. Describe the benefits you would receive from becoming a more playful person.

Work and Play

1. Describe the dichotomy between work and play in our culture. Are these really incompatible with each other? Can a playful attitude actually help you be more effective on the job?

2. Do you have fun at work? What would it take to make your job fun? Answer both in terms of changes in yourself and changes in the work environment.

3. How are play and a lighter attitude on the job viewed where you work? If you do your job well and work hard, would such an attitude be viewed positively or negatively?

4. What are some of the stereotypical views (e.g., immature) of adults who bring a lighter approach to their work, and to their life generally?

5. What "signals" have you noticed at work which suggest that a playful attitude would not be well-received on the job—regardless of how well you do your work?

6. Discuss the notion of seriousness in connection with competence, professionalism, and responsibility. Do these three qualities require that you always be serious on the job?

7. On your job, what are the ways in which seriousness is modeled and reinforced on a daily basis?

8. How does Terminal Seriousness set you up for greater stress on the job, and in life generally?

9. Discuss the difference between taking your work seriously and taking yourself seriously.

Current Playfulness

1. How often are you playful in everyday life?
2. When you are playful, who are you generally with, and what are the circumstances?
3. When you are serious, who are you generally with, and what are the circumstances?
4. What makes you uncomfortable about being playful (if that's true)?
5. How important is it for you to learn to become more playful? Why?
6. All things considered, what do you expect your biggest obstacle to be in adopting a more playful attitude toward life?
7. What would you like to achieve in the next two weeks, in terms of cultivating a playful attitude?

Early Development and Influences

1. How playful/serious were you as a child? As an adolescent?
2. When did you lose the playfulness of your childhood?
3. What early events helped make you a less playful person than you would like to be? Focus specifically on parents and teachers, along with other pertinent life experiences.
4. What remarks did your parents make suggesting that you should "straighten up and get serious?" (E.g., "Wipe that stupid grin off your face," or "If you play all the time, you'll never amount to anything.")

GROUP SESSION

Opening Fun Activity

Have a game or fun activity prepared to put the group in a playful frame of mind. Consider having a "twit race," as shown on the old Monty Python television programs. Or assume that the Minister of Silly Walks has come to your meeting and requested that everyone walk across the room with their best silly walk. Assign someone to be prepared for an opening activity for the next meeting.

Discussion of Homeplay for Step 1

Any aspect of the Homeplay for Step 1, or insights gained since the last group meeting, should be discussed before moving on to Step 2. Some possibilities for discussion are listed below.

1. Share with a partner the ways in which you immersed yourself in humor during the past week.
2. What new insights have you had about your sense of humor, as a result of doing the Homeplay for Step 1?
3. Now that you've spent a week or two thinking about your sense of humor, have your goals in going through the 8-Step Program changed?
4. You can also use the beginning of this session to discuss any topics from Step 1 that you didn't get to last time.

Discussion of Step 2

Use the general material presented for Step 2, or any of the items from the Humor Log Exercises to generate a discussion of play and a playful outlook on life. Be sure to also talk about the general importance of a playful attitude for improving your sense of humor. After you leave this meeting, remember to stay in touch with your telephone partners.

HOME PLAY

Your goal during Step 2 is to be more playful than you usually are. You want to develop this quality to the point that you have the choice of being playful or serious, rather than have it be determined by the circumstances or mood of the moment.

1. Take a silly photo of yourself.

    Go to a photomat or use a polaroid camera to take a photo of yourself making a silly face or doing something silly. Keep the photo with you or put it in a place where you'll see it every day. Use it as a reminder to maintain a playful attitude (while continuing to be responsible and do your job well) when you choose to, rather than having it depend on how things are going.

2. Make a list of things you have fun doing and do two of them each day.

    Doing things that are fun automatically leaves you in a more playful mood. The best way to assure that you do this is to make a list of things that are fun to do. When possible, do something from the list both during the day and in the evening.

3. Spend time watching young children play.

    If you have forgotten how to be playful, think back to what you were like as a child. To help you remember, go to a park or preschool center and watch young children play. Also look at photographs of yourself as a child.

    If you have young children of your own, be more attentive to the way they play. Pay special attention to their spontaneity, joy, and absorption in the moment. Note how they get upset, but then leave it behind and start playing again. Look for their sense of fun and aliveness, and build those qualities into your own life.

4. Put reminders to be playful in key places (bathroom mirror, refrigerator, office, car, etc.).

    You'll need constant reminders that you're trying to adopt a more playful attitude and style of relating to people. Your natural tendency will be to fall into your usual serious demeanor, regardless of whether it's on the job, at home, in the car, or dining out. Bumper stickers, buttons, and cartoons on your refrigerator, on your desk, etc., work well as reminders. Be sure the cartoons make you smile every time you see them.

5. Find an activity or prop that helps get you in a playful mood.

    I have a collection of "animal noses." My favorite is an elephant nose, attached to glasses. Even if I'm alone, it's impossible for me to look in the mirror with this nose on, and not break into a grin. Other people who see me wearing it also smile or laugh. Their reactions help me lighten up. As you use your own props, notice how it helps you pull out of a serious or somber mood, and create a lighter, more positive mood.

6. Tell your friends, spouse, girl/boyfriend, and co-workers that you're making an effort to lighten up and be more playful. Tell them why. Ask for their support.

   NOTE: Be sure to continue taking your work and responsibilities seriously while cultivating a playful attitude. You can have a playful attitude and still be professional and competent. Be sensitive to where this attitude is and is not appropriate.

7. Hang around positive people.

   In a Peanuts cartoon, Linus asks Lucy, "How did you like Disneyland?" Lucy coolly answers, "I didn't. They didn't have marmalade for my toast." It's difficult to be playful when you're around negative, complaining, irritable people all the time. They will get annoyed at your light, playful demeanor, and try to bring you down to their level of upset. So think of all the friends and co-workers you have who are upbeat, positive, and playful, and spend as much time as you can around them.

8. Make it a point to do something playful that is out of character for you every day (e.g., face the rear of the elevator while everyone else is facing the front, wear a funny prop, pay a toll for the person in the car behind you, etc.). Be creative in thinking of ways of expressing your playfulness, but avoid tasteless pranks.

9. Catch people in the act of being playful.

   Be on the lookout for playfulness in adults. Keep a tab of the number of examples you spot each day. If possible, keep track of any factors that seem related to who is playful and who is not (e.g., men vs. women, different age groups, upper-, mid-, or non-management employees, etc.).

10. Follow your instincts about when it is and is not appropriate to be playful. If people aren't used to playfulness from you, it can backfire. Choose situations where you know you'll be comfortable, even if things backfire.

STEP 3

A. Laugh More Often and More Heartily
B. Begin Telling Jokes and Funny Stories

> ❝*What soap is to the body, laughter is to the soul.*❞
> (Yiddish proverb)

> ❝*Were it not for my little jokes, I could not bear the burdens of this office.*❞
> (Abraham Lincoln)

Zen Buddhists believe that if you start the day off with a laugh, you'll be fine the rest of the day. Twenty years spent as a researcher studying humor and laughter have led me to respect the wisdom of this view. When you lighten up and have free access to joyful laughter, you become more stress resistant. In fact, you can think of laughter as a "stress deodorant." It protects you from stress in several ways. It helps you maintain a frame of mind more conducive to handling problems, offers a means of releasing tension and upset before they get a chance to escalate to stressful levels, produces muscle relaxation, and helps keep problems in perspective. Humor and laughter help keep you from getting bent out of shape when the inevitable hassles and problems of the day attack from all angles at once. If you're lucky, one application of this deodorant in the morning will get you through the day. Chances are, however, that you'll require repeated applications.

You may not think of laughter as an important part of your sense of humor to work on. But some of humor's most important health benefits stem from laughter itself. In addition to the benefits listed in the previous paragraph, belly laughter strengthens the immune system and lowers the level of stress hormones circulating in the blood. It's also energizing, helping you fight burnout and lethargy at the end of the day. Most people say they just feel better after a good laugh, sometimes even euphoric. (See Part I for a discussion of these benefits.) Learning to laugh more often and more heartily, then, is essential to taking full advantage of the health-promoting and stress-reducing power of humor.

A staff member at a hospital told me following a seminar that she was asked while under hypnosis to start laughing, and to just keep on laughing. She did this for several minutes. When brought out of the hypnotic state, she reported having "the best feeling I've ever had in my life." She said she felt totally relaxed, but also "energized and up." You'll find the same effect occurring even when you're not hypnotized.

The second part of Step 3 focuses on joke and story telling. You don't have to be a good joke teller to use humor as a coping tool and receive the health benefits it offers. It is included in this program, however, because many people want to learn to tell jokes. Also, it's is a useful social skill, and helps sustain the overall development of your sense of humor. You may have long ago given up on being able to tell a joke or funny story well. Perhaps you've tried in the past, only to find people looking at you blankly. So you decided that some people just didn't know how to tell jokes—and you're one of them!

Or maybe you've just never made the effort. In that case, you'll be pleasantly surprised at how easily you can weave jokes into conversations without really appearing to tell a joke—once you make the effort to memorize jokes and practice telling them. For example, if you're in the midst of a conversation about the harmful effects of smoking, you can directly ease into lines like this: "A smoker I know has read so much about the harmful effects of smoking that he decided to give up reading."

A Jewish doctor who removed foreskins dies, and his wife discovers a bag of 100 of them in a drawer. His daughter takes them, saying, "I know a guy who makes things, maybe he can do something with them." So she gives them to this guy, and comes back a couple of weeks later to see what he's done with them. He shows her a wallet. "A wallet?" she says, "100 foreskins, and that's it?" "Ah, but when you rub it, it becomes a suitcase."

You may choose to split your work on these two aspects of humor, spending a week or two on each one. They go together very naturally, though, so you should have no trouble learning to become more emotionally expressive when you find something funny, at the same time that you learn to become a better joke or story teller. If you're already a great joke teller, or if you already have a great belly laugh, then you can spend less time with this step—or skip it completely.

Laugh More Often and More Heartily

In most of my humor seminars, I do an exercise in which the entire audience does 20 to 30 seconds of belly laughter. Many in the audience say they haven't had a real belly laugh in months—sometimes years! So the exercise allows everyone to see first-hand the cathartic release, relaxation, and good feeling that comes from hearty laughter. While I do have a routine that gets everyone laughing, I purposefully keep the exercise a bit artificial, asking them to force laughter if they have to. This shows that you can even get the benefits of laughter when you're faking it. When you find real events in your life to laugh at, you will notice these benefits even more. The exercise also demonstrates the importance of initially pushing yourself to laugh harder than you normally do. This is an essential insight if you're not a laugher, since it gives you the incentive you need to fake it until laughter starts to feel more natural and to flow without effort.

> **Even if there's nothing to laugh about, laugh on credit.**
>
> (Anonymous)

Research has demonstrated that going through the motions of the behavior associated with a particular emotion actually causes you to experience that emotion to some extent. That is, by acting as if you're angry or happy, you actually begin to feel angrier or happier. Even making the facial expression that generally accompanies an emotion increases the extent to which that emotion is felt—especially happiness.[1] Laughter has the power to pull your emotions back in a more positive direction, even when you're exposed to something that would normally make you angry or anxious.[2] It helps you take control of your emotional state, and that very control reduces stress.

These findings support the familiar advice to "Let a smile be your umbrella," or "Put on a happy face." Your emotional memories are connected to physical movements, so the movements themselves revive part of the experience of past similar emotions. They may not be as strong, but if you have a strong emotion that's close to the surface, going through such actions can bring it back vividly. To get a sense of how this works, do exercise #3 under "Belly laughter" in the "Group Session" at the end of Step 3.

Laughter and Emotional Expression

Have you ever felt angry, anxious, or depressed, and really wanted to pull out of it? You knew you'd be more effective if you could just stop feeling this way—even though you were perfectly justified in having the feeling. But how do you try not to feel angry when you're honestly upset? How do you try not to feel depressed when you're really down? Besides, isn't it healthier to let these feelings out?

It's certainly important to express your feelings, and not swallow them up. Suppression of emotion is never healthy. But you may find that the events in your life leave you in a constant state of anger or anxiety. Expressing these feelings makes you feel better, but that doesn't change the fact that you're always upset or tense. Humor helps you defuse these negative emotions by replacing them with something more positive.

Just as you don't want to deny your feelings, you don't want to deny or hide from the problem which is producing them. Keep in mind that humor and laughter can also be used as a means of escaping problems, and of avoiding any attempts to confront them. If you use humor in this way, it will work against you, rather than for you. The healthy way to use humor is to use the improved frame of mind it gives you to move ahead and deal with the problem effectively.

> **Time spend laughing is time spent with the gods.**
>
> (Japanese saying)

When you have a good laugh, it generates a positive mood which is totally incompatible with the negative mood you were in. I recently had a woman say to me after a seminar, "You know, I almost didn't come because the entire day was a complete disaster. But I can see now that it was precisely because of my rotten day that I needed to be here. In the last two hours, I totally forgot about the lousy day I had."

Don't expect to magically reverse a negative emotion by just smiling or laughing. That's unrealistic. If you have cancer, or have just lost a loved one, you won't turn depression or grief into joy by smiling or laughing. You shouldn't even try to. These emotions are appropriate under the circumstances. But the time will come when you feel that you need to get on with living your life. If the negative emotion persists long beyond what you consider to be a normal period, try surrounding yourself with humor, and force yourself to laugh. Your body won't know the difference, and you'll nudge yourself toward a more positive mood, while getting the same benefits you get from natural belly laughter.

This will seem artificial at first, but a funny thing happens after you force hearty laughter a few times. You start to feel its positive effects immediately, just as a smile somehow pulls you in the direction of feeling better. Laughter also helps focus your attention on the positive aspects of your life, which further boosts your morale and mood.

Of course, the benefits you receive will be even greater when the laughter is genuine and in response to something you really find funny. But if belly laughter is not something you've done much of in the past, you'll have to make the effort to force it at first, even if it seems artificial. You can start by practicing in situations where you are alone (e.g., in your car or house), if you feel uncomfortable laughing in public. This may seem strange at first, but it will start breaking down the barriers to hearty, unrestrained belly laughter.

> **God is a comedian playing to an audience that is afraid to laugh.**
> (Voltaire)

You should also make the effort to laugh more heartily when you do find something funny. The easiest way to practice this is in situations where your own laughter gets lost in the laughter of a crowd (e.g., at a party or movie). Make it a point to notice how you feel after a good laugh in these situations. Non-laughers often say that this helps them become more expressive in general—both with positive and negative emotions.

> **I can't express anger. I grow tumors, instead.**
> (Woody Allen, in the film, *Manhattan*.)

If you have suppressed strong feelings about something for any length of time, laughter can trigger their expression—even if it's negative, and you're in a totally positive mood at the time. Have you ever had the experience of bursting into tears in the middle of a good laugh (at the movies, for example)? If so, you probably had some basic sadness or grief within you which had not been expressed. The fact that you suddenly began crying "for no reason" may have surprised you. But you can be sure that if you cried, you needed to.

Tears are just as therapeutic as laughter. Now that you think about it, don't you feel better after the tears? This is just one of the ways in which laughter helps sustain a sense of well being. I often do programs for cancer patients, many of whom have been emotionally unexpressive throughout their lives. They have suppressed their feelings for so long that emotions just stay all bottled up inside. But laughter pops the cork of that bottle and opens up the floodgates of emotion. For many, the first real belly laugh causes them to cry. They then open up and talk about their feelings, and this opens the door to a more positive focus in coping with the disease.

An 80-year-old woman said her cancer had been in remission for over 30 years. I asked her what she attributed her long life to. She said, "Well, I haven't died."

Even when laughter does not lead to crying, you can still feel a powerful cathartic release of pent-up tension, frustration, anger, or anxiety. We all carry within us emotional residues of stress. For some, it shows up as anger; for others, it's anxiety or depression. These emotions build up and take their toll as you go through a typical high stress day. Anything you can do to weaken them would be of tremendous value in your life. Laughter has the power to do this.

> **"***Laughter lets me relax. It's the equivalent of taking a deep breath, letting it out and saying, 'This too will pass.'***"**
> (Odette Pollar)

In hospitals, patients are often given a cathartic to clean out the bowels and purge the intestinal tract of harmful toxins. But just as a build up of physical toxins in your body can damage your physical health, so can a build up of psychological toxins (unexpressed negative emotions) damage both your mental and physical health. Freud noted nearly a century ago that humor provides a cathartic release of pent-up negative emotions. Laughter is an extraordinary cleansing agent—a kind of emotional laxative. Are you taking full advantage of it?

Have you ever had the experience of having a good belly laugh while really angry? If so, what happened to the anger? If you're like most people, it gradually disappeared, like butter on a hot grill. Laughter gives you an emotional boost that is simply incompatible with anger. There is every reason to believe that the stress levels in our lives will continue to escalate in the future, so you can't afford to not take advantage of this built-in stress reducer that nature has provided you.

If you have a cassette deck in your car, you have an ideal means of practicing laughing every day. By listening to comedy tapes on the way to and from work, you can regularly strengthen the habit of laughing, making a natural and hearty laugh more and more accessible. This will help you ease into laughing more freely in social situations.

> **"***There are three things which are real: God, human folly, and laughter. The first two are beyond our comprehension. So we must do what we can with the third.***"** (John F. Kennedy)

As you work on belly laughter for the next week or two, keep an eye out for the "anti-laughter police." Every organization has them. These are people who know that if you're laughing, you can't possibly be working or taking your job seriously. You'll recognize them from the hostile glances thrown your way when you are caught laughing.

Use their reactions as a reminder that you work in a setting where laughter is not viewed positively. At the same time, remember that they may be right. Learning to judge when laughter is and is not inappropriate is an essential humor skill to develop. So be sure to choose the right time and place to work on Step 3.

> **"*The unexamined life is not worth living.*"**   (Socrates)

> **"*Life without laughter is not worth examining.*"** (Paul McGhee)

Humor Log Exercises

On Laughter

1. When you have a good belly laugh, how does it make you feel? Before you answer this, get a partner and do nonstop belly laughter for 20-30 seconds (do whatever is necessary to keep yourselves laughing). Then pay attention to any physical or other changes you notice, and write them down here. (Add any changes you remember experiencing in past bouts of laughter.)
2. Name three people you know who you consider to be "good laughers." Compare their personalities to others who laugh less often or less heartily
3. Have you ever had the experience of laughter suddenly turning into crying? Why does this sudden reversal of emotions occur? How do you feel after such a laugh/cry?
4. Many consider laughter on the job inappropriate in any situation. Describe areas of your job or work setting where laughter would be inappropriate, even if you did find something funny. Under what circumstances would laughter be acceptable?
5. Assume that you have a job that requires you to be on the phone a lot. Your boss has suggested that you have a brief laugh as you lean over to pick up the phone (but stop before you answer it). What effect might this have on how you're perceived by the caller?
6. Many of the health benefits associated with humor result directly from laughter. Describe how laughter helps promote health and well being, and how it helps reduce stress.

Current Laughter

1. How often do you have a real belly laugh?
2. Describe your typical laughter (quiet, explosive, etc.).
3. On a typical day/week, how many times do you laugh out loud?
4. How emotionally expressive are you in general? Is your laughter "style" consistent with this? Do you think learning to do belly laughter more often can help you become more emotionally expressive in general?
5. What would you like to gain from Step 3, in terms of how often you laugh, and how heartily you laugh?

Early Development and Influences

1. During your childhood and adolescence, did you laugh a lot? (Ask your parents, if you don't remember.)
2. Describe your mother's and father's laughter, both in terms of how often and how heartily they laughed.
3. What influence do you think the laughter patterns shown by your parents had on your own laughter?
4. Describe your parents' general emotional expressiveness, and how that might have influenced your emotional expressiveness.
5. Did your parents ever get upset at your laughter (e.g., because you were laughing too much, or too loudly)? How often? How did this influence the development of your own laughter style?

Psychoneuroimmunology and Laughter

A new area of medical research, given the unwieldy name of psychoneuroimmunology, has blossomed in the past 10-15 years (see Chapter 2). "Psycho" refers to the mind, "neuro" to the central nervous system, and "immunology" to the immune system. This exciting new field studies the mind-body connection, and has demonstrated that your mental and emotional state have a significant impact on your health and well being. While this may seem obvious to you, it was long believed in medical circles that the mind and body were independent, and that there were no mechanisms by which your thoughts, beliefs, moods, and emotions could influence your health. But psychosomatic research over the past several decades has shown that chronic negative emotions can cause a wide range of health problems. And more recent research has shown that positive emotions and an optimistic daily outlook help sustain physiological and biochemical conditions within our bodies that promote good health.

> **❝** *There is no medicine like hope, no incentive so great, and no tonic so powerful as the expectation of something tomorrow.***❞**
> (O. S. Marden)

The research findings from psychoneuroimmunology, and the clinical experience of Bernie Siegel, O. Carl Simonton, and other physicians, have led a growing number of nurses, doctors, and patients all over the world to the conclusion that hope, determination, and an optimistic outlook play an important role in battling cancer and other diseases. Bernie has seen first-hand that each person makes an important contribution to their own health and healing. They do this by maintaining a set of attitudes, emotions, and belief systems which either support the body's basic healing mechanisms, or hinder them. Your sense of humor is one of your most powerful allies in supporting them.

If you have a negative, pessimistic outlook on life, you can generally find things to justify it. After all, life is full of injustice. And the more support you find for your outlook, the more it feeds your pessimism. But if you make the effort, you can often find a positive, as well as a negative, aspect of the same bad situation. So you have a choice of focusing your attention on the negative or the positive. We've all heard about seeing the glass as "half full" or "half empty." Which kind of person are you?

John and Sal were two cancer patients who had gotten to know each other in the hospital, because they both had the same kind of pancreatic cancer. One day John saw Sal sitting on his bed looking depressed. So he walked in and said, "What's the matter, Sal? You look terrible." Sal said, "My doctor just told me that three out of every four people who have the cancer we have don't make it." "No, no," said John, "That's not what my doctor told me. He said one out of every four survive, and you could be that one."

The percentages are the same, but the way John's doctor communicated the news gave John a better chance of surviving than the way Sal's doctor gave him the news. John's doctor knew that focusing on the positive would give John hope and optimism, and nurture conditions within his body which would improve his chance of overcoming the disease.

It will work the same way in your life. Doing things which help you maintain an optimistic frame of mind on a day-to-day basis will help you manage the stress in your life more effectively. This, in turn, will enable you to be more effective on the job. Choosing to see the glass as half full will support your efforts to become a more optimistic person. And your sense of humor will help you see the glass as half full.

> *"A merry heart does good like a medicine. A brittle spirit dries the bones."* (Proverbs 17:22)

> *"He that is of a merry heart has a continual feast."* (Proverbs 15:15)

> *"Ye shall laugh."* (Luke 6:21)

> *"He that sitteth in Heaven shall laugh."* (Psalms 2:4)

When you wake up in the morning, what you put into your stomach determines your energy level until lunch. The experiences you create for yourself in the first hour of the day also strongly influence your mood and general effectiveness throughout the morning. To assure that you start off positively, try listening to comedy tapes on your morning walk, as you're getting ready for work, or in the car on the way to work. Make it a point to have a good belly laugh—even if you have to force it. If you're in a bad mood, this will help pull you out of it.

Think of this as a means of jump-starting a positive mental attitude. If you can get yourself thinking funny—and laughing—in the morning, your days will always start off better. You'll arrive at work with a positive focus. And if you manage to find your own humor as the day goes on, you'll sustain this focus throughout the day.

The handle used in Nintendo and other computer games for kids is called a joy stick. This makes sense if you watch kids playing the games. Start thinking of your sense of humor as the "joy stick of life." You always have access to it, and if you learn how to use it well, it guarantees that you'll always have joy and fun in your life. Like Gilda

Radner, the *Saturday Night Live* star who died from cancer, you'll have a life full of joy, regardless of how long you live.

Laughter and Optimism

"God is dead!" Nietzsche, 1891.
"Nietzsche is dead!" God, 1900.

Folk wisdom has always reminded us of the importance of a positive, optimistic outlook in life. This is sometimes referred to as PMA—positive mental attitude. It is no surprise, then, that one of the most popular books of all time is Norman Vincent Peale's *The Power of Positive Thinking*. The basic notion behind PMA is that if you can get yourself thinking positive thoughts, positive emotions will follow. Hopefully, action consistent with the good feelings will also follow. But you know from your own experience how difficult it is to maintain an optimistic outlook when life serves you one lemon after another. A good laugh gives you an optimism booster shot. And don't forget about smiling. A big smile always increases your face value.

> *❝The optimist proclaims that we live in the best of all possible worlds, and the pessimist fears this is true.❞*
> (James Branch Cabell)

What does it mean to be upbeat and optimistic? Is it a naive Pollyana-type view that everything will somehow be OK? Are optimistic people out of touch with real everyday problems? Are they the ones who always have a plastic smile on their faces, no matter what happens? We all know people who show a simplistic, passive optimism, and just sit back and hope for the best, but this kind of optimism will not serve you well in a stress-prone world.

It is a more active form of optimism that helps you cope, one in which you use a positive outlook as a basis for engaging in action. Confident in your ability to achieve your goal, you first find out what needs to be done, and then do it. This leads to a sense of control which is lacking in naive optimism. And it is this sense of control which helps you be more effective, even in the midst of obstacles. In this more active approach to optimism, you acknowledge life's problems and inconsistencies, but choose to focus on the positive, rather than the negative, because it's more adaptive to do so.

> *❝Humor is a great thing, the saving thing, after all. The minute it crops up, all our hardnesses yield, all our irritations and resentments flit away, and a sunny spirit takes their place.❞*
> (Mark Twain)

A close relationship generally exists between our thoughts, emotions, and actions. We act in ways that reflect what we think, believe, and feel, and the outcome of these actions triggers new thoughts and feelings. So we have an endless cycle of connections between thoughts, feelings and behavior that looks like this:

When you're in a good mood, and all is going well, your thoughts and emotions serve you well by producing effective behavior that handles any problem that comes up. This action, in turn, generates new positive thoughts and emotions. Stress disrupts the cycle, however, by creating strong negative emotions which make it difficult to handle even easy problems effectively. Your judgment and ability to focus clearly on the problem deteriorate as your anger, anxiety, sadness, or depression increases. And when you handle the problem poorly, this generates more negative thoughts and emotions, creating a vicious cycle.

Thoughts
↓
Feelings & Emotions
↓
Behavior
↓
Thoughts

Life is like an elevator. Some days you go up, some days you go down, and some days you get the shaft.

Once things start going badly, you start thinking the worst, and get even more caught up in your anxieties, anger, or depression. And it's difficult to break out of it. But this is precisely where you'll discover the real coping power of your sense of humor. Humor and laughter give you a tool to quickly cut through the negative chain of thoughts, emotions, and behavior, and substitute a positive chain in its place. When you develop your skill at finding something to laugh at in the midst of your problems, it gives you more control over your ability to handle those problems by creating an emotional state which is more conducive to effective problem-solving.

> ❝*Most folks are about as happy as they make up their minds to be.*❞
> (Abraham Lincoln)

Humor Log Exercises

On Optimism

1. What does it mean to have a optimistic or pessimistic outlook on life?
2. "A smile can be heard on the phone." Discuss the meaning of this statement.
3. What does it mean to "see the glass half full" or "half empty?" How would you describe yourself in this respect?
4. How can your sense of humor help you see the glass as "half full?"

Current Optimism

1. Is your general approach to life one of optimism or pessimism? Give specific examples of your behavior which support this.
2. Do you generally see the glass half full or half empty?
3. List two recent instances in your life in which something you did or experienced boosted your a) optimism or b) pessimism.
4. How would your life change if you were able to adopt a more optimistic, positive attitude?

Early Development and Influences

1. During your a) childhood and b) adolescence, were you generally more positive and optimistic or negative and pessimistic?
2. Describe your mother and father in terms of their typical level of optimism or pessimism as you were growing up.
3. What influence, if any, did your parents have on the level of optimism or pessimism with which you approach your life? Who else had a significant impact on this aspect of your personality?

Begin Telling Jokes and Funny Stories

> *"A joke is not a thing, but a process, a trick you play on the listener's mind. You start him off toward a plausible goal, and then by a sudden twist, you land him nowhere at all or just where he didn't expect to go."*
>
> (Max Eastman)

Art Buchwald has said, "I learned quickly that when I made others laugh, they liked me. This lesson I will never forget." Everybody likes people who make them laugh, but becoming a good joke teller will do more than make you popular and entertaining. It will also improve your communication skills and help you manage conflict more effectively, both within your family and at work. A former assistant secretary general of the United Nations noted that jokes are even used in diplomatic negotiations and receptions to ease tensions.[3] Henry Kissinger, President Nixon's secretary of state, frequently used jokes to break through the icy tensions surrounding negotiations with the Soviets during the cold war. (I know, it's hard to imagine Kissinger telling jokes; but if he can do it, you can do it.)

> *"I don't make jokes. I just watch the government and report the facts."*
>
> (Will Rogers)

More recently, President Reagan showed himself to be a master at using jokes and spontaneous humor to ease tensions and conflict. After being shot during his first term, he calmed the nation's anxiety by casually announcing to his surgeons as he was wheeled into the operating room, "Well, I hope you guys are all Republicans." He also relayed this message to his wife: "Honey, I forgot to duck."

During Reagan's run for a second term, there was some concern about his advancing age and whether this might interfere with his ability to remain effective on the job. Prior to the presidential debates with Walter Mondale, everyone knew that Mondale would raise the issue of age, but Reagan quickly defused the issue by beating Mondale to the punch, saying, "I'm not going to raise the question of age in this campaign. I'm not going to exploit for political gain my opponents youth and inexperience."

If you've never tried to tell jokes in the past, start with one joke—and be sure you think it's funny! The first thing to do is memorize it. How many times have you heard people start to tell a joke, only to forget the punchline? This is the most common mistake made by novice joke-tellers. One way or another, they butcher the punch line. If this sounds like you, begin by telling the joke to a few close friends, your spouse, or anyone else with whom you feel totally comfortable. This will minimize your embarrassment, in case you do botch it up. A good friend, remember, is anyone who—when you make a fool out of yourself—feels you haven't done a permanent job.

> **"***If you want someone to laugh at your jokes, tell him he has a good sense of humor.***"**
> (Herbert V. Prochnow)

After practicing with your friends, begin telling the joke to work associates (when the circumstances are appropriate, of course). A good way to create opportunities to practice your jokes is to simply ask people if they've heard any good jokes lately. Those who like jokes will welcome the opportunity to tell a few. And after they've told one, you'll have a natural opportunity to tell one yourself. This also gives you a chance to learn some new jokes. For example, early in Clinton's Presidency, the policy regarding gays in the military was a very controversial issue. So you might have picked up the following joke. "You know, I think this problem of gays in the military is really overblown. I don't think you'll ever have to worry about gays leaving their buddies behind." How could I resist telling this joke to my friends?

People are especially fond of using humor to express their views about politics and other issues. A Republican friend of mine recently said to me, "Did you hear that they doubled the security on Hillary Clinton? They realized that if something happened to her, Bill would become president." This came up passing during a conversation about politics, but can you think of a more effective way of communicating your feelings about the level of influence the First Lady was having on our lives in 1993 and 1994? After Step 3, you'll be smoothly integrating such remarks into your own conversations.

If someone else tells a joke that you think is especially funny, write it down at that moment. Keep a small notebook in your pocket for just such occasions. If you don't write it down, you'll forget it. Or you may remember part of it, but not know it well enough to repeat to someone else. Consider putting the joke on a 3" x 5" index card or in your computer when you get a chance. Develop a collection of jokes you like. This will keep you focused on building up your joke repertoire.

When I heard the following joke, I didn't even hesitate. I immediately grabbed a piece of paper and scribbled it down.

A couple that had been married 55 years was watching a faith healer on TV. The evangelist said, "I can heal you tonight brothers and sisters! I can heal you tonight! If you want to be healed, put one hand on the television and the other on what you want to heal."

So the woman put one hand on the TV and the other on her tired old heart and prayed along with him.

The man looked over and thought to himself, "Well, what have I got to lose?" So he put one hand on the TV and snuck the other between his legs.

His wife looked over at him and said, "He said he could heal, not raise the dead."

You may want to remember certain jokes because they demonstrate a point that you know you'll want to make from time to time. You'll be amazed at the impact the joke has when it's directly linked to the topic you're discussing at the moment. I loved this joke, and (sometimes) use it in talks to senior citizens when I want to lead into stereotypes about sexuality among the elderly, or concerns about aging.

If you have no way of writing the joke down, make it your top priority to remember the punch line. This is the most crucial part of the joke. You'll be able to reconstruct the joke well enough later to make it funny—even if it's not exactly the way you heard it.

Uncle Remus (of Brer Rabbit fame) said that "Everybody's got a laughin' place," a special place where you can go when you need a good laugh, and you know you'll be able to get it. If you develop the habit of writing down the jokes you like, and of putting them in a box, you can always go to the box (or your computer) and pull one out when things are going badly, and you need a good laugh.

When you get to the point where you feel comfortable telling one joke, simply add another. Adding only one or two jokes at a time to your repertoire, and practicing them a lot before learning new ones, will assure that you won't forget the old ones as you add new ones. Be sure you're comfortable with the first jokes before adding others. Being relaxed and confident about joke telling is an essential part of being a good joke teller.

> **"**Act as if you enjoy telling the joke, which suggests you know how to do it.**"**
> (Leo Rosten)

You can make many jokes funnier by changing some of the details so they're more salient to the person or group you're telling them to. Will Rogers once said, "I'm not a member of an organized political party . . . I'm a _____." You could say either "Republican" or "Democrat," depending on who you're talking to. If you are going to put down a group, however, make sure the person or group you're talking to is not a member of it, or doesn't identify positively with it. Otherwise, the joke will not only fall flat, you'll also offend your audience.

Everyone knows someone who just can't tell a joke. The following classic joke pokes fun at these people.

> **A new convict is sitting in his cell at the state prison. Suddenly, someone yells out, "42!" The whole cell block starts laughing. Someone else yells, "125!" Again, everyone laughs. "74!" Mass hysteria. This goes on all afternoon, and the new guy can't figure it out. He asks his cell mate what's so funny.**
>
> **He says, "We've been telling the same jokes so long that everybody knows all the jokes. So we just gave them numbers, and call out the numbers."**
>
> **So the new guy thought he'd get into the act, and called out, "82!" But nothing happened. Total silence. He tried again, "77!" Again, no reaction. He asked his cell mate why nobody laughed. "Well," his partner answered, "Some people just don't know how to tell a joke."**

In the movie *Punchline*, an aspiring comedian (played by Tom Hanks) has consistent success on stage until some "significant" people come to check him out for a possible shot at the big time. He uses material that has always worked for him in the past, but nothing works for him on the one evening that it's essential that he get good laughs. Everything he does is flat. The reason? The pressure caused him to loose his spontaneity and playfulness. He's not relaxed and natural. The more desperate he gets to produce something that's funny, the worse it gets.

You may experience a form of performance anxiety yourself if you're new at telling jokes. That's why you want to start with a single joke or two, and tell it over and over among friends until you feel totally comfortable with it, and know how people are generally going to react. This experience among friends will strengthen your ability to keep a naturally playful demeanor in delivering the joke to strangers, as well.

You may want to choose a few jokes told by your favorite comedians, and imitate their style and delivery. Just as artists copy the masters before they develop their own style, you can copy good joke tellers' style before developing your own.

While working on jokes, try your hand at stories, as well. The following is one of my favorites.

> **During World War II, a British pilot is shot down and captured by the Germans. He has serious injuries from the crash, and the Germans say, "We're going to have to amputate your right leg." The pilot says, "OK, if you've got to do it. But do me a favor. Could you just drop the leg along with your bombs the next time you bomb London? At least part of me would be home." The Germans say, "Ya, we can do that for you."**
>
> **A week later, it's the same story with his left leg. Again, he asks the Germans to drop the leg over London on their next bombing mission, and the Germans say, "Ya, we can do that for you."**
>
> **A couple of weeks later, they tell him they're going to have to amputate his right arm, and he again asks if they can drop his arm over London. To his surprise, this time the Germans say "Nein, this we cannot do." So he asks, "Why not? You were willing to drop each leg over London."**
>
> **The German says, "The Gestapo thinks you're trying to escape!"**

In collecting and memorizing stories, always ask yourself, "What point can I make using this story?" For example, in this case, you could use the story to illustrate how absurd our reasoning can become when we get caught up in our own limited view of things. A line of reasoning that makes sense in some situations can be complete nonsense in others.

When personalizing jokes, be sure that the changes you make don't destroy the humor. Otherwise, you'll be in the position of the Englishman who comes to the United States and decides that he want to learn a typical American joke to take back home, because he thinks Americans have a great sense of humor. Somebody gives him the following joke:

"What does a fat man do after he runs for a bus?
He takes off his hat and pants."

When he gets back to England, he says, "I heard this terrific joke in America. What does a stout fellow do after he runs for a tram? He takes off his cap and trousers."

One of the most important rules in this list is to always keep in mind when humor is and is not appropriate. If the person you tell the joke to has just received some bad news, you'll be seen as unsympathetic and uncaring, at best. The same principle holds if you're the bearer of bad news yourself. Don't try to ease the pain by making light of the situation. It's the recipient of the bad news who must decide that it's OK to joke about it.

Failure to be sensitive to the social situation can put you in the position of the politician who would always walk over and start telling stories whenever he saw a little group of people gathered together. After capturing people with his story, he'd make his political pitch. It worked pretty well most of the time, but one day he ran into a group that just wouldn't warm up to him. He said, "What's the matter with you folks? You act like you were at a funeral." A member of the group looked up at him and said, "Brother, this is a funeral."

You should also be careful about telling put-down jokes. If you develop the habit of repeating put-down jokes you find funny, it's just a matter of time ·until you offend somebody. Jokes which disparage others may make you feel better, but they can also create a disruptive force—especially when told in groups. The best rule of thumb here is to restrict the butt of put-down jokes to any group that you know is viewed negatively by those hearing the joke (e.g., a competing company, political party, or other organization).

A week or two is enough time to work on joke telling, as long as you make it a point to tell one or more jokes to several people every day. If you want to become especially good at telling jokes or stories, you'll want to spend as much time as possible learning and telling them. The more often you do it, the better you'll get. Even if you don't ever plan to be a joke teller, you will benefit from telling them. It will keep you focused on humor as you move on to the more difficult steps to follow.

❝*Forgive, O Lord, my little jokes on Thee, and I'll forgive Thy great big one on me.*❞
(Robert Frost)

General Rules for Communicating Humor

If you have little or no experience at telling jokes and stories, use the following guidelines to maximize your chances of success.

1. Don't try to tell jokes/stories that you don't know well.
2. Don't tell a joke you don't find funny yourself.
3. Don't laugh at your own joke (especially in advance).
4. Don't announce, "This is a joke," or "I'm not very good at telling jokes, but . . ."
5. Don't apologize if others don't laugh.
6. Don't try to explain the joke if people don't laugh. It still won't be funny.
7. Use gestures and facial expressions while telling the joke.
8. But don't feel obliged to act funny while telling the joke.
9. Be clear about which words need emphasis.
10. Don't drag it out! Remember, brevity is the soul of wit.
11. Be sure the punchline is at the end. Don't telegraph what's coming.
12. When the joke invites visualization, pause where appropriate to allow your audience to imagine the situation.
13. Don't overdo puns. They're generally less funny to the hearer than to the teller.
14. Keep your humor positive.
15. Avoid put-down or other potentially sensitive or offensive humor—especially among people you don't know. Remember that others' sensitivities may differ from your own. You may offend people, and not know it.
16. Avoid racial and sexist humor.
17. Always know your audience before attempting "risky" humor.
18. Be sensitive to the social situation; know when any humor at all, or a particular joke/story, would be in bad taste.
19. Know when to stop joking and be serious. Nothing is more frustrating than trying to communicate with someone who refuses to take you seriously.
20. Personalize or localize jokes when possible. Use names, activities and locations familiar to your audience.

Humor Log Exercises

On Joke/Story Telling

1. What are the qualities of a good/poor joke/story teller?
2. Why is it so difficult to remember jokes and stories? What can you do to help yourself remember them?
3. How important do you think joke telling is, in comparison to skills associated with the other steps in this program?

Current Joke/Story Telling

1. How often do you tell jokes or funny stories on a typical day? Would you like to do so more often?
2. How would you describe your skills as a joke/story teller? If you're not good at it, what generally goes wrong?
3. What improvements would you like to make in your joke-telling skills?

Early Development and Influences

1. How often did you tell jokes or funny stories during your a) childhood and b) adolescence? Again, ask your parents for a different perspective on this. (If your parents are no longer living, ask anyone else who was around you a lot as you were growing up.)
2. Do you now tell jokes more often or less often than you did as a child/adolescent? When/why did this change occur?
3. How often did your mother and father tell jokes or funny stories when you were growing up? What impact did this have on you?
4. How do you recall your parents reacting to the riddles/jokes you told as a child? Did they generally react positively or negatively? Did this have any effect on the development of your joke-telling skills or habits?

GROUP SESSION

Opening Fun Activity

Discussion of Homeplay for Step 2

1. Open with a request for a show of hands of those who contacted their telephone partner during the week to discuss the Homeplay. Remember that regular contact with your partner boosts the benefits received from this program, since it helps keep you actively engaged.
2. Share with a partner your list of "fun things to do." Which of these activities were most effective in sustaining a playful attitude?
3. What progress did you make toward becoming more playful? What new insights did you have regarding your playfulness?
4. Discuss your observations of young children playing. What qualities did they show in their play that you lack?
5. What props or reminders did you use to help establish the habit of adopting a playful outlook in life?
6. How did your friends, family, and colleagues react to your efforts to become a more playful person?

Belly Laughter, Optimism, and Joke Telling

Use any of the material discussed in Step 3, along with the Humor Log Exercises, to generate issues for group discussion. Also try the following exercise (to be led by one group member). Leave as much time between suggestions as seems appropriate. Introduce any other variations that make sense to you.

"Close your eyes . . . Let a big smile slowly grow on your face . . . Now let your face go back to its usual expression . . . Now go back to the smile . . . Go back and forth between these two expressions. Notice any changes in how you feel . . . Now clench your jaw and fists . . . Notice how that feels . . . Keep your jaw and fists clenched, and start breathing quick, short breaths . . . Notice how that feels . . . Now think back

140

to a time when you had a good long belly laugh. It could be a very recent time, or a time from your childhood . . . Picture the situation as vividly as you can . . . What other people are there? . . . What happened that got you started laughing? . . . Let out a little giggle when it feels right to do so . . . Let the giggle build up, and gradually lead into belly laughter . . . Now think back to a particular time when you were really depressed . . . Hold your body in the way you usually do when you're depressed . . . Say 'I'm depressed' to yourself (and mean it) . . . Turn to the person on your right and left and say, 'I'm so depressed.'. . . Hang your head down . . . Hunch your shoulders over . . . Keep your arms close to your body . . . Stand up right at your chair . . . Take a few depressed shuffling steps, without leaving your chair . . . Now start exaggerating your depressed behavior . . . Let your shoulders drop lower than anyone would ever do . . . Make your depression really extreme . . . Now start adding some silliness to your depression . . . Be playful as you act depressed . . . Now forget about being depressed, and just start being silly in any way that suits you . . . And that's a good place for us to stop."

After completing this exercise, discuss the impact of making yourself engage in such behaviors as smiling, tightening your jaw and fists, laughing, acting depressed, and exaggerating depression in a playful way. What emotions did these actions make you feel (if any)? Can you influence how you feel by simply getting yourself to behave in a way associated with one emotion or another? What implications does this have for the value of forcing yourself to smile or laugh more than you usually do?

Arrange to have present at this session some audio tapes of comedians. Include a range of sexual, put-down, ethnic, political, etc., types of humor. Discuss what you like and don't like about particular jokes or routines. Great insight about your own sense of humor, and the nature of humor in general, can be gained simply by exploring personal differences in what people find funny. This will also help you focus on the kinds of jokes you should tell.

Use the same audio tapes to talk about differences in the delivery of different comedians. Discuss qualities they show in telling jokes that reflect their skill as joke tellers.

Also use jokes told by members of your group as a basis for discussing what is and is not funny (to you). Give feedback on how well they told the jokes. How could they do it differently for greater impact?

Ask for volunteers to tell jokes in ways that assure that the joke won't be very funny. Then discuss what was wrong with the delivery.

Come prepared to tell a joke at the next meeting. In the meantime, be sure to stay in contact with your telephone partners until that meeting.

HOME PLAY

Laughter

1. Laugh more often and more intensely than you usually do.
2. Seek out social situations (e.g., movies and parties) where you will have the opportunity to practice belly laughter without feeling conspicuous.
3. Get a few comedy audio tapes and practice laughing when alone in your car. Force it if you have to. This will gradually make it easier to belly-laugh spontaneously and naturally.
4. Put reminders to laugh more in places at work, at home, and in your car where you're sure to see them. Leave them up until laughing starts to seem more natural and spontaneous.
5. Use silly props to help keep you in a frame of mind which is naturally conducive to laughter. Laughter comes more easily when you feel light and playful than when you are more serious.
6. Hang around people who make you laugh.
7. Tell friends, family members, and colleagues at work that you will be making an effort to laugh more than you usually do. Also tell them why, and ask for their support.
8. At some point, try forcing yourself to laugh (get a friend to join in with you) when you're angry, anxious, or depressed. Notice the effect this has on your emotional state.

Optimism

1. Be positive and optimistic. Ask yourself, "What would an optimistic, positive person do/say here?"
2. Seek out positive people. Spend more time around them.
3. Observe the effect of seeking out positive people/situations upon your mood and general sense of well being.
4. Each time you sit down to a meal, make a list of (or think about) the positive things you've noticed since the last meal (no traffic, no wait for the bus/subway, beautiful day, good feedback at work, met an interesting person, etc.).

Joke Telling

1. Learn and tell one new joke each day. Be sure you think it's funny. Rehearse it. Be sure you have it memorized before telling it to someone else. Tell it to as many people as you can.

2. Ask your friends and people you work with to tell you their favorite joke or funny story. Develop the habit of asking them periodically if they've heard any good jokes lately. People welcome the opportunity to tell jokes, and it opens the door for you to practice telling your own jokes. Be on the lookout for jokes you find especially funny. When you hear a joke you want to remember, do either of two things:

   A. Keep a little notebook with you, and immediately (or as soon as possible) write it down. You can even ask the person to repeat it so you can get it written down.

   B. If the joke is not long, and you can easily remember it, tell it to someone else at the first opportunity. This will help solidify it in your memory. Once you've told it three or four times, you'll have it.

3. Listen to tapes of your favorite comedians. Select a few of their jokes that you think are funny, and practice telling them to your friends. Imitate the delivery style on the tape.

4. Continue to focus on being more playful than you have been in the recent past. Make it a point to be in a playful mood when practicing your joke-telling.

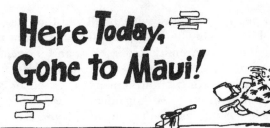

STEP 4

Play with Language
Puns and Other Verbal Humor

> ❝ Wit is the sudden marriage of ideas which, before their marriage, were not perceived to have any relationship. ❞
>
> (Mark Twain)

> ❝ Wit consists in knowing the likeness of things that differ and the difference between things that are alike. ❞
>
> (Madame de Stael)

Playwright George Bernard Shaw once wrote to Churchill:

**"Dear Mr. Churchill,
Enclosed are two tickets to my new play, which opens Thursday night. Please come and bring a friend, if you have one."**

Churchill sent back the following reply:

**"Dear Mr. Shaw,
I am sorry, I have a previous engagement and cannot attend your opening. However, I will come to the second performance, if there is one."**

As a child growing up in the 1950s, I loved to watch Groucho Marx on his television show, *You Bet Your Life*. One day he was interviewing a woman from Iowa, and she said she had eight children. Groucho said, "Eight kids. That's amazing. How come you have so many children?" The woman answered, "Well, I guess my husband just likes me." Without hesitation, Groucho quipped, "I like my cigar too, but sometimes I take it out!"

Churchill, Shaw, and Groucho were known for their quick wit. You're probably not yet ready for this level of spontaneous wit, but if you have immersed yourself in humor during the past few weeks, and are now both more playful and more comfortable telling jokes than you used to be, then you are ready to take the first step toward creating your own humor. Many people want to skip the first three steps, because they seem to have little direct bearing on humor skills. But I can assure you that—in the long run—you'll make faster and more lasting progress if you take Steps 1, 2, and 3 "seriously." They give you the basic foundation you need to benefit from Step 4—especially if you haven't used humor much in your life.

While humor doesn't have to be expressed through language, it generally is. In addition to relying on words for jokes and stories, we use language to make light of difficult situations, and to poke fun at ourselves. When funny things happen in everyday life, they may not depend on language, but we use language to communicate them to others, and to think about them ourselves.

Learning to create your own verbal humor will be of tremendous value in using your sense of humor to cope with life stress. The basic strategy adopted here is to begin with simple forms of verbal humor and practice them when you're not under stress. Once you develop the habit of playing with the meanings of words, this skill gradually will start showing up under more stressful situations.

I have done many stress management programs for firemen, policemen, and others who regularly are called on to risk their lives in emergency situations. These people frequently are obliged to pull dismembered bodies from a wreckage, or otherwise function in emotionally wrenching situations. I always encourage them to give special attention to Step 4 as a means of developing verbal humor skills which they can they use to relieve the terrible emotional stress they confront when they work with charred and shattered bodies and lives.

Ignoramus: Someone who doesn't know something you've just learned.

"What's the difference between ignorance and apathy?"
"I don't know and I don't care."

As you work on Step 4, ideas for verbal humor eventually will begin to show up automatically. I went to a free prostate cancer screening at my local hospital recently. The screening included a digital examination of the rectum. After filling out the forms, I immediately was taken in for the examination and blood tests, and was on my way out five minutes later. As I was leaving, I found myself saying to the receptionist, "That's the quickest in and out I've ever seen in a hospital." It was a simple play on words which popped into my mind with no effort on my part (it was funnier in context than it is here). The receptionist, who had had a hectic day, had a good laugh and welcomed the next patient with a smile on her face.

Even simple puns, which often aren't very funny, can help you lighten up a high stress situation—once you develop the ability to be spontaneously "punny" in difficult situations. If you spend two weeks focused on the activities and exercises described here, you gradually will become a person who effortlessly plays with words. And if you continue to practice word play throughout the 8-Step Program, you will find it easier to create your own puns and other forms of verbal humor as you go along.

Puns: The Foundation for Your Verbal Sense of Humor

"A friend of mine was engaged to a beautiful contortionist . . . until she broke it off."

We all grew up enjoying puns. In my generation, they took the form of moron jokes and knock-knock jokes. The following will be forever etched in my memory.

> **Why did the moron bury his car? The motor was dead.**
>
> **Why did the moron tiptoe past the medicine cabinet? He didn't want to wake up the sleeping pills.**
>
> **Why did the moron jump off the Empire State Building? He wanted to try out his new spring suit.**
>
> **What is black and white and red (read) all over? A newspaper.** (You should be able to think of other answers to this one.)
>
> **Knock knock. Who's there? Gorilla. Gorilla who? Gorilla (girl of) my dreams, I love you.**
>
> **Knock knock. Who's there? Arthur. Arthur who? Arthur any stars in the sky tonight?**

Although we associate these simple forms of humor with childhood, puns also play a prominent role in adult humor. Every president triggers new jokes when he comes into office. When President Clinton took over, there were endless pun-based jokes about him.

> **Now that Clinton has been elected president, he'll have flowers on his desk every day.** (He was alleged to have had an affair with a woman named "Flowers.")
>
> **There'll be no Thanksgiving celebration in Little Rock this year, because the turkey's gone to Washington.**
>
> **President Clinton is walking away from the Arkansas State Fair holding a pig under his arm. A farmer walks up and says, "Hey Bill, what's with the pig?" The president says, "I got it for Hillary." The farmer hesitates a minute, reflecting, and then says, "Good swap."**

We've all heard the phrase, "The pun is the lowest form of wit." So why use puns as the starting point for improving your verbal sense of humor? Because this is where you probably left off in developing your sense of humor. Children begin to understand puns around the first grade and go through a period of several years tirelessly telling riddles based on puns. The reason children all over the world love riddles at this age is that this is when they first acquire the intellectual ability to keep two meanings of a word in mind at the same time—a prerequisite for understanding puns.

The ability to simultaneously keep two things in mind is a basic component of what the famous Swiss psychologist Jean Piaget called "concrete operational thinking." A younger child may know both meanings of a word, but can only focus attention on one at a time. The discovery of two possible meanings—the correct one being determined by the context of the sentence—creates the mental experience of ambiguity. It is this exciting discovery that leads children to love telling riddles and other jokes, tricking the person who hears them. Interest in riddles fades by the end of elementary school because they just aren't as funny as they used to be. They're too simple!

> *"Hanging is too good for a man who makes puns; he should be drawn and quoted."* (Fred Allen)

Yet each of us knows a chronic punster who hits us with one pun after another. And the predictable reaction? A groan! While there are exceptions, most puns just aren't very funny to adults, precisely because they're so simple. It's no coincidence that the word "pun" forms the first half of the word "punish." And that's exactly what you're doing to your listener when you overuse puns. Tell anyone you catch overdoing puns that if they do one more, you'll see that they do time in a "punitentiary."

The reason persistent punsters never get the message that their puns aren't very funny is that they really are funnier to the person who creates them than they are to those who hear them. It's more difficult to have the quick insight that leads to a pun than it is to understand it when someone gives it to you on a silver platter. People who are always thinking of puns tend to be impressed with how clever they are—and they really are more clever than the rest of us, at least in this sense. But that doesn't change the fact that their puns generally aren't very funny.

> *"In the beginning was the pun."* (Samuel Beckett)

So we're left in the paradoxical position of puns being funniest to the person who produces them. As Oscar Levant once put it, "A pun is the lowest form of humor—when you don't think of it first." Why, then, should you spend a lot of time developing this skill if no one's going to appreciate it? Because your ability to play with words will serve you well when you're under stress. Remember, the purpose of this program is to help you learn to use your sense of humor to cope with difficult life situations, not to entertain other people with your finely-honed wit—although this also will occur as you move through the program.

Think back to when you were a child. How often did you make up your own puns? If you were like most kids, the answer is "rarely, if ever." You just kept repeating the jokes and riddles you heard. When you did make up your own, they bombed. Instead of laughter, you got strange looks from people. This is why special attention is given to puns here. In addition to directly serving you in coping with stress, puns are also an excellent way to begin sensitizing yourself to other incongruities and ambiguities in life.

Types of Puns

Several kinds of word play can be classified as puns.

1. Same spelling, same pronunciation.

    In some puns, the key word is spelled and pronounced the same way for both meanings.

    Working in the garment district is a seamy business.

    What did Samson die of? Fallen arches.

2. Different spelling, same pronunciation.

    When ordered to row the lifeboat, the first-class passenger harrumphed, "Do I have a choice?" "You certainly do," replied the sailor, "either oar."

    To be successful, a doctor has to have a lot of patience.

    Every time the prince found a girl he thought might be Cinderella, he went down to defeat. (This is not a pure case.)

3. Different spelling, different pronunciation.

    Note that each of the key words in these examples are themselves real words.

    Death is just around the coroner.

    Male jogger to female jogger: "My pace or yours?"

    Someone who's always telling the same joke has a one-crack mind.

    The Eskimos are God's frozen people.

    Oliver Wendel Holmes once said that he was grateful for small fevers.

How to Develop Your Ability to Create Puns and Other Verbal Humor

There are several things you can do to improve your ability to come up with your own spontaneous puns and other verbal humor. If you practice the exercises included here, playing with language soon will become second nature to you. This is the point at which it will become a useful tool in helping you manage stress. The basic principle in Steps 4, 5, and 6 is that you must practice the skills discussed when you are not under stress before they can help you cope with stress.

An Exercise in Multiple Meanings

People who are good at creating their own spontaneous humor generally are very quick at seeing other possible meanings of a key word or phrase during conversations. The rest of us know these other meanings but don't have the habit of seeing them, because the context always makes the true meaning clear. If you've never been a playful thinker, your starting point should be to focus your attention on extra meanings of a word as soon as it's spoken.

A good way to heighten the quickness of your thinking along these lines is to take words associated with common objects or events and try to think of two or more ways of interpreting them. This does not produce jokes, but strengthens your ability to see and create extra meanings. And a greater awareness of multiple meanings will enable you to create your own spontaneous jokes. Just to give you the idea, here are a few examples:

Chair
- Something you sit on
- A position or title (e.g., chair of a committee)

Table
- A piece of furniture
- To table a motion
- Water level

Book
- A written document
- A record of bets
- A set of cards
- Engage someone's services

Fan
- Something used to keep you cool
- Someone who follows sports
- To spread something out
- To strike out (baseball)

To practice this exercise, look at objects in the room you're now in to come up with words which have two or more possible meanings. Also try to imagine verbs which lend themselves easily to double meanings. Write down both meanings. But don't stop at two; be sure to look for more. Remember, though, that many words only have one meaning.

Also remember that this exercise is designed to build up a preliminary skill for creating your own humor, not to be funny itself.

To accelerate your progress, make a game out of this. Practice the exercise while driving, waiting for the bus, walking down the street, or in any other situation where you have a few spare moments. This has far more value than you would guess. It strengthens the habit of having surplus meanings quickly pop into mind. You may have to force yourself to do the exercise at first, but you'll quickly reap the rewards. These extra meanings are precisely what you need to make up your own puns or jokes. As you get better at the exercise, you will also get better at coming up with your own spontaneous humor.

Look for Ambiguity in Everyday Conversations

One of the best ways to start developing basic skills in playing with language is to make a conscious effort to find ambiguity in everyday conversations—both your own and those of others. Don't worry about whether it's funny or whether it's intended as a joke. Just be on the lookout for words where a second interpretation is possible. The context of ambiguous statements almost always makes the intended meaning clear. But remember, humorists trick us by using the other meaning, even if it makes no sense in the context given.

You never know when you'll accidentally say something which could be interpreted another way. I once did a program for a group in a church basement, and had just finished talking about looking for ambiguity in conversations. I noticed a small organ over in one corner of the room during the break and innocently said to the minister (who was participating in the workshop), "Gee, what a beautiful little organ you've got." Five women standing nearby cracked up. They immediately began to practice what I had been preaching.

Most of the time, the extra meanings you notice won't be very funny. Don't worry about it. You're taking the initial steps needed to put the detection and creation of puns on automatic pilot. If you spend a week or so devoting some time every day to listening actively for ambiguity (at lunch, with friends, listening to the radio in your car, etc.), you'll quickly get better at spotting double meanings, even when you're not looking for them. They'll just jump out at you. For example, a friend of mine heard this announcement from a pilot just after takeoff from Chicago: "We'll be cruising at 37,000 feet and briefly pass out over the lake." She thought the remark was very funny, but noticed that no one else seemed to have spotted the unintended meaning.

When you find yourself grinning at such unintentional puns, you'll know you've taken an important step toward creating them yourself. You'll be in the middle of a conversation, and puns will just pop into your mind. The first time this happens, you may get just as excited as when you first discovered puns as a child.

A doctor was asking a woman questions in an attempt to find clues about the cause of her persistent abdominal pain. He asked, "Are you sexually active?" She answered, "No, I just lay there." I'm sure the doctor controlled his laughter, but I hope he was laughing on the inside. Another doctor told a 16-year-old that she had acute vaginitis. She looked down with embarrassment and said, "Thank you."

❝*There is a foolish corner in the brain of the wisest man.***❞**

(Aristotle)

Since you are not used to seeing ambiguity in language, it will take an active effort to get into the habit of doing so. To speed up the process, use the same notebook you used to copy down jokes you like. Every time you hear or see a word (on signs, in conversation, in a newspaper, etc.) whose meaning is ambiguous, write it down, along with enough of the context to enable you to remember it later. This will strengthen the habit of noticing them, even if you never tell them to anyone else.

At the end of the day, consult your notebook and think back about the ambiguities you noticed that day. Ask yourself which ones were funny and which weren't. This will further strengthen the habit of looking for them. Part of the Homeplay for Step 4 invites you to be on the lookout for such ambiguities.

A few examples are given here to give you the basic idea. Take the underlined word, or set of words, and substitute another word, or set of words, which has basically the same meaning. But the word(s) you substitute should produce an ambiguity in the meaning of the sentence. For example, you could take the phrase, "He went lion hunting with a group of friends," and change it to, "He went lion hunting with a club." The second sentence is ambiguous, while the first one is not. Avoid looking at the ambiguous versions (which follow immediately after the set of unambiguous versions) until you've tried to create your own ambiguous way of restating the sentence.

Unambiguous Sentences

1. She helped the boy **put on** the hat.
2. He laughed **in** school.
3. He saw a **ferocious** fish.
4. The **sailor's fat wife** likes to cook.
5. The duck **can now be eaten.**
6. The mayor asked the police to **not allow** drinking while driving.

Ambiguous Versions

1. She helped the boy with the hat.
2. He laughed at school.
3. He saw a man-eating fish.
4. The fat sailor's wife likes to cook.
5. The duck is ready to eat.
6. The mayor asked the police to stop drinking while driving.

Look for Humor in Newspaper Headlines

Most newspapers have adopted the habit of inserting word play into some of their headlines. Developing the habit of looking for double meanings in headlines, will further strengthen your own sensitivities to ambiguity.

The following exercise involves real headlines taken from newspapers. Jay Leno has published several books based on headlines. A key word or two has been left out of each headline. Your task is to fill in the blank with a word that makes the headline funny. Make the effort to come up with your own answer before checking the answers given below. Use the clue given only if you need it. Remember, your answer could be different from the one given here, but be just as funny. You'll know you're making progress when the humor in such headlines begins to automatically pop out at you in reading your own newspaper. As you become familiar with the pattern of word play used here, try coming up with your own headlines. You can use this skill to build some fun into office memos, announcements of meetings, etc.

Puns

1. **"Condom week starts out with a _____."**
   CLUE: It's a good start. The word is also slang for "having sex."
2. **"Man shoots alligator ____ pajamas."**
   CLUE: This is a little word, but still makes it funny.
3. **"Organ recital fades after _____ beginning."**
   CLUE: An excellent or solid beginning.
4. **"Pants man to expand at the _____."**
   CLUE: A men's clothing store is enlarging the store—not at the front, but . . .
5. **"'Family _____ fire just in time,' chief says."**
   CLUE: They find or spot the fire.
6. **"Trees can _____ wind."**
   CLUE: Weaken or reduce. Think of a childish prank that's always in bad taste (actually, another sensory system is closer).
7. **"Drought _____ coyotes to watermelons."**
   CLUE: Causes them to start eating watermelons.
8. **"Ban on nude dancing ____ Governor's desk."**
   CLUE: This is another little word, but it does carry the pun.

Absurdity

9. **"Furniture drive for _____ launched."**
   CLUE: What group of people does it make sense to raise money for, but not furniture?
10. **"Man _____, _____; death by natural causes ruled."**
    CLUE: Pick any cause of death that is anything but a natural cause.

Stating the Obvious

11. **"Researchers call _____ a threat to public health."**
    CLUE: The most extreme assault on one's body that you can think of.
12. **"'Death row inmates no longer allowed day off after _____,' official says."**

CLUE: What is the one condition in which a day off would be irrelevant?

13. **"Commissioner says _____ is needed to end drought."**

CLUE: What's always needed in a drought?

14. **"Women's Club to hold June meeting in _____."**

CLUE: None needed.

Answers

1. Bang	8. On
2. In	9. Homeless
3. Firm	10. Shot, stabbed
4. Rear	11. Murder
5. Catches	12. Execution
6. Break	13. Rain
7. Turns	14. June

Look for Word Play on Public Signs

Humor is often used on public signs to capture attention. For example, a sign in a funeral parlor said, "Ask about our layaway plan." A jewelry story in a mall had a sign out front saying, "Ears pierced while you wait." A furniture store displayed a sign saying, "Modular sofas—only $299. For rest or foreplay."

The signs listed on the next page were found in a broad range of business establishments. To practice your skill at thinking in terms of puns, first cover the right column and try to guess what kind of business would be associated with each sign in the left column. The businesses in the right column are listed in the incorrect order. Draw a line from each sign to the business that makes sense of the pun in the sign. (The answers are listed below.)

Answers

1C, 2G, 3I, 4B, 5F, 6J, 7H, 8A, 9K, 10E, 11D.

Daffynitions

In daffynitions, the idea is to use some aspect of a word to come up with a really daffy definition of the word. This is a common feature of Johnny Hart's *"B.C.,"* in the comic section of your newspaper. In the paper on the day I wrote this, the word "privatize" was defined in *B.C.* as "Mike Hammer, Sam Spade, and Philip Marlowe." In another, "loin cloth" was defined as "what you have to do if you want to work in the garment district."

Daffynitions are an admittedly low level of humor, but learning to generate them on your own is an excellent way to build your ability to see ambiguity and play with language. Again, you can do this any time you're in a situation where you have a few minutes with nothing to do (waiting in line, riding a bus, waiting for your meal in a restaurant, etc.). Just look around the room for ideas for different verbs and nouns, and find as many as you can which are conducive to daffynitions.

Sign	Location
1. **Ask about our layaway plan.**	A. Plumber's truck
2. **Get lots for little.**	B. Hair stylist
3. **Come in and have a fit.**	C. Funeral parlor
4. **Curl up and dye.**	D. Lumberyard
5. **Medium prices.**	E. Restaurant
6. **Better laid than ever.**	F. Fortune teller
7. **Litany candles?**	G. Real estate office
8. **A flush is better than a full house.**	H. Catholic church
9. **If you're at death's door, let our doctors pull you through.**	I. Shoe store
10. **Don't stand outside and be miserable. Come in and get fed up.**	J. Poultry farm
11. **Come see, come saw.**	K. Hospital

Oar: What you are when you borrow something.

Oblate: When you don't go to sleep until the wee hours.

Oboe: When you've borrowed someone's bow.

Ode: Made a long time ago.

Odor: A person who sings odes.

Offense: Where something that used to be on the fence is when it falls.

Ooze: What people say when they see a beautiful sunset.

Oppose: What you do when you go to a photographer.

Orchid: A kid who likes to row boats.

Oregon: Row the boat one more time.

You can use newspapers, magazines, or any other printed matter as a source of words to play with.

A dictionary is the best starting point for this exercise. Take your own dictionary, and go through the pages at random looking for words which seem ideal for daffynitions. I'm picking up the dictionary as I'm writing this, and I've opened it up at random to "O." Here's what I've come up with:

I purposefully wrote down the first thing that came into mind as I thought of these words. With a little effort, I could have come up with funnier lines. You'll also note that other answers are possible for many of them. The point is that, if you do the same thing and just verbalize the first daffynition that you think of, you'll get better at having this kind of word play occur to you automatically. Come up with your own Daffynitions of the following: alarms, arrears, crock, debate, delight, fungi, insane, mutilate, vitamin, and zebra. (See end of next section for answers.)

Practice Generating Your Own Punchlines

The best way to learn to generate your own puns and other jokes, of course, is to practice creating your own punchlines. The following examples are given to help you see how you will benefit from creating your own punchlines . Fill in the blank with any word or phrase which creates ambiguity within the context of the other information given. There often is more than one acceptable answer for these jokes, so if yours differs from the one given, do not consider it wrong. Also, don't worry about how funny your answer is. If it creates ambiguity, that's all that matters at this point.

1. (A classic) **"Waiter, what's this fly doing in my soup?"**
   "I don't know sir, but it looks like _____."
   CLUE: Look for a second meaning of "doing."

2. What would it take to legalize marijuana these days?
   A _____ session of congress.
   CLUE: What are marijuana cigarettes called?

3. A couple of women walk into a club for men only, and the waiter says, "I'm sorry ladies, we only serve men here."
   One woman replies, "_____."
   CLUE: Look for a second meaning of "serve."

4. Did you hear about the two angels who got kicked out of heaven? They were trying to _____ a _____.
   CLUE: This is a double pun. A familiar phrase meaning to "earn a profit."

5. What do Saddam Hussein and his father have in common?
   Neither one _____ in time.
   CLUE: Find a sexual meaning. And remember that Iraq eventually withdrew from Kuwait.

6. **What does a grape say when you step on it?**
   Nothing, it just gives a little _____.
   CLUE: You probably don't need one. In case you do, think of a term for an unpleasant way young children cry.

7. **How are a duck and an icicle alike?**
   They both grow _____.
   CLUE: What duck product is used in ski jackets?

8. (Item on a news broadcast) **"The Detroit Police Department reported today that someone broke into police headquarters during the night and damaged their toilet facilities. The sabotage remains a mystery, and at present the police have nothing to _____."**
   CLUE: None needed.

9. **They've developed a new potency pill for men, but it has one drawback. If it's swallowed too slowly, the user winds up with a _____ neck.**
   CLUE: A slang term used to refer to a dead person.

10. **One bachelor asks another, "Well, how did you like your stay at the nudist camp?"**
    "Well, it was OK after a while. The first three days were the _____."
    CLUE: Most difficult.

Answers

1. The backstroke	6. Wine
2. Joint	7. Down
3. Good, we'll take two	8. Go on
4. Make a prophet	9. Stiff
5. Pulled out	10. Hardest

Answers to Daffynitions

1. What an octopus is.
2. What we often forget to wash behind.
3. A Japanese device for telling time.
4. What you turn on to see in de room.
5. A guy who knows how to have a good time.
6. Where Parisians swim on hot days.
7. What tomcats do at night.
8. What you do when guests visit.
9. What you put on de hook.
10. The biggest bra they make.

Exaggeration

Exaggeration is another technique that will serve you well under stress. If you exaggerate your problem to extremes—to the point that it becomes ridiculous—it's easier to find a way to laugh at it because it seems less threatening. It helps you let go of the problem instead of carrying it around. Therapists know the value of exaggeration. Every year, more therapists are learning to use it to help patients cope. Alan Fay points out in his book, *Making Things Better by Making Them Worse*, that therapists sometimes use exaggeration to pull patients out of depression. One woman was very depressed about her husband's heart attack and death. She felt responsible, because she had been pressuring him to do work around the house when he got home. A logical approach by the therapist failed to take away her guilt. She kept saying, "If only I had treated him better . . ."

One day, after a remark like this, her therapist said, "That's right. We have to face the fact that you killed him. It was clearly a case of murder. The only decent thing to do is turn yourself in at the nearest police station." She chuckled and improved quickly after this.

If you're prone to being anxious in the midst of everyday problems and hassles, try exaggerating the way you usually react. For example, shake your hands, breathe rapidly, pace back and forth, shouting something like, "Oh my God! Oh my God! This is it! This is the end! I'm dead. I'll never get out of this!" For extra effect, say it in a high-pitched, or otherwise silly, voice.

> **❝Comedy has to be truth. You take the truth and put a little curlicue at the end.❞**
> (Sid Caesar)

A nurse used exaggeration to help pull a cancer patient out of his depression. One day the patient was walking down the hall with his head down, shoulders drooping, obviously depressed. The nurse moved up beside him and just walked along with him, looking at the floor with her head even lower than his, her shoulders and arms drooping even lower toward the floor. As they walked along, a big grin came across his face. He straightened up and was in a much better mood the rest of the day. The exaggeration made him realize that he was feeling sorry for himself. It made him see how he must have looked, and brought him back to a more positive focus.

Exaggeration is commonly used by comedians. Johnny Carson was famous for his "It was so hot/cold/small/large that . . ." lines. Here are some examples.

> I had a cavity so deep that my dentist sent me to a podiatrist.
>
> The town I grew up in was so conservative, you had to have a prescription to buy a condom.
>
> My ranch is so big that when I go for the mail I have to stay overnight in a motel.
>
> It was so hot that when the dogs chased cats, they both walked.
>
> She was so chubby, she had to have her hula hoop let out.
>
> He's so old, the bank mails him a new calendar one month at a time.
>
> Sampson was so popular, he brought down the house. (Notice how this exaggeration joke differs from the others.)
>
> He's so clumsy, he trips over cordless phones.
>
> I had so many pimples when I was a kid, the blind always wanted to read my face.
>
> He was so rich, he bought his dog a boy.

Michael Iapoce, in his book *A Funny Thing Happened on the Way to the Board Room*, describes an excellent 5-step technique for learning to create your own exaggeration jokes.

1. Pick a subject.
   It could be yourself, your mother-in-law, school, your job, marriage, your car, anything at all. Let's say you pick your car.
2. Make a list of associations to this subject, using only nouns.
   For "car," you might come up with door, headlights, engine, trunk, windshield wipers, gas tank, license plate, speedometer, wheels, dash, chrome, paint, hood, mechanic, glove box, tow truck, etc.
3. Pick an adjective to describe the subject.
   It might be old, slow, small, economical, etc. Let's say you pick "old."
4. Make another list of associations for the word selected in step 3.
   These generally should be nouns, but some verbs also will work. For old, you could include wrinkles, Geritol, fossils, antiques, Roman numerals, grey hair, arthritis,

stone carvings, hieroglyphics, Dead Sea Scrolls, liver spots, petrified wood, prunes, bifocals, false teeth, etc.

5. Find words within the two lists that you can meaningfully connect.
   Connect them in a statement that makes sense in an exaggerated or absurd way. Practice this exercise by using one of the terms listed in step 4 to complete the following sentences. Cover up the right column below now, and try to come up with your own answer (sometimes more than one answer works).

My car is so old that the:

1. Headlights . . .	have bifocals.
2. Wheels . . .	are carved in stone.
3. Gas tank . . .	uses prunes.
4. Speedometer . . .	is in Roman numerals.
5. Paint . . .	has wrinkles.
6. Engine . . .	runs on Geritol.
7. Chrome . . .	has liver spots.
8. Dash . . .	is petrified wood.
9. License plate . . .	is carved in stone.
10. Trunk . . .	contains dinosaur eggs.

Now repeat the exercise on your own in your Humor Log. To maximize your benefit, repeat it several times. (Note: this is much more fun when done with another person.)

Finding Connections Between Apparently Unrelated Terms

More creative individuals are better than others at finding meaningful links between ideas or events which initially seem to have no connection at all. Creative insights may show up in science, literature, the arts . . . and in humor. Researchers have long known that a close relationship exists between humor and creativity. Creative people tend to be more strongly drawn to humor, and there is even evidence that working at improving your humor skills increases your creativity in general.[1]

Thus, any efforts you make to improve your ability to find meaningful links between events where the connection is not at all obvious should improve your ability to generate unusual connections in humor. And working on your verbal humor skills should also enhance your creative thinking abilities in a broader sense.

The following exercise, developed by Art Gliner, is designed to develop your skill at finding connections between apparently unrelated terms. It is similar to the exaggeration exercise described above. It allows you to practice making unusual associations in a funny way. Start out with a familiar subject, such as golf, music, cars, marriage, nuclear war, etc. Then write down 10-20 words or ideas which are related to this subject. If we choose golf, the terms might be club, golf cart, ball, putt, sand trap, fairway, hole in one, eagle, birdie, green, iron, wood, hook, slice, tee, drive, divot, bogey, handicap, etc.

Then choose a major event going on in the world at the moment, such as the poor economy, a national disaster, the Somali food mission, the invasion of Kuwait by Iraq, or the fall of communism. Then take the golf terms and search for a way to relate them to the world event you've chosen. Let's say you've selected Iraq's invasion of Kuwait.

Select from the following golf terms (or a variation of the terms) to fill in the blank for the sentences listed below:

ball, birdie, bogey, cart, chipper, club, divot, drive, eagle, fairway, green, handicap, hole in one, hook, iron, nineteenth hole, pin, putt, rough, sand trap, slice, tee, wood.

1. Get _____ on freedom.
2. What did every Kuwaitee want to do when they saw the tanks roll in? _____ a _____.
3. The Kuwaitees were really _____ off about the attack.
4. Iraqi armor _____ into Kuwait, causing Kuwaitees to run to their cement shelters. So they were somewhere between Iraq and a hard place. (Sometimes you have to reach for them.)
5. Iraq's attack was no _____ to deal with Kuwait.
6. When the Kuwaitees lined the streets as the tanks rolled into town, they shouted, "Save gas! Drive a _____!"
7. The Kuwaitees told a lot of jokes about the Iraqis during the war. What kind of jokes were these? _____-down jokes.
8. When the Iraqis said they were going to try a(n) _____ shot, no one expected it would come from a tank.
9. The Iraqis were _____ with envy at all the riches of the Kuwaitees.
10. The Kuwaitees told a lot of crude jokes about the oil fires set by the Iraqis. But they'd have to be refined to repeat here. (It's not a golf joke, but it's too good to leave out.)

Answers:

1. Hooked	6. Ball
2. Putt a hole in one	7. Putt
3. Teed	8. Iron
4. Sliced	9. Green
5. Fairway	

Try this exercise yourself, using other terms. Again, don't be overly concerned about how funny your ideas are at this point. As you can see from my example, some ideas will be funnier than others. But don't close out ideas that you don't think are funny enough. After you do the exercise several times, you'll find the percentage of funny associations gradually increasing. Each time you repeat the exercise, you'll build your verbal humor skills. This is an especially effective technique to use in groups.

Nonsense and Opposites

> ❝*A little nonsense now and then is relished by the wisest men.*❞
> (Ronald Dahl)

I know someone who frequently complains that jokes just "make no sense!" She just looks puzzled, while those around her are rolling on the floor laughing. Actually, you rarely come across true nonsense humor, because jokes generally do make sense in an odd, unexpected way. A man is reading the newspaper and sees a headline stating, "Most accidents occur within 10 miles of home." He throws the paper down and says, "That's it! We're moving!" This seems to be nonsense. But there is a way in which the idea of moving does make sense; namely, if you assume that the report refers to his particular home. You get the joke when you realize this.

A little boy tells his mother he wants to watch the eclipse of the sun. The mother says, "Ok, but don't stand too close." Again, we understand that this comes from the general rule that if you stand too close to something dangerous, you could get hurt. But this makes no sense at all when applied to the sun.

Chances are that you will never use much nonsense humor in your everyday life after you finish this program, but learning to be comfortable thinking in terms of nonsense will be of great value in developing your sense of humor. It will help you break through a barrier that limits many people in the development of their sense of humor—the idea that life is always supposed to make sense. As you become more comfortable with the idea that the world is not always reasonable, a whole new world of humor will open up to you.

> "*Nonsense is an assertion of man's spiritual freedom in spite of all the oppressions of circumstance.*"   (Aldous Huxley)

> "*It is far better to have a firm anchor in nonsense than to put out on the troubled seas of thought.*"   (John Kenneth Galbraith)

The following exercises give you an opportunity to explore this aspect of your sense of humor. One technique is to form a group of 4 or 5 people. Have a dictionary handy and look for unfamiliar words. One person selects a word, and the others write down a definition that is purposefully as absurd or nonsensical as possible. The goal is to come up with a definition that others will think is funny. After everyone has written down their definition, the person who selected the word reads all of the definitions given, and everyone votes for the funniest definition. Each person keeps track of the number of votes their own answers receive, and continues to record these throughout the game. Group members take turns choosing the word to be defined. After two rounds (or one, if the group is large), the person who has received the most votes for funniest definition wins the game. Doing this in the context of a game makes it more fun, and shows you the broad range of nonsensical definitions that are possible, but that you didn't think of. Hearing other people's answers also stimulates your own ability to think of funny definitions.

Find a partner for the following game. Partner A will start out with the following statement: "I live in a crazy house. In my house all the _____ . . ." Partner A will then choose any familiar item around the house (an object or person) to fill in the blank. Partner B's task is then to say something about that object or person that is either complete nonsense, or just the opposite of what is known to be true.

Here are some examples that have come into my mind as I'm writing this.

I live in a crazy house. In my house the

- Dishes clean themselves.
- Kids make their own bed.
- Oven makes ice cubes.
- Kids insist on taking baths.
- Toilets speak German.
- Carpets are on the ceiling.
- Microwave plays rock music.
- Plants salute the flag.
- Windows are made of bricks.
- Carpets are on the walls.

As with previous exercises, I did not screen these to be sure they're funny; in fact, several of them are not. You will have a tendency to hesitate and try to think of a really "good" answer (i.e., one that's very funny). As with the other exercises, it is important to forget about funniness and just say whatever pops into your mind. Sometimes it will be funny, and sometimes it won't. The more of these you do, the more you will find yourself quickly screening out the kinds of answers you initially were giving, in favor of answers that are more likely to be funny. The benefits received from this exercise depend on your willingness to adopt the habit of quickly giving an opposite or nonsense answer, not on the funniness of your answers.

For a variation of this idea, change the setting to where you work. For example, "I work for a crazy company. At my company, the photocopy machines give coffee refills, free weekends in Rio, etc.). At my company, the desks are on the ceiling." This last example is not at all funny, but it's absurd, so it's a good answer. This will seem awkward at first, but you soon will soon get easier. Don't give up before it becomes fun.

Once you become more familiar with thinking in terms of nonsense, you may start building nonsense into your own spontaneous humor. Some of this may be complete nonsense, like the idea of creating a male tampon. Most of it, though, will probably be humor that seems to be pure nonsense at first, but really does make sense in an unexpected way. For example, did you hear about the test-tube baby that was born with a glass eye? The idea of a baby being born with a glass eye is complete nonsense, and yet there is a meaningful connection to the fact that it's a test-tube baby.

Create Your Own Captions

Another enjoyable way to strengthen your ability to create funny lines is to create your own captions for cartoons. This exercise works best in groups, or with a partner. Each person should bring in a cartoon. Cut off the caption and pass the cartoon around the group. The goal is to come up with as many ideas as possible for a funny caption. Each person should make the effort to create their own caption. Your ability to come up with funny captions will improve as you see the broad range of ideas generated, some of which will be "off the wall." This often works best if the ideas are written down and then discussed anonymously. The group then can select the funniest caption.

"Ruts are coffins with the ends kicked out of them."
(Anonymous)

You also will benefit from this exercise by doing it alone. Take any book of captioned cartoons and make up your own caption for each cartoon. Cover the caption before you read it, and write your own before looking at the one created by the cartoonist. In thinking of your own captions, be sure to keep in mind all the techniques described above.

Other Verbal Humor Techniques

There are many other techniques we haven't considered here, including switching or substitution, reversal, changing cliches, "toppers" (ways of building on a joke you've just done), and more. In all cases, remember to keep the element of surprise or the unexpected in your punchlines. At an Irish funeral, a man is asked to say a few kind words about the deceased. He says, "No, I really can't. I never knew him well." After persistent prodding, he agrees. He gets up and says, "His brother was a lot worse!" Decide for yourself just what technique is used here. What makes it funny?

As the storm raged, the captain realized his ship was sinking fast. He called out, "Anyone here know how to pray?"

One man stepped forward, "Aye Captain, I know how to pray."

"Good," said the Captain, "you pray while the rest of us put on our life jackets—we're one short."

"$200! That's a lot to pay for a sweater!" said a customer.

"Not really," said the salesman. "The sweater's wool was shorn from sheep whose habitat is the most inaccessible area of the Himalayas. It is truly an amazing yarn."

"And," said the customer, "You tell it so well."

Many jokes will be hard to classify as examples of any specific technique. See if you agree with a friend on the technique involved in this joke. "Did you hear about the woman who had three breasts? She had quadruplets." My advice is to not be overly concerned about techniques. As you spend more time with jokes, different techniques will just pop into mind without having to think about it.

After 20 years of marriage, a couple amicably agrees to get a divorce. As they share a bottle of champagne to celebrate their agreement, the husband says, "There's one thing I've always wanted to ask you, but I never had the nerve. Since we're splitting up now, it can't possibly hurt me, so tell me, why is it that five out of our six children have black hair, while little Tommy has blond hair? Whose child is Tommy, anyway?"

"Well, if you really want to know," says the wife, "Tommy is your child."

Step 4

The following exercise samples a range of different techniques. Try to create your answer without using the clue. If you can't come up with anything, use the clue to generate an answer before checking the answers below. The last seven jokes here are "Dumb men" jokes, a variation on the familiar "Dumb blond" jokes.

1. "I'm on a new seafood diet. I _____ food and I eat it."
   CLUE: Find a pun based on the sound of the key word.

2. When the police asked the drunk what he was doing on the roof of the bar, he explained that someone said that drinks were _____.
   CLUE: A familiar phrase when you're not paying.

3. What do you get when you cross a birth control pill with LSD? A _____ without the kids.
   CLUE: None necessary.

4. A couple makes love, and in the afterglow he says, "Honey, have you ever wondered what it feels like to be a man?" She smiles sweetly and says, "No dear, I haven't, _____?"
   CLUE: She's putting him down.

5. A psychiatrist gives his client a battery of tests and then tells him, "I hate to tell you this, but the tests clearly show that you're hopelessly insane."
   "What?" says the client, "I want a second opinion!"
   "Ok," says the doctor, you're _____."
   CLUE: Play with the notion of a second opinion.

6. A lusty young farmer is showing an attractive woman around his farm. Hoping to turn her on, he shows her his prize bull mating with a cow. "Ain't that something?" he says. "Yes, it's really impressive," she answers.
   He then looks her up and down and says, "I'd sure like to do that myself."
   "Well why don't you?" she says, "It's _____."
   CLUE: What's the best way for her to switch the focus of attention and get even?

7. Everyone who cheats on their diet gains in _____."
   CLUE: Eventually.

8. At what time of night do babies always wake up? In the _____ hours of the morning.
   CLUE: A variation of a familiar term meaning "early."

9. The Reverend Henry Ward Beecher
   Called the hen a most elegant creature.
   The hen, pleased with that
   Laid an egg in his hat.
   Thus did the hen _____.
   CLUE: Play with the person's name to complete this limerick.

10. A man is about to undergo serious surgery following an accident. He asks his doctor if he'll be able to play golf after the operation. The doctor says, "Yes, I guarantee it!" The patient says, "That's fantastic, because I've _____."
    CLUE: Reverse a basic assumption you're making about the patient.

11. Jean Paul Sartre arrives in Heaven and says to God, "It's not what I expected." God asks, "Well what did you expect?" And Sartre answers, "_____."
    CLUE: This is a bit esoteric. What did Sartre write about?

12. A man keeps going to the doctor because his eye hurts, and the doctor finally discovers the problem. He says, "Your eye hurts only when you drink tea, so don't drink tea."

The patient says, "But I love tea."

"Ok," answers the doctor, "then just take the _____ first."

CLUE: Although he develops an eye problem when he drinks tea, it's not from ingesting the tea.

13. Why are all dumb blond jokes one liners? So _____ can understand them.

    CLUE: None needed.

14. What is the difference between Government bonds and men? Government bonds _____.

    CLUE: How are men who never grow up referred to?

15. What is a man's idea of helping with the housework? Lifting his _____ so you can _____.

    CLUE: A part of the house we clean every week or so.

16. How was E. T. different from men? E. T. _____ home.

    CLUE: What are men always (stereotypically) forgetting to do?

17. What did God say after He created man? I can _____ than this.

    CLUE: He created an imperfect being.

18. What's the best way to get a man to do situps? Put the _____ between his toes.

    CLUE: What does the average man do when he gets home from work?

19. Why is it essential that there are female astronauts? If the crew gets _____ in space, at least the women will ask _____.

    CLUE: What are men often accused of rarely doing when traveling in unfamiliar territory?

Answers:

1. See	6. Your cow
2. On the house	7. The end
3. Trip	8. Wee-wee
4. Have you?	9. Reward Beecher
5. Ugly too	10. Never played golf in my life
11. Nothing	16. Phoned
12. Spoon out	17. Do better
13. Men	18. Remote control
14. Mature	19. Lost . . . directions
15. Legs . . . vacuum	

Conversation-Between-Two-Objects Game

Find another person to play this game with. Pick any two objects and pretend that each of you is one of those objects. Develop your own spontaneous funny conversation by speaking from the vantage point of that object. Talk about how the object feels, the kind of experiences it has, the injustices it suffers, its disappointments, sources of joy, etc. Just let your mind go in any silly or absurd direction that comes up. Practice saying anything that comes into your mind; don't worry about whether or not it's funny. Remember to vary your voice in any way that makes sense, given the object you're speaking for.

Humor Log Exercises

On Play with Language

1. Why do we generally groan at puns?
2. When do children start to understand puns?
3. Are all riddles and puns alike? How would you classify them?
4. Why do puns generally seem funnier to the person who creates them than to the person s/he tells them to?
5. Can learning to create your own puns help sensitize you to spotting other forms of humor in everyday life? How?
6. How will learning to play with language help you cope with stress?
7. If you were to become more skilled at creating humor, how might that improve your effectiveness on the job?
8. List a few situations where you've seen co-workers make witty remarks that were inappropriate. Why were they inappropriate?

Current Verbal Sense of Humor

1. Do you enjoy puns and other forms of word play? Why (not)?
2. How often do you produce original puns in conversations?
3. What is the most common form of verbal humor you initiate?
4. Do you prefer to make up your own spontaneous verbal humor or tell memorized jokes and stories?
5. How often do you create your own verbal humor at work? What keeps you from doing this more often on the job?
6. How important is it for you to improve your skill at creating puns and other verbal humor?

Early Development and Influences

1. Did you go through a period around 1st-3rd grade during which you constantly told riddles? If possible, ask your parents, or anyone else who knew you as a child. What prompted you to tell fewer riddles and jokes as you got older?
2. Was there any other period in your childhood or adolescence during which you told a lot of jokes?
3. As you look back at your life (including your adult years), at what age were you most prone to creating your own spontaneous verbal humor? Why do you think you did more then than you do now?
4. When you told jokes while growing up, were they generally memorized, or did you often create your own spontaneous jokes?
5. When you did initiate some form of humor as a child or adolescent, what kind of humor was it generally?
6. Who had the greatest (positive or negative) influence on your ability to create verbal humor?
7. How did your mother and father influence your ability to create humor?

GROUP SESSION

Opening Fun Activity

Open the meeting by asking each person to tell a recently learned joke.

Discussion of Homeplay for Step 3

1. Laughter

   What were your experiences in your efforts to laugh more often and more heartily? How did you go about it? Did you force laughter at first? Did this forced laughter help you "break through" so you could laugh more openly and heartily? Did it seem unnatural? Did laughter gradually become easier and more comfortable? What situations did you use to practice laughter? What reminders did you use?

2. Optimism

   How successful were you at being more positive and optimistic? How did you go about it? What problems did you encounter? How did other people react to you?

3. Telling Jokes/Stories

   What was your experience in starting to tell jokes? How many did you learn? Who did you tell them to? How did they react? How comfortable did you feel doing this? Did you ask others about their favorite jokes? Did you get a notebook, and write down the jokes you liked soon after you heard them? What difficulties did you have, either in remembering or telling the jokes? What insights did you gain about joke telling? In what ways are you now better at telling jokes than you were?

Puns and Verbal Humor

Be prepared to talk about the issues raised in the Humor Log Exercises. Also practice or discuss the exercises presented above during the session. Come prepared with your own variations of these exercises. Give special consideration to the following:

1. The exercise in "Multiple Meanings" provides a good starting point. Break into smaller groups of 4 or 5 people. Take turns giving a target word. One person names a common word, of which s/he can think of at least two meanings. The person to

his/her left then gives one meaning, the next person gives a second, etc., until no one can think of any more meanings. Remember that although these are not jokes, it helps stimulate the habit of quickly thinking of alternative meanings. The exercise moves more quickly if someone brings a prepared list of words.

2. If you want to play a version of "Daffynition," make it a point to have a dictionary available at this session (to make it easier to come up with words conducive to good daffynitions). Play the game in groups of 8-10 people. Group members will take turns saying a word for which they have a daffynition in mind. The rest of the group then says out loud whatever daffynition comes to mind. As soon as no more ideas come forth, the next person proposes a new word to be given a daffynition. Doing this in a group will help you get started creating them on your own.

3. Bring in a few examples of jokes based on puns. Have everyone in the group rate how funny they are, using a 5-point funniness scale (1 = not funny at all, 2 = a little bit funny, 3 = moderately funny, 4 = funny, 5 = very funny). Look for any patterns in what you and the group find funny, and discuss any differences you note.

4. Repeat 3) using other types of verbal humor.

5. Practice creating your own joke by starting with a key phrase or word which could be interpreted in more than one way. Use the words or phrases listed below to get started. Come to the group session with one or two of your own which the group can use to create jokes.
   a. "The competition was too stiff."
   b. "Bear with me."
   c. "It was a pleasure having you."
   d. "Perfect score."

6. Do the "Cartoon Caption" exercise, described above.

7. Try the 5-part technique for creating your own exaggeration jokes, described above.

8. Consider allowing those who wrote a funny story about their family or job to read it to the entire group. The group may choose to present their own ideas about funny additions to the story.

9. To get started practicing exaggeration, describe any familiar event and exaggerate some of the details related to the event. For example, if the topic is your wedding day, describe the size of the church, the number of people present, the temperature in the church, the behavior of your spouse at the reception, etc.

   You can also take turns initiating the first half of a classic exaggeration joke, such as, "It was so hot that," "She was so tall that," "He was so determined to succeed that," "I was so hungry that," etc. Everyone else in the group should then come up with a completion of the sentence which provides a clear exaggeration. Don't worry about whether it's funny at this point. Just get used to exaggerating.

10. Play the game of "I work for a crazy company" (or "I live in a crazy house"), described above.

11. Get a partner and spend time on the "Conversation-between-two-objects game."

12. Stay in touch with your telephone partners.

HOME PLAY

1. Complete as many of the above exercises as you can. The more effort you put into it, the more rapidly your verbal humor skills will develop. Spend as much time as necessary to give yourself the feeling that you've made real progress on Step 4 before going on to Step 5.

2. Do the "Exercise in multiple meanings" at least once each day. Do it when you're in your car, waiting in lines, eating alone, riding the bus, etc. Write yourself reminders to do this, and put them in places where you're sure to see them. Writing the meanings down is not essential. But be sure to probe your mental dictionary for extra meanings. Even if you only have a few minutes, you'll benefit from this exercise.

3. Look for ambiguous words or phrases in conversations. Put reminders to do this in places where you'll see them. Whenever possible, write them down (this will help strengthen the habit of looking for them) in the same pocket-size notebook you used to record jokes. Include enough of the context to enable you to fully remember them later. At the end of the day, consult your notebook and think about the ambiguities you noticed that day. Ask yourself which ones were funny and which weren't.

4. Also record any examples of word play you notice in newspaper headlines and on signs. Jot these down in your notebook.

5. Create at least five daffynitions each day. Do this whenever you have a few spare moments (at lunch, waiting in the doctor's office, in elevators, etc.). Jot your daffynitions down in your notebook. Make a game out of it by engaging others in it.

6. Be on the lookout for communications in which you can take what is said literally and produce a comic effect. For example, if someone told you to "keep your eye on the ball . . ." Also keep looking for funny literal interpretations of headlines (e.g., "Drought turns coyotes to watermelons.").

7. Generate as many spontaneous puns as you can during conversations. Start with family members or friends (anyone you trust, or with whom you feel you can take risks). Don't worry about how funny they are. Just get into the habit of playing with words.

8. Find some time to work on the "Exaggeration exercise" described in Step 4. Since this exercise is a little more difficult, do it with a friend in order to make it fun.

9. Also try the exercise on "Connections between apparently unrelated terms" at least once. This is time consuming and a little more difficult, so try it with friends.

10. Get a book of captioned cartoons and create your own captions. Be sure to cover the existing caption first, or you'll find yourself unable to think beyond the caption given. Do this with a friend or two, if possible. Get into the habit of looking at the cartoons in your daily paper, and of creating your own caption for at least one of the cartoons every day.

11. Continue being playful and laughing more than you usually do. Also continue learning new jokes when the opportunity arises, but do not make it your main focus.

STEP 5

Find Humor

In Everyday Life

"You can't really be strong until you see a funny side to things."

(Ken Kesey)

One of the most effective ways to get the health benefits of humor, and to eventually learn to use humor to cope with stress, is to improve your skill at finding a funny side of things that happen in everyday life. If you have done the Homeplay for the first four steps, you should already be better at doing this. Becoming more playful puts you into a frame of mind that makes it easier to see the funny side of things. Even when you are being serious, it's probably much easier now to switch gears and become playful than it was before you started the 8-Step Program. And while you may not realize it yet, joke telling and looking for word play in everyday conversations, newspapers, and on signs, also helps you get started seeing the funny side of situations that have nothing to do with language.

The goal of Step 5 is to sensitize you to the opportunities for humor on your job, at home, in the grocery store, in your relationships, and in every other facet of your life. You will learn to spot humor where you least expect it. I was recently watching a PBS television program on "Madness" and the history of psychiatric approaches to treating it. A standard format is always used to acknowledge the sponsors at the end of the program. The announcer read: "Madness is made possible by the Corporation for Public Broadcasting and viewers like you." I howled with laughter, as I scrambled to write it down before I forgot it.

You are exposed to such opportunities for humor every day, but you're simply not seeing them. The first time I noticed a pay phone on a plane, I was seized with a mid-flight urge to call Dominos Pizza and have a pizza delivered. A flight attendant told me that a man once complained to her about the design of the lavatories on the plane. He said that some turbulence had occurred while he was urinating, and he didn't have anything to hang on to. She had to restrain herself from saying, "Well, blame Mother Nature, it's not our fault."

You soon will have thoughts like this popping into your own mind, as you work on Step 5. But you will have to spend a couple of weeks—maybe a month—making an active effort to find humor everywhere you go before you begin to notice it without looking for it. Developing this skill when you're not under stress is one of the most important things you can do to prepare yourself to find humor when you are under stress.

I heard this same flight attendant walk down the aisle with a cup of decaffeinated coffee asking, "Who asked for the unleaded?" Most of the people within ear shot of her flashed a big smile. It was a brief comment, made in passing while carrying out her regular duties. It took no extra time, but added just a little bit of happiness to the lives of the passengers. It's these seemingly minor everyday opportunities for humor that are the most important to work on.

> **"All eyes are on Mrs. Kennedy as she picks her seat."**
> (Radio commentator's words about Jacqueline Kennedy
> at a public event in the 1960s.)

I was listening to the radio recently and heard a discussion of President Reagan's Memoirs, which were about to be published. Did you immediately see the potential for humor when you read the preceding sentence? The very notion of Reagan's Memoirs made me laugh. Was Reagan known for having a good memory when he was in the White House?

It's easy to find ready-made humor these days. We have sit coms and comedy films on television, funny TV ads, stand-up comics on TV and in clubs, regularly appearing cartoons by *The Far Side*, *Doonesbury*, *Ziggy*, and more, and funny newspaper columnists (e.g., Erma Bombeck). In fact, a humor revolution exploded in the 1980s, as humor became big business. But while the packaged humor that is thrown at you daily does help ease stress, it's not the most effective way to manage stress through humor. It comes at the end of the day, and not when you're in the situations that cause stress (at least job-related stress). And it has no meaningful connection to those situations. Also, it's passively received humor, rather than actively produced.

To use humor to cope, you need to take a more active role in creating or finding your own humor. You can't carry *Saturday Night Live* tapes or *All in the Family* reruns around with you all the time and throw them in the VCR when your problems escalate. But you can learn to look for humor in the situation of the moment and use that humor to take control over the upset. The key is to realize that **improving your sense of humor is not a spectator sport**! We all love to be entertained by humor, but humor won't transform the quality of your life until you take an active role in discovering and creating it yourself.

The problem is that you may still be at ground zero when it comes to finding humor in your own life. You never see it because your head is full of more important things, like what you're going to have for lunch, when the coffee machine will get fixed, and the fact that you drive your son's friend more often than his parents drive your son when the two of them have to go somewhere.

> **❝** *From there to here and here to there, funny things are every-*
> *where.* **❞**
> (Dr. Seuss)

Maybe you're so busy that you feel you can't afford to waste time looking around for what's funny. By the time you get to Step 8, you'll see that you can't afford **not** to look for humor. Once you learn to use humor to maintain a more upbeat, positive mood, and see how it helps you both take control over your emotional reactions to stress and remain productive on the job when everything's going wrong, you'll wonder why you didn't do this years ago. You'll be saying, "I can't believe I've been missing this."

Be sure to start looking for the light side of non-stressful situations before doing so in stressful ones. This includes simply spotting life's oddities when they occur. For example, Charlie Chaplin once entered a Charlie Chaplin look-alike contest, and came in third. During his acting years, Ronald Reagan once was turned down for the role of a presidential candidate in *The Best Man*, by Gore Vidal, because he didn't have a "presidential look."

In the summer of 1993, a New York couple was mugged and had their money, jewelry, some clothes, and a pair of tickets to a Yankee baseball game stolen. They reported the theft to the police. On a hunch, the couple went with the police to the game that the tickets were for. Incredibly, the muggers were sitting in their seats—and were wearing some of the stolen clothes! Who could fail to see the humor in this?

Some things will just strike you as incongruous, but won't make you laugh. Even these situations nurture your sense of humor. For example, after the World Trade Center bombing in 1993, what was the first thing that hundreds of people did after struggling to get through the heavy smoke that nearly took their lives? They lit up a cigarette.

Five or six railroad cars filled with chlorine derailed recently, posing a threat to the surrounding community. A string of barriers was set up to prevent anyone from getting near the restricted zone. No one was allowed near because of the danger. But then the Governor showed up, and the on-site coordinator gave him a close-up tour of the scene. I immediately thought of the way canaries used to be taken into mines.

I recently spotted an article in the newspaper about a company in Colorado called "Dog-Gone." This enterprising company developed a vacuum system for sucking prairie dogs out of their holes and into a large tank on a truck. "The animals are deposited alive 'but somewhat confused'" into the tank. The mere image of a giant vacuum cleaner sucking prairie dogs out of their holes is enough to make me chuckle.

Looking for humor will take extra time and mental effort at first. But after a couple of weeks of putting "finding humor" on the front burner, you'll discover that it takes less and less time and effort. Soon, it will take no extra time at all. You'll notice things that make you laugh while remaining fully engaged in the activity of the moment. That's when humor really begins to serve you, and becomes a tool for dealing with stress. At that point, humor gives you back the energy that stress-induced anger, anxiety, and depression steal from you. The more you immerse yourself in Step 5, the more quickly you will see this change in yourself.

What Is a Humorous Perspective?

Many attitudes can serve as a starting point for viewing the world. Think about people you know well. How many different attitudes can you distinguish among them? Among those with a generally negative attitude, you may find a tendency to be hostile, pessimistic, detached, fearful, resentful, paranoid, accusing, and so forth. All of these negative attitudes make it more difficult to find humor.

Those with a persistent positive attitude may be caring or compassionate, optimistic, friendly, altruistic, or playful. Any kind of positive attitude makes it easier to notice humor, but a playful attitude is essential (see Step 2). It is a playful frame of mind that leads you to see the light side of life, naturally and effortlessly.

We also can talk about attitude in the sense of perspective. First, there's perceptual perspective. The fact that two people are standing/sitting in different positions means that they see the same object differently. In the film *Dead Poet Society*, a teacher (Robin Williams) asks his students to get on top of their desks and look around the room. The lesson is that our perception of the world changes when we adopt a different physical vantage point for looking at it.

Intellectual perspective also determines how we view things. During the 1992 Clarence Thomas—Anita Hill controversy surrounding Thomas' confirmation as a member of the U.S. Supreme Court, men and women generally had very different perceptions of who was telling the truth and who was lying, or bending the truth. They approached the hearings with different attitudes and ideas about men and about sexual harassment, and these different starting points led them to perceive the same events in different ways.

> **"*An egg is funny. An orange is not.*"**   (Fred Allen)

Similarly, Republicans and Democrats, and Christians, Muslims, and Jews generally see the same event differently because different beliefs, attitudes, and values serve as starting points for them. An artist, brick layer, and real estate salesman view the same building in very different ways. It's not that one is right and the other wrong; they just focus on different things.

Intellectual perspective also is important in another way. Look around the room you're in right now and find five things that are round. Now look for five things that are red. These things were there all along, but you didn't see them—because you weren't looking for them. You didn't have a mind-set to see "round" or "red."

The same thing happens with humor. You are surrounded by situations all day long where you might find something funny, **if you have a mind-set to look for it**. In working on Step 5, do the humor-equivalent of asking yourself, "What are the round things in the room?"

Emotional perspective also has an impact on both how you see things in general and your likelihood of finding something funny at any particular moment. You've probably heard the phrase, "Looking at the world through rose-colored glasses." When you're in a good mood, you view the world through a kind of filter that makes everything look better than it does when you're in a bad mood. You see things entirely differently if you've just won the lottery than if you've just been fired or laid off.

> **"*Pointing out the comic elements of a situation can bring a sense of proportion and perspective to what might otherwise seem an overwhelming problem.*"**   (Harvey Mindess)

❝Here's my advice: Go ahead and be wacky. Get into a crazy frame of mind, and ask what's funny about what you're doing.❞

(Roger von Oech)

So what does it mean to have a humorous perspective on things? How does the head bone get connected to the funny bone? How do humorists think that's different from the way you think? First, they have the ability to quickly switch from a serious frame of mind to a playful one. This makes it easy for them to see a light side of things that others miss. Secondly, they have more unusual associations to events, and are more willing than the rest of us to turn the world upside down for the fun of it. They enjoy toying with crazy ideas. This helps sustain a high level of mental flexibility and creativity.

People with a well-developed humorous vantage point on life enjoy creating absurdities in their own minds. One of my favorite comedians is Sid Caesar. He can take a common innocuous situation and make it absurd. In a skit on the old *Show of Shows*, he took his child to the movies on a cold winter day, and put so many clothes on him that you could hardly see the child. When they got back home, he took off the child's hat, ear muffs, mittens, coat, another coat, boots, leggings, sweater, a second sweater . . . When he finished, there was no child there.

A bank robber in a small town was caught recently after signing his name to a withdrawal slip just prior to the holdup.

A drunken man walked into the Emergency Room of a hospital one Saturday evening complaining of a backache. He asked a nurse on duty if he could make a phone call first. When he turned around and walked toward the phone, the nurse noticed a knife stuck in the middle of his back.

Evander Hollyfield's trainer made the following statement a few years ago about an upcoming fight with Mike Tyson: "It's not a matter of life and death; it's more important than that."

A man in Texas had been hiding from the law for 17 years. He finally got caught when he contacted the FBI to find out if they were still looking for him.

After his surgery for gallstones, a man awakened in his hospital room to discover the stones on the same tray on which his medications had been placed. A nurse had put them there so he could see the cause of his torture. With some effort, he was finally able to get them down.

In another skit, he played a woman putting on her make-up. He draws a line on the right eyebrow, and then the left. After scrutinizing them, he decides the right one is too short, so he lengthens it. Then the other one is too short, so he lengthens it. This continues to the point where he finally has lines coming all the way down the sides of his cheeks. And the audience is howling.

Humorists also have a built-in tendency to see and enjoy the incongruities, ironies, absurdities, and ridiculous aspects of real life. They thrive on the oddities of things that happen and that people do, like the following:

The humorist has a keen eye for such events, and never tires of looking for them. Learning to spot them yourself is one of the most important skills you can develop. If it helps, try assuming that God has a great sense of humor, and that He has set up opportunities for you to laugh every day. Your job is to enjoy the chances He gives you.

I recently saw a man in a supermarket trying to get coffee from a coffee machine that wasn't working. He had put two quarters in, but all it gave him was a persistent clicking sound—and no coffee. He got very annoyed and shouted for someone to come fix the machine. I can still see his bulging eyes as the store employee started pulling out the quarters that were dropping into the coin return slot with every click. The machine was still spewing out quarters as I walked away chuckling.

Shit Happens!

Taoism: "*Shit happens.*"

Confucianism: "*Confucius say, 'Shit happens.'*"

Islam: "*If shit happens, it is the will of Allah.*"

Buddhism: "*If shit happens, it is not really shit.*"

Zen Buddhism: "*What is the sound of shit happening?*"

Hinduism: "*This shit has happened before.*"

Catholicism: "*If shit happens, you deserve it.*"

Protestantism: "*Let this shit happen to someone else.*"

Judaism: "*Why does this shit always happen to us?*"

Existentialism: "*Shit is what's happening. Dig it!*"

A few weeks later, I discovered how he felt. I went to a cash machine (ATM) to make a withdrawal, and spent several minutes trying to make it work—to no avail. I kept getting a "temporarily out of service" message on the screen. Finally, I banged on the wall. After a brief exchange of shouts, a guy came out front, lifted up the cash door, and removed a wad of $20 bills that had somehow gotten jammed in the distributor. I stared with my mouth hanging open, in disbelief. A part of me was angry, but I burst out laughing as I walked to my car, and the words burned in my mind, "All I had to do was open that door . . ."

Humorists also have fewer "sacred cows" than the rest of us. Sacred cows create sensitive zones. And your sense of humor is usually the victim when you enter one of these zones. You will start getting rid of your own sacred cows during Step 6.

Humor, like beauty, is in the eye of the beholder. The opportunity exists to find both humor and beauty around you every day, if you just learn to look for it. All you need is a mind set to detect it. Humorists adopt an attitude in life which enables them to keep their sense of humor when the rest of us lose it. If you're having difficulty adopting this attitude, try imagining that you're a common, everyday object, and describe a typical day in the life of that object. Describe its experiences, how it feels, its complaints, the stressors in its life, etc. When possible, illustrate what you're saying with body language or actions. Feel free to exaggerate and be absurd.

Life is full of absurdity, the humorist might say, and it's much more adaptive to laugh at it than to cry, get depressed, or get angry. Those with a comic vision of life know that life is not fair or just, so you have to make the best of it. As an insightful philosopher once said, "Shit happens!"

Going through the 8-Step Program gradually shifts your intellectual and emotional perspective on things that happen to you, or that you observe, so that you increasingly come to adopt a humorous perspective on life. You become more attuned to the incongruous, bizarre, ironic, and absurd aspects of everyday life. This is the point at which your sense of humor becomes an effective coping tool.

Laughing *with* and Laughing *at* Others

Humor has incredible power to draw people together, to create a bond among those who share it—even among strangers. But it also can be destructive and create divisions. Which of these occurs often depends on whether you're laughing with or at others. Laughing with has a positive focus, characterized by support, caring, and empathy. Laughing at, on the other hand, generally communicates a sense of contempt and insensitivity, exclusion, one-upmanship, and even abuse. Laughing with focuses on the situation, while laughing at centers more around the person. Laughing with is constructive, while laughing at is destructive.

Children often are viewed as having a cruel sense of humor, because they have no qualms about laughing directly at others—in their presence! We've all seen young children laugh at someone's unusual physical features (e.g., a large nose or an odd walk resulting from a physical deformity). They eventually learn that this is inappropriate and inhibit laughter, even though they still find it funny.

Laughing *with* Others Vs. Laughing *at* Others

Laughing with	Laughing at
Positive & friendly	Negative & hostile
Caring & empathetic	Contemptuous
Sensitive	Insensitive
Constructive	Destructive
Supportive	Unsupportive
Egalitarian	Superiority
Inclusive	Exclusive
Brings people closer	Divides people
Strengthens teambuilding	Weakens teambuilding

As you focus on finding the funny side of everyday life, you're bound to find situations where your laughter is at someone else's expense. People all over the world laugh at jokes which disparage others. My own view, however, is that if put-down jokes are the only jokes you like, and if you mainly find humor in the mistakes, predicaments, or embarrassment of others, this is not a sign of a healthy sense of humor. But we all find ourselves laughing at others from time to time, so a bit of humor etiquette is worth discussing here.

If the humor comes from something you've just witnessed, always remember to put yourself in the place of the person being laughed at. Keep in mind whether your laughter would be offensive or embarrassing to him/her. When in doubt, go ahead and enjoy the funniness of the situation in your own mind; just hold off laughing until later. But funny is funny! So don't worry about whether humor itself is appropriate. Your sense of humor is just as valid as the next person's. But nobody likes being laughed at, so wait until the proper moment to let your laughter loose.

The day will come, of course, when you'll blow it and be unable to hold back laughter at someone's blunder or circumstances. You'll laugh when it's clearly inappropriate to do so. The best way out of this is to simply say, "I'm sorry, I couldn't help laughing. It reminds me of a funny thing that happened to me . . ." If you can then relay a funny incident along the same lines, you eliminate the impression that you're laughing at, instead of with, the other person. You're laughing at the embarrassment and humor of a shared experience.

Even if you're not laughing at someone, the situation itself may dictate that you not laugh. Chapter 2 describes the case of an anesthesiologist who was seen laughing by a family member of a man who had just died on the operating table. There was nothing wrong with the doctor's laughter; it reduced his own stress, putting him in a better position to go on and deal effectively with the next patient. But laughing within view of a family member was clearly inappropriate. His mistake was getting caught. Make sure you don't!

Getting Started

How do you get yourself to the point where you notice the funny side of things if you're not used to doing it? There are several easy things you can do.

Put Up "What's Funny About This?" Reminders

If you never find anything funny about your life, the best way to begin is by doing something that helps you remember to look for humor. Put up reminders in key places (refrigerator, desk, car, etc.) to actively look for humor in situations where you don't normally see any.

Focus on daily routines and circumstances. At the beginning, you'll have to be very specific and ask, "Is there anything weird, incongruous, surprising, ironic or absurd about this?" Or you may be more comfortable simply asking yourself, "OK, if I were Steve Martin (substitute your own favorite comedian), what would I find funny about this?" With practice you won't have to consciously ask yourself. You automatically will notice the light side of situations.

I went to my local YMCA to work out a few weeks ago and overheard a conversation between a mother and her 5-year-old daughter, who had been taking swimming lessons for several weeks. She had a swimming test that morning, and ran excitedly toward her mother when she came to pick her up, shouting, "Mommy, mommy, I did real good!" Her mother also got excited, and said, "Oh, Amy, that's wonderful. You passed your test?" The daughter responded with, "No, but I did real good!" It was the mother's reaction that gave me a good laugh. Clearly she and her daughter had different definitions of "real good."

Have a chuckle at the things children say out of naivete. A friend of mine heard her daughter say, "there's today, tomorrow, and tonow." I was on a plane recently, and a young child in the seat behind me had never been on a plane before. It had been clear weather the entire flight, but as we approached Orlando we passed through some white, fluffy clouds. I overheard her say, "Look, mommy, it's snowing! It's snowing!"

A hospital in New Jersey had a separate division of the hospital on Madison Avenue, in another part of the city. A shuttle bus carried employees back and forth between the main hospital and the Madison Avenue building. Painted in large letters on the side of the vans were the words, "MAD Employees Shuttle."

Make it a point to ask yourself, "What's funny here?" even for mundane occurrences. For example, how many married couples have you met where the husband seems not to hear a word his wife is saying, while she remembers everything he says? How many men have you met who can tell you more than you'd ever want to know about batting averages, world series, and Super Bowl winners for the past 25 years, but can't remember their own anniversaries? How many women do you know who can tell you what you were both wearing on your first five dates, but can't tell you how long the red light on the dash in the car has been flashing?

If you can't find anything funny, change the question to, "How could I change this situation so that it would be funny?" Again, feel free to exaggerate or distort circumstances, including what people are doing and saying, so that it does become funny. This is a great habit to develop for those social situations where you're bored, but have to go through the motions of being interested. You'll have a great time, and will be adding to your humor skills at the same time.

Ask Friends and Colleagues About the Humor They See

Some of your friends or colleagues may already have a well-developed sense of humor, and may be very good at noticing the funny side of things. Seek these people out while working on Step 5, and spend more time with them than you normally do. Whenever you see them, make it a point to ask about the funny things they've noticed recently. Talk to co-workers on breaks, at lunch, or whenever the opportunity for casual conversation arises, about the humor they've noticed. People who enjoy humor usually enjoy sharing it, and the funny things they notice will help sensitize you to seeing humor in the same things yourself.

A friend of mine who works in a hospital told me recently that someone had posted on a bulletin board an article which said that "Research shows that the first five minutes of life are very risky." Someone had penciled in below it, "The last five minutes aren't so hot either." She also said that the intensive care unit of the hospital is often referred to as either the "intensive scare" or "expensive care" unit.

Someone else told me about a couple of horses named "We're Not Sure" and "Who You Gonna Call?" entered in the same race. Amazingly enough, they finished first and second. The announcer called out, "As they come to the wire, it's Who You Gonna Call and We're Not Sure!"

> **"If you smoke, don't exhale."**   (Sign observed in a taxi.)

Write it Down

Whenever you notice anything that strikes you as funny, write it down at the first opportunity. Use the same notebook used for earlier steps. If you don't have time to get the details down at the moment, write down a key word or phrase as a reminder to record it in detail later. This will help keep you from forgetting it.

I recently was out on my daily morning walk/jog when I spotted a very overweight woman walking toward me at a fast pace. There was no doubt that she was walking for the exercise, but I couldn't help noticing her clutching a doughnut in each hand as she puffed by me. I found this very odd, so I turned around and followed her for about half a mile. She never did eat the doughnuts, but I chuckle to this day when I remember the earnest look on her face and the apparent lack of awareness of how odd this must appear. The doughnuts may have been her reward at the half-way point; maybe she never did eat them. She reminded me of all the people I've known who have salad, a baked potato, and diet coke for lunch, but who also add high fat salad dressings to the salad, pile melted cheese, butter or sour cream onto the baked potato, and finish off with a little piece of pecan pie.

One of the most innovative uses of humor I've seen came up in a junior high school basketball game recently. The evening sports news showed highlights of a game that was tied with about 3 seconds to go. One of the teams had the ball out of bounds under its own net. Just before the ball was thrown in, one of the players on the in-bounding team got down on his hands and knees and started barking like a dog. The other team was momentarily distracted, and another offensive player took the pass right under the basket and made an easy shot to win the game. It was hilariously funny and creative. I wrote it down immediately.

"I think I have old-timers disease."
(Remark by an elderly patient, overheard in a hospital.)

The reason for writing things down is not to share them with others later (although this is a good idea), but to reinforce the habit of noticing humor. Even if you only do this for 2–3 weeks, it will be enough to start developing the habit.

Share the Humor You Observe

Sharing the funny things you see with friends, family, and colleagues is another powerful way to build up the habit of noticing humor. If you've recorded several funny incidents in your notebook, choose one to share with others. Make it the one you feel most comfortable with—for whatever reason. Also make sure you found it very funny yourself. Mention it to everyone you come in contact with. By telling the same story over and over again, you'll rapidly improve your ability to make it interesting as you tell it. As soon as you feel like you've mastered that one, start with another one and repeat the same procedure.

> **"***I see humor as food . . . An adequate share of humor and laughter represent an essential part of the diet of the healthy person.***"**
> (Norman Cousins)

You may be uneasy about doing this at first, since many of the funny things that you see just won't be as funny when you describe them to someone else. Situational humor often is of the "You-had-to-be-there" type. It's impossible to recapture everything that happened, and you certainly can't recapture the mood and other intangibles that combined to make the situation really funny. No matter how well you tell the story of what happened, it may just leave people looking at you with a puzzled look, saying "Oh, I see." Don't be discouraged if this happens to you. Remember that your goal here is not to become skilled at making other people laugh. The goal is to become more adept at observing things that **you** find funny, because this helps sustain your own health and well being. As you get better at spotting your own humor, you'll also get better at deciding which incidents will and will not be funny to someone else.

A woman explained that she left her parrot in its cage hanging from a nearby tree as she set about mowing the grass in a small cemetery. At a point at which she was some distance from the cage, an elderly woman walked over to one of the recent graves. As she kneeled there, holding flowers and lost in

her own grief, she was startled to hear a nearby voice saying, "Helloo-oo." She looked around and found no one, and yet there it was again: "Helloo-ooo." She glanced around again—more frantically this time—and had an uneasy look as she realized she was alone. When she spotted the parrot, she broke out in uncontrollable laughter.[1]

This is a good example of humor that had to be much funnier to both the elderly woman and the grass mower (who eventually came over and heard from the visitor what had just happened). While the story is funny, because we can picture the frightened woman's reaction, it had to be funnier if you were there. It would be very difficult to capture in words everything that made her burst out laughing.

The best way to make progress in describing funny incidents is to do so with a partner who is also working on the 8-Step Program. Giving each other feedback about whether the incident was funny as described, and about what was missing in the telling of the story, will speed up your progress in learning what's crucial to the story and what's not. You want to get the key points in, without dragging them out. If you don't have a partner going through the program with you, find a friend or family member with whom you can practice sharing funny observations. Make sure you're comfortable enough with this person to not be embarrassed if the story backfires.

Pretend You're Allan Funt

Steve Allen once said that "Nothing is funnier than the unintended humor of reality." One of the most popular programs in television history was based on this very idea. Allan Funt's *Candid Camera* captured viewers of all ages—people who loved to see the range of funny ways in which people react in unusual situations. Many other countries now have their own version of *Candid Camera*, supporting the idea that reactions to the unexpected is a universal source of humor.

One of my favorite *Candid Camera* episodes involves a car that was specially constructed to allow it to separate in the middle without collapsing. At one point, the front half of the car simply drives away, leaving the back half behind. Thinking about people's startled reactions of disbelief continues to make me chuckle 30 years later. I'll also never forget the "Talking mailbox" episode, in which a microphone/speaker system installed in a mailbox enabled the mailbox to engage puzzled letter-depositors in conversation. (This was a much more startling event in 1960 than it would be today.)

> **"***Life literally abounds in comedy, if you just look around you.***"**
> (Mel Brooks)

One of the best ways to develop this aspect of your sense of humor is to pretend that you're producing your own *Candid Camera* program. The only difference is that you won't be setting up the situations, as Allan Funt did. Your job is just to be on the lookout for unexpected situations and watch people's reactions (including your own) to them. Learn to relish the surprise and puzzlement that people show. You may choose to have a separate *Candid Camera* section of your notebook in which you jot down notes about funny reactions to everyday events.

Remember that Your View of What's Funny Is Just as Valid as the Next Person's

How often have you found yourself laughing at a joke or incident, while others nearby react with indifference? Did you find yourself feeling ill at ease? Or maybe you've found yourself thinking, "What's wrong with him? That's not funny!" In the 1970s, the hard-driving, hostile humor of comedian Don Rickles made just as many people angry as it left howling with laughter. We all have our sensitive zones which keep us from laughing at things others find funny.

A common sensitive zone concerns funerals. Have you ever had the urge to laugh at a funeral? If you have, you probably also tried to resist it—or got stern looks from others if the laughter leaked out. In a recent letter to "Dear Abby," a man wrote that he was an altar boy at a funeral as a child, and was holding an incense burner as people filed by the coffin. A mourner who was a heavy breather walked in front of him. His nose whistled every time he exhaled. After about 10 whistles, he couldn't take it any more, and his body shook with laughter—rattling a chain on the incense burner with each laugh. The nuns kicked him out of the group of altar boys, but he laughs at the incident to this day.

At another funeral, an elderly woman was attending the military funeral being held for her 97-year-old husband. The unexpected shots which were fired as part of the ceremony so startled the woman that she fell out of the folding chair she was sitting in. At that point, one of the small children present said, "Gee . . . they shot grandma!" How could anyone resist laughing at this—even at a funeral?

People who work in disasters and other emergency situations laugh at things that you would find horrifying (see Chapter 2). They're generally careful not to tell others about the things they laugh at, since they know that anyone who lacks their experiences with death and dying couldn't possibly relate to their macabre humor. But your inability to see the humor of the situation doesn't make it any less valid as humor for them.

Remember, then, that humor—like beauty—is in the eye of the beholder. It's not written down in tablets of stone somewhere that "This is funny! Thou shalt laugh at this! Thou shalt not laugh at that!" There is no right or wrong when it comes to what's funny. It doesn't matter if no one else finds it funny. They also will be laughing at things you don't laugh at. Your sense of humor is just as valid as the next person's. To become more comfortable at finding humor where others don't, start thinking of yourself as simply being more skilled than others at lightening up and seeing the humor life offers.

What Are You Looking For?

Pay special attention to things that are unusual, incongruous, bizarre, absurd, or simply unexpected. Look for them at work and at home, in your relationships and in casual acquaintances, when traveling or in the midst of your daily routine. Also look for:

Coincidences

Develop the habit of looking for odd coincidences that occur. We all have coincidences that occur in our lives. The phone rings as soon as you sit down on the toilet. Or it rings the moment you get outside and lock your door. You're waiting and waiting for the bus, and it's nowhere in sight. So you duck into a store to get a newspaper, and return just in time to catch sight of the rear of the bus leaving the bus stop. You're in heavy traffic on the freeway, and you notice that the other two lanes have been moving faster than yours for several minutes. The moment you force your way into that lane, it slows down and the lane you just left speeds up.

You take the shortest line at the check out, but one customer in front of you writes a check that has to be cleared by the manager, and the other doesn't have enough cash to cover everything he bought . . . and they have products that aren't recognized by the bar scanner . . . and the check-out person runs out of quarters . . . and you notice that you would have been out five minutes ago, had you gotten into the long line.

You go to your favorite restaurant and arrive at the door at the same time as another couple. You hold the door open for them to enter first. That couple orders the last of your favorite entre.

If you've made progress in Steps 1–4, you'll welcome these coincidences with a grin and a chuckle at the way the world works. Murphy's Law states that "If anything can go wrong, it will go wrong." Create your own variation of this law: "The improbable always happens." Instead of getting annoyed at coincidences, make a game of them, and be on the lookout for as many as you can find each day. Have an ongoing duel with friends and colleagues to see who can come up with the most unlikely occurrence of the day. Maybe your luggage came off the plane first (I'll bet it has never happened to you). Maybe you walked up to a Coke machine and found several quarters sitting in the coin return. Be sure to note the positive coincidences, as well as the negative ones.

Irony

Irony is a special kind of coincidence. It is not always easy to see, but learning to appreciate it—and to find a light side of it—can help you cope with unwanted outcomes. We call an event ironic when some aspect of it is just the opposite of what was expected, usually through some quirk of timing. Let's say that you win a week's free vacation in Cozumel, Mexico. But the day before you are to arrive, a hurricane sweeps in and wipes out your hotel and all the main tourist areas. You finally buy your wife an expensive set of clip-on ear rings, and give them to her on the very day she finally gets around to having her ears pierced. You finally get the raise you've been waiting for, but your rent, health insurance, and auto insurance go up at the same time. Or you see a newspaper headline indicating that a fire boat (used to extinguish fires) caught fire and was destroyed.

Irony doesn't have to make you laugh to be appreciated. Before becoming a professional speaker, I had an academic career doing research on humor. I grew up watching Soupy Sales get hit with cream pies, and had always wanted to throw a pie at someone. My opportunity came at the opening ceremony of the Second International Conference on Humor and Laughter, held in Los Angeles in 1979. The organizer of the conference was just finishing his opening speech following a dinner which got the conference started. A fellow researcher (Jeffrey Goldstein) and I had made arrangements with the hotel manager to provide us with a couple of cream pies. As the talk wound down, we headed toward the podium, walking by the 500 people present—armed with one pie each behind our backs. The speaker had a nervous, puzzled look as we got closer, and his eyes doubled in size as we raised our pies and let him have it.

184

The audience was reeling with laughter, thinking that this had all been planned as part of the show. But my own reaction startled me. After eagerly anticipating the pie throw all evening—and after years of waiting—what I experienced was totally incompatible with humor. Just as I released the pie, it felt hostile! My playfulness completely disappeared. It felt like an attack (the speaker was not in on the game). To this day, I have never thrown another pie. I have been hit with them, however, and that's much more fun—at least when you expect it. I found it very ironic that something I had long looked forward to doing was anything but fun.

Rigidity of Behavior

We're all creatures of habit. Many people adopt particular ways of doing things, and get so comfortable with them that they continue with those ways, even when another approach obviously makes more sense. Last fall, as I was heading into my local library, I noticed a man with a portable leaf blower blowing the leaves off the walkway in front of the library. There were several circular benches surrounding trees where he was working, and he was having trouble getting the leaves blown out from under these benches. For some reason, the leaves were clinging to the ground. I watched in amazement as he spent 10 minutes going from one side to the other, blowing at them from all directions. The funny part to me was that if he had simply used the rake at his side, he easily could have removed the resistant leaves in 15 seconds.

Some behavior isn't really rigid, but still is funny just because some people insist on doing things one way, while others insist on the opposite way. I lived in Lubbock, Texas for 8 years, and often ate in a nearby cafeteria. The same woman worked in the meat section throughout this period. I would often go in and ask for the "salmon," pronouncing the word as if there were no "l." She would always repeat the word saying the "l," and this went on for years. We each persisted in trying to correct the other's error, without ever raising the question of how the word should be pronounced. Sometimes I would stretch it out and say "saaaamon," but she always stuck the "l" in at the first opportunity. I don't know who was being most rigid here, but I always found the salmon game amusing.

If you put both socks on before putting your shoes on, it can strike you as funny to see someone else put the left sock and left shoe on, followed by the right sock and right shoe. I still chuckle when I see people put on a sweater by putting their head through first, and then sticking their arms through. Spoons should be stored in the drawer with the handles to the right, not the left. Tooth paste should be squeezed neatly from the end, not squished out from the middle. What couple has not gone through the routine of where the toilet seat should be left when not in use?

Continue Looking for Unintended Verbal Humor

While working on Step 5, do not stop looking for verbal humor—especially where you know it's not intended as a joke. This will support your skills at spotting situational humor. Two doctors sharing an office in Mississippi have the names "Dr. Drinkwater" and "Dr. Wetmore." Anyone with a well developed sense of humor can't help but grin at this coincidence.

People often butcher the English language in ways that are very funny. The following quotes were taken from insurance forms, and eventually were published in the *Toronto Sun*, July 26, 1977.

> **"I was thrown from my car as it left the road. I was later found in a ditch by some stray cows."**
>
> **"The pedestrian had no idea which direction to run, so I ran over him."**
>
> **"I was sure the old fellow would never make it to the other side of the road when I struck him."**
>
> **"An invisible car came out of nowhere, struck my car, and vanished."**
>
> **"I was on my way to the doctor with rear end trouble when my universal joint gave way, causing me to have an accident."**
>
> **"A pedestrian hit me and went under my car."**
>
> **"A truck backed through my windshield into my wife's face."**
>
> **"Coming home, I drove into the wrong house and collided with a tree I do not have."**
>
> **"I collided with a stationary truck coming the other way."**

Sensitizing yourself to the humor in people's misuse of language will serve you well when you're under stress, so practice finding these language distortions when you're not under stress. Nurses often can find humor right in patients' medical charts. The following statements were taken directly from patients' medical records.

> **"Patient suffers from headaches while menstruating from the top of her head."**
>
> **"Patient referred to hospital by private physician with green stools."**
>
> **"Patient complains of abdominal cramps, with BMs on one hand, and constipation on the other."**

> "Patient says he urinates around the clock every two hours."
>
> "R$_X$: Mycostatin vaginal suppositories #24. Insert daily until exhausted."
>
> "Discharge status: Alive, but without permission."
>
> "Patient says she is suffering from shortness of breasts."

And don't stop looking for humor when you go to church on Sunday. The following announcements were actually printed in church bulletins.

> "The ladies of the church have cast off clothing of every kind, and they may be seen in the church basement on Friday afternoon."
>
> "On Sunday, a special collection will be taken to defray the expense of the carpet. All those wishing to do something on the carpet, please come forward and get a piece of paper."
>
> "This being Easter Sunday, we will ask Mrs. Johnson to come forward and lay an egg on the altar."
>
> "Thursday, at 5:00 p.m., there will be a meeting of the Little Mothers Club. All wishing to become Little Mothers will please meet the minister in his study."
>
> "Wednesday, the Ladies Literary Society will meet. Mrs. Thomas will sing, 'Put me in my little bed,' accompanied by the pastor."
>
> "For those of you who have small children and don't know it, we have a nursery downstairs."
>
> "A harvest feast will be held in the church October 28. A traditional New England boiled sinner will be served."
>
> "Jamie Smith was baptized last Sunday. Spongers are Marion and Chuck Graves."

Young children's everyday conversations provide one of the best sources of unintentional verbal humor. If you spend much time around children, you might hear gems like these:

> **A little boy and girl were getting a bath at the same time. The girl says, "Can I touch it?" The boy answers, "No, 'cause you broke yours."**
>
> **A mother trying to save money on the bus (children have to pay if they're over five) hurries her daughter past the driver, but he says, "Just a minute little girl, how old are you?" "Four and a half," says the girl. "And when will you be five?" "Just as soon as I get off this bus."**

Finally, keep looking for humor in signs, ads and newspaper headlines, as suggested in Step 4. You might be lucky enough to catch gems like the following:

> **"Dog for sale. Eats anything. Especially fond of children."**
>
> **"Bras half off."**
>
> **"Braille dictionary for sale. Must see to appreciate,"**
>
> **"Eat here. Get gas."**
>
> **"We skid you not."** (In an ad for tires.)
>
> **"A recent report indicated that some college graduates cannot even read or right."** (Editorial.)
>
> **"Quality dry Cleaners. 25 years on the same spot."** (Sign in front of a dry cleaners business.)
>
> **"If you're at death's door, let our doctors pull you through."** (Sign in front of hospital.)

Continue looking for humor in television, radio, and print advertising. Advertising agencies know that humor is very effective in getting and holding attention, so this provides a regular opportunity to maintain your focus on finding humor. Discuss with your friends which TV ads are and are not funny—and why. If you spend much time watching television, this will give you a daily basis for finding and thinking about humor.

The New York Racing Association faced the problem of how to get rid of 250 thousand cubic yards of thoroughbred manure. It ran an ad in the *New York Times* saying, "Our horses leave a lot to be desired. If you're a large scale manure user, call . . ." As a result of the ad, they wound up being mentioned all over the country in newspapers, magazines, and even on talk shows. A follow-up article four months later indicated that while they had been paying a lot of money to get rid of the stuff, they now couldn't get enough manure to keep up with the sales demand.

A brief article reprinted from a midwestern newspaper had the following headline: "Cows let chips fall where they may." The senior class of a small-town high school sponsored a game of "cow bingo" to raise funds for an all-night graduation party. A large field was divided into a grid pattern, and cows were let loose on the field, letting cow chips fall where they may. Numerous prizes were offered to the winners of the four-hour contest. While this is not a case of humor in the usual sense, I find it wonderfully funny. Be sure that you also keep an eye out for off-beat things that you think are funny—even if no one agrees with you.

> **"** *The most completely lost of all days is the one on which we haven't laughed.* **"**
> (French proverb)

Humor Log Exercises

On Seeing the Funny Side of Life

1. What does it mean to cultivate a humorous perspective on life?
2. How do humorists view the world? What do they notice that others do not notice? How do anger, anxiety, or depression keep you from noticing these things?
3. Look around the room and find five things that are blue (or have any other quality which you name). These things were in the room all the time, but you never noticed them. How does the same thing occur with humor?
4. Do you agree or disagree with the view that humor is really a form of intellectual play, or play with ideas? Elaborate.
5. Why is it that when you describe to someone else a funny experience you've had, it's generally not as funny to them as it was to you? What does the phrase "you had to be there" mean?
6. Will cultivating a mind-set to laugh at the absurdities of life lead you to give up trying to change conditions in your own life that need to be changed? Will it cause you to hide from problems instead of dealing with them? Why (not)?
7. The Homeplay asks you to record in your Humor Log the funny things you notice while working on Step 5. How will the act of writing them down help develop this part of your sense of humor?

189

Humor and Creativity

Learning to think more creatively helps open your eyes to humor that you've been missing all along. These exercises help stimulate your own creative abilities as they apply to humor.

1. Practice letting your imagination go in an "absurd creativity exercise." Pick any object and record as many absurd, silly, nonsensical, and impossible ways you can think of to use the object. Don't judge them as good or bad, and don't worry about whether they're funny. Just come up with as many uses as you can, no matter how far-fetched they seem. In fact, the more absurd, the better. Do this with several different objects.

2. Be creative in thinking of other ways to practice your absurd/nonsense creativity abilities. For example, think of as many ways as you can in which life would be different if you had a third arm. Where would it be placed? How would it change your life? How would life be different if you could see though objects? If you walked on your hands, instead of your feet?

3. Another way to work on your humorous creativity is to write down a list of ridiculous images. Include anything at all that comes to mind. The only requirement is that these things never occur together. Don't worry about how bizarre they are. Everything is fair game for this exercise. As I'm writing this, the following have popped into mind.

     An octopus doing the twist (have I seen too many "Far Side" cartoons?)
     A pencil sharpener in a "cow pie"
     A computer with warts
     A bathtub full of spam
     A pickup loaded with giraffes
     A lemon pie threatening a water buffalo
     A telephone massaging a duck

This exercise may or may not produce ideas which make others laugh. They may not even make you laugh. I forced myself to write the above six items without stopping my typing. Doing the same thing yourself will build up your facility of bringing nonsensical ideas together. Later, you will learn to screen out the ones which are and are not funny.

Current Ability to Find Humor in Everyday Life

1. How often do you find humor in everyday life (e.g., several times a day, once a day/week/month)?
2. Where are you most likely to notice humor (at work, parties, home, etc.? Why do you find more humor there than in other situations?
3. Who are you most likely to be with when you find things to laugh at? Why does this person help see the funny side of life?
4. What's the funniest thing that has happened to you at work?
5. Think about the day-to-day routines and operations associated with your present job. Find at least two aspects of these routines which are really pretty absurd or ridiculous, now that you think about it. Also write down why they're absurd.

6. What's the funniest thing that has happened on any prior job?

7. What's the funniest thing that has happened to you in your marriage, or in any other intimate relationship?

8. What funny things have you noticed about the differences in the way men and women react or do things?

9. What impact does your daily mood or stress have on your tendency to notice the funny side of situations and events?

10. What are the conditions under which you are most and least likely to appreciate the humor around you?

11. What would it take to develop the habit of noticing the light side of things that happen in your life every day?

12. If you were to pick out one experience in your life which would be a good candidate for "Candid Camera," what would it be?

13. If you generally do not notice funny things in your life, why do you think that is?

14. Can you learn to perceive humor in your everyday life if you've never been good at it before? What kind of changes do you need to make in order to get better at this?

Early Development and Influences

1. How good were you at spotting funny incidents during your childhood? Adolescence?

2. What's the funniest thing you can remember happening during your childhood? Adolescence?

3. How good were your mother and father at finding humor in everyday life as you were growing up?

4. Who were the best models you had for learning how to laugh at life (include friends, teachers, and relatives, as well as your parents)? Answer separately for childhood and adolescence.

5. Did your parents (or anyone else) ever talk to you about the importance of learning to see the "light side" of life when you were growing up? If so, what did they say?

6. What influence did television (or radio) have on your sense of humor when you were growing up?

7. Overall, what has had the greatest impact on your current ability to notice the light side of everyday situations?

8. If you were to give advice to other parents about the value of helping their children learn to find humor in the things that happen in everyday life, what would it be? Why would you give this advice?

GROUP SESSION

Opening Fun Activity

Discussion of Homeplay for Step 4

(General suggestion: To further develop your skills at creating spontaneous verbal humor, look for ambiguous words in your discussion throughout this session. Interrupt—within limits—and point them out as they occur. This will help everyone in the group see that the potential for puns and other verbal humor is always present.)

Discuss the following with a partner. Then open it up for a group discussion.

1. Bring in examples of word play you noticed in newspapers and on signs, and share them.
2. How successful were you at noticing ambiguity in conversations?
3. How well did you do at generating puns and other verbal humor?
4. Did you do the exercise in "multiple meanings" every day? Did it help you start thinking in terms of double meanings?
5. Share a couple of daffynitions that you created.
6. As you worked on Step 5, how difficult was it to maintain the gains you made during Steps 1-4?
7. Discuss any other aspect of your efforts to improve your verbal sense of humor that you think would be of interest to the group.

Finding Humor in Everyday Life

1. Draw from any of the issues raised in Step 5 as a starting point for discussion. Each group member should also select one or two suggestions from the Humor Log Exercises for detailed discussion within the group. Make a special effort to try the "Absurd Creativity Exercise," using 3 or 4 people per group. Also try the "Ridiculous Images" exercise within the group.
2. Remember to stay in touch with your telephone partners.

HOME PLAY

1. Assume that there's a general conspiracy among everyone you come in contact with to create situations and events to make you laugh. Like beauty, humor is in the eye of the beholder. But if you don't look for it, you won't find it. Go out expecting to find something funny, even in commonplace situations. Ask yourself, "What's funny here?" Or, "What could be funny here?"

   What are you looking for? Anything incongruous, absurd, ironic, or that you find funny for any reason. Watch what people do and say. Look at how they handle unexpected circumstances.

2. Keep your notebook with you at all times. Write funny things down as you see them. Find something to record every day. Look for things at work, at home, in the supermarket, while driving—everywhere you go, and in everything you do. Update the notebook daily (in the evening, during the day at meals, on breaks, or whenever you have a spare moment).

3. Maintain a playful frame of mind. This will help you see humor in situations that arise.

4. Continue doing the things you did for Step 4. This will help you sustain a playful frame of mind and set you up to find more unexpected incidents funny.

5. Put up reminders at home, at the office, and in your car to look for humor. Keep a pair of "Groucho glasses" or other props handy as a reminder to be on the lookout for humor.

6. To help sensitize yourself to seeing funny things, change your daily routines. Brush your teeth with the other hand. Put your clothes on in a different order. Wave to people you don't know, etc. Breaking up old patterns of actions helps break up old patterns of thinking, and it will lead you to become more observant of unusual things.

7. Ask friends or colleagues what funny things they have observed or had happen to them lately. You'll find that they often see humor that passes you by. This will broaden your own sense of humor by making you aware of funny incidents that you've never noticed before.

8. Specifically ask friends and colleagues about what they find absurd, ridiculous, or bizarre about the policies, rules, and expectations associated with their job, about politics, or any other aspect of life.

9. Make it a point to share the humor you observe with your friends, family, and coworkers. This will strengthen the habit of finding humor.

10. When watching television sit coms, relate funny situations that arise to incidents in your own life. Has anything like this ever happened to you?

11. When looking for humor, don't intellectualize it; and don't try to decide, "Is this really funny?" Trust your instincts. It will either be funny or it won't.

12. Don't compare what you find funny to what others find funny. If you find it funny, it's funny.

13. If you're going through the 8-Step Program with a group, be prepared to share at the next meeting a funny incident you observed during the week.

STEP 6
Take Yourself Lightly
Laugh at Yourself

❝ *So many tangles in life are ultimately hopeless that we have no appropriate sword other than laughter. I venture to say that no person is in good health unless he can laugh at himself.* ❞
(Gordon W. Allport)

❝ *What is a sense of humor? . . . a residing feeling of one's own absurdity. It is the ability to understand a joke—and that the joke is oneself.* ❞
(Clifton Fadiman)

Eleanor Roosevelt once said that "You don't grow up until you have your first good laugh at yourself." The ability to laugh at your own flaws, weaknesses, and blunders has long been recognized as a sign of maturity. And yet it is one of the most difficult aspects of your sense of humor to develop. That is why it is not introduced here until you have progressed in developing other aspects of your sense of humor. You will need the foundation provided by Steps 1–5 if your sense of humor generally disappears when you're the butt of the joke. But you'll be richly rewarded by your efforts at Step 6. You may find that learning to laugh at yourself is just as important as the money you're spending on a therapist.

What Prevents You From Laughing at Yourself?

We all slip on psychological banana peels from time to time. At some point in your life, you've committed a faux pas that triggered immediate laughter in everyone around you; and yet you found nothing to laugh at. Your embarrassment or upset made it impossible to adopt the playful attitude required to see the light side of an awkward moment. I discovered this in the 11th grade. We were about to have an exam in my physics class, taught by the dreaded "Colonel Burns." A small teacher's office was located between our classroom and the next classroom, and a friend of mine noticed that the exams were just sitting on top of the desk—with the Colonel nowhere in sight.

We all glanced at each other, eyebrows raised. With hardly a word spoken, we knew what we had to do, even though the exam would start in five minutes. For reasons that are no longer clear to me, I was nominated to go in and scan the test, as "lookouts" were set up at each door to signal the teacher's return. Somehow I never heard the shouted whispers of "he's coming!" I suddenly found myself looking up at the Colonel with a test in my hand. After recovering from my initial startle, I found myself saying, "I saw these tests sitting on the desk, so I thought I'd better hide them until you got back; some of these guys will do anything to cheat."

Half the room started snorting and grunting, the way you do when you're trying to swallow your laughter. Even the Colonel could not suppress a rare half-grin. It was only years later, upon remembering this incident, that I really saw the absurdity of what I said, and could laugh at it myself. I had not intended to be funny; the words just happened to come out that way. I was so embarrassed and humiliated that my sense of humor completely abandoned me.

If you think of the blunders you've made, you'll find that what keeps you from seeing a funny side of them at the moment is your own emotional reaction. You get embarrassed, angry, anxious, or depressed about what happened, and your sense of humor is the victim of these emotions. If the same thing were to happen to someone else, you'd have a good chuckle at it, because you wouldn't be trapped in your own embarrassment or annoyance.

Your ultimate goal should be to learn to laugh in the midst of the embarrassing situation—or soon afterwards. Right now, you probably only see the humor of it later, as the embarrassment fades. But this is a good starting point, since some people never see the funny side of blunders and embarrassing incidents—even years later. With some effort, you will learn to see the funny side of the situation closer and closer to the incident itself.

A couple of years ago, my parents were taking me to the Daytona Beach airport, following a Christmas visit with them. My father, in his early 80s at the time, sometimes got the urge to go the bathroom, and couldn't afford to waste time getting there when the urge came. We were only three miles from the airport when he said, "I think you'd better find a gas station." I found one a mile down the road, and he hustled into the bathroom—and almost made it. I happened to have a pair of bermuda shorts with me, and handed them to him through the door. Since the men's room was located inside, dad had no choice but to walk by the attendant to get back to the car. You can imagine his embarrassment at having to walk by this guy who just stared as an 80-year-old man who walked in wearing long green pants came out wearing tan bermuda shorts, looking like he hadn't been in the sun in 10 years. I thought the man's puzzled reaction was very funny. Dad thought it was anything but funny—until a few weeks later, when it became a great story about the perils of growing old.

When you get to the point that you can laugh at your blunders, you leave them behind you. Why carry this emotional baggage around with you for months—or longer? The past is past, and there's nothing you can do about it. But you can do something to prevent your memory of it from haunting you, simply by seeing the light side of it. This new humorous vantage point puts the incident in its proper perspective and lets you get on with life.

We Take Ourselves Too Seriously!

Oscar Wilde offered a keen insight about how to live your life when he said, "Life is too important to be taken seriously." In this paradoxical statement, he did not mean that life doesn't matter. He didn't mean that you shouldn't keep your promises, have integrity, or meet your responsibilities. I believe he meant that if you are serious about everything, the quality of your life suffers. Think about the people you work with who are always serious. Do they look like they enjoy life? Probably not. They no doubt did when they were kids, as we all did, but being serious all the time robs them of whatever joy and aliveness they once had. It slowly erodes the capacity to have fun. It also sets them up for extra stress in their life. If you consider yourself a generally serious person, this should give you all the incentive you need to become more playful. If you view life as precious, you have every reason to overcome Terminal Seriousness. Remember, TS is the #1 symptom of Acquired Amusement Deficiency Syndrome.

> ❝ *What is funny about us is precisely that we take ourselves too seriously.* ❞
> (Reinhold Neibuhr)

Each of us has sensitive areas where it's difficult to lighten up about ourselves. In your case, maybe it's a physical feature. You don't like the fact that you're too skinny, fat, tall, or short, or that you have a bald spot, dark spots under your eyes, etc. You can joke about most things, but not that! Or maybe you feel clumsy or uneducated, or annoyed by your unassertive style. Perhaps your accent embarrasses you. You will confront these no-laugh zones head-on in Step 6. You will experience a sense of exhilaration and liberation as you become more comfortable with joking about the things that used to simply annoy or embarrass you.

A woman who had been a nun found any kind of discussion related to sexual issues terribly embarrassing. She helped ease herself out of this by playfully telling her friends, "You know, sex is really a lot like praying . . . Oh God! Oh God!"

As you get better at poking fun at yourself, you will learn to use it to your advantage. It was noted earlier that President Reagan's advanced age was a major issue when he ran for reelection. Many felt that he was simply too old for the job. He diffused the issue by poking fun at his age. For example, at one point in the campaign he said, "Well Andrew Jackson left the White House at the age of 75, and he was still quite vigorous. I know, because he told me."

Former President Jimmy Carter showed his lighter side on the *Late Show* with David Letterman September 28, 1993 when Letterman asked him what he thought about the appropriateness of former President Reagan accepting $2 million from Japan for a talk soon after leaving the Presidency. Carter hesitated a bit, as if he felt in an awkward position. My own impression was that he disapproved of the action. But he said he wasn't a judge and didn't like to comment on the behavior of other presidents, "But if any of you know of another opportunity for $2 million . . ." The audience laughed, and the joking remark helped him ease his way out of a potentially embarrassing situation. While we generally think of President Carter as a serious person, he clearly has access to playfulness when he needs it.

What Does it Mean to Take Yourself Lightly?

Do you know why angels can fly?
Because they take themselves so lightly.

Have you ever thought about what it means to take yourself lightly? It does not mean:

1. You have a low opinion of yourself.
2. You're putting yourself down.
3. You're incompetent, unprofessional, immature, or irresponsible.
4. You're never serious.

You can take yourself lightly and still hold yourself in high esteem, command respect, and be competent. In fact, the ability to laugh at yourself generally enhances others' perception of these qualities within you—as long as you don't overdo it! If you direct all your humor at yourself, it will work against you, rather than for you. People will begin to see you as unsure of yourself, and as having a poor self-image. And this may lead them to doubt your competence. The key is to show that you are capable of laughing at yourself, not to do it all the time.

Some people who are good at poking fun at themselves never seem to get serious about anything. This is obviously not your goal in Step 6. You want to achieve a good balance between being serious and being playful. You want to be serious when the situation calls for it, but be capable of lightening up and laughing at yourself when the opportunity presents itself.

Taking yourself lightly does mean:

1. Recognizing that you are not the center of the universe.

   In one sense, of course, you are the center of the universe—**your** universe. But in the broader scheme of things, you are a minor speck. Acknowledging this helps many people lighten up about themselves and about minor problems.
   When you make a mistake or do something embarrassing, the rest of the world generally doesn't care. So don't brood about it; just accept it for what it is and go on.

2. Recognizing that your own attitude or perspective is just one among many that are possible.

   This is difficult for many people. You have to "step out of yourself" to really appreciate other perspectives. For example, going to a foreign country helps you see your own country in a new light; you begin to realize that each culture develops its own way of making sense out of the world, and that no single one is more "right" than another. The same applies to different religions.
   In the same fashion, you can broaden your perspective on ways of reacting to life's embarrassing moments, or to some hated personal flaw, by observing how other people adapt to them. Watching other people find a light side of embarrassing moments, or otherwise poke fun at themselves, is very illuminating. It shows you

that you don't have to punish yourself for your blunders; you can find a way to laugh at them and move on.

3. Refusing to carry around a sense of heaviness (e.g., due to anger, anxiety, depression, or embarrassment) when you make a mistake or blunder.

   We have already seen that humor and laughter help eliminate these negative feelings in a direct way by providing a cathartic release of pent-up feelings. But learning to take yourself lightly also makes these feelings less likely to occur. It insulates you from them by substituting a more positive, upbeat mood that simply is incompatible with their occurrence. You can't be heavy when you're having a good laugh.

4. Seeing the funny side of your own circumstance or behavior.

   When you're good at laughing at yourself, it's just as easy to see the humor of the situation when you commit a blunder as when someone else does. Your ego isn't threatened, so you're free to laugh at the situation itself—even though your own behavior caused the situation to occur. And remember, you're laughing at things you do and that happen to you, not at who you are.

Mastery and Laughing at Yourself

Put-down humor was very popular in the 1970s and 1980s. But as the country became more sensitized to ethnic, racial, and gender differences, the offensive quality of such humor received more attention. This led to a sharp reduction in mass media humor disparaging racial, ethnic, or other groups. And yet, most of us continue to enjoy humor victimizing groups we don't particularly care for. Democrats still enjoy humor putting down Republicans, and Republicans enjoy humor at the expense of Democrats. Will Rogers was once asked if he was a member of an organized party. His response was, "No, I'm a Democrat."

One of the oldest theories of humor, superiority theory, argues that we enjoy put-down humor because it makes us feel superior to the butt of the joke. This theory argues that we have a basic need to feel superior, and that humor provides an easy and effective way to achieve this feeling. If this is the kind of humor you enjoy the most, remember that it is certain to be divisive in groups where not everyone shares your views.

If humor does make you feel superior to the person or group you laugh at, can it also help you feel superior to your problems if you laugh at them? Step 7 (also see Chapter 2) will demonstrate that joking about problems or stressful situations does help you master them; it creates a feeling of being superior to them, instead of being at their mercy.

Think about laughing at yourself along the same lines. By learning to poke fun at your anxieties, concerns, and self-dislikes, and by finding a light side of mistakes, you elevate yourself above them. You feel superior to them, and in control of them. And this enables you to leave them behind, instead of carrying them around in the form of regrets, upsets, or anxieties. Obviously, this is very adaptive and helps you lead a more stress-free life.

When you can joke about your weaknesses and mistakes, it's a way of admitting that you have them, without letting them hold you down. You develop a kind of upset-free coexistence with them. And once you learn to live with them, you'll find that they simply aren't the problem they used to be. A woman told me that her mother's hand would sometimes tremble to the point that she couldn't hold things in it. When this happened in social situations, she would ease the embarrassment by saying (in the style off former President Reagan), "There you go again."

Part of humor's power to help you cope stems from its ability to leave you at peace with the reality of the situation, regardless of whether it's some quality of yourself or an upsetting event that has occurred. There's real strength in just accepting things as they are—when you can't change them—and letting them be. When they can be changed, humor puts you in a frame of mind more conducive to action by reducing the emotional upset of the moment.

The serenity prayer of Alcoholics Anonymous says,

"God grant me the serenity to accept the things I cannot change, courage to change the things I can, and wisdom to know the difference."

Alcoholics and drug addicts beginning a 12-Step Recovery Program find very little to laugh at in the early stages of recovery. One of the earliest goals of recovery programs is to get the person to simply admit and accept that s/he is an alcoholic or addict. Once this is achieved, it's easier to see humor in some of the crazy things they used to think and do. For example, one recovering alcoholic told me that he never considered it strange to walk across an 8-lane expressway to take a shorter route to get to a liquor store. He now laughs at the crazy things he used to do to get alcohol, or while drunk. For example, he can now see the humor is the claim he often used to make that "someone spilled a drink on me" whenever someone noticed the smell of alcohol around him.

When you laugh at a personal blunder, an oddity of your physical appearance, or a disability you have, you also put those around you at ease. Others initially may feel embarrassed or awkward, but once they see that you can joke about it, they relax. They feel more at ease because they can see that you're at ease about it. I have a friend who is blind and unmarried. Four years ago, he had a T-shirt made up with the following message on the back: "For a real blind date, call . . ." It eliminated the discomfort others often felt around him, got him some laughs—and some dates!

My family moved out of Detroit onto a farm when I was eight years old. My only friend within miles stuttered. He was embarrassed by this for years, and people who didn't know him well felt ill at ease when he stuttered. He eventually learned to put people at ease by saying, "Is there an echo here?"

The key to learning to laugh at yourself sounds very simple; just accept what is—especially things that are unchangeable. As you take a few steps toward self-acceptance, it gets easier to lighten up about non-sensitive areas. But you still won't find anything funny when your sensitive zones are involved. Rest assured, though, that every step you make toward laughing at minor embarrassments and non-sensitive areas takes you a step closer to laughing at your sensitive zones. You'll know you're making progress when you feel the enlivening sense of liberation that occurs when you can laugh freely at yourself.

W. Mitchell is a well known professional speaker whose main message is, "It's not what happens to you; it's what you do about it!" Mitchell became a human torch following an accident in which the gasoline from the motorcycle he was riding spilled on him and caught fire. Most of his face was burned off, and his hands were so seriously burned that he was left with stubs where his fingers and thumbs used to be. He describes the first point at which he was able to laugh at himself after the accident as a turning point in his life. A few weeks after the accident, a plastic surgeon came by his hospital room and said, "Your face has been burned off by the fire. We're going to have to give you a new one. What did you look like before the fire?"

When Mitchell showed the plastic surgeon his driver's license photo, the doctor looked at it, hesitated, and then took another long look. Finally, he shook his head and said, "Well I know we can do better than this!" Mitchell, who had remained immobile during the conversation, because it was too painful to move, could not help but laugh. It was the first time he'd been able to laugh since the fire. Years later, he said that this laughter put his new life circumstances in perspective. It catapulted him out of self-pity and made him realize that "It's not what happens to you; it's what you do about it!" He realized that the fire didn't destroy his life; it simply changed his options of paths to follow. The path he chose was to become a public speaker and use his own life as an example to help others take control of their lives.

It's difficult to laugh at yourself when life deals you a disfigured body, but humor helped Mitchell see that the limitations in his life lasted only as long as he let them. It wasn't fair or just for him to have to cope with losing his face and hands. You may not see it as fair that you have a weight problem, no hair, or such poor vision that you need thick glasses. If it's a condition that's unchangeable, the time comes when you have to face up to the fact that "that's the way it is; now what am I going to do about it?" Your sense of humor helps you get on to living your life with joy and aliveness, even in the midst of the harsh realities that life may have imposed upon you.

Luckily, the link between acceptance and humor is a two-way street. That is, accepting the things you don't like about yourself helps you joke about them. But joking about them also takes you a step closer to complete acceptance. It offers a "back door" approach to living joyfully with your difficult-to-accept qualities.

As you move toward self-acceptance, a curious thing happens. You begin to see the absurdity of the things you used to be so sensitive about. Again, this is real progress. It is a sign that this part of your sense of humor has fully bloomed. When I was a senior in college, I worked in a private treatment center for disturbed children. One afternoon, during nap time, I took a nap myself. I woke up to see one of the kids looking down at my face saying, "Hey, your face is an upside down triangle." I got up, looked in the mirror, and saw that he was right—and I didn't like it!

From that "point" on, my self-image included a pointy chin. I grew a beard a few years later and kept it for 18 years. The day finally came when I had to shave the beard in order to convince myself that I fully accepted my chin as it was, pointy or not. I had always justified my beard by saying that I looked better with it. But I was also hiding an embarrassing part of myself.

I now see the whole thing as very silly, and can laugh at it. But it wasn't funny then. What pointy chins do you have in your own life? Think about how your sensitivities about your body or other aspects of yourself have influenced your life. Some may even have become a driving force in your life. As you learn to lighten up about yourself, the power these sensitive zones hold over your life will gradually diminish.

Is Laughing at Yourself the Same as Putting Yourself Down?

You can poke fun at yourself in a way that is either full of fun, acceptance, and positivity, or that's bitter, rejecting, and negative. It's all in the spirit you bring to it. If it comes out of bitterness and self-dislike, you genuinely put yourself down—and lower your self-esteem in the process. In this case, humor makes no positive contribution to your health and well being.

Some people who laugh at themselves are really putting themselves down or criticizing themselves. There is no lightness, even though they're joking. But others manage to laugh at themselves in a way that is not at all negative—a way that shows that they accept what has happened and are at peace with it. It is this playful acceptance that establishes a healthy foundation for poking fun at yourself.

In 1988, while running for the presidency, Vice President George Bush was describing his partnership with Ronald Reagan over the preceding eight years. He said, "We've had triumphs. We've made mistakes. We've had sex." The audience exploded with laughter, leaving him no time to correct himself and say "setbacks." Having prepared for just such a moment, however, his comeback was, "I feel like the javelin thrower who won the toss and elected to receive." By poking fun at his embarrassing choice of words, he turned a negative into a positive. If anything, the blunder gained him points in the eyes of the television audience, because he showed he was quick on his feet and could handle people laughing at him.

> **❝** *We should be proud of who we are. Then we can laugh at ourselves. Being natural, being yourself goes right to the heart of humor.* **❞**
> (Willard Scott)

> **❝** *There is hope for any man who can look in a mirror and laugh at what he sees.* **❞**
> (Anonymous)

Former Vice President Dan Quayle suffered the great embarrassment of pointing out to a child in a spelling contest that he had forgotten to put the "e" on "potatoe." Given the public image that the vice president had already developed, this was terribly embarrassing. A new rash of Quayle jokes immediately popped up around the country. In one joke, Dan Quayle was asked how to spell "Mississippi." "You can't fool me," said Mr. Quayle, "Do you mean the state or the river?"

A few months later, he capitalized on this blunder in his acceptance speech for the 1992 vice presidential nomination. He said: "Clinton and Gore claim to be moderates. Well, if they're moderates, I'm a world champion speller!" The audience loved it. Was he putting himself down with this comment? Not at all. By joking about his spelling error, he was showing confidence, not self-disdain. He was rising above the error by laughing at it. And this served to improve his image in the eyes of others, not lower it. Even democrats had to grin and acknowledge that this was a smart thing to do.

Quayle continued to poke fun at his spelling skills after President Clinton unveiled his new economic plan in February, 1993: "Now they're calling taxes 'contributions.' And these are the same guys who said I needed a dictionary."

Can You Laugh When You're the Butt of the Joke?

To help assess your own ability to laugh at yourself, think back to situations where you've been the butt of the joke. Did you stiffen up, or feel embarrassed or insulted? If so, you have a lot of work to do on Step 6. Sometimes, of course, people disguise real hostility in making you the butt of their jokes. If you feel that's the case, there's no reason to share their laughter. Most of the time, however, it comes out of good-natured fun. And if you can't laugh when others poke fun at you in the spirit of good times, you'll certainly have trouble poking fun at yourself.

> **"***If you are willing to make yourself the butt of a joke, you become one of the guys, a human being, and people are more willing to listen to what you have to say.***"** (Larry Wilde)

The Jews, more than any other people, have mastered the art of self disparagement. They learned long ago that poking fun at yourself helps you adapt to things that can't really be changed, and invites others to laugh along with you. As you start learning to laugh at yourself, remember that "The not-easily offended shall inherit the mirth."

How to Start Laughing at Yourself

So how do you learn to laugh at yourself, if you've never been good at it? The steps discussed here are presented in a specific order. I've found this order to be the most effective, but if another order works better for you, don't be rigid about sticking to this one. The important thing is to start doing as many of these things as you can. The more you do, the greater and more rapid your progress will be.

Make a List of Things You Don't Like About Yourself

Think about the things you don't like about yourself. What are your sensitive zones? Where do your emotional reactions cause you to completely lose your sense of humor? There are two reasons for making this list. First, you need to be specific in targeting aspects of yourself about which you want to lighten up—areas where you're humor impaired. At this point, however, just make the list. Don't try to laugh at yourself yet.

Secondly, for some people, the mere act of creating the list has a surprising effect. A smile creeps onto their face as the list gets longer and longer. By the time they get to the 10th or 15th thing, they see the absurdity of all the things they don't like about themselves. If you're one of these lucky ones, you'll master this step much more quickly.

Divide the List into "Heavy" and Minor Items, and into Things You Can and Cannot Change

To assure your success at Step 6, slowly ease into poking fun at your self-dislikes. Starting with mildly sensitive areas gradually prepares you for laughing at those "heavy" areas where your sense of humor has always abandoned you in the past.

Separating your list into things that can and cannot be changed helps you take action when change is possible. It also helps you discover that your sense of humor is your best friend when you're stuck with an unchangeable situation, and have to learn to live with it. In the case of my pointy chin, nothing short of plastic surgery was going to change it. It was "pointless" to beat myself up about something that was never going to change. Acknowledging this made it much easier to laugh about it.

Admit Your Weaknesses and Self-Dislikes

" When we admit our schnozzles, instead of defending them, we begin to laugh, and the whole world laughs with us."
(Jimmy Durante)

As Jimmy Durante (a comedian from the 1940s who was known for his big nose) suggests, you begin by simply admitting that you are the way you are. That doesn't mean you like it. You're just stating what's so. Admitting your schnozzles opens the door toward acceptance of them. In some cases, acceptance quickly follows. In others, it takes months.

I felt embarrassed about being skinny during high school, and it kept me from going out for basketball. Several years later, I realized the absurdity of avoiding basketball, just to avoid being seen in the skimpy uniforms. No one cares about your body type if you're good at the game. Once I admitted that I had an image of myself as a skinny person, and that I didn't like this self-image, it opened the door to becoming OK with being thin. My sensitivity about it disappeared, and I could joke about it. This is no different from my discovery that accepting my pointy chin freed me up so that I carried my chin only on my face, and not in my mind.

Share One Item on Your List with Someone Every Day, Starting with Minor Items. Don't Try to Joke About It.

There is real power in sharing your self-dislikes with others. Some of the barriers to self-acceptance quickly drop just by coming out of the closet of self-dislike and announcing to anyone who'll listen that you're skinny, fat, a workaholic, and so forth. That is why meetings of Alcoholics Anonymous always begin with people going around the group saying, "My name is _____, and I'm an alcoholic." They understand the power of publicly admitting something about yourself that's difficult to face up to—and difficult to accept. It helps break down the barriers to overcoming alcoholism.

It also helps to verbalize the way you feel about it. Just speak what's true for you (what's so), and don't worry about what comes afterwards. If you've never experienced what happens when you do this, be sure not to skip this step. You'll see that the more sensitive the area, and the more difficult it is to share, the greater the release you experience from talking about it in public. And the larger the group you share it with, the stronger the effect. But you'll also benefit from sharing it over and over again with one person at a time.

The mere act of admitting to someone else that, for example, you don't like your ears, that you've always been embarrassed by them (because they stick out), starts breaking down the barriers to acceptance of that part of yourself and to lightening up about them. But you don't even have to joke about them at this point; just express how you feel. The ability to joke about them soon will follow. If it worked for Ross Perot, it will work for you.

Begin Sharing Your Blunders, Mistakes, and Embarrassing Experiences

You can work on this while sharing things you don't like about yourself. Start with past embarrassments. The longer ago they happened, the easier they'll be to discuss. You may even find them funny now. You gradually will get better at discussing these incidents soon after they occur.

Start with experiences that are not closely related to your sensitive zones. Then share those that are more difficult to admit. Again, don't worry about whether there's anything funny about it. Just get into the habit of sharing it (e.g., "You won't believe what I did today . . .").

Sometimes, of course, these will be funny in their own right. One day a nurse walked into a patient's room, and found the patient—an older man—in the bathroom, bent over the toilet bowl. He had vomited a tremendous amount, and the toilet bowl was filling up. So she flushed it. The man immediately started shouting something incomprehensible. By the time he repeated it two or three times, she could finally make it out: "My teeth are in there!" Look for the flushed teeth in your own life, and start telling people about them.

Learn a Few Self-Disparaging Jokes

You're now ready to start poking fun at yourself. An easy way to start is to tell self-disparaging jokes related to the whatever you're sensitive about. So be on the lookout for such jokes, and write them down when you hear them. Make it a point to memorize a few. When opportunities arise, tell them to your friends. Any kind of self-put-down joke is a good start, but move quickly to jokes that tap into your own sensitivities. This will help get you used to the feeling of poking fun at yourself and will ease you into coming up with ways of doing so on your own. Be sure to distinguish between doing this in good fun and really putting yourself down. Laughing at yourself elevates your self-esteem; putting yourself down lowers it.

Try learning a few jokes which put down either your profession or some other group you identify with. If you're a lawyer, for example, you might start with this joke:

God and Saint Peter were talking about the problems in heaven. God says, "We're losing money every day. We've got to get things straightened out."

Saint Peter asks, "What should we do?"

God says, "Get a lawyer to handle it."

Saint Peter looks at Him and says, "Now where are we going to find a lawyer up here?"

If you're constantly embarrassing yourself by forgetting things, practice telling the following joke:

A couple who both had Alzheimer Disease was watching TV. A commercial came on and the wife asked her husband if he'd like some ice cream. As she walked out of the room, he said, "You'd better write it down."

"Don't worry," she said, "I can remember that."

Ten minutes later, she came back with scrambled eggs, and her husband said, "I told you you'd forget the toast!"

Be on the lookout for stand-up comedians who specialize in material along these lines. For example, if you get uptight about your own competence, and feel people at work don't respect your skills, you might listen to tapes of Rodney Dangerfield ("I don't get no respect."), and learn some of his lines. Memorize these and start telling them to your friends. It will ease you into coming up with your own ways of laughing at yourself.

Begin Joking About Your Blunders and Things You Don't Like About Yourself

Choose one of the minor items on your list. Put it on the "front burner" for a day, and look for opportunities to poke fun at it. If this is difficult, start by poking fun something that doesn't bother you at all (your hair color, your weight, the fact that you wear glasses, etc.). Then proceed to more sensitive areas when it feels right to do so.

> **"** *To make mistakes is human; to stumble is commonplace; to be able to laugh at yourself is maturity.* **"**   (William Arthur Ward)

During the 1992 presidential race, Ross Perot's ears gave cartoonists a field day. The entire nation roared its approval during one of the presidential debates when Perot spontaneously came up with the line, "I'm all ears." In your case, maybe it's your nose, your double chin, your squeaky laugh, or the way you walk. Be on the lookout for other people's lines that help you poke fun at that part of yourself as you continue to work at coming up with your own.

Additional Helpful Suggestions

There are several other things you can do to support your efforts to learn to laugh at yourself.

206

Recognize That No One Is Perfect

One of the most important insights you can have about yourself is that you're allowed to be imperfect. Every one makes mistakes and has flaws.

> **A speaker says to his audience, "We've all heard the phrase, 'Nobody's perfect.' If there's anyone here who's perfect, just raise your hand, because I'd really like to meet a perfect person."**
>
> **No one raises their hand at first. But then he notices a middle-aged man way in the back waving his hand back and forth. "Great!" says the speaker, "We've finally found a perfect person. Tell me sir, are you really perfect?"**
>
> **"No, no, no," said the man, "I'm raising my hand for my wife's first husband."**

Requiring perfection of yourself on the job, in your relationships, or in developing your sense of humor, sets you up for extra frustration, anger, anxiety, and depression. And that translates into extra stress! You expend incredible energy in connection with your real and imagined weaknesses and blunders. As you carry the tension, anxiety, depression, or anger around, it inevitably starts dragging you down. But as soon as you can say, "Yeah, I blew it!" or "OK, I'm a complete klutz . . . but I'm a lovable Klutz," you feel lighter and act lighter. You'll come closer to "letting go."

This, in turn, gives you even more freedom to laugh at yourself. The comedienne Carol Burnett was once eating in a restaurant when an elderly woman approached and touched Carol's face with her hands. She traced the profile of her face, saying, "I'm sorry, I don't see so good." Carol answered, "Count your blessings. I don't look so good."

Have a Planned Funny Response for Embarrassing Moments

If you have a funny phrase or action ready for your next embarrassing moment, it will help you react in a lighter manner—even if you don't feel like doing so. You've probably already witnessed some of the standard reactions to embarrassing incidents. They include taking a bow (e.g., after you've dropped your food tray), saying, "For my next trick," or "No applause, please." Or you can be more creative with things like, "And now for something completely different" (from Monty Python), "You may think that was an accident, but my department is now doing research on reactions to awkward incidents," or "I'm training for the clumsy olympics." You're sure to be successful with, "I didn't do it . . . and I'll never do it again."

Maybe you'll feel more comfortable imitating the voice of Elmer Fudd, Donald Duck, Bugs Bunny, John Wayne, Woody Allen, or any other famous figure. Try pulling a Ronald Reagan, saying in the Reagan style, "There I go again." This will get a grin from those around you and will shift attention away from the awkwardness of the moment, transforming it into an occasion for mirth.

> **A woman who married a man 20 years younger than herself got tired of the same old embarrassing questions and raised eye brows, so one day she responded with, "Well 20 goes into 40 a lot more than 40 goes into 20."**

If the same embarrassing incident occurs often, make an extra effort to have a light response ready the next time it occurs. If you're always forgetting things, for example, the next time it happens you might use this line: "My memory is really very good; it's just very short."

Hang Around People Who Are Good at Laughing at Themselves

An excellent way to make progress at Step 6 is to think of the people you know who are very good at poking fun at themselves—who don't take themselves seriously all the time. Hang around these people more, and imitate them in any ways that feel comfortable to you. When you see them do something you think would work for you, write it down. Talk to them about how poking fun at themselves makes them feel and why they're good at it, while you aren't.

Exaggerate!

Exaggeration is a classic comedy technique, and it can help you learn to laugh at yourself. Find some way to exaggerate the part of yourself that you're sensitive about, or the mistake you've made. If it's your inability to gain weight, turn to the person next to you when you find yourself in front of a mirror and say, "My God, I'm so thin I disappear when I turn sideways." You might also try, "I'm so skinny I put my bra on backwards yesterday . . . and it fit better!" Or if the problem is being overweight, try, "I'm one of the few people I know who is taller lying down than standing up."

Phyllis Diller, Woody Allen, and Rodney Dangerfield based much of their comic style on exaggeration of their most prominent features. For example, Phyllis Diller once said that she was so ugly that a Peeping Tom asked her to pull her shade down. Rodney Dangerfield's parents were so poor that he had to wear his father's hand-me-downs. He had to unzip his fly every time wanted to blow his nose. Use the material of these and other comedians as a source of ideas for how to exaggerate about yourself.

Consider playing a game of "Poor me!" with yourself or with a friend. Just start naming all the things that are wrong in your life, and exaggerate every one of them to absurd proportions. Try acting depressed when you say them. Let your chin hang low, and let your shoulders droop. Keep exaggerating one thing after another until the silliness of it hits you. Throw in Woody Allen's line, "If it weren't for bad luck, I'd have no luck at all."

> **"***If I were given the opportunity to present a gift to the next generation, it would be the ability of each individual to learn to laugh at himself.***"**
> (Charles Schulz)

Sometimes a friend or spouse can help you out. A woman came home from her hair dresser very depressed about her new hair style, but her hair was cut so short that she was stuck with it. She told her husband that she felt ugly, and no amount of reassurance by him could convince her otherwise. He finally took a new tact and said, "You know, now that I really look at it, I can see that you're right. It's disgusting. You look terrible. Let's get you a wig before anyone realizes the damage that's been done." She broke up laughing and soon lost her concern about being ugly.

If you find it difficult to exaggerate about yourself, ask someone else to do it for you. For example, have a friend say to you, "You know, you're right, we've got to face up to the fact that you're incredibly skinny/fat. In fact, we really ought to document this, because nobody would believe it. Let's take a photograph and send it to *Ripley's Believe it or Not.*"

Humor Log Exercises

On Laughing at Yourself

1. How would you interpret the phrase, "Life is too important to be taken seriously?"
2. How might taking yourself seriously all the time have a negative effect on your life?
3. What does the phrase "Take yourself lightly" mean?
4. What does it mean to "take yourself lightly, but take your work seriously?"
5. Why is it easier to laugh when things that happen to other people than when the same things happen to you?
6. Who do you know whom you consider to be very good at laughing at their own flaws or mistakes? Write down a couple of examples you've witnessed that demonstrate this ability.
7. Why do many people experience a sense of liberation and freedom when they first learn to laugh at themselves?
8. How does laughing at yourself produce a feeling of "mastery" or "superiority?"
9. Sometimes laughing at yourself is healthy and adds to self-esteem and your ability to cope. But it also can be unhealthy and reduce your self-esteem and ability to cope. How do these two cases differ?
10. Write down the names of any people you know who a) do, and b) do not belittle or put themselves down when poking fun at themselves. What's different about the two groups?
11. Can being a perfectionist weaken your sense of humor? How?
12. Do you think that men or women are generally better at laughing at themselves? Why do you think this is?

Current Ability to Laugh at Yourself

1. In comparison to other people you know, how good are you at laughing at yourself?
2. Why is this so difficult to do?
3. List in your Humor Log any physical characteristics you have which you don't like, separating them into minor and strong dislikes. Put a "C" beside those you consider changeable, and a "U" beside those you consider unchangeable.
4. In which of these areas do you expect to have the most difficulty learning to lighten up?
5. In which do you consider it most important to learn to lighten up?
6. List in your Humor Log any behaviors that are typical of you, but that you don't like. Again, distinguish between minor and strong dislikes. Also put a "C" beside those you consider changeable, and a "U" beside those you consider unchangeable.

7. In which of these areas do you think you'll have the most difficulty learning to lighten up?

8. In which is it most important to learn to lighten up?

9. Go back and place a check mark next to the items listed above that you've been able to joke about in the past. As you work on Step 6, place a check mark next to other items when you manage to poke fun at them.

10. Look at your list of physical or behavioral qualities that you don't like about yourself, and check those about which you can honestly say, "I'm _____, and I don't like the fact that I'm _____. But I accept the fact that that's the way it is. I'll change the parts I can; but otherwise, I'm just going to accept it, learn to live with it, and move on with my life."

11. Have any of your sensitive zones had a significant influence on your life over the years? What kind of influence?

12. Is it easier to laugh at your blunders or mistakes when alone or with other people? Why do think that is?

13. List a few embarrassing situations where you have been able to laugh at yourself in public in the past.

14. List a few embarrassing situations where you were unable to laugh at yourself, but wish you could have.

15. List any awkward or embarrassing moments that come up from time to time on your job or elsewhere, and that could come up again at any point. Write down in your Humor Log a couple of "saving" funny remarks you could make the next time these occur.

16. How easy is it for you to laugh when you're the butt of someone else's joke?

17. In what ways do you feel you have to be perfect? Is it easier or more difficult to poke fun at yourself in these areas?

18. Some people are able to ease into poking fun at themselves by memorizing a few self-putdown jokes. If you were to do this, what kind of joke (in terms of content) would you be looking for (e.g., laughing at one's baldness, eating habits, etc.)?

19. What specific goals would you like to achieve in working on Step 6?

Early Development and Influences

1. Young children are often very direct and cruel in laughing at others. How good were you at "taking it" when kids laughed at you?

2. What aspects of yourself were you especially sensitive about during your childhood and adolescence? Were you ever able to see humor in connection with these sensitive areas?

3. Has it gotten easier or more difficult to laugh at yourself as you've gotten older? Why do you think that is?

4. Who had the greatest positive and negative influence on your present ability to laugh at yourself?

5. How good were your mother and father at poking fun at themselves?

6. Let's assume that you would like to help your own children learn the skill of laughing at oneself, so that they'll have access to it as a coping skill when they grow up. What is the most important thing you can do to help them develop this skill?

GROUP SESSION

Opening Fun Activity

Discussion of Homeplay for Step 5

1. How successful were you at noticing funny things this past week?
2. Pair up with a partner and share the funniest incident you've observed since the last meeting.
3. Where did you find the most humor? At home? Work? Elsewhere?
4. What reminders did you use to help remember to look for humor?
5. Did you ask friends and colleagues to tell you about the funny things they've seen recently?
6. Did you get better at noticing humor as the week went along?
7. Discuss any difficulties you encountered in sharing a funny event with someone else. Was it as funny to them as it was to you?
8. Take a particular funny incident and describe it to the group (or a partner) twice; first in a way that captures the essence of what made it funny, then in a way that leaves out some key aspect of what made it funny. Discuss these "key" aspects. This will help make you conscious of the things you have to include to complete the picture for someone who wasn't there.

Laughing at Yourself

Use any of the issues discussed in Step 6, or the Humor Log Exercises, as a basis for discussion. Also consider the following.

1. Break up into small groups. Think of a situation in your past which was very embarrassing at the moment, and which you did not find funny. Describe it to the group. The group should come up with some way in which you could have used your sense of humor to lighten up in the situation.

211

2. Share with a partner a case where you've observed someone really putting themselves down while poking fun at themselves. How might this lower self-esteem and influence others' view of you?

3. Share one of your strongest self-dislikes with a partner. If possible, make it something you've never shared with anyone before. Discuss how you felt after sharing it.

4. Now imagine that part of yourself in an exaggerated way. Try to make an exaggerated statement about it to your partner. (e.g., "My chin is so pointy, I get stab wounds in my chest when I look at my feet.")

5. Remember to contact your telephone partners to support their efforts on Step 6.

HOME PLAY

1. Complete the seven steps described above in "How to start laughing at yourself."
   Spend as much time as necessary to feel comfortable with each one.

   a. Make a list of things you don't like about yourself.
   b. Divide the list into "heavy" and minor items, and into things you can and cannot change.
   c. Admit your weaknesses and self-dislikes.
   d. Share one item from your list with someone each day, starting with minor items.
   e. Begin sharing blunders, mistakes, and embarrassments.
   f. Learn a few self-disparaging jokes.
   g. Begin joking about your blunders and things you don't like about yourself.

   Start joking about those areas that seem easiest to joke about. Also poke fun at past
   embarrassments. Remember that embarrassing events often are funny days or weeks
   later.
2. Ask other people to describe their own funny experiences with personal blunders
   and embarrassments. This will help you learn to see the light side of your own.
3. Keep an eye out for embarrassing situations experienced by others. Think about
   how you would react if it happened to you. Look for a funny side of the situation.
   (Note: do not tell them how funny you think it is.)
4. Take two in which you tend to be a perfectionist and find a way to poke fun at
   them. Encourage your friends to also poke fun at you in these areas.
5. Collect jokes or funny stories in which the butt of the joke is your own political
   party, ethnic identity, etc. This will help ease into taking yourself less seriously.
6. Seek out any comedians who do self-disparaging humor, and spend some time
   listening to them. Pay attention to your reaction as you listen to or watch self-disparaging humor.
7. Seek out self-disparaging jokes which relate directly to your sensitive zones. Practice
   telling them to others.
8. Jot down a few words in your notebook (either at the moment or later) each time
   you manage to laugh at yourself in some way.

STEP 7

Find Humor in the Midst of Stress

> **"***You cannot prevent the birds of sorrow from flying over your head, but you can prevent them from building nests in your hair.***"**
> (Chinese proverb)

In the book, *One Flew Over the Cuckoo's Nest*, McMurphy (played by Jack Nicholson in the film) says, "When you lose your sense of humor, you lose your footing." Another character says about McMurphy, "He knows you have to laugh at the things that hurt you, just to keep yourself in balance, just to keep the world from running you plumb crazy." This is great wisdom from someone who lives in a psychiatric institution. Your sense of humor is one of the most potent tools you have to cope with those days when life seems determined to deal you enough stress to make you crazy.

Empowerment has become a major buzzword in corporations, as companies have recognized the value of granting more decision-making power to employees at all levels of the organization. If you haven't already done so, start thinking of humor in terms of empowerment. Your sense of humor empowers you to take charge of tough, stressful situations.

President Abraham Lincoln once read something to his advisors which he found very funny, but they didn't laugh. He said, "Why don't you laugh? With the fearful strain that is upon me night and day, if I did not laugh I should die, and you need this medicine as much as I do." When the president has a good sense of humor, we all benefit. It eases our tensions about the country's problems. As Robert Orben, a former director of the White House Speech Writing Department, once said, "A sense of humor implies a confident person . . . If you can joke about a tough situation, you're saying, 'Yes, it's serious, but I'm in control.'"

Like tea bags, people never discover how strong they are until they get into hot water. If you've made a real effort to develop the skills associated with Steps 2–6, you should already be able to withstand much hotter water than you used to. You're now ready to take the final step toward using your sense of humor as a coping tool.

Your Sense of Humor: The Secret Ingredient for Making Lemonade

We've all heard the expression, "When life deals you lemons, make lemonade." What no one told you, however, is that the secret ingredient in making good lemonade is your sense of humor. It can take a sour event in your life and make it sweet(er). By learning to find a light side of the situation, you can transform the hand you've been dealt. So don't let the fact that you're miserable keep you from getting some fun and joy out of life.

We saw earlier that humor has the power to transform a negative mood into a positive one. It substitutes a frame of mind that is more conducive to finding solutions to the problem of the moment. It also eases your tension and upset and gives you a greater sense of control over your lemons. As you get better at making good lemonade, you'll find yourself serving it to others—comfortably and naturally—giving them the same benefits of humor that you enjoy yourself.

> **"**Life is full of misery, loneliness, and unhappiness, and it's all over much too quickly.**"**
> (Woody Allen)

The French writer and philosopher Voltaire once said, "It is because they can be frivolous at times that the majority of people do not hang themselves." Hopefully, you're not ready to hang yourself because of the stress in your life. But if you're like most people, your stress level has been going up in recent years—especially on your job. The mushrooming growth of the stress management industry provides ample evidence of the increasing stress in our lives. We have seen a proliferation of stress management techniques, such as progressive relaxation, deep breathing, meditation, biofeedback, yoga, and more.

Amazingly, we have completely neglected one of the most effective stress reducers available to us—our sense of humor. This natural stress remedy is one of the most important tools you have for maintaining a more relaxed and joyous life, a life that always has room for fun, even in the midst of stress from jobs, relationships, health—from life, in the 1990s.

The problem, of course, is that your sense of humor abandons you right when you need it the most. Even if you've consistently done the Homeplay for Steps 1–6, you probably still lose your sense of humor when things start going wrong. Step 7 gives you control over when you use your sense of humor, instead of having it be at the mercy of your mood at the moment. You may even achieve the coolness of the New York hot dog vendor who had a guy aim a gun at him in a robbery attempt. The vender come up with the following line: "Now what do I need a gun for on a job like this? Try selling it to that cop over there." The gunman panicked and ran off—even though there was no cop.

During Step 5, you worked on finding humor in situations where you had few emotional obstacles to doing so. Now that you've learned to enjoy humor in connection with your sensitive zones, you're ready to start looking for humor on days like the following.

We've All Had Days Like This

It's Monday morning, and you have an important meeting to attend, so you absolutely have to be there on time. Imagine that the following sequence of events happens to you. We've all had days like this, so think about how you react when it happens to you.

Since it's crucial that you not be late, you give yourself two hours to get there—twice the time you really need. You head out the door, but can't find your keys. You don't panic, because you've allowed for this. After looking everywhere twice, you start to feel anxious. But just then, your son finds them on his way out to school—in the front door! You grab them and smugly congratulate yourself on having decided to start early. You get to your car and find that a freezing rain has fallen during the night, covering everything with a layer of ice. Not only do you have to scrape the ice off the windshield, you can't even open the door; it's frozen shut. After making your feelings about this situation known to everyone in the neighborhood, it finally occurs to you to go back inside and get a screw driver. You return to the car and force the door open as you lift the handle. You're in!

After one block, you glance at the gas gauge. Less than one eighth of a tank! You'll never get there without stopping for gas. You pull into the first gas station your see. One of the attendants has called in sick, so there's only one guy operating the pumps. You jump out and pump the gas yourself. As you run in to pay for it, you find two other people waiting to pay. They each have credit cards. One guy has his card rejected . . . and doesn't have the cash to cover his gas.

Finally, your turn comes. You have no choice but to use your credit card. As the attendant is writing up your slip, the phone rings. It's her boss. She feels obliged to give him her full attention and stops writing. You grab the slip and fill it out yourself. Your jaw is clenched as you head out the door. You mutter your appreciation to the attendant as you head back to your car.

You pull back on the road just in time to catch a red light. A school bus turns in front of you. There's so much traffic that you can't pass. The bus makes 11 stops before you get around it. You've also managed to hit every light red! But you're almost to the interstate and you know you're home free from there.

> **"** *When you're down in the mouth, remember Jonah. He came out ok.* **"**
> (Thomas Edison)

As you approach the entry ramp to the freeway, the lights start flashing and the gate comes down in front of the one set of railroad tracks you have to cross—the ones you've crossed every day for a year without ever seeing a train. It's a freight train unloading a few cars nearby. Two minutes later, the end of the train is in sight. Then it comes to an agonizing halt . . . and starts backing up! Does this sound familiar so far?

You finally get across the tracks and onto the freeway, and you're cruising at 60 mph. You come over a little hill and are stunned by a string of red lights—break lights—as far down the road as you can see. It's an accident. Traffic is backed up over a mile.

You realize now that you're running out of time and that it'll be close. You notice that the other lane is moving faster, so you force your way into that lane as the driver you cut in front of compliments you on your maneuver. Within seconds, that lane slows down and the cars from the lane you just left zip by. You're determined to prove that you made the right decision, so you stay put, as traffic from the original lane continues to pass you. Just before you reach the site of the accident, a wrecker pulls the damaged car off the road and traffic speeds up again.

You've got 15 minutes until your meeting begins. As you exit the freeway, you run into construction; two lanes have been funneled into one. So you take an alternate route, where traffic is moving freely. You hear sirens in the distance. They are getting closer, but your path is finally clear. No problem! Five minutes to go, but you're a mile away from your destination.

The sirens are getting very loud now. Suddenly, from out of nowhere, two fire engines career around the corner and stop at the intersection in front of you. Another one emerges behind you and blocks your only escape. You look up and realize that the fire is in the building you just happen to be in front of at that moment. Three cars are trapped between the fire trucks, and yours is one of them.

Every one of these incidents has occurred in my life at one time or another, although not all on the same trip. I came close, though, the day I got surrounded by fire engines in New York, after every traffic problem imaginable made me late for my meeting. At some point, you've had your own version of this episode. How did you react?

My own reaction was to burst out laughing when the fire trucks surrounded me. I couldn't believe it. The gathering crowd looked at me oddly, thinking I was laughing at the fire. But all the tension and upset that had built up in the previous hour and a half just exploded in the form of a good belly laugh. After the laughter, I stopped worrying about the fact that I was late and focused my attention on the problems this would cause and how I would deal with them.

> **"***God is a comedian playing to an audience that is afraid to laugh.***"**
> (Voltaire)

I broke through the blockade and arrived 10 minutes late. I later realized that the fire trucks actually helped me; they reversed the bad mood I would have been in when I arrived at the meeting. The belly laugh didn't get me there any faster, but instead of arriving tense, upset, and unable to concentrate, I walked in relatively relaxed and able to focus on the tasks at hand.

The real power of humor and laughter shows up when you learn to use it under stress. It keeps the problem in perspective, dissipates negative emotions (anger, anxiety, depression) that burgeon up within you when things go wrong, and puts you in a frame of mind that is much better equipped to handle the situation.

Donovan the bartender is walking to his pub one day when a perfect stranger walks up to him and gives him a punch in the face, trying to start a fight. He says, "That'll teach you O'Brien!" To which Donovan roars with laughter, after recovering from the shock.

"Why are you laughing?" asks the stranger. "Do you want me to hit you again?"

"No, please," comes the reply, "It's just that the joke's on you . . . I'm not O'Brien."

Does Stress Happen to You? Or Do You Create It?

There is a general consensus in the stress management industry that "you create your own stress." If you've never heard this idea before, it probably makes no sense to you. After all, you didn't create the tornado that wiped out your house, the extra work you inherited when your colleague was laid off, or the increase in your insurance payments. You never create the events themselves, but you do determine how stressful they are—depending on how you interpret and react to them.

If you've ever been in a situation where several people have had identical stressors (e.g., cancer, loss of a job, or impossible job demands), you've probably noticed that they handle it in very different ways. Some get so angry, anxious, or depressed that their relationships collapse, they lose their effectiveness on the job, and their life falls apart in general. Others have the same initial upset, but quickly face up to the reality of the situation and get on to coping with it.

> **❝Perhaps I know why it is man alone who laughs; he alone suffers so deeply that he had to invent laughter.❞**
> (Friedreich Wilhelm Nietzsche)

One way we create stress is by constantly worrying about things that might happen. Unforeseen and unwanted events occur in all of our lives. You want to take reasonable precautions against these, but you must also learn to accept the fact that you can't control everything. The key to effective living is managing unwanted events once they occur. Learning to lighten up in the midst of your problems helps you do exactly that.

Humor Helps You Overcome the Law of Psychological Gravity

The Law of Psychological Gravity says that people become heavier when they're under stress. When you have one terrible day after another, you can feel yourself start to drag. You become emotionally heavy. For some, this heaviness takes the form of anger. For others, it shows up as anxiety, depression, or general sadness. Regardless of how it shows in you, it weighs you down on your job and in your relationships; and it robs you of effectiveness in both. But your sense of humor overcomes this law, preventing the weight build-up (or reducing it if it has already occurred) and improving your effectiveness on the job and in life generally.

I recently witnessed the anti-gravity power of humor while visiting my parents a few months ago. My father is in his mid-80s and has a number of health problems and physical limitations. As he often says, "My day is full of misery; you just don't know what it's like. My job is to put in my 24 hours and get through the day." I've heard him say many times, "I just ain't no good any more." He says it's hard for him to keep his spirits up, because he has nothing to hope for. He knows that things are never going to get better; they can only get worse.

But a funny thing happened when the in-home-care lady who had been helping my mother was replaced. The new lady had a good sense of humor and often engaged my father in playful banter and good-natured ribbing. The impact on his mood was immediately apparent. You can imagine how wonderful it was to see a playful grin come across his face when the new woman began talking about how the two of them had "a thing" going, and that she hoped my mother wouldn't be too jealous.

> **"*If I had no sense of humor, I should long ago have committed suicide.*"**
> (Mohandas K. Gandhi)

He even started telling jokes and funny stories. He asked me one day, "Did you hear about the fellow who bowled 301?" "301? That's impossible!" I said. He couldn't keep from grinning as he added, "Well did you ever see anyone who bowled three hundred and lost?" (The ambiguity here only works orally.) Since he rarely tells jokes, I saw this as a direct effect of the new aide's ability to bring out his own playfulness.

On the same trip, I had some animal noses and a silly-looking "Smile on a Stick" sitting around the house. On Christmas day, I took some photographs of him and my mother wearing these and making silly faces. From that point on, whenever friends or relatives would come over, he would grab the Smile on a Stick and suddenly turn toward the guest, holding it under his nose with his eyebrows sharply raised. Or he would hand them the nose-photos and wait for their reaction. These simple little props brought several moments of joy to his difficult, dreary days. This is just one of the ways in which humor adds to the quality of your life. It may or may not add years to your life, but it will certainly add life to your years.

Bounce-Back-Ability

Your sense of humor gives you what I call "bounce-back-ability." By this point in your life, you have developed a good set of coping skills, so that problems generally only get you down momentarily. You're able to bounce back quickly and do whatever is required to deal with them. But some days are tougher than others, and it takes every bit of energy you can muster to bounce back and cope. You can do it, but it takes a committed effort on your part, and it leaves you emotionally drained.

And then there are other days—you know the ones I mean—where your problems just seem to overwhelm you, maybe because they all happen at once. No matter what you do, you just can't bounce back and squeeze the lemons thrown your way. Your resistance is weakened, and you become a victim of the Law of Psychological Gravity.

This is precisely where you sense of humor can help. It helps you bounce back in situations where you'd otherwise succumb. Just as the elasticity of a ball enables it to absorb the energy created by gravity and produce the force necessary to bounce back up against the pull of gravity, your sense of humor gives you the elasticity you need to absorb psychological gravity and bounce back in a more positive direction.

> **"*I have seen what a laugh can do. It can transform almost unbearable tears into something bearable, even hopeful.*"**
> (Bob Hope)

You will feel the force of gravity pulling you down as you first start trying to use your sense of humor in the midst of stress. It will seem unnatural as you ask yourself, "OK, what's funny about this situation?" Because you know there's absolutely nothing funny about it! This soon will pass, however, as you learn to distinguish between the seriousness of the situation and the little things that still could be funny to someone who had the habit of noticing them.

Finding something to laugh at during hard times does not mean you're failing to take the situation seriously. You will learn that having a good laugh actually helps you handle the problem—if you're determined to deal with it effectively to begin with. Meetings in corporations often begin with a joke or funny story, because it makes the meeting flow better, and more gets accomplished. The same thing happens when you manage to have a good laugh in the midst of a personal conflict. It helps you bounce back and deal with the conflict more effectively.

The Importance of Learning to Actively Use Humor

We noted in Step 1 that there are passive and active ways of showing a good sense of humor. You can enjoy humor without ever initiating it yourself. You can also laugh at your friends' jokes, listen to TV sit coms, collect Far Side cartoons, and listen to comedy tapes. These all offer some relief from stress. But you won't always have a friend around when you need a good laugh, and you can't pop a *Saturday Night Live* tape into your VCR when things get bad at work. To fully benefit from the stress-reducing power of humor, you need to take control of your opportunities for laughter by coming up with your own humor. As noted in Chapter 3, humor helps you cope only if you actively use your sense of humor when under stress.

In the 1950s, Eve Arden, star of the popular *Our Miss Brooks* television program, demonstrated this active use of humor when a practical joke was played on her during a stage performance. A fellow actor had arranged to have the phone unexpectedly ring in the middle of a monologue by Eve. She picked up the phone, paused a moment, and handed it to her leading man, saying, "It's for you."

Humor as Verbal Aikido

Aikido is a martial art in which you use an attacker's own force to disarm him and defend yourself. Instead of countering his force by striking back, you add to it or deflect it in a slightly different direction. If someone rushes toward you, you use his own energy to thrust him aside.

Joel Goodman noted some years ago that humor can be used as a kind of verbal aikido. In the midst of a conflict, humor can be used to disarm a verbal attack in a way that establishes a more positive—even playful—atmosphere for resolving the conflict, and doesn't put the other person down. It removes the bitterness from the air and leaves both parties in a better position to deal with the problem at hand.

For example, Robert F. Kennedy was asked in the early 1960s why he felt qualified to become attorney general for the United States. His answer was, "If a person wants to become attorney general, that person should first go to a good law school, study hard, get good marks, establish a reputation, and most important of all—have a brother who is president of the United States." The remark totally defused the implicit suggestion that it was inappropriate for a brother of the president to receive the post.

In the fall of 1993, many public schools in New York City were late in opening for classes because of a scandal in which schools which had presumably been tested for the presence of asbestos were found not to have been tested. In the midst of tension-filled meetings between parents and school authorities, one group of parents congregated around a school wearing T-shirts which said, "We're doing asbestos we can." They provided a welcome release of the tension and upset felt by both sides.

A group of bus drivers got tired of people in cars behind them honking their horns all day long. So they got the bus company to put a big sign on the back of the busses saying, "Honk if you love life!" Drivers stopped honking as soon as the signs went up.

How Does Your Sense of Humor Help You Cope with Stress?

We all know people who suffer more than their share of traumas, but manage to draw from some inner strength that enables them to not only go on, but to do so with a positive attitude. A strong religious faith can provide this, but your sense of humor can do so as well. How does it do this? How does your sense of humor help you cope?

> **❝** *The world breaks all of us, but some of us become stronger in the broken places.* **❞**
> (Ernest Hemingway)

Relaxation

Stress causes you to get upset or anxious, and these feelings increase muscle tension. This increased muscle tension can, in turn, help sustain or even increase your anger or anxiety. A vicious cycle is created in which your upset feeds on itself. Since relaxing the body has been shown to produce calmer thoughts and emotions, this has become the main goal of all stress management techniques.

Laughter produces muscle relaxation automatically and naturally (see Chapter 1). That's why children fall down on the ground during fits of laughter, and why you fall backwards in your chair when you laugh. Muscles that don't directly participate in laughter relax while you're laughing. Then when you stop laughing, the muscles that had been contracting tend to relax—just as any muscle involved in vigorous exercise relaxes when you stop working it. You don't have to learn to produce this relaxation effect. Nature has built it into your body. As you laugh more often, you will become more relaxed—whether you're trying to or not.

That's why you were encouraged to become more expressive in your laughter in Step 2. You need to become more comfortable with belly laughter and build up the habit of laughing (when it is socially appropriate). This makes laughter an effective stress-reducing tool when you really need it. Of course, there are some risks to doing this. Muscles may relax that you don't want to relax. If you've ever fallen into hysterical laughter after two or three beers at a party, you know what I mean.

Emotional Release

Have you ever noticed how your emotions gradually escalate during a typical high stress day? You can feel the tension, anxiety, anger, or general upset increase as the day goes along. The upset may reflect a few key events, or an accumulated effect of simply having too many things to do, with too little time to do them. The longer this goes on, the greater the build up of emotional tension. If you have no way of releasing this tension, you soon feel like you're going to explode. Maybe you do explode. You kick the dog, slam your fist against the wall, shout insults at colleagues, or just scream! These reactions generally aren't very adaptive, even if they do make you feel better.

Therapists offer one source of release by providing an environment in which you can talk about the causes of your stress and develop better ways of dealing with it. Humor is certainly no substitute for therapy, but you don't always have access to your therapist, and you may not have anyone else available with whom you can talk it out. Laughter provides an immediate release of tension. You feel a tremendous weight being removed from your shoulders when you have a good belly laugh. It's hard to hang on to your anger and anxiety when you're laughing. That's one reason most people say they just feel better after a good laugh.

You can obtain this cathartic release of anger and tension to some extent by forcing yourself to have a good laugh, as suggested in Step 3. The greatest release occurs, however, when you find or create something to laugh at that you find genuinely funny. Step 7 gets you to the point that you can do this.

John Glenn was the first American astronaut in space, and there was a great deal of nervousness before the flight. When he was later asked what he was thinking about before the launch, he said: "I looked around me and suddenly realized that everything had been built by the lowest bidder." This joke to himself eased his pre-launch nervousness.

The available evidence suggests that humor is effective in reducing feelings of both anger[1] and anxiety,[2] although it may be less effective in lowering anxiety.[3] One study found humor to be just as effective as progressive relaxation procedures in reducing anxiety.[4]

As noted in Chapter 3, hospital nurses work in a very high stress environment. Most nurses quickly learn that they need a good laugh several times a day, just to release the emotional build-up that goes along with confronting one life-threatening situation after another all day long. They often tell each other jokes like the following just to keep stress levels manageable.

> **Three people died and went to hell. When they got there, the devil gave them a choice of the room in which they would spend eternity. All the rooms were bad, but one was less bad than the others. It was a room in which people were standing in sewage up to their knees. So they all three chose this room. As they were walking away, the devil said, "OK, coffee break's over, back on your heads."**

The reason nurses love this joke is that it pretty much sums up their job. Laughing at this joke, or at other unplanned funny events, provides a release for their frustrations, and allows them to stay focused on doing their usual good job. It will do the same for you.

This cathartic release of negative emotions provides a kind of emotional cleansing, allowing you to leave the past in the past—instead of carrying it up front in the present.

222

Hospitals often give patients a cathartic to induce a bowel movement. It purges the system, removing poisons from the body. Laughter does the same thing, emotionally. Unexpressed negative emotions become poisons if you allow them to build up. They sour your attitude toward life and your job, and kill your ability to experience joy, spontaneity, aliveness, and fun. So think of laughter as a kind of "emotional movement." And just as you need a good B.M. every day to stay healthy, you also need a good E.M.

Increased Energy/Decreased Burnout

Anger and anxiety are energy-sapping emotions. If your job causes you stress day after day, week after week, the anger, anxiety, or depression you live with drains the energy you need to be perform effectively. It also lowers your morale and job satisfaction and sets you up for burnout.

As you learn to lighten up on the job, you'll have more energy and experience less burnout. Laughter recharges your batteries. It fights burnout by giving you back the energy you're supposed to have, and by making work more enjoyable. It restores energy by cutting through energy-sapping emotions and replacing them with energizing ones. In short, it revitalizes you. People who are able to incorporate humor and a sense of fun into their job look forward to going to work and are more effective when they get there. This alone reduces job stress.

> **"***I've developed a new philosophy . . . I only dread one day at a time.***"**
> (Charlie Brown)

This increased energy is surprising, because belly laughter is a real physical workout. Your heart rate goes up, you start sweating, and you may even get sore muscles. This should leave you tired and less energetic; but most people report the opposite. This energizing effect is most noticeable when you actively find humor in a situation yourself, but even listening to others' humor causes you to feel more vigorous and less fatigued.[5]

Maintenance of Perspective

Roseanne Roseanna Danna (Gilda Radner), of *Saturday Night Live*, used to say, "It's always something; if it's not one thing, it's another!" If this sums up your life, you may be getting too caught up in minor hassles, while losing sight of the big picture. Your battery is dead! The photocopy machine at work is jammed! You're out of coffee! Someone cut in front of you in line. Your suit/dress isn't ready when it's supposed to be. You got in the shortest line, and the long line is moving faster.

As you learn to lighten up in life, you realize that these problems are just not worth the toll taken by getting all bent out of shape by them. Humor enables you to take an emotional step back from them; and from this more distant vantage point, they lose their emotional control over you, leaving you in a better position to take effective action to deal with them.

Do you catastrophize your problems, acting as if each one is the end of the world? During my years as a university teacher, I once had a student who was in the last semester of her senior year, and she had to pass my course to graduate. The only problem was that she had an "F" going into the final exam. She came into my office one day, burst into tears, and blurted out: "If I don't pass your test, I won't graduate! And if I don't graduate, I won't get a job! And if I don't get a job, I'll become a bag lady and live in the streets and be miserable for the rest of my life!" It was all I could do to resist laughing at this spectacle, but she failed to see the humor of it. She had completely lost perspective, and was pinning her entire life on the outcome of that course.

> **"** *Humor is the healthy way of feeling a 'distance' between one's self and the problem, a way of standing off and looking at one's problem with perspective.* **"**
> (Rollo May)

Dr. Robert Elliott, former Director of the National Center of Preventive and Stress Medicine, said in 1983 that we all need to develop some means of maintaining a broader perspective on our problems. Your sense of humor is one of the best tools you'll find for doing this. As you get better at learning to lighten up, you automatically become more adept at keeping your focus on the big picture as you see your daily hassles for what they are—problems to be dealt with in the most effective way possible.

We've all heard the phrase, "Don't sweat the small stuff."

It was noted in Chapter 2 that cancer patients who have defeated their cancer are very good at doing this. Their cancer has given them a different perspective on the daily hassles that used to cause them stress. They don't deny these hassles. They just accept them and get on to dealing with them. They've learned that life is too important to let yourself to be in a stew all the time about minor matters. Why wait until you get cancer to learn this lesson? Developing your sense of humor helps you become someone who no longer sweats the small stuff.

The letter reproduced on the following page clearly demonstrates the importance of perspective.

Substitution of a Positive Mood for a Negative One

Anything which helps you maintain a more positive, upbeat, optimistic mood or outlook in life puts you in a better position to cope with life's trials. But extended periods of stress can cause you to fall into a negative mood. This adds to your stress by making you less efficient in dealing with it. But if you can find some humor in the situation, it helps prevent this mood disturbance from occurring.[6] Genuine humor and laughter are simply incompatible with anger and upsets.

Negative moods (especially depression) also weaken your motivation to take action. You feel there's no point, since you always fail anyway. You're more likely to feel powerless and decide that things are hopeless. The improved mood that humor creates stimulates hope and motivates you to take action.

Even if you're not very good at using your sense of humor to cope, but really enjoy humor and often find humor in everyday situations when you're not under stress, then these two aspects of your sense of humor are enough to help keep you in a more upbeat, positive mood.[7]

For many, a bad mood from stress shows up as depression. The power of humor to counter depression was evident in a patient in a hospital who was given limited

Dear Mom and Dad,

I'm sorry for not writing, but hope you will understand. Please sit down before you read further.

I'm doing much better now after recovering from the concussion I received jumping from my dorm window when it caught fire last month. I can almost see normally now, thanks to the loving care of Norman, the janitor who pulled me from the flames. He more than saved me; he's become my entire life. I've been living with him since the fire. We're planning to get married. We haven't set a date yet, but plan to have one soon, before my pregnancy shows.

Yes, I'm pregnant. I knew how excited you'd be for me, given how much you wanted to be grandparents. We'd be married by now, if it weren't for Norman's infection that prevented him from passing the blood test. I caught it from him, but the doctors are sure it won't affect the child.

Although he's not well educated, I know your own tolerance will make it easy for you to accept Norm.

Your Loving Daughter,

Mary

P.S. There was no fire. I had no concussion. I'm not pregnant. And there is no Norman. But I'm getting an "F" in biology, and I wanted you to see that grade in its proper perspective.

chances of survival. One day a clown visited the hospital, gave her several good laughs, and raised her spirits. She decided then and there that "They're going to take me out of here in a wheel chair, not in a box." To this day, she continues to avoid the box and loves life.

> **❝**[Humor] does put you in a good mood . . . Usually when people are sick, or have something wrong, they get depressed. They can't do this, they can't do that . . . But if you start to laugh, it'll change your mood. It's a feeling of 'I can, I can,' instead of 'I can't.' Because depression is 'I can't,' and laughing is 'I can.'**❞**[8]
>
> (Sid Caesar)

Again, research has shown that humor is an effective means of staving off, and bringing you out of, mild (non-clinical) levels of depression.[9] And it is precisely when you're under high stress that finding humor in the situation helps keep you from getting depressed.[10] So this again demonstrates the importance of developing your humor skills.

In one innovative study, young women in different phases of their menstrual cycle were asked to select from among comedy, drama, and game show programs for an evening of television viewing. Premenstrual and menstrual women preferred comedy over the other choices to a greater extent than did women mid-way through their menstrual cycle.[11] The researchers conducting the study concluded that this choice was due to "a desire to overcome the hormonally-mediated noxious mood states that are characteristically associated with the premenstrual and menstrual phases of the cycle."

Finally, among a group of 35 patients in a rehabilitation hospital, 91% said that laughter puts them in a good mood.[12] If laughter can improve the mood of patients with brain or spinal cord injuries, severe arthritis, neurological disorders, and amputations, it can also improve your mood.

> ❝*Most folks are about as happy as they make up their minds to be.*❞
>
> (Abraham Lincoln)

Increased Sense of Control

A perceived lack of control, or a sense of helplessness, is probably the most important single cause of stress. An unwanted event occurs, but you feel powerless to change it—possibly because several problems develop at the same time. As noted in Chapter 2, finding something to laugh at in the midst of the problem helps you feel more in control, because you really are taking a form of control over your emotional reaction to the situation. Rather than allowing the circumstances to generate feelings of frustration/anger, tension/anxiety, or depression, you create a positive mood which supports your effort to deal with the problem.

A recovering alcoholic put it this way halfway through the 8-Step Program:

> "*I take control by looking in the mirror and having a good laugh before I walk out the door in the morning. I leave with the intent of passing on a smile to whoever I meet. It changes everything . . . A good laugh helps me take charge of the things that used to upset me. I can get into the nuttiest traffic situation now, and it doesn't bother me. I just let them be who they are, and I go on my way. Before, every little thing that happened on the road upset me. But if I can manage to find a bit of humor in things, it keeps me in a good mood. By the time I get home, I may be tired, but I'm not beaten or depressed or angry. And it's all under my control.*"

Are you a thermostat or a thermometer? A thermometer just reflects temperature as a function of what's happening around it. Something happens that you don't like, and your temperature goes up. You get angry. A thermostat can be set in advance to operate at a given temperature. Learning to lighten up in difficult situations provides you a skill that enables you stay cool, while the thermometers around you are heating up.

Carol Burnett grew up in an alcoholic family, and her parents argued all the time. One day she began giving points during the arguments, depending on how well each was doing. By making a game of it, she managed to take a measure of control over a very stressful situation. She stopped being a passive victim of the violent emotions around her, and took charge of at least her own emotional reactions.

> **"***Humor is an affirmation of dignity, a declaration of man's superiority to all that befalls him.***"** (Romain Gary)

During the Gulf War with Iraq, Israeli radio sponsored a nation-wide contest—an anagrams game—while citizens were anxiously sitting in their sealed rooms awaiting the Scud missiles to fall. The game was to see who in the country could come up with the greatest number of words from the letters of the name Saddam Hussein. This playful distraction helped the entire country regain control over it's emotional state in a time of great national crisis.

We noted in Step 6 that a very old theory of humor argues that we laugh at situations, events, and jokes which make us feel superior. The enjoyment of put-down jokes can, in part, be explained in this way. We feel superior to the person or group put down in the joke. But the same idea applies to stressful situations. When you find something to laugh at in the midst of difficult circumstances, you will notice a change in yourself. You'll feel like you've beaten it, like you've risen above it.

In support of this view, researchers conducting a study (described in Chapter 2) of Israeli soldiers concluded that humor increased the soldiers' feeling that they were in control of whatever situations came up, and that this enabled them to perform at a higher level.[13] It will work the same way for you on your job. Consistent with this idea, a humor training workshop has been shown to strengthen the general belief that important events in our lives are under our own control, rather than a result of outside forces or luck.[14]

Feeling a sense of control also contributes to the activation of your healing systems when you are physically sick. Humor is one means of generating this, but it can also come from love, faith (in your doctor, a medicine, or God), meditation, exercise, good nutrition, or other coping skills.[15] If you believe you can have impact on a stress-inducing situation, this enhances the operation of the body's self-healing mechanisms.

Distraction

Distraction is one of the mechanisms by which humor helps substitute a positive for a negative mood. It breaks through the cycle of negative thoughts leading to negative emotions, which trigger even more negative thoughts, and so forth. This vicious cycle keeps you trapped in negativity, but laughter breaks through the cycle and focuses your attention in a more positive direction. This, in turn, leaves you in a better state of mind to take action. Instead of thinking, "Ok, this is it; I'm in big trouble now," "I'll never have enough money," "I always have bad luck," or "No one likes me," you are more likely to think, "Ok, that's the way it is; now what? How do I deal with this?"

You will recall from Step 2 that one of the most fundamental characteristics of play is it's tendency to fully engage you in the activity itself. You become fully immersed in things that are intrinsically enjoyable or fun. Since humor is really a form of mental play, it's not surprising that it helps you at least momentarily forget your worries and concerns.

> **"*A smile confuses an approaching frown.*"**
> (Anonymous)

The power of humor to distract can also help in connection with threats to physical health. Norman Cousins used to tell the story of a man who suddenly developed a wildly beating heart (paroxysmal tachycardia), a condition that sometimes requires immediate medical attention.[16] His wife phoned the family doctor, who instructed her to do anything she could to keep him from panicking, because that could make the problem worse and cause complications. She immediately played an old *Candid Camera* videotape, in which Buster Keaton is seated at a lunchroom counter and having a difficult time keeping his glasses and toupee from repeatedly falling into his soup. Her husband laughed and laughed, and when the doctor arrived, his pulse was back to normal. The doctor said that the wife's quick thinking averted a potentially serious situation.

How to Practice Finding Humor in the Midst of Stress

This is the most difficult part of your sense of humor to develop. But if you have spent at least a week on each of the previous six steps, you are now in a position to lighten up under stress. If you were suffering from Acquired Amusement Deficiency Syndrome (AADS), you've overcome it. You have developed the ability to be more playful and can readily switch back and forth between seriousness and playfulness. You are more sensitized to the funny side of life and have developed the habit of seeking out ambiguities, incongruities, and ironies in your own life. You have even become more expressive of your appreciation of humor; that is, you are laughing more often and more heartily than you did two months ago. All of these skills prepare you for what you probably really wanted to do from the beginning—use your sense of humor to cope with stress.

> **"*If you don't learn to laugh at trouble, you won't have anything to laugh at when you grow old.*"**
> (Ed Howe)

While working on Step 7, just keep doing what you've been doing up to this point. You already have all the skills you need to use humor to deal with minor hassles. But they don't get you very far under conditions of high stress. The key to success at Step 7 is to find humor in connection with minor hassles and problems first, and then move on to more stressful situations. There are several things you can do to speed up this process.

Seek Out Friends Who Are Good at Finding Humor Under Stress

Determine in advance which of your friends and co-workers are sufficiently positive and up-beat to help you find a light side of difficult situations when they arise. Spend more time around these people, and seek them out when you're under stress. Also ask them about how they've used humor to cope in the past. Agree to help each other lighten up when one is under stress, and the other is not.

Look for the Light Side of Other People's Problems. (Do Not Tell Them!)

It's always easier to see a funny side of other people's problems than it is your own. This may take the form of thinking of a funny line. For example, a woman called a doctor and shrieked that her daughter had swallowed paint thinner. The thought flashed into his mind: "For God's sake, don't let her light a cigarette!" But he kept the idea to himself and simply asked what she had given the child. Once the child was clearly ok, he might then have considered sharing his joke with the mother—if he had had some prior history of playful interaction with her. Otherwise, humor would never be appropriate in this situation.

> **"Everything is funny as long as it happens to someone else."**
> (Will Rogers)

> **"Human life is basically a comedy. Even its tragedies often seem comic to the spectator, and not infrequently to the victim."**
> (H.L. Mencken)

Also be on the lookout for humor resulting from ineffective or "stupid" behavior shown by people in difficult situations. For example, there was a convict from Texas who had been running from the law for 15 years. He finally got caught when he called the FBI to find out if they were still looking for him.

Observe How Other People Use Humor to Cope with Stress

Make it a point to watch how others handle stress using humor. If you have friends who are good at this, ask them to share incidents where their sense of humor has helped them cope. This is especially useful at work.

It was noted in Chapter 3 that cancer patients often say that humor and a positive attitude got them through their battle with the disease. If you know someone with a good sense of humor who is fighting a serious disease, spend more time around them. And don't forget about children. Erma Bombeck talks about a 3-year-old cancer patient who had lost her hair, but had a little fuzz reappearing on her head. One day "she observed with curiosity her father's balding head as he bent over to tie his shoe. 'Daddy,' she asked, 'Is your hair coming or going?'"[17] An adult cancer patient often borrowed Carl Reiner's line, saying that "Anyone who wears hair during the daytime is overdressed."

You can also watch the newspapers for stories about how people use their sense of humor in the midst of stress. For example, after a tornado in Texas, a family put up a sign in front of where the house used to be saying, "Gone with the wind." Another tornado victim had his car smashed by a large tree. He put a sign on it saying, "Compact car."

Steve Allen, long known for his quick wit, describes in his book, *How to be Funny*, how he handled an embarrassing situation during his old radio days.

> **Jim Moran . . . was on, pushing Persian rugs. He entered, dressed as an Arab, leading an enormous camel. Well, right in the middle of our conversation, the camel began to urinate all over the linoleum floor. Camels have a tremendous capacity to store water, of course, so when they empty their bladders, it takes a while—much longer than for, say, a horse or an elephant.**
>
> **Anyway, the audience got hysterical. So Jim and I stopped the conversation. The camel went on for about five minutes. The longer he relieved himself, the more the audience laughed. Stagehands came out with buckets and mops to clean up the mess, which was about to spill out into the audience.**
>
> **After everything was mopped up, the linoleum—originally a dark brown color—was about eight shades lighter, since the waxy buildup, or whatever, had been removed. It had now been reduced to a pale shade of yellow. Suddenly, that transformation struck me funny and I said: "Say, homemakers, having trouble keeping kitchen floors spotlessly clean?"**
>
> **The laughter was loud and long.**

While you can't expect to match Steve Allen's quick wit at this point, it shows you what's possible, even in the most unpredictable and awkward of situations.

Look for Humor in Stressful Situations in Your Own Past

Have you ever noticed that things that upset you at the moment often seem funny days or weeks later? The upset disappears with time, allowing your mood to improve to the point where you can see the humor of the situation. Making the effort to see a funny side of past problems gradually will help you find humor in problems as they're occurring.

How many times have you thought to yourself, "Some day we'll look back at this and laugh." Why wait? The fact that you say it is a good sign, since it shows that you recognize the potential for humor in the situation. But the trick is to learn to laugh at strange, bizarre, incongruous, unexpected, and ironic turns of events as they are happening.

Look for Tomorrow's Humor in Today's Crises

This is the logical next step after looking for the funny side of past problems and of the problems of other people. Ask yourself, "What will I find funny about this next month? What's absurd, incongruous, or ironic here?" Even if you don't find anything funny at the moment, develop the habit of asking the question. Or ask yourself, "If someone else were looking over my shoulder, what would they find to laugh at?" Or, "What would _____ (name your favorite comedian) find funny about this?"

Make a List of Minor Hassles and Problems that You Encounter on a Typical Day. Start Looking for Humor in These Situations.

This may include traffic, annoying colleagues, deadlines, spilling food on yourself on the way to a meeting, having someone forget an appointment, hitting a long check-out line, finding that your child has not done what s/he was supposed to do, etc. To assure success, start off with minor stressors. As you think back to the last time these things happened, is there anything about them that now seems funny to you? Be on the lookout for these same funny things when the next opportunity arises.

Take the initiative in using your joking skills in these situations. If you find yourself in a hospital for a few days, you might answer a knock at the door by saying, "who's there, friend or enema?" If you're deadly serious about your golf game, and having a bad day, you might lighten things up by saying, "You know, nothing increases my golf score like witnesses."

Keep a "Lighten-Up!" Prop Handy

This might be a clown nose, Groucho glasses, a photograph of yourself making a face, your favorite cartoon, etc. (You can use the same props you used for Step 2.) You might wear one of my buttons saying, "Lighten Up!" or "Humor Me! I'm Recovering from Terminal Seriousness." Or you can put up a funny sign in your office. Signs I've seen recently include "Are we having fun yet?" and "People who think they know everything are particularly annoying to those of use who do." Although crude, my favorite is a bumper sticker which says, "Unless you're a hemorrhoid, get off my ass!" Use these props to help create a mood conducive to finding humor under stress.

I have a pair of glasses with an elephant trunk where the "Groucho nose" should be. Whenever I put them on, I can't help but grin (it helps, of course, to check yourself out in a mirror); nor can those around me. A woman who attended one of my programs took my advice about props to heart and began wearing an animal nose whenever she was in a sour mood. She was amazed to discover that it really worked! Many people reacted playfully to her or said something silly about the nose. Their reactions pulled her out of her upset in a way she could never do on her own. She couldn't believe that something so simple could be so effective.

Putting on a clown nose or nose glasses is also a good way to defuse arguments among spouses or friends. It reminds you that this person is your friend and that you want to focus your upset on the issue, not on the person. Remember, though, that this can backfire if the other person decides that you're not taking him/her seriously. You can eliminate this problem by communicating in advance your plan to grab a funny prop whenever the dispute gets out of hand. After you've each had a good laugh, you'll find it much easier to deal with your differences.

> **❝*The one serious conviction that a man should have is that nothing is to be taken too seriously.*❞**   (Samuel Butler)

Keep your props in a place where you know you'll see them (in your pocket, on your desk, in your car, on the refrigerator, etc.). Keeping a cartoon with you at all times works very well for some. It should bring a grin to your face every time you look at it and symbolize your commitment to take things a little less seriously.

I use Gary Larson's *The Far Side* cartoons for this purpose. I used to carry in my wallet a cartoon showing two people and a dog just walking along. All three of them have bull's eye targets drawn on their heads, and the viewer is up high and looking down. The caption reads, "How birds see the world." I cannot help but laugh every time I see this cartoon, because I got hit by an especially disgusting bird dropping when I was 17. It doesn't change the problem at hand, but it does put me in a better frame of mind to deal with it.

My current cartoon prop shows a woman in a dentist chair, with the usual array of equipment hanging out of her mouth. Her right hand, however, has a firm grip on the male dentist's private parts. The caption reads, "We aren't going to hurt each other, are we doctor?"

Signs Observed on Office Desks

"There will be no crisis next week . . . My schedule is already full."

"Due to current financial constraints, the light at the end of the tunnel will be turned off until further notice."

"You want it by when?" (Shows cartoon figure on floor, laughing.)

Use Funny Visual Imagery

Research in the past decade or so has clearly documented the impact of visual imagery on both your mind and body. You can influence your emotional state by conjuring up images associated with a given emotion. Actors do this all the time in order to create a convincing level of communication to the audience.

The classic example of visual imagery is to imagine yourself going to the refrigerator, pulling out a lemon, cutting it in two pieces, and then putting one of the pieces into your mouth and sucking on it. Most people picture the lemon vividly and salivate, just as if they had bitten into a real lemon.

As you work on Step 7, practice conjuring up funny visual images as a means of influencing your sour mood. Jot down a few experiences from your past which make you smile every time you think of them. Or create in your own mind a silly or ridiculous situation which you will intentionally call forth the next time any regularly occurring source of stress occurs. This is especially effective when the image involves particular people with whom you often have conflict. The classic approach to this is to imagine the other person in underwear, but use any imagery that works for you. I am especially fond of visualizing and hearing people as animals. The sillier the animal, the better this works.

Choose an animal which bears some resemblance to a dominating physical or behavioral quality of the person. I once had a tall gangly department chair whom I often imagined as a chicken. I could almost hear real chicken sounds coming from her mouth as she spoke, and imagined her laying an egg every time she said something I disagreed with. I sometimes saw her on her tip toes, with wings extended and flapping. It helped me rise above the situation, and enabled me to avoid getting emotionally caught up in conflict.

Unwanted noise drives me crazy, especially when I'm trying to sleep. I once had an apartment in which a heavy-footed man lived on the floor immediately above me. He would invariable come home about the time I was going to bed. His midnight plodding would upset me to the point that it was impossible to get sleepy—even after he went to bed! I finally discovered that I could keep from getting upset by imagining him as a rotund elephant with big ears flopping where his arms should be. I pictured him doing ridiculous things in his apartment, and sometimes laughed out loud. This helped me stay in a playful frame of mind until he stopped walking around. This mood always made it easier for me to fall asleep.

Practice Seeing the Glass Half-Full, Instead of Half-Empty

We've all heard this idea, but have you ever tried to put it into action? First, decide which kind of person you are. Do you generally see the empty or the full part of the glass? If you focus on the empty part, your first step is to acknowledge your tendency to take positive things for granted, while focusing on the negative. In Step 3, you were asked to develop the habit of adopting an optimistic outlook, rather than a pessimistic one. You now should take this a step further by looking for a positive side of things when under stress. Again, begin with minor hassles before trying it with major stressors.

Two older men suffering from the same pancreatic cancer were on the same floor of a hospital and chatted occasionally. One day one of them spotted the other sitting on his bed, head down, looking very depressed. He walked in and asked:

> **"What's the matter? Why so glum?"**
> **"My doctor just told me that 70% of the people who have what we have don't make it," said the second.**
> **"Oh no, that's not what my doctor said," replied the first. "He said that 3 out of every 10 survive!"**

The following story offers a different slant on seeing the glass half-full:

> **A woman discovers one day that her husband wants to leave her. She goes through six months of depression. One day a friend drags her to a therapist, and she goes through her tale of woe. The therapist says, "Look, you don't need therapy. You just have a decision to make. You can either spend the rest of your life in your house moping around and being miserable, or you can open your door, go outside, and yell, 'Next!'."**

Remind Yourself that Something Good Often Comes Out of a Bad Situation

I have had many occasions in my life where an unwanted outcome turned out to be a blessing in disguise. My entire career in psychology was indirectly due to my poor grades in chemistry and calculus during my freshman year of college. At the beginning of my sophomore year, my advisor (a mathematician) saw my grades and asked if I'd thought about another major. I had peeked through (but not read) my older brother's psychology text the preceding summer and found it interesting. So I said "psychology," more to avoid the embarrassment of the moment than because of any real interest in pursuing psychology as a major. (If my brother had had an astronomy book, I'm sure I would have said "astronomy.")

If I had not had such terrible grades my freshman year, I might have continued on to an engineering career—which I would have detested. Had I not failed calculus, I would never have gotten interested in research on humor. I would never have written this book or developed a career as a professional speaker on humor and stress. So what seemed like a disaster at the time turned out to have been the best thing that could have happened.

When you look back on your own past disappointments and problems, search for unexpected positive outcomes. Then do the same thing with problems as they're happening. Adopt a wait-and-see attitude when things don't go the way you want them to. Become a "good things" detective, searching for positive outcomes that might occur—while still acknowledging the bad side of the situation.

The following story, told by Dr. Bernie Siegel, illustrates the value of adopting a wait and see attitude.

> **There's a man who has a farm, and his whole livelihood depends on his horse, which plows the fields. One day he's out plowing, and suddenly the horse drops dead. The people of the town say, "Gee, that's tough." And the man says, "We'll see."**
>
> **A few days later, someone feels sorry for him and gives him a horse. The townspeople say, "What a lucky guy." And the man says, "We'll see."**
>
> **A couple of days later, the horse runs away and everyone says, "You poor guy." And the man says, "We'll see."**
>
> **A few days later, the horse returns with a second horse, and everyone says, "What a lucky guy!" And the man says, "We'll see."**
>
> **The man had never had two horses before, so he and his son decide to go riding, but the boy falls off his horse and breaks a leg. The townspeople say, "Poor kid." And the man says, "We'll see."**
>
> **The next day, the militia comes into town grabbing young men for the army. But they leave the boy behind, because he has a broken leg. Everyone says, "What a lucky kid!" And the man says, "We'll see."**

This story clearly shows that our lives are a constant mix of good and bad things happening. You can get bent out of shape when bad things occur, or wait and see what good things will come about as a result of them. You can choose to focus on the negative or to anticipate the positive. As you get better at looking for the good side of bad situations, you'll find your sense of humor coming back to you. You'll start making lemonade out of the lemons you're dealt.

Exaggerate Your Problems!

An excellent way to shake yourself out of an upset when you're under stress is to exaggerate the problem. Make it much worse than it really is. Blow it out of proportion, so that you have no choice but to see it as laughable.

A nurse who found a cancer patient walking down the hallway, head hung low, walked up beside him and—without saying a word—did exactly what the patient was doing, but more so. She walked even slower, held her head even lower, and had an Emmet Kelly look of sadness on her face. The patient, seeing himself in this new light, got a big grin on his face, straightened up, and walked with a much lighter pace. He got the point!

Have a Planned Playful Reaction to Fall Back On

An excellent way to practice pulling yourself out of a stress reaction is to have a planned silly behavior or statement to fall back on. This can be absolutely anything, as long as it has the power to draw you back into a playful frame of mind. One woman I know turns her tongue upside down to talk when she find herself getting stressed out. It sounds so silly to her that she can't help but grin—in spite of her problems. She first discovered talking like this when a bug flew into her mouth. Now, talking with her tongue upside down reminds her of how hilarious it was trying to talk with a bug in her mouth. She even brought a smile to her father's face by talking this way after he had a stroke.

Another friend imagines an elf sitting on her shoulder, and speaks in a high pitched, silly voice, saying "Now you've done it! You're in big trouble now! You'll never get out of this one!" She says this regardless of who's around, and it always works to ease her tension enough to cope better with the problem at hand.

It's much easier to have a light reaction prepared, of course, if the same problem comes up repeatedly. A teenager who bagged groceries in a supermarket would occasionally have groceries fall through the bottom of the bag. When this happened, he'd say, "They just don't make 'em like they used to; it's supposed to break as you carry it into your house."

An IRS representative was constantly bombarded with complaints and angry questions from groups he spoke to. This got in the way of good communication, so one day he came prepared with a couple of funny lines. First he said, "Well, they're written by the same people who write instructions for assembling toys." A few minutes later, he added, "Next year they'll be a lot simpler; you'll just put your income on one line and your tax due on another line—it's the same number!" From that point on, the anger was gone and people's attention was more sharply focused on the issues they were there to discuss.

I often break myself out of an upset by just shaking my head and cheeks (keeping the cheeks in a loose and relaxed position) sideways and blowing air out of my mouth in a way that sounds like Donald Duck. By vocalizing at the same time, I get a different funny effect. (I generally only do this when I'm alone.) Create a silly reaction of your own that will work for you.

If you have predictable sources of stress, make it a point to plan for them. For example, if your boss often asks you to get something done by 3 p.m. today, and you already have more things to do than you could get done by 3 p.m. tomorrow, you might consider one of the following responses:

"No problem! Could you unplug that clock for awhile?"

"Hey, I can do the work of two people. My mother always told me I had a split personality."

"My friends warned me to watch out for bosses who wanted a quickie."

"No problem, I'll just call the V.P. and tell her that her job will have to wait."

"If I asked my husband to make love to me 10 times by 3 p.m., could he do it?"

"Great, I Was wondering how I'd occupy myself today."

"No problem! Miracles are my specialty."

Let's assume that you're in a restaurant, and the waiter spills coffee or soup on you. Instead of your usual reaction, what playful remark could you make? Here are a few ideas to stimulate your thinking, but make an effort to come up with your own.

"There must have been a misprint in my horoscope today. It said a hot deal would fall into my lap today, not a hot meal."

"100 restaurants in this town, and I had to get a juggler for a waiter."

"I said fill it, not spill it."

"No problem. My wife was just saying, I should have taken a shower."

"That's nothing! You should see how they (the pants) look when *I* make dinner."

"No problem! My wife says I'm always hot about something."

"Hey, that's the most excitement I've had in my lap all week."

"That'll teach me to order the chef's surprise!"

"Listen, cancel that order for the egg drop soup."

Some additional ideas for planned verbal silliness are:

"For an encore, I will now challenge a piranha to a chicken-eating contest."

"Beam me up Scotty!"

"I try to take one day at a time, but lately several days have attacked me at once."

"I didn't do it! It's not my fault! . . . and I'll never do it again!"

"For my next trick . . ."

"I haven't had a drink to drop until now." (When you've just spilled an alcoholic drink.)

Try off-the-wall segues, like

"Speaking of sex . . ."

"And now for something completely different."

"It could be worse. I could be pregnant."

"It's always something . . . If it's not one thing, it's another"

"I'd rather kiss a snake."

You also may want to memorize "laws" in the tradition of Murphy's Law. The following may be especially helpful on bad days. Note that each one is better suited to some embarrassing or problem situations than others.

Law of Selective Gravity: "An object will fall so as to do the most damage."

Jenning's Corollary to the Law of Selective Damage: "The chance of the bread falling with the buttered side down is directly proportional to the cost of the carpet."

Probable Dispersal Law: "Whatever hits the fan will not be equally distributed."

Zymurgy's First Law of Evolving Systems Dynamics: "Once you open a can of worms, the only way to re-can them is to use a larger can."

Navy Law: "If you can keep your head when all around you are losing theirs, you don't understand the situation."

Howe's Law: "Every man/woman has a scheme that will not work."

Boren's First Law: "When in doubt, mumble."

Hoare's Law of Large Problems: "Inside every large problem is a small problem struggling to get out."

Additional Suggestions

When it comes to ideas for using humor to cope, you're limited only by your own imagination. Try viewing your everyday life as having the same properties as a joke. The setup in a joke gets you thinking in a certain direction, but then the punchline sends you in a new, unexpected direction. How often have you had days where everything is fine and going in the expected direction, and wham! Something happens, leaving you no choice but to move in a new direction to find a way to cope. You get a flat tire, lock yourself out, forget an important meeting, or have a proposal rejected. Look for a punchline in these real-life situations, and use it to keep the event from setting you back. A broad range of ideas is listed below. These work for some people, and may work for you. Use the list to stimulate your own thinking about approaches you'd like to try.

13 Tips for Easing Life's Strains

1. When something goes wrong, say in a silly manner, "It's all my/your fault. If I/you had only _____ (say anything absurd), this would never have happened."

2. In the midst of a family argument, everyone starts talking at the same time, speaking in complete gibberish.

3. When your young child is upset about something, say in a serious tone, "Hmmm, this is serious. Don't you dare grin."

4. Put on an animal nose in difficult situations.

5. Agree in advance to switch sides in the middle of an argument if it starts to get nasty.

6. Blow bubbles in traffic.

7. Use any object as a microphone and act like a commentator discussing how bad things are.

8. Play a game of "It could be worse," and make ridiculous or exaggerated statements about what could still happen.

9. If you're a hospital patient, ask entering nurses, "Who is it, friend or enema?" If you're about to have surgery, invite fellow patients to your "coming out" party.

10. If you're a patient about to get a shot, take the initiative and say, "Don't worry, you won't feel a thing."

11. Start imitating a familiar person while talking about a heavy problem (include comedy characters, like Lily Tomlin's telephone operator or Gilda Radner's Roseanne Roseanna Danna).

12. When an impossible conditions arises, playfully announce, "Now here's an opportunity for real personal growth."

13. Have a "Whine along" session with co-workers. Take turns whining your complaints to the melody of a familiar tune.

Humor Log Exercises

On Using Humor to Cope

1. Why is it so hard for most people to keep their sense of humor during stressful times?

2. Describe your own views regarding the ways in which humor can help you cope with stress.

3. How do Steps 1-6 help lay the foundation for using your sense of humor when under stress?

4. Comment on the idea that situations which are not, in themselves, funny can have a funny side. Describe an example of this in your own life.

5. People who are regularly exposed to serious injury, death, and dying tend to have a macabre sense of humor, laughing at things that most of us would find horrifying. Why does this occur? What special role does humor serve in these cases?

6. Why does this form of black humor show up in jokes all over the country every time a major disaster occurs?

7. What obstacles to using humor under stress can you expect to encounter if you've never tried this before?

8. Most of us are not very good at solving problems when under stress; we see things more narrowly, and are less creative. How can humor and laughter in the midst of stress lead to more innovative thinking and more effective problem solving?

9. If you look for things to laugh at in the midst of stress, does this mean that you are running away from the problem?

10. A sense of humor helps you keep everyday hassles and problems in perspective. What do we mean by keeping problems in perspective?

11. Much of our stress comes from conflict with other people. With whom do you have the most conflict in your life? How might you use your sense of humor to deal with this conflict?

12. Name two people you know who actively use their sense of humor to cope with stressful events. Describe a specific case where you've seen them initiate humor in a difficult situation.

13. Considering the different skills you've developed while working on Steps 2-6, which ones do you expect to be especially helpful to you in dealing with stress?

14. Describe two conflicts which often come up at work or at home. How might you use humor to help diffuse the conflict in the future?

15. To what extent do you think that passive exposure to the humor of others can help you handle the stress in your life more effectively?

16. Why should an active use of humor be more effective than a passive enjoyment of humor in helping you cope with stress?

17. Can you think of any reasons why parents might hesitate to use a joking remark in front of their children in the midst of a family conflict? How could these reasons be satisfactorily overcome?

18. What do you think is the best thing you can do to help your child learn to use humor as an effective coping skill?

Current Ability to Find Humor in the Midst of Stress

1. How would you describe your present skills at finding a light side of a) mildly and b) highly stressful situations?

2. Describe a recent stressful event which best demonstrates your present use (or lack of use) of humor to cope.

3. How has your ability to use humor to cope already improved as a result of your efforts at the Homeplay for Steps 1-6?

4. What obstacles do you expect to encounter in learning to actively use humor when under stress?

5. Disregarding your use of humor, how well do you generally cope with stressful events in your life?

6. Is your typical reaction to stress to get angry, anxious, or depressed? Describe an example of finding humor in the midst of this emotion, and discuss how it changed your emotional state.

7. Have you ever used humor in difficult situations to hide from the problem, or deny it? If so, what needs to be changed in order to use humor in a positive, constructive manner?

8. What are your goals in working on Step 7?

Early Development and Influences

1. How much stress was there in your family as you were growing up (both during childhood and adolescence)?

2. What was the most common source of stress during each period?

3. What was the most difficult thing for you to adjust to in the following areas: a) parents, b) brothers and sisters, c) friends, d) school, and e) dating?

4. How often did you use humor to cope when you were growing up?

5. Describe one example of a situation in both your childhood and adolescence where you used your sense of humor to cope.

6. Think of an example from each period of a stressful situation in which you would like to have come up with a humorous remark to handle a problem, but were unable to do so. What might you have done or said to handle the situation in a lighter manner?

7. How would you describe your typical emotional reaction to difficult situations when you were growing up?

8. How good were your parents at using humor in the midst of family conflicts? Give an example which demonstrates both your mother's and father's use (or lack of) use of humor.

9. List any other significant adults during your childhood who showed a good sense of humor in the midst of stress.

10. Did your parents ever react negatively to some effort at humor on your part in the midst of a family conflict? Positively? Describe the situation and their reaction.

11. Did your parents ever talk to you about the value of looking for a light side of problems? If so, how valuable was this in the development of your sense of humor?

GROUP SESSION

Opening Fun Activity

Discussion of Homeplay For Step 6

1. Share with a partner your experiences in learning to laugh at yourself. Describe specific cases where you were and were not successful.
2. If time permits, also share with a partner
   a. Your list of things you don't like about yourself.
   b. Whether you shared items from this list with others during the week, and whether you were able to poke fun at any of them.
   c. Your success at finding humor in a blunder or embarrassing event.
   d. Obstacles you discovered in trying to poke fun at yourself.
   e. Self-disparaging jokes that you learned.
3. Do you now have a better understanding of the idea that you can take yourself lightly, while taking your work and responsibilities seriously? Discuss this with a partner.

Finding Humor in the Midst of Stress

Discuss any of the issues raised in connection with Step 5, giving special attention to the Humor Log Exercises.

1. Describe a specific stressful situation from your own experience, preferably one that occurs often. The group should discuss ways in which you could use humor to lighten up in that situation.
2. If you're going through the 8-Step Program with co-workers at your place of employment, break up into small groups and try to come up with your own "Murphy's Laws" (see above) which apply to your company or work situation.
3. Remember to contact your phone partners this week. Be sure to support each other's efforts and successes at using humor to cope.

HOME PLAY

In general, just keep doing what you've been doing through the first six steps. Maintain a commitment to deal effectively with the cause of the stress, but don't lose access to your playfulness in the process. Look for a positive side of the situation (even if you have to stretch). Find ways to play with language. Look for incongruity, irony, absurdity, bizarre aspects, coincidences, etc. Poke fun at yourself. Start doing this with minor problems, and gradually build up to bigger ones.

1. Make a list of commonly occurring hassles and problems. Be determined to find a way to maintain a lighter attitude when these come up, while remaining committed to handling the problem. Give special attention to sources of stress at home and at work.
2. Think about what it means in these particular situations to see the glass "half full" instead of "half empty."
3. Ask friends (especially those with whom you've shared humor before) to help you find a light side of difficult situations when they arise.
4. Practice finding humor in connection with other people's problems (keep it to yourself). Then look for similarities to your own situation.
5. Look for humor in past stressful situations of your own.
6. Develop the habit of asking, "What will I find funny about this next week?"
7. Keep a prop handy which reminds you to "Lighten Up!"
8. Look for cartoons related to daily job hassles and sources of stress. Post them in an easily visible place so you and others can use them to release tension on bad days.
9. When your stress centers around your boss, or some other person to whom you may not feel free to fully express yourself, visualize him/her in some ridiculous way (e.g., as a pig oinking, a sheep bleating, in underwear, etc.) the next time a conflict situation comes up.
10. Think of some kind of silly behavior or statement you can use to help maintain a playful outlook the next time a problem arises.
11. Ask yourself, "How would Charlie Chaplin (or your favorite comedian) react in this situation?" Imagine you're that person.

12. Write down in your notebook incidents where you are able to be more playful or find a light side of a difficult situation. Don't worry about how funny it is. Note even minor examples of showing your sense of humor when under some stress.

13. Follow as many suggestions as you can in the section on "How to practice finding humor in the midst of stress."

14. People often get annoyed when they see someone adopting a light and playful attitude as they skillfully go about dealing with the problem at hand. If this form of motivation works for you, see how many people you can annoy in this fashion. Watch for their reaction as you playfully stay cool in the midst of conflict.

15. If you're going through the 8-Step Program as part of a group, come to the next meeting prepared to share a way in which you've found or created humor in the midst of stress.

STEP 8
Integration of Steps 1–7
Using Humor to Survive and Cope

"If you want to rule the world, you must keep it amused."
(Ralph Waldo Emerson)

"I try to think of humor as one of our greatest . . . national resources that must be preserved at all costs." (James Thurber)

Putting It All Together

Step 8 gives you the opportunity to assess how far you've come since starting on Step 1, and to put all the steps together and begin using humor to survive, and even thrive, in the midst of life stress. As you've put different aspects of your sense of humor on the "front burner" from one week to the next, you've may have lost some of the gains made on earlier steps. You now know that it takes more than a week or two to make the skills associated with each step a permanent part of your personality. By reexamining where you stand on each step, you'll see which areas of your sense of humor still need more work, and can give them special attention.

During Step 8, you'll also be asked to consciously work on each of the steps at the same time. This will further strengthen all of the skills you've been developing, helping to put them on "automatic pilot." That is, it will make them available when you need them, with no real effort on your part. This is the point at which you know that your sense of humor will always be there to help you cope. It will serve you as a life preserver when you're drowning.

In addition to helping you cope with stress, humor and laughter will now also help prevent stress from occurring. So you can **think of your sense of humor as a stress deodorant!** If you're lucky, one application in the morning will get you through the day. Chances are, however, that with your life, you'll need repeated applications all day long. You now have the skills to make this happen.

Humor Log Exercises

The following questions related to each of the first seven steps of the program invite you to think about the progress you've made on each step, and how these skills have influenced other aspects of your life. Use the information gained to decide for yourself where the strong and weak parts of your sense of humor lie.

> **There's this guy who's a big shot in guns. And yet he gets fired several times a day. He works for the circus, getting shot out of a cannon. Finally, he decides he's had it and quits. His boss says to him sadly, "I hate to see you go. We'll never find another guy of your calibre."**

Once you've completed this assessment of your progess, map out where you feel you've made the most and the least gains. Select the areas you consider the weakest, and spend a week or so just on those areas before moving on. Go back and reread everything associated with those steps, including the Homeplay. If possible, spend a week or so on each step you repeat. If you're going through the program with a group, do this on your own after the group meetings are finished.

Use your Humor Log to keep a daily log of the number of times you use skills associated with each step each day. Be sure to use this daily log. It will help assure that you do the Homeplay, and will show you which set of humor skills you seem to be most comfortable with. It will also reveal which humor skills you draw on when you're under stress.

Assessment of Your Progress

Step 1

1. Compare the general extent to which you now build outside sources of humor into your life to the extent to which you did so before starting this program. How much more daily exposure to humor do you now have?
2. Answer the same question with respect to specific sources of humor, including television, movies, print cartoons, stand-up comedy, and funny friends.
3. How has immersing yourself in humor for the past few months influenced your sense of humor?
4. What insights about the nature of your sense of humor have you had as a result of this immersion in humor?

Step 2

1. What progress have you made in overcoming Terminal Seriousness?
2. In what situations do you still find it difficult to adopt a lighter, more playful attitude?
3. Given your experience in the past few weeks, how important do you now think playfulness is for developing your sense of humor?
4. If you've made the effort to adopt a more playful style at work, how successful has this been? How is it now being received?
5. If you've made the effort to adopt a more playful style in your personal relationships, how would you describe its effect?

Step 3

1. Describe how your laughter has changed as you've gone through this program—both in terms of how often and how heartily you laugh.
2. How important a role does an occasional belly laugh play in managing your mood and helping you cope with stress?
3. Compared to before you started the 8-Step Program, how often do you now tell jokes or funny stories?
4. In what ways are you now a better joke teller than you used to be?
5. To what extent has joke telling helped you deal with stress?

Step 4

1. How have your skills at creating your own verbal humor improved?
2. At present, what is your most common way of playing with language (e.g., puns, exaggeration, nonsense, etc.)?
3. To what extent does coming up with your own spontaneous puns or other verbal humor now help you cope with stress?

Step 5

1. Describe your progress in finding humor in everyday life situations at work, at home, and elsewhere.
2. Where have you been most and least successful at finding a funny side of things?
3. To what extent has your ability to find humor in everyday life circumstances helped you cope with stress?

Step 6

1. How much improvement have you shown in your ability to laugh at yourself as a result of this program?
2. List the areas where you've been most and least successful in learning to poke fun at yourself.
3. To what extent has being able to laugh at yourself helped you cope with stress?

Step 7

1. How much progress have you shown in using your sense of humor to cope with stress during the 8-Step Program?
2. Which of the steps has been most useful in helping you cope?

3. Which step would you like to continue working on to get even better at using humor to cope?
4. In what areas of your life have you been most/least successful in using your sense of humor to cope?

Use the following daily log for a two-week period to record the number of times you use any of the skills associated with Steps 2-6. Indicate in the parentheses provided how many of those helped you cope with a difficult or stressful situation. Do this every evening before going to bed. Recording these will clarify to you which parts of your sense of humor are serving you best as a coping tool.

Frequency of Use of Humor Skills

Week 1

Mon: Step 2 ___( ) Step 3 ___( ) Step 4 ___( ) Step 5 ___( ) Step 6 ___( )
Tues: Step 2 ___( ) Step 3 ___( ) Step 4 ___( ) Step 5 ___( ) Step 6 ___( )
Wed: Step 2 ___( ) Step 3 ___( ) Step 4 ___( ) Step 5 ___( ) Step 6 ___( )
Thur: Step 2 ___( ) Step 3 ___( ) Step 4 ___( ) Step 5 ___( ) Step 6 ___( )
Fri: Step 2 ___( ) Step 3 ___( ) Step 4 ___( ) Step 5 ___( ) Step 6 ___( )
Sat: Step 2 ___( ) Step 3 ___( ) Step 4 ___( ) Step 5 ___( ) Step 6 ___( )
Sun: Step 2 ___( ) Step 3 ___( ) Step 4 ___( ) Step 5 ___( ) Step 6 ___( )

Week 2

Mon: Step 2 ___( ) Step 3 ___( ) Step 4 ___( ) Step 5 ___( ) Step 6 ___( )
Tues: Step 2 ___( ) Step 3 ___( ) Step 4 ___( ) Step 5 ___( ) Step 6 ___( )
Wed: Step 2 ___( ) Step 3 ___( ) Step 4 ___( ) Step 5 ___( ) Step 6 ___( )
Thur: Step 2 ___( ) Step 3 ___( ) Step 4 ___( ) Step 5 ___( ) Step 6 ___( )
Fri: Step 2 ___( ) Step 3 ___( ) Step 4 ___( ) Step 5 ___( ) Step 6 ___( )
Sat: Step 2 ___( ) Step 3 ___( ) Step 4 ___( ) Step 5 ___( ) Step 6 ___( )
Sun: Step 2 ___( ) Step 3 ___( ) Step 4 ___( ) Step 5 ___( ) Step 6 ___( )

Based on the above information, which parts (check the numbers associated with each step) of your sense of humor are used most/least often on a daily basis?

GROUP SESSION

Opening Fun Activity

Discussion of Homeplay for Step 7

1. Share a successful and unsuccessful attempt at lightening up in the midst of stress.
2. Humor can be thought of as an attitude, a way of looking at things which keeps you from being overwhelmed by the stressful event. Discuss this idea in light of specific stressors you've encountered.
3. Along the same lines, use a specific stressful situation in your life to discuss the idea that events which are not, in themselves, funny can have a funny side.
4. Describe to the group specific stressful situations that have come up since the last session. Give the group the task of deciding how you could have used humor in this situation, or reacted in a lighter and more effective way.
5. How successful were you at seeing the glass "half full," instead of "half empty?"
6. How successful were you at finding a funny side of other people's problems? Did this help you lighten up when you had the same problem?
7. What props or cartoons did you use to help you maintain a lighter attitude in difficult situations?
8. Was it easier to use humor to deal with stress at home or at work?
9. Which steps of this program were most useful in helping you cope with stress? Which humor skills did you use most often?
10. All things considered, how has this program influenced the general level of stress in your life?

Progress in Improving your Sense of Humor

1. Share your feelings about how you've benefitted from this Program.
2. In what areas have you made the most/least progress in improving your sense of humor?

3. If you've already completed the post-test, share the results with a partner. Discuss difference scores for each area, and communicate any insights you gained from the post-test.

Continuing to Improve Your Humor Skills

1. What do you plan to do in the months ahead to assure that you continue building on the humor skills you now have?
2. Discuss how you can continue to support each other in improving your sense of humor after the group stops meeting. Make it a point to contact members of your telephone team from time to time.
3. Be sure to spend a couple of weeks on Step 8, even if you don't have a 9th group meeting to discuss your efforts.
4. Remember, s/he who laughs, lasts.

HOME PLAY

You have focused on one humor skill at a time to this point. Even when you tried to maintain what you were doing on one step, while moving on to the next one, you probably found that it was difficult to do. To effectively use humor to cope, you need access to the skills associated with each step in any given situation. Step 8 allows you to consolidate the gains you've made and make them an integral part of yourself. Practice all of the skills you've worked on in the past. Give special attention to areas you consider your weak points. Refer back to the Homeplay related to those areas to which you want to give extra attention.

Take the Sense of Humor Post-Test

After completing Step 8, take the post-test provided at the end of the book. If you have been completing the 8-Step Program with a group, and the group is having only 8 meetings, complete the post-test prior to the 8th meeting so that you can discuss it in the group. Do not consult your answers on the pre-test until after you've completed the post-test. Then compare your pre- and post- test scores, using the difference score procedure provided. Describe in your Humor Log any insights you gain about your progress in the program using these difference scores. Pay attention to specific items on the humor test, in addition to the total scores. If you've been going through the 8-Step Program alone, make it a point to discuss these difference scores, along with any insights you have with some of your friends or co-workers.

Homeplay for the Months Ahead

You can now see that it takes time and effort to change your old habits relating to humor and laughter. You've made some progress, but you'd probably like to make more. One way of doing so is to start back at the beginning, and repeat each of the steps. You'll find that the skills will become more firmly entrenched into your personality the second time around.

Another way to continue benefiting from the program is to simply extend Step 8 into the months and years ahead. Make it a point periodically to think about whether you're being as playful as you want to be, making enough effort to play with language, laugh at yourself, and look for humor—especially on your bad days.

Like any skills, if you don't use them, they can atrophy. So you'll need to make a commitment to continue building humor into your life, both by creating it yourself and looking for it in everyday life. Of course, as the following story illustrates, it's not always easy to keep your commitments.

> **An elderly woman was taking care of her 3-year-old grandson one day. They went to the beach, and as the child made sand castles, the grandmother dozed off. As she slept, a huge wave dragged the child out to sea. When she awoke, she was devastated. She fell on her knees and prayed. "God, if You save my grandson, I promise I'll make it up to You. I'll join whatever club You want me to. I'll volunteer up at the hospital. I'll give to the poor and do anything else You ask."**
>
> **Suddenly, a huge wave tossed the child back on the beach at her feet. She saw that there was color in his cheeks, and that he was breathing. He was alive! She put her hands on her hips, looked skyward, and said sharply, "He had a hat, You know!"**

To help sustain the development of your sense of humor, create a Mirth Aide Kit, using the props, audio tapes, cartoons, and anything else you've collected in the past few months that helps you laugh when you're having a bad day. Keep a separate kit at home and at work, or wherever you know you'll need it the most.

You should also consider putting this book aside for a year, and going through the entire program again at that time. If possible, do it with a partner. Whichever option you choose for continuing to make the 8-Step Humor Training Program work for you, remember to make it **fun,** not work.

In the months ahead, use your sense of humor to provide a daily emotional cleansing. You cleanse your body every day by washing it, and you nourish it by eating. You keep it in good condition to perform physical tasks by exercising it. You nourish your mind by reading, listening to the news, and talking to people.

What daily activities do you engage in to cleanse and nourish your emotions? Establishing loving relationships with others helps, but you also need a regular means of letting go of the negative emotions that accumulate on high stress days. Laughter provides an emotional release that is just as cleansing as the soap on your body. It is nourishment for your soul. And when you experience this cleansing yourself, you'll inevitably pass it on to others. So do what you can to put more MIRTH ON EARTH.

It's All in Your Hands

There was a man who for many years was known across the land for his great wisdom. He would go from town to town and give people advice about their love life, their job, raising a family—about any problem at all. He's a sage, and he's loved in every town he goes to—except one. There are two men in this town who are jealous of all the attention and respect he gets. So they try to make him look bad, even though they, themselves, could never achieve his level of wisdom.

The wise man is coming to their town the next day. And one of the men comes to the other and says, "You know, I've finally figured out a way to make him look bad." And his friend says, "Well, what are we going to do this time?" The first says, "Well, I'm going to be the first one in line tomorrow. And I'm going to say, 'Wise man, many of us in this town think you've lost your wisdom. In fact, we think you're getting senile. To prove your wisdom once and for all, just answer the following question.'"

So his friend says, "Well, what's the question?" "Well, I'm going to have a little butterfly in my hands, and I'm going to ask him whether the butterfly is alive or dead. If he says it's dead, I'll just open up my hands, and it'll fly away. But if he says it's alive, I'll just gently crush my hands together, and everybody will see a dead butterfly." His friend gets really excited and says, "So no matter what he says, he's going to be wrong."

Well, they couldn't wait until the next day's confrontation. Everything goes according to plan, and they are the first ones in line. There are several hundred people there, and when the wise man shows up, the second man causes a big ruckus to get everyone to gather around. The first man says, "Wise man, many of us in this town think you've lost your wisdom. In fact, we think you're getting senile. To prove your wisdom once and for all, just answer the following question." And he put his hands up and said, "Is the butterfly in my hands alive or dead?"

The wise man doesn't even hesitate. He looks him in the eye and says, "The answer to that question is very simple. It's all in your hands . . . It's your choice."

Think of the butterfly as your sense of humor. You know from your own experience that your sense of humor is easily crushed by the stress from your job, your relationships, your financial problems, your health problems—from all the areas in your life where things can go wrong. But if you nurture it and use the 8-Step Program to build it up, it can also help you survive any problem thrown your way. It can carry you to heights that make it easier to cope. It can provide you with joy and a love of life even in the midst of hard times. It can give you a sense of control over your daily mood, and leave you in a frame of mind that is better equipped to handle problems effectively. It can help you cope! This book provide you with the steps you need to follow to learn to use humor to cope with life stress. Whether or not you allow the butterfly to die or develop and thrive is all in your hands . . . It's your choice.

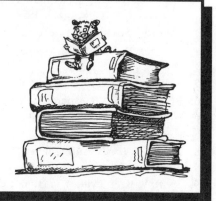

Footnotes

Introduction

1. Nevo, O. et al. The development and evaluation of a systematic program for improving your sense of humor. In Ruch, W. (Ed.) *The Sense of Humor: Explorations of a Personality Characteristic.* New York: Mouton de Gruyter, 1998.

2. Lowis, M.J. & Nieuwoudt, J.M. Humor as a coping aid for stress. *Social Work,* 1994, 30, 124–131.

3. Gunderson, A.L. A comparison of the effect of two humor programs on self-reported coping capabilities and pain among the elderly. Unpublished Master's Thesis, Montclair State University, 1998.

4. Ruch, W. & Carrell, A. Trait cheerfulness and the sense of humour. *Personality and Individual Differences,* 1998, 24, 551–558.

Chapter 1

1. LaBarre, P. Lighten up! Blurring the line between fun and work not only humanizes organizations, but strengthens the bottom line. *Industry Week,* Feb. 5, 1996, p. 53.

2. LaBarre, 1996, p. 53.

3. LaBarre, 1996, p. 54.

4. McKenna, J.F. April foolin'. *Managing Office Technology,* April, 1997, p. 10.

5. *New York Times,* May 14, 1989. Business section, p. 2.

6. Abramis, D.J. Fun at work. *Personnel Administrator,* November, 1989 (a), 60–63.

7. Lancaster, H. Your career may be a laugh track away from the fast track ("Managing Your Career" column). *Wall Street Journal,* March 26, 1996.

8. Flynn, G. Remedy cures work doldrums. *Workforce,* February, 1998.

9. Levering, R. & Moskowitz, M. The 100 best companies to work for in America. *Fortune,* Jan. 12, 1998, pp. 84–96.

10. Smith, A.L. Are we having fun yet? *Business Quarterly,* Spring, 1997, 9–10.

11. Abramis, D. Building fun into your organization. *Personnel Administrator,* October, 1989 (b), 68–72.

12. Abramis, D. All work and no play isn't even good for work. *Psychology Today,* March, 1989 (c), 34–38.

Abramis, D. Fun at Work. Paper presented at the Humor Project Conference, Saratoga Springs, New York, April, 1992.

13. Caudron, S. Humor is healthy in the workplace. *Personnel Journal,* 1992, 71, 63–68.

14. Twidale, H. Nowadays, being "old sourpuss" is no joke. *Working Woman,* March, 1986, p. 18.

15. *San Jose Mercury News,* July 30, 1986, p. 14.

16. Blumenfeld, E. & Alpern, L. *Humor at Work.* Atlanta: Peachtree, 1994, p. 2.

17. Humor is no joke in workplace (staff article). *Christian Science Monitor,* August 21, 1995, p. 8.

18. Peters, T. *The Pursuit of Wow! Every Person's Guide to Topsy-Turvy Times.* New York: Vintage, 1994.

19. Swift, W.B. & Swift, A.T. Humor experts jazz up the workplace. *HR Magazine,* March, 1994, p. 72.

20. *Fortune,* May 4, 1994.

21. Pollio, H. & Bainum, C. Are funny groups good at problem solving? A methodological evaluation and some preliminary results. *Small Group Behavior,* 1983, 14, 379–404.

22. Vinton, K.L. Humor in the workplace: Is it more than telling jokes? *Small Group Behavior,* 1989, 20, 151–166.

23. Section on The Expert Manager. Humor on the job—avoid it to your detriment. *Executive Female,* 1997, 20(4), p. 23.

24. Survey reported in the *St. Petersburg Times,* September 30, 1994, p.10h.

25. Weiss, W.H. Humor on the job. *Supervision,* November, 1997, 9–11.

26. Filipczak, B. Are we having fun yet? *Training,* April, 1995, 48–56.

27. Filipczak, 1995.

28. Lancaster, 1996.

29. Abramis, 1989 (a).

30. Fry, P.S. Perfectionism, humor, and optimism as moderators of health outcomes and determinants of coping styles of women executives. *Genetic, Social & General Psychology Monographs,* 1995, 121, 213–245.

31. Von Oech, R. *A Whack on the Side of the Head.* New York: Warner, 1990.

32. Posen, D.B. Stress management for patient and physician. *Canadian Journal of Continuing Medical Education,* April, 1995.

33. Levy, S. Working in Dilbert's world. *Newsweek,* August 12, 1996.

34. Baumohl, B. When downsizing becomes "dumbsizing." *Time,* March 15, 1993, p. 55.

35. Levy, 1996, p. 57.

36. Levy, 1996, p. 53.

37. Black, D. Scots' stress levels higher than average. *The Herald,* June 29, 1995.

38. Gerstner, J. Good communication, bad morale. *IABC Communication World,* March, 18–21, 1994.

39. Baumohl, 1993, p. 55.

40. Paxton, L. Foregoing the American Dream. *Chicago Tribune,* September 17, 1994, p. 21.

41. LaBarre, 1996.

42. Ziv, A. Facilitating effects of humor on creativity. *Journal of Educational Psychology,* 1976, 68, 318–432.

43. Glynn, M.A. The perceptual structuring of tasks: A cognitive approach to understanding task attitudes and behaviors. Unpublished doctoral dissertation. New York: Columbia University, 1988.

44. Isen, A.M., et al., Positive affect facilitates creative problem solving. *Journal of Personality and Social Psychology,* 1987, 52, 112–131.

45. Duncan, W.J. & Feisal, J.P. No laughing matter: Patters of Humor in the workplace. *Organizational Dynamics,* 1989, 17, 18–30. (Quote on p. 18.)

46. Ziv, A. Using humor to develop creative thinking. In P.E. McGhee (Ed.), *Humor and Children's Development: A Guide to Practical Applications.* New York: Haworth, 1989.

47. Duncan, W.J. Perceived humor and social network patterns in a sample of task-oriented groups: A reexamination of prior research. *Human Relations,* 1984, 37, 895–907.
    Blau, P. *The Dynamics of Bureaucracy.* Chicago: University of Chicago Press, 1955.

48. Malone, P. Humor: A double-edged tool for today's managers? *Academy of Management Review,* 1980, 5, 357–360.

49. Duncan & Feisal, 1989.

50. Levy, 1996, p. 56.

51. Malec, W.F. A funny thing happened on the way to quality. *Public Utilities Fortnightly,* April 1, 1992.

52. Baron, R. Reducing organizational conflict: An incompatible response approach. *Journal of Applied Psychology,* 1984, 69, 272–279.

53. Consalvo, C.M. Humor in management: No laughing matter. *Humor: International Journal of Humor Research,* 1989, 2, 285–297.

54. Kushner, M. *The Light Touch.* New York: Simon & Schuster, 1990.

55. McCormack, M. *What They Don't Teach You at the Harvard Business School.* New York: Bantam Books, 1984, pp. 46–47.

56. Paulsen, T.L. *Making Humor Work.* Los Altos, CA.: Crisp Publications, 1989, p. 50.

57. O'quinn, K. & Aronoff, J. Humor as a technique of social influence. *Social Psychology Quarterly,* 1981, 44, 349–357.

58. Callahan, J. A lesson from the Leonards. *Convenience Store News,* May 3, 1993.

59. Clouse, R.W. & Spurgeon, K.L. Corporate analysis of humor. *Psychology: A Journal of Human Behavior,* 1995, 32, 1–24. (Quote on p. 20.)

60. Lancaster, 1996.

61. Fisher, A. What's so funny jokeboy? *Fortune,* Dec. 9, 1996, p. 220.

62. Editorial. Laugh, for heaven's sake. *Industry Week,* July 20, 1992, p. 7.

63. Pickard, J. You cannot be serious! *People Management,* Dec. 18, 1997, 3(25), p. 34.

64. Abner, M. Corporate America takes fun seriously. *Women in Business,* 1997, 49(5), p. 42.

65. Paulsen, 1989, p. 48.

66. LaBarre, 1996, p. 53.

67. Section on The Expert Manager. Humor on the job—avoid it to your detriment. *Executive Female,* 1997, 20(4), p. 23.

68. Kennedy, M.M. *Across the Board,* June, 1995, 11–12.

69. Kennedy, 1995.

70. Duncan, W. J. & Feisal, J. P. No laughing matter: Patterns of humor in the workplace. *Organizational Dynamics,* 1989, 18–30.

71. Freiberg, K. & Freiberg, J. *NUTS! Southwest Airlines Crazy Recipe for Business and Personal Success.* Austin, TX: Bard Press, 1996, p. 67.

72. Freiberg & Freiberg, 1996, p. 64.

73. Abramis, 1989 (b).

74. Schlegel, S. Humor at work. *Trenton Times,* March 20, 1994.

75. McKenna, 1997, p. 10.

76. Filipczak, 1995.

77. Glanz, B. *Care Package for the workplace.* New York: McGraw-Hill, pp. 26–27.

Chapter 2

1. Goldstein, J.H. Therapeutic effects of laughter. In W.F. Fry & W.A. Salameh (Eds.), *Handbook of Humor and Psychotherapy.* Sarasota, FL: Professional Resource Exchange, 1987.

2. Paskind, H.A. Effects of laughter on muscle tone. *Archives of Neurology and Psychiatry,* 1932, 28, 23–628.
   Prerost, F.J. & Ruma, C. Exposure to humorous stimuli as an adjunct to muscle relaxation training. *Psychology: A Quarterly Journal of Human Behavior,* 1987, 24, 70–74.
   Fry, W.F. Jr. Humor, physiology, and the aging process. In L. Nahemow, K. McCluskey-Fawcett, & P. McGhee (Eds.), *Humor and Aging.* New York: Academic Press, 1986.

3. Prerost & Ruma, 1987.

4. Langorch, W., et al. Behavior therapy with coronary heart disease patients. *Journal of Psychosomatic Research,* 1982, 26, 465–484.

5. Blanehard, E., et al. Sequential comparisons of relaxation training and biofeedback in the treatment of three kinds of chronic headache. *Behavior Research and Therapy,* 1982, 20, 469–481.

6. Leboeuf, A. The effects of EMG feedback training on state anxiety. *Journal of Clinical Psychology,* 1977, 33, 251–253.

7. Berk, L.S., et al. Neuroendocrine and stress hormone changes during mirthful laughter. *American Journal of the Medical Sciences,* 1989, 298, 390–396.
   Yoshino, S., et al. Effects of mirthful laughter on neuroendocrine and immune systems in patients with rheumatoid arthritis. *Journal of Rheumatology,* 1996, 23, 793–794.

8. Jemmott, J.B. & Locke, S.E. Psychosocial factors, immunologic mediation, and human susceptibility to infectious diseases: How much do we know? *Psychological Bulletin,* 1984, 95, 78–108.
   Kiecolt-Glaser, J., et al. Modulation of cellular immunity in medical students. *Journal of Behavioral Medicine,* 1986, 9, 5–21.

9. Vollhardt, L.T. Psychoneuroimmunology: A literature review. *American Journal of Orthopsychiatry,* 1991, 61, 35–47.

10. Dillon, K.M., et al. Positive emotional states and enhancement of the immune system. *International Journal of Psychiatry in Medicine,* 1985, 5, 13–18.
    Lefcourt, H., et al. Humor and immune system functioning. *International Journal of Humor Research,* 1990, 3, 305–321.
    McClelland, D. & Cheriff, A.D. The immunoenhancing effects of humor on secretory IgA and resistance to respiratory infections. *Psychology and Health,* 1997, 12, 329–344.

11. Berk, L.S., et al. Immune system changes during humor associated with laughter. *Clinical Research,* 1991, 39, 124A.

12. Lambert, R.B. & Lambert, N.K. The effects of humor on secretory immunoglobulin A levels in school-aged children. *Pediatric Nursing*, 1995, 21, 16–19.

13. Berk, L.S., et al. Eustress of humor associated with laughter modulates specific immune system components. *Annals of Behavioral Medicine*, 1993, 15 (supplement), p. S111.

14. Berk, et al., 1993.

15. Berk, L.S., et al. Eustress of mirthful laughter modifies natural killer cell activity. *Clinical Research*, 1989, 37 (No. 1), p. 115A.
    Berk, et al., 1993.

16. Itami, J., et al. Laughter and immunity. *Japanese Journal of Psychosomatic Medicine*, 1994, 34, 565–571.
    Kamei, T., et al. Changes of immunoregulatory cells associated with psychological stress and humor. *Perceptual and Motor Skills*, 1997, 84, 1296–1298.

17. Levy, S.M., et al. Prognostic risk assessments in primary breast cancer by behavior and immunological parameters. *Health Psychology*, 1985, 4, 99–113.

18. Bellert, J.L. Humor: A therapeutic approach in oncology nursing. *Cancer Nursing*, 1989, 12, 65–70.

19. Berk, et al., 1989, 1993.

20. Kiecolt-Glaser, et al., 1986.

21. Gruber, B.L., et al. Immune system and psychologic changes in metastatic cancer patients while using ritualized relaxation and guided imagery: A pilot study. *Scandinavian Journal of Behavior Therapy*, 1988, 17, 25–46.

22. Callen, M. *Surviving AIDS*. New York: Harper Collins, 1990.

23. Berk, L.S. & Tan, S.A. A positive emotion, the eustress of mirthful laughter, modulates the immune system lymphokine interferon-Gamma. Research Perspectives in Psychoneuroimmunology. *Psychoneuroimmunology Research Society Program Abstracts*, June, 1996

24. Berk, et al., 1991.
    Berk, et al., 1993.
    Berk & Tan, 1996.

25. Dillon, et al., 1985.
    Dillon, K.M. & Totten, M.C. Psychological factors, immunocompetence, and health of breast feeding mothers and their infants. *Journal of General Psychology*, 1989, 150, 155–162.
    McClelland, D.C. & Cheriff, A.D. The immunoenhancement effects of humor on secretory IgA and resistance to respiratory infections. *Psychology and Health*, 1997, 12, 329–344.

26. Lefcourt, et al., 1990.
    McClelland & Cheriff, 1997.

27. Martin, R.A. & Dobbin, J.P. Sense of humor, hassles, and immunoglobulin A: Evidence for a stress-moderating effect of humor. *International Journal of Psychiatry in Medicine*, 1988, 18, 93–105.

28. Stone, A.A., et al. Evidence that secretory IgA is associated with daily mood. *Journal of Personality and Social Psychology*, 1987, 52, 988–993.
    Valdimarsdottir, H.B. & Bovbjerg, D.H. Positive and negative mood: Association with natural killer cell activity. *Psychology and Health*, 1997, 12, 319–327.

29. Irwin, M., et al. Life events, depressive symptoms and immune function. *American Journal of Psychiatry*, 1987, 144, 437–441.

30. Linn, B.S., et al. Anxiety and immune responsiveness. *Psychological Reports*, 1981, 49, 969–970.

31. Jabaaij, L., et al. Influences of perceived psychological stress and distress on antibody response to lose dose rDNA hepatitis B vaccine. *Journal of Psychosomatic Research,* 1993, 37, 361–369.

32. Stone, A.A., et al. Evidence that secretory IgA antibody is associated with daily mood. *Journal of Personality and Social Psychology,* 1987, 52, 988–993.

33. Martin, R.A. & Lefcourt, H. Sense of humor as a moderator of the relation between stressors and moods. *Journal of Personality and Social Psychology,* 1983, 45, 1313–1324.

34. Siegel, B.S. *Peave, Love and Healing.* New York: Harper & Row, 1989,

35. Labbott, S.M., et al. The physical and psychological effects of the expression and inhibition of emotion. *Behavioral Medicine,* 1990, 16, 182–189.

36. McClelland & Cheriff, 1997.

37. Adams, E.R. & McGuire, F.A. Is laughter the best medicine? A study of the effects of humor on perceived pain and affect. *Activities, Adaptation, and Aging,* 1986, 8, 157–175.

38. Cogan, R., et al. Effects of laughter and relaxation on discomfort thresholds. *Journal of Behavioral Medicine,* 1987, 10, 139–144.
    Zillmann, D., et al. Does humor facilitate coping with physical discomfort? *Motivation and Emotion,* 1993, 17, 1–21.
    Weisenberg, M., et al. Humor as a cognitive technique for increasing pain tolerance. *Pain,* 1995, 63, 207–212.

39. Nevo, O., et al. Humor and pain tolerance. *International Journal of Humor Research,* 1993, 6, 71–78.

40. Kelly, M.L., et al. Decreasing burned children's pain behavior: Impacting the trauma of hydrotherapy. *Journal of Applied Behavior Analysis,* 1984, 17, 147–158.

41. Hudak, D.A., et al. Effects of humorous stimuli and sense of humor on discomfort. *Psychological Reports,* 1991, 69, 779–786.

42. Yoshino, et al., 1996.

43. Leise, C.M. The correlation between humor and the chronic pain of arthritis. *Journal of Holistic Nursing,* 1993, 11, 82–95.

44. Ljungdahl, L. Laugh if this is a joke. *Journal of the American Medical Association,* 1989, 261, 558.

45. Schmitt, N. Patients' perception of laughter in a rehabilitation hospital. *Rehabilitation Nursing,* 1990, 15 (No. 3), 143–146.

46. Trice, A.D. & Price-Greathouse, J. Joking under the drill: A validity study of the humor coping scale. *Journal of Social Behavior and Personality,* 1986, 1, 265–266.

47. McCaffery, M. Nursing approaches to non-pharmacological pain control. *International Journal of Nursing Studies,* 1990, 27, 1–5.

48. Berk, et al., 1989.
    Yoshino, et al., 1996.

49. Kogan, R. & Kluthe, K.B. The role of learning in pain reduction associated with relaxation and patterned breathing. *Journal of Psychosomatic Research,* 1981, 25, 535–539.
    French, A.P. & Turpin, J.P. Therapeutic application of a simple relaxation method. *American Journal of Psychotherapy,* 1974, 28, 282–287.

50. Fry, W.F., Jr. & Savin, M. Mirthful laughter and blood pressure. Paper presented at the Third International Conference on Humor, Washington, D.C., 1982.

51. Lefcourt, H.M., et al. Humor as a stress moderator in the prediction of blood pressure obtained during five stressful tasks. *Journal of Research in Personality,* 1997, 31, 523–542.

52. Carroll, D., et al. The relationship between socioeconomic status, hostility, and blood pressure reactions to mental stress in men: Data from the Whitehall II study. *Health Psychology,* 1997, 16, 131–136.

53. Curtis, A.B., et al. Job strain and blood pressure in African Americans: the Pitt County study. *American Journal of Public Health,* 1997, 87, 1297–1302.

54. Fry, W.F., Jr. Humor, physiology, and the aging process. In L. Nahemow, K.A. McCluskey-Fawcett & P.E. McGhee (Eds.), *Humor and Aging.* San Diego: Academic Press, 1986, pp. 81–98.

55. Cousins, N. *Head First: The Biology of Hope.* New York: Dutton, 1989, p. 126.

56. Carroll, J.L. & Shmidt, J.L. Correlation between humorous coping style and health. *Psychological Reports,* 1992, 70, 402.
    Simon, J. M. Humor and its relationship to perceived health, life satisfaction, and morale in older adults. *Issues in Mental Health Nursing,* 1990, 11, 17–31.

57. Fry, P.S. Perfectionism, humor and optimism as moderators of health outcomes and determinants of coping styles of women executives. *Genetic, Social and General Psychology Monographs,* 1995, 121, 213–245.

58. Schmitt, 1990.

59. Moyers, B. *Healing and the Mind.* New York: 1993.
    Goleman, D. & Gurin, J. (Eds.) *Mind/Body medicine: How to Use Your Mind for Better Health.* Yonkers, NY: Consumer Reports Books, 1993.

60. Pert, C. The chemical communications. In B. Moyers, 1993.

61. Kemeny, M. Emotions and the immune system. In B. Moyers, *Healing and the Mind.* New York: 1993.

62. Cluff, L.E., et al. Asian influenza: Infection, disease and psychological factors. *Archives of Internal Medicine,* 1966, 117, 159–164.

63. Kiecolt-Glaser, J., et al. Psychosocial modifiers of immunocompetence in medical students. *Psychosomatic Medicine,* 1984, 46, 7–14.
    Locke, S.E., et al. Life change stress, psychiatric symptoms and natural killer cell activity. *Psychosomatic Medicine,* 1984, 46, 441–453.

64. Justice, B. *Who Gets Sick: How Beliefs, Moods, and Thoughts Affect Your Health.* Los Angeles: Tarcher, 1987.

65. Pert, C., 1993, p. 176.

66. Pert, C., 1993, p. 190.

67. Pert, C., 1993, p. 190.

68. Stone, et al., 1987.

69. Jabaaij, et al., 1993.

70. Linn, et al., 1981.

71. Bovbjerg, D.H. & Valdimarsdottir, H. Familial cancer, emotional distress, and low natural cytotoxic activity in healthy women. *Annals of Oncology,* 1993, 4, 745–752.

72. Stone, et al., 1987.
    Stone, A.A., et al. Daily events are associated with a secretory immune response to an oral antigen in humans. *Health Psychology,* 1994, 13, 440–446.

73. Valdimarsdottir & Bovbjerg, 1997.

74. Rees, W.D. & Lutkins, S.G. Mortality of bereavement. *British Medical Journal,* 1967, 4, 13–16.
    Helsing, K.J., et al. Factors associated with mortality after widowhood. *American Journal of Public Health,* 1981, 71, 802–809.

75. Shekelle, R.B. Psychological depression and 17-year risk of death from cancer. *Psychosomatic Medicine,* 1981, 43, 117–125.

76. Temoshok, L. Clinical psychoneuroimmunology in AIDS. Paper presented at annual meeting of the Society of Behavioral Medicine, San Francisco, 1986.

77. Associated Press. Pessimism can be deadly for heart patients. *The New York Times,* April 16, 1994, p. 8.

78. Associated Press. *The New York Times,* 1994, p. 8.

79. Luborsky, L., et al. Herpes simplex virus and moods: A longitudinal study. *Journal of Psychosomatic Research,* 1976, 20, 543–548.

80. Scheier, M.F. & Carver, C.S. Optimism, coping and health: Assessment and implications of generalized outcome expectancies. *Health Psychology,* 1985, 4, 219–247.

81. Peterson, C. & Bossio, L.M. Health attitudes: Optimism, hope, and control. In Goleman & Gurin, 1993.

82. Cohen, R., et al. Psychological stress and susceptibility to the common cold. *New England Journal of Medicine,* 1991, 325, 606–612.

83. Cluff, et al., 1966.

84. Verthein, U. & Kohler, T. The correlation between everyday stress and angina pectoris: A longitudinal study. *Journal of Psychosomatic Research,* 1997, 43, 241–245.

85. Justice, 1987.

86. Friedman, H.S. & Booth-Kewley, S. The disease-prone personality. *American Psychologist,* 1987, 42, 539–555.

87. Turk, D.C. & Nash, J.M. Chronic Pain: New ways to cope. In Goleman & Gurin, 1993, p. 115–116.

88. Mossey, J.A. & Shapiro, E. Self-rated health: A predictor of mortality among the elderly. *American Journal of Public Health,* 1982, 72, 800–808.

89. Gottshalk, L.A. Hope and other deterrents of illness. *American Journal of Psychotherapy,* 1985, 39, 515–524.

90. Green, E. & Green, A. *Beyond Biofeedback.* New York: Delta, 1975.

91. Weinstock, C. Recent progress in cancer psychobiology and psychiatry. *Journal of the American Society of Psychosomatic Dentistry and Medicine,* 1977, 24, 4–14.

92. Cousins, 1989, p. 126.

93. Kemeny, 1993.

94. Pettingale, K.W., et al. Mental attitudes to cancer: An attitudinal prognostic factor. *Lancet,* 1985, 8, 750.

95. Temoshok, 1986.
    Solomon, G.F., et al. An intensive psychoimmunologic study of long-surviving persons with AIDS. *Annals of the New York Academy of Sciences,* 1987, 496, 647–655.

96. Peterson & Bossio, 1993.

97. Cousins, 1989.

98. Peterson, C., et al. Pessimistic explanatory style is a risk factor for physical illness: A thirty-five year longitudinal study. *Journal of Personality and Social psychology,* 1988, 55, 23–27.

99. Peterson & Bossio, 1993.

100. Mason, T., et al., Acceptance and healing. *Journal of Religion and Health,* 1969, 8, 123–142.

101. Melnechuk, T. Emotions, brain, immunity and health: A review. In M. Clynes & J. Panksepp (Eds.), *Emotions and Psychopathology*. New York: Plenum, 1988, 181–247.

102. Peterson & Bossio, 1993.

103. Goleman, D. & Gurin, J. What is mind/body medicine? In D. Goleman & J. Gurin, 1993.

104. Callow, K.A. Effect of specific humoral immunity and some non-specific factors on resistance of volunteers to respiratory coronavirus infection. *Journal of Hygiene*, 1985, 95, 173–189. Jemmott, J.B. III & McClelland, D.C. Secretary IgA as a measure of resistance to infectious disease: Comments on Stone, Cox, Valdimirsdottir, and Neale. *Behavioral Medicine*, 1989, 15, 63–71.

105. Smith, D.J. & Taubman, M.A. Effect of local deposition of antigen on salivary immune responses and reaccumulation of mutans streptococci. *Journal of Clinical Immunology*, 1990, 10, 273–281.

106. McClelland & Cheriff, 1997.

107. Dillon & Totten, 1989.

108. Annie, C.L. & Groer, M. Childbirth stress: An immunologic study. *JOGN Nursing*, 1991, 20, 391–397.

109. Hehl, F.J. Beziehungen zwischenkorperlichen Beschwerden und Humor. *Zeitschrift fur Klinische Psychologie, Psychopathologie und Psychotherapie*, 1990, 38, 362–368.

110. Hehl, F.J. & Ruch, W. The location of sense of humor within comprehensive personality spaces: An exploratory study. *Personality and Individual Differences*, 1988, 6, 703–715.

111. Friedman, M. & Rosenman, R.H. *Type A Behavior and Your Heart*. New York: Knopf, 1974, p. 298.

112. Goldstein, J.H., et al. Humor and the coronary-prone behavior pattern. *Current Psychological Research Review*, 1988, 7, 115–121.

113. Schmitt, 1990.

114. Darrach, B. Send in the clowns. *Life Magazine*. 1990, 13(10), 76–85.

115. McGhee, P.E. Rx: Laughter. *RN Magazine*, July, 1998, 50–53.

116. Bittman, B., et al. SMILE: Subjective Multidimensional Interactive Laughter Evaluation. Computer software program (for Windows 3.1 or 95). To order, contact Touchstar Productions, 800–759–1294.

117. Dreher, D. Mind-body interventions for surgery: Evidence and exigency. *Advances in Mind-Body Medicine*, 1998, 14, 207–222.

118. Mumford, E., et al. The effects of psychological intervention on recovery from surgery and heart attacks: An analysis of the literature. *American Journal of Public Health*, 1982, 72, 141–151.

119. Devine, E.C. Effect of psychoeducational care for adult surgical patients: A meta-analysis of 191 studies. *Patient Education and Counseling*, 1992, 19, 129–142.

120. Devine, E.C. & Cook, T.D. Clinical and cost-savings effects of psychoeducational interventions with surgical patients: A meta-analysis. *Research in Nursing and Health*, 1986, 9, 89–105.

121. Dreher, 1998.

122. Melnechuk, 1988.

123. Holden-Lund, C. Effects of relaxation with guided imagery on surgical stress and wound healing. *Research in Nursing and Health*, 1988, 11, 235–244.

124. Rotton, J. & Shats, M. Effects of state humor, expectancies and choice on post-surgical mood and self-medication: A field experiment. *Journal of Applied Social Psychology,* 1996, 26, 1775–1794.

125. Adams & McGuire, 1986.

Chapter 3

1. Martin, R.A., & Lefcourt, H.M. Sense of humor as a moderator of the relation between stressors and moods. *Journal of Personality and Social Psychology,* 1983, 45, 1313–1324.

2. Masten, A. Humor and competence in school-aged children. *Child Development,* 1986, 57, 461–473.

3. Kobasa, S.C. Stressful life events, personality and health: An inquiry into hardiness. *Journal of Personality and Social Psychology,* 1979, 37, 1–11.

   Schaffer, M. *Life after Stress.* NY: Plenum, 1982.

4. Lipson, J.G. & Koehler, S.L. The psychiatric emergency room: Staff subculture. *Issues in Mental Health Nursing,* 1986, 8, 237–246.

5. Robinson, V. *Humor and the Health Professions.* Thorofare, NJ: Slack, 1991.

6. Johnson, W. To the ones left behind. *American Journal of Nursing,* 1985 (August), p. 936.

7. Palmer, C.E. A note about paramedics' strategies for dealing with death and dying. *Journal of Occupational Psychology,* 1983, 56, 83–86.

8. Herrman, J.D. Sudden death and the police officer. *Issues in Comprehensive Pediatric Nursing,* 1989, 12, 327–332.

9. Durham, T.W., et al. The psychological impact of disaster on rescue personnel. *Annals of Emergency Medicine,* 1985, 14, 664–668.

10. Rosenberg, L. A qualitative investigation of the use of humor by emergency personnel as a strategy for coping with stress. *Journal of Emergency Nursing,* 1991, 17, 197–203.

11. Burkle, F.M. Coping with stress under conditions of disaster refugee care. *Military Medicine,* 1983 (Oct.), 148–800–803.

12. Ritz, S.E. Survivor humor and disaster nursing. In K. Buxman (Ed.), *Humor and Nursing,* in press.

13. Farberow, N.L., & Frederick, C.J. *Training Manual for Human Service Workers in Major Disasters.* National Institute of Health, DHHS Publication (ADM), 90–538.

14. Ritz, S. Lighten up, seriously! *Laughing Matters,* 1993, 9 (#2), 47–52.

15. Weinrich, S., et al. Nurses respond to Hurricane Hugo victims' disaster stress. *Archives of Psychiatric Nursing,* 1990, 4, 195–205.

16. Coffee, G. *Beyond Survival.* New York: Putnam, 1990, pp. 131–132.

17. Anderson, T. *Den of Lyons.* New York: Crown, 1993.

18. Victoroff, D. New approaches to the psychology of humor. *Impact of Society on Science,* 1969, 19, 291–298.

19. Obrdlik, A.J. "Gallows humor"—A sociological phenomenon. *American Journal of Sociology,* 1942, 47, 709–716.

20. Nevo, O., & Levine, J. Jewish humor strikes again: The outburst of humor in Israel during the Gulf war. *Humor: International Journal of Humor Research,* 1993.

21. Palmer, L. The nurses of Vietnam, still wounded. *New York Times Magazine,* Nov. 7, 1993, pp. 36–43, 68, 72–73.

22. Bizi, S., et al. Humor and coping with stress: A test under real-life conditions. *Personality and Individual Differences*, 1988, 9, 951–956.

23. Glenn, N.D., & Weaver, C.N. The contribution of marital happiness to global happiness. *Journal of Marriage and the Family*, 1981, 43, 161–168.

24. Sarason, I.G., & Sarason, B. (Eds.) *Social Support: Theory, Research, and Application.* The Hague: Nijhoff, 1985.

25. Lauer, R.H., et al., The long-term marriage: Perceptions of stability and satisfaction. *International Journal of Aging and Human Development*, 1990, 31, 189–195.

26. Ziv, A., & Gadish, O. Humor and marital satisfaction. *Journal of Social Psychology*, 1989, 129, 759–768.

27. Rust, J., & Goldstein, J.H. Humor in marital adjustment. *Humor: International Journal of Humor Research,* 1989, 2, 217–224.

28. Jacobs, E. The functions of humor in marital adjustment. *Dissertation Abstracts,* 1985, 46 (5-B), 1688.

29. Lefcourt, H. M. , & Martin, R. A. *Humor and Life Stress: Antidote to Adversity.* New York: Springer-Verlag, 1986.

Step 2

1. Angier, N. The purpose of playful frolics: Training for adulthood. *The New York Times,* Oct. 20, 1992.

2. McGhee, P. E. Development of the creative aspects of humor. In P.E. McGhee & A.C. Chapman (Eds.), *Children's Humour.* Chichester, England: Wiley, 1980.

3. Ziv, A. Using humor to develop creative thinking. In P.E. McGhee (Ed.), *Humor and Children's Development: A Guide to Practical Applications.* New York: Haworth, 1989.

4. Bryant, J., & Zillmann, D. Using humor to promote learning in the classroom. In P.E. McGhee (Ed.), 1989.

Step 3

1. Levenson, R.W., et al. Voluntary facial action generates emotion-specific autonomic nervous system activity. *Psychophysiology,* 1990, 27, 363–384.

2. Santibanez, H., & Bloch, S. A qualitative analysis of emotional effector patterns and their feedback. *Pavlovian Journal of Biological Science,* 1986, 21, 108–116.

3. Muller, R. *The World Joke Book.* New York: Amity House, 1988.

Step 4

1. Ziv, A. Using humor to develop creative thinking. In P. E. McGhee (Ed.), *Humor and Children's Development: A Guide to Practical Applications.* New York: Haworth, 1989.

Step 5

1. John, G. The warmth of the unlikely. *The Christian Science Monitor,* Aug. 6, 1993, p. 16.

Step 7

1. Retzinger, S. The resentment process: Videotape studies. *Psychoanalytic Psychology,* 1985, 2, 129–151.

   Prerost, F.J., & Brewer, R.E. Humor content preferences and the relief of experimentally aroused aggression. *Journal of Social Psychology,* 1977, 103, 225–231.

2. Yovetich, N.A., et al. Benefits of humor in reduction of threat-induced anxiety. *Psychological Reports,* 1990, 66, 51–58.

3. Nezu, A.M., et al. Sense of humor as a moderator of the relation between stressful events and psychological distress: A prospective analysis. *Journal of Personality and Social Psychology,* 1988, 54, 520–525.

4. White, S., & Winzelberg, A. Laughter and stress. *Humor: International Journal of Humor Research,* 1992.

5. Aiello, J.R., et al. How funny is crowding, anyway? Effects of room size, group size, and the introduction of humor. *Basic and Applied Social Psychology,* 1983, 4, 193–207.

6. Martin, R.A., & Lefcourt, H.M. Sense of humor as a moderator of the relation between stressors and moods. *Journal of Personality and Social Psychology,* 1983, 45, 1313–1324.

   Labbott, S.M., & Martin, R.B. The stress-moderating effects of weeping and humor. *Journal of Human Stress,* 1987, Winter, 159–164.

7. Lefcourt, H.M., & Martin, R.A. *Humor and Life Stress: Antidote to Adversity.* New York: Springer-Verlag, 1986.

8. Caesar, S. Comments made at the Power of Humor and Play Conference, Anaheim, 1988.

9. Nezu, et al., 1988.

   Danzer, A. J., et al. Effect of exposure to humorous stimuli on induced depression. *Psychological Reports,* 1990, 66, 1027–1036.

10. Nezu, et al., 1988.

11. Meadowcraft, J.M., & Zillmann, D. Women's comedy preferences during the menstrual cycle. *Communication Research,* 1987, 14, 204–218.

12. Schmitt, N. Patients' perception of laughter in a rehabilitation hospital. *Rehabilitation Nursing,* 1990, 15 (No. 3), 143–146.

13. Bizi, S., et al. Humor and coping with stress: A test under real-life conditions. *Personality and Individual Differences,* 1988, 9, 951–956.

14. Wooten, P. Effect of humor training for health professionals. Paper presented at 8th International Conference on Humor, 1991.

15. Justice, B. *Who Gets Sick: How Beliefs, Moods, and Thoughts Affect Your Health.* Los Angeles: Tarcher, 1987, p. 307.

16. Cousins, N. *Head First: The Biology of Hope.* New York: Dutton, 1989, p. 138.

17. Bombeck, E. *I Want to Grow Up, I Want to Grow Hair, I Want to Go to Boise.* New York: Harper & Row, 1989.

Pre-Test

The pre-test of your attitude, mood and sense of humor will provide you with 1) a good picture of your present sense of humor, including its strengths and weaknesses, 2) a basis for determining what aspects of your sense of humor you want to target for special effort, and 3) a base line for comparison with the post-test, so that you can determine how much you've gained by completing the 8-Step Program.

A separate test of your attitude (playful vs. serious) and mood (positive vs. negative) is provided, because your daily attitude and mood influence how easy it is to use your sense of humor when you need a good laugh. Once you've completed the pre-test, do not look at your answers until you've completed Step 8 and the post-test.

Peer/Spouse Rating

In addition to completing the pre-test yourself, ask two other people (or more) who know you well, and who have daily contact with you, to rate your sense of humor using the same pretest. Make photocopies of the pre-test and ask them to simply substitute your name where it says "I." You should be aware that there is a tendency for friends or colleagues to give you ratings that are higher than the way they actually perceive you. Mention this tendency to them, and ask them to rate you as honestly as possible. Otherwise, the information you get will be of little use to you. You should also be careful to rate yourself as honestly as possible. No one else will see your ratings, so rate yourself as you really are, not as you'd like to be.

Having other people rate you will give you a better picture of your current sense of humor. You'll be surprised to see that others may have a very different perception of your sense of humor than you do. Again, you can use this information to select specific steps of the program for extra attention.

One of the raters should be someone you work with—but make sure it's someone who will feel comfortable about rating you honestly. This should also be someone by whom you will not be offended if s/he rates you in a way that does not match your own view of yourself. If possible have two different people at work rate you.

If you are married, ask your spouse to rate you. If his/her ratings differ from yours, be careful not to allow this to generate discord. Use the differences as a starting point for a discussion of why s/he sees you differently than you see yourself.

Assessing Your Sense of Humor

Use the 7-point scale provided just below each question to answer that question. In the space to the left of each item, indicate the extent to which you agree with the statement by writing a 1, 2, 3, etc. in that space. Avoid the tendency to give what you consider a "good" answer. Be honest with yourself.

Playful/Serious Attitude

____ 1. I am in a serious frame of mind most of the time.

1	2	3	4	5	6	7
Strongly Agree		Mildly Agree		Mildly Disagree		Strongly Disagree

____ 2. I am a very spontaneous person.

1	2	3	4	5	6	7
Strongly Disagree		Mildly Disagree		Mildly Agree		Strongly Agree

____ 3. I think it's important to always adopt a serious demeanor at work.

1	2	3	4	5	6	7
Strongly Agree		Mildly Agree		Mildly Disagree		Strongly Disagree

____ 4. I have a lot of fun in my life.

1	2	3	4	5	6	7
Strongly Disagree		Mildly Disagree		Mildly Agree		Strongly Agree

____ 5. I prefer friends who are generally pretty serious.

1	2	3	4	5	6	7
Strongly Agree		Mildly Agree		Mildly Disagree		Strongly Disagree

____ 6. I prefer spending time with people who are good at what they do, but know how to have fun and enjoy life.

1	2	3	4	5	6	7
Strongly Disagree		Mildly Disagree		Mildly Agree		Strongly Agree

____ 7. I get annoyed by people who are playful at work.

1	2	3	4	5	6	7
Strongly Agree		Mildly Agree		Mildly Disagree		Strongly Disagree

____ 8. I often adopt a playful attitude in everyday life.

1	2	3	4	5	6	7
Strongly Disagree		Mildly Disagree		Mildly Agree		Strongly Agree

____ Total PSA score (add items 1–8)

Positive/Negative Mood

_____ 1. I would describe my current outlook on life as

1	2	3	4	5	6	7
Very Pessimistic		Pessimistic		Optimistic		Very Optimistic

_____ 2. These days, my typical mood is

1	2	3	4	5	6	7
Very Negative		Negative		Positive		Very Positive

_____ 3. These days, I am generally

1	2	3	4	5	6	7
Very Sad		Sad		Happy		Very Happy

_____ 4. I have a lot of joy in my life.

1	2	3	4	5	6	7
Strongly Disagree		Mildly Disagree		Mildly Agree		Strongly Agree

_____ 5. I often get very frustrated on my job.

1	2	3	4	5	6	7
Strongly Agree		Mildly Agree		Mildly Disagree		Strongly Disagree

_____ 6. I am often depressed.

1	2	3	4	5	6	7
Strongly Agree		Mildly Agree		Mildly Disagree		Strongly Disagree

_____ 7. I am often anxious.

1	2	3	4	5	6	7
Strongly Agree		Mildly Agree		Mildly Disagree		Strongly Disagree

_____ 8. I am often angry.

1	2	3	4	5	6	7
Strongly Agree		Mildly Agree		Mildly Disagree		Strongly Disagree

_____ Total PNM score (add items 1–8)

Sense of Humor Scale

Use the 7-point scale provided here to answer the rest of the items below. Again, avoid the tendency to give what you consider a "good" answer. Be honest with yourself.

1	2	3	4	5	6	7
Strongly Disagree		Mildly Disagree		Mildly Agree		Strongly Agree

Enjoyment of Humor

_____ 1. I generally look for sit coms or other funny programs to watch on TV.

_____ 2. When I pick up magazines, I generally look at the cartoons in them first.

_____ 3. When I go to the movies, my preference is generally to see a good comedy.

____ 4. It is important for me to have a lot of humor in my life.
____ Total EH score (add items 1–4)

Laughter

____ 5. I have a good belly laugh many times each day.
____ 6. I have a heartier, more robust laugh than most people.
____ 7. I feel comfortable laughing, even when others aren't.
____ 8. One or both of my parents laughed a lot when I was growing up.
____ Total L score (add items 5–8)

Verbal Humor

____ 9. I often tell jokes.
____ 10. I often tell funny stories.
____ 11. I often create my own spontaneous puns.
____ 12. I often make other spontaneous witty remarks (other than 9–11).
____ Total VH score (add items 9–12)

Finding Humor in Everyday Life

____ 13. I often find humor in things that happen at work.
____ 14. I often find humor in things that happen at home.
____ 15. I often find humor in things that happen outside of work & family settings.
____ 16. I often share with others the funny incidents I observe, or that happen to me.
____ Total FHEL score (add items 13–16)

Laughing at Yourself

____ 17. I have no trouble poking fun at my physical imperfections.
____ 18. I often find humor in my own embarrassing incidents or personal blunders.
____ 19. I often share with others the humor in my blunders/embarrassing incidents.
____ 20. I find it easy to laugh when I am the butt of the joke.
____ Total LY score (add items 17–20)

Humor Under Stress

____ 21. My sense of humor rarely abandons me under stress.
____ 22. I often use my sense of humor to control the effect of stress on my mood.
____ 23. I often use humor at work to reduce stress and stay effective on the job.
____ 24. My sense of humor is my most effective tool in coping with life stress.
____ Total HUS score (add items 21–24)
____ Total Sense of Humor score (add items 1–24)

This is your Humor Quotient. Lowest possible score = 24. Highest = 168. Your goal should be to score somewhere between 140–168. For the Playful/Serious Attitude and Positive/Negative Mood Scales, your goal should be to raise your score up to 50 or higher.

Post-Test

The post-test is identical to the pre-test. It should be completed only after you've completed all 8 steps of the program. Use the past few weeks as the basis for determining your rating of each item. Do not look at your pre-test answers before completing the post-test. You may notice a tendency to try to remember how you rated each item the first time, so that you can be sure to mark it a little higher this time. Doing this will simply make it more difficult to see how much progress you've made. So you should again rate yourself as honestly as you can. Ask the same people who rated you on the pre-test to do so again using the post-test. They should also be careful to avoid rating you higher just because they know you've been working at improving your sense of humor. Remind them to simply substitute your name for "I." Do not allow them to see their pre-test ratings of you until after they've completed the post-test.

Assessing Your Sense of Humor

Use the 7-point scale provided just below each question to answer that question. In the space to the left of each item, indicate the extent to which you agree with the statement by writing a 1, 2, 3, etc. in that space. Avoid the tendency to give what you consider a "good" answer. Be honest with yourself.

Playful/Serious Attitude

_____ 1. I am in a serious frame of mind most of the time.

1	2	3	4	5	6	7
Strongly Agree		Mildly Agree		Mildly Disagree		Strongly Disagree

_____ 2. I am a very spontaneous person.

1	2	3	4	5	6	7
Strongly Disagree		Mildly Disagree		Mildly Agree		Strongly Agree

_____ 3. I think it's important to always adopt a serious demeanor at work.

1	2	3	4	5	6	7
Strongly Agree		Mildly Agree		Mildly Disagree		Strongly Disagree

_____ 4. I have a lot of fun in my life.

1	2	3	4	5	6	7
Strongly Disagree		Mildly Disagree		Mildly Agree		Strongly Agree

____ 5. I prefer friends who are generally pretty serious.

1	2	3	4	5	6	7
Strongly Agree		Mildly Agree		Mildly Disagree		Strongly Disagree

____ 6. I prefer spending time with people who are good at what they do, but know how to have fun and enjoy life.

1	2	3	4	5	6	7
Strongly Disagree		Mildly Disagree		Mildly Agree		Strongly Agree

____ 7. I get annoyed by people who are playful at work.

1	2	3	4	5	6	7
Strongly Agree		Mildly Agree		Mildly Disagree		Strongly Disagree

____ 8. I often adopt a playful attitude in everyday life.

1	2	3	4	5	6	7
Strongly Disagree		Mildly Disagree		Mildly Agree		Strongly Agree

____ Total PSA score (add items 1–8)

Positive/Negative Mood

____ 1. I would describe my current outlook on life as

1	2	3	4	5	6	7
Very Pessimistic		Pessimistic		Optimistic		Very Optimistic

____ 2. These days, my typical mood is

1	2	3	4	5	6	7
Very Negative		Negative		Positive		Very Positive

____ 3. These days, I am generally

1	2	3	4	5	6	7
Very Sad		Sad		Happy		Very Happy

____ 4. I have a lot of joy in my life.

1	2	3	4	5	6	7
Strongly Disagree		Mildly Disagree		Mildly Agree		Strongly Agree

____ 5. I often get very frustrated on my job.

1	2	3	4	5	6	7
Strongly Agree		Mildly Agree		Mildly Disagree		Strongly Disagree

____ 6. I am often depressed.

1	2	3	4	5	6	7
Strongly Agree		Mildly Agree		Mildly Disagree		Strongly Disagree

____ 7. I am often anxious.

1	2	3	4	5	6	7
Strongly Agree		Mildly Agree		Mildly Disagree		Strongly Disagree

_____ 8. I am often angry.

1	2	3	4	5	6	7
Strongly Agree		Mildly Agree		Mildly Disagree		Strongly Disagree

_____ Total PNM score (add items 1–8)

Sense of Humor Scale

Use the 7-point scale provided here to answer the rest of the items below. Again, avoid the tendency to give what you consider a "good" answer. Be honest with yourself.

1	2	3	4	5	6	7
Strongly Disagree		Mildly Disagree		Mildly Agree		Strongly Agree

Enjoyment of Humor

_____ 1. I generally look for sit coms or other funny programs to watch on TV.
_____ 2. When I pick up magazines, I generally look at the cartoons in them first.
_____ 3. When I go to the movies, my preference is generally to see a good comedy.
_____ 4. It is important for me to have a lot of humor in my life.
_____ Total EH score (add items 1–4)

Laughter

_____ 5. I have a good belly laugh many times each day.
_____ 6. I have a heartier, more robust laugh than most people.
_____ 7. I feel comfortable laughing, even when others aren't.
_____ 8. One or both of my parents laughed a lot when I was growing up.
_____ Total L score (add items 5–8)

Verbal Humor

_____ 9. I often tell jokes.
_____ 10. I often tell funny stories.
_____ 11. I often create my own spontaneous puns.
_____ 12. I often make other spontaneous witty remarks (other than 9–11).
_____ Total VH score (add items 9–12)

Finding Humor in Everyday Life

_____ 13. I often find humor in things that happen at work.
_____ 14. I often find humor in things that happen at home.
_____ 15. I often find humor in things that happen outside of work & family settings.
_____ 16. I often share with others the funny incidents I observe, or that happen to me.
_____ Total FHEL score (add items 13–16)

Laughing at Yourself

_____ 17. I have no trouble poking fun at my physical imperfections.
_____ 18. I often find humor in my own embarrassing incidents or personal blunders.
_____ 19. I often share with others the humor in my blunders/embarrassing incidents.

_____ 20. I find it easy to laugh when I am the butt of the joke.
_____ Total LY score (add items 17–20)

Humor Under Stress

_____ 21. My sense of humor rarely abandons me under stress.
_____ 22. I often use my sense of humor to control the effect of stress on my mood.
_____ 23. I often use humor at work to reduce stress and stay effective on the job.
_____ 24. My sense of humor is my most effective tool in coping with life stress.
_____ Total HUS score (add items 21–24)
_____ Total Sense of Humor score (add items 1–24)

This is your Humor Quotient. Lowest possible score = 24. Highest = 168. Your goal should be to score somewhere between 140–168. For the Playful/Serious Attitude and Positive/Negative Mood Scales, your goal should be to raise your score up to 50 or higher.

Comparison of Pre-Test and Post-Test Scores

	Pre-Test	Post-Test	Difference
Playful/Serious Attitude	_____	_____	_____
Positive/Negative Mood	_____	_____	_____
Enjoyment of Humor	_____	_____	_____
Laughter	_____	_____	_____
Verbal Humor	_____	_____	_____
Finding Humor in Everyday Life	_____	_____	_____
Laughing at Yourself	_____	_____	_____
Humor Under Stress	_____	_____	_____

Area of greatest gain:

Area of least gain:

Areas you'd like to continue to improve:

What They Say About Paul McGhee

Comments by Dr. McGhee's clients

Corporate

*"Thank you for offering such a memorable program here at the corporate headquarters of Bristol-Myers Squibb. **Even after several weeks, I still hear employees talking about your presentation** and your suggestions for reducing stress."*   (Gail Rosselot, Coordinator of Health Promotion, Bristol-Myers Squibb)

*"We were apprehensive about whether or not we had a funny bone, but **you really cracked us up!**"* (Laura Davis, Quality Committee Chair, The CIT Group)

*"Paul, I cannot thank you enough for your hilarious, energetic presentation on using laughter as a stress management tool. **Every member who attended the meeting has taken the time to express not only how much they enjoyed your presentation, but also how valuable they felt your message** was to those of us on the 'firing line' every day."*   (Marie A. Cunningham, Board of Trustees, Building Owners and Managers Assn. of New Jersey)

*"**Your presentation was extremely helpful to our staff**. . . . We all have enjoyed the book [Health, Healing and the Amuse System] and many of us have taken your thoughtful concepts to heart, not only at work but in our everyday lives."*   (Dana Zerfas Butler, U.S. Department of Justice)

*"You showed us ways to lighten up on the job, which can be powerful tools in helping us all to sustain high levels of performance--even on our worst days. **I am sure your program will have a lasting impact on our group.**"*   (Sandy Ratcliffe, Asst. Manager of Conventions, Pfizer, Inc.)

*"Thank you so much for a wonderful presentation. As reflected in the attached evaluation composite, the audience loved your silliness and your emphasis on improving our daily lives through humor . . . **It truly was an enlightening and uplifting two hours.**"*   (Lila Gabriel, Training & Dev. Coord., Holmes Regional Corporate Educational Services)

*"**Spending an afternoon learning how to 'lighten up' proved to be a powerful tool** for all who attended. It certainly made our software conversion on January 4th go so much more smoothly from the 'stress level' perspective."*   (Scott R. Williams, Director of Procurement, Public Service Electricity & Gas Company)

"The audience was hysterical at both your words and animation. . . . Your presentation was excellent and I would be happy to recommend you to any group. . ." (Earl S. Glover, Executive Director, Arkansas Ready Mixed Concrete Assn.)

"Everyone at the meeting really enjoyed your program. I have gotten a considerable amount of positive feedback from the leaders." (J. Marie Taylor, Director of Customer Service and Quality, AlliedSignal, Inc.)

"Your ability to teach people to add humor to their lives, in order to cope with stress on the job, was invigorating. Everyone that attended your workshop seemed to leave with a smile on their face. We heard from many of the participants that they had not had such a good laugh in a long time." (Carolyn DeCarbo, Vice President Elect, New Jersey School Food Service Assn.)

"Our president . . . said, 'not only is he an entertaining speaker, but his message is profound.' . . . You were definitely worth waiting for." (Alice Blomquist, Wellness and Human Performance Division, William Rainey Harper College)

"I was particularly impressed with the way in which you wove information on the jobs of our staff into the presentation. This lent credibility and relevance to the program." (Richard J. Albano, Director of Special Education, Lower Pioneer Valley Educational Collaborative)

"Everyone was still talking about the session on Monday morning." (Elizabeth J. Clapham, Manager of Recruitment Benefits, Visions Federal Credit Union)

"Paul, you've helped us on the road to lighten up, which will improve morale and productivity." (Richard Hamrick, Senior V. P. of Finance & Administration, Miller Enterprises, Inc.)

"You've helped make our industry's 101st Annual Convention a big success!" (Robert O. Lehrman, President, Community Bankers Association of New York State)

"Your presentation received the highest scores of the day. You certainly were a hit with the audience." (Joan Wainwright, Conference Chair, New Jersey Healthcare Public Relations & Marketing Assn.)

"We just wanted to let you know that your keynote session at our department meeting was a huge success. We had been looking for a different learning experience with a focus on creating a healthier work environment. Your program on the use of humor to reduce stress and improve productivity really fit the bill." (Mary Anne Robinson & Marty Morehouse, Corporate HR/Communications, Allied Signal, Inc.)

"Excellent way to start the conference . . . . Original, informative and entertaining." (Dorothy M. Klein, Government Finance Officers' Assn. of New Jersey)

"You left a lasting impression in the minds of our conference participants, and they will be talking about your insightful views of the work world for years to come." (Jim Morford, President, & Linda Doherty, Vice President, New Jersey Food Council)

"Your method of presentation of these fundamental [humor] skills kept the audience's attention for the entire hour." (John A. Kennedy, CEO, Arkansas Workers' Compensation Commission)

Healthcare

"I have yet to meet anyone who attended your keynote speech who didn't rave over your presentation. . . . But now you have created a dilemma for the 1999 Conference Committee. **How can we ever top your 1998 keynote presentation?"** (Daisy Horn, Executive Director, New Jersey Assn. of Community Providers)

"The returned evaluations have been nothing short of raves." (Frank Dimaiolo, Chairman of Professional Education Committee, American Cancer Society)

"Your talk, 'Humor as Survival Training for Office Nurses,' was more than we could have expected. . . You were able to give practical advice they could take back to the office and put into practice. **The feedback from participants was glowing.** *We look forward to a repeat performance in the future!"* (Mary Ann Jones, Founder, American Assn. of Office Nurses)

"The entire audience extremely enjoyed your presentation. Below are a few of their remarks. 'This was wonderfully magnificent. Absolutely great and I will incorporate it into my practice and life.' **'Excellent!' 'Something like this should be included in every conference. You could not have chosen a better speaker.'** *'Paul McGhee was wonderful!' 'Excellent presenter. Very helpful information, presented with a lasting impression.' 'Marvelous!!' 'I feel energized.' 'Outstanding!'"* (Carol A. Jones, Co-Chair, Allied Health Committee, American Academy of Allergy, Asthma, & Immunology)

"You provided . . . a wonderful evening of entertainment and a keen insight into the benefit of humor and laughter in the workplace. **The response . . . was overwhelmingly positive."** (Peter W. Diestel, Vice President, Association of Healthcare Executives of New Jersey)

"The best program on this topic yet! *The program should be mandatory for all employees."* (Charlain Andres, Education Coordinator, Carrier Foundation)

"Your presentation was not only informative, but much enjoyed by all in attendance. **My only regret is that I did not have it videotaped . . ."** (G. Gordon McCormick, M.D., Conference Chairman, Spohn Health System)

"A tremendous program and presentation! For 90 minutes, Dr. McGhee had our attendees literally 'rolling on the floor.' *I have now heard Dr. McGhee three times, and each time he brings a fresh and exciting message."* (Forest Eichmann, Past President, New Jersey - National Emergency Number Assn.)

" You connected with the staff and customized the content to our organizational needs and issues. *Participants left the programs feeling energized and positive, as well as seeing humor as a critical skill to develop in the workplace."* (Kimberly McNally, Manager of Educational Services, Valley Medical Center)

"You were great!! There have been many comments made about your [National Cancer Survivors' Day] presentation; they were all positive and glowing. The attendee's commented on your humor, warmth and your 'belly laugh.'" (Carol Rogers, FNP, Lourdes Hosp. Regional Cancer Center)

"Participants were stopping us hours after you left expressing how much they enjoyed your presentation." (Maria R. Anan, Kessler Institute for Rehabilitation)

*"When I went to the conference, I was feeling drained and exhausted from six months of chemo-therapy and two months of radiation. My body was aching and so were my spirits. . . . You got us laughing! Your polished presentation as a stand-up comic with a message had us all laughing with such gusto, and I could feel myself being slowly drawn out of my apathy into a renewed sense of energy and joy. . . . **After an hour of real laughter, I could feel the weight being lifted off my chest** . . . and I began to look around the room with a new sense of enthusiasm and interest."*   (Adele Fuller, cancer patient)

"Your seminar on laughter and humor . . . was not only totally enjoyable but gave us the means to deal with stress and conflict in our daily lives. I am still getting comments from people who say they 'laughed so hard it hurt.'"   (Anne Sullivan, Training Coordinator, Franklin Delano Roosevelt VA Hospital)

*"Of all our presenters, **you received the greatest number of 'excellent' evaluations.**"*
(Estere Pilgrim, Managing Director, The Wellness Project)

"Your presentation was a huge success! *. . . all in attendance thoroughly enjoyed your presentation and gained valuable humor skills and ideas to utilize in their career as well as in their own lives."*   (Laura R. Schilpp, Director of Membership, Home Health Assembly of New Jersey)

*"Your presentation entitled 'Using humor to cope in Alzheimer's Disease caregiving' was **most inspiring and extremely helpful** to all who attended that day."*   (Fred Brand, Manager of Family Service Programs, Alzheimer's Assn.)

*"Thank you so much for the energizing and enlightening program you shared with the Living with Cancer Family Support Groups. Many of the participants shared that the 'remedy' of laughter, which seems so difficult to find during the course of cancer treatment, **has been used many times since your presentation to help lighten otherwise dismal events.**"*   (Gayle Joannides, Living with Cancer Coordinator, St. Clares Riverside Hospital)

*"A very sincere 'thank you' for a wonderful program. The audience was not only impressed by your knowledge, but also by your warm, witty and genuine style. **I know you positively impacted many lives, and I feel that for many, the results will be long-lasting.**"*   (Susan Carroll, Manager of Community Relations, University Behavioral Center)

*"You did an excellent job of relating your message to the emergency management community . . . . **You made us look good!**"*   (Elizabeth Armstrong, Executive Director, National Coordinating Council on Emergency Management)

*"We notice that many of our employees are now more aware of how humor can play a most important role in everyday activities. **Your presentation showed us the importance of humor in our personal lives, as well as in our interaction with our patients and their families.**"*   (Ruth Laing, Assistant Vice President, Muhlenberg Regional Medical Center)

*"Who would think that so much humor could be found in head injury. **We'll be laughing for months**, not only from the memories of your message, but from the **lessons you taught us about the value of fun and laughter in the recovery process.**"*   (Elynor Kazuk, Executive Director, Florida Head Injury Foundation)

*"Remember me? I was the handicapped lady that was talking to you. **I don't know what you did, but you changed my life.** I look at life differently now, where I can do anything I put my mind to."* (Maureen Maher, hospital patient)

Partial Corporate Client List

Paul McGhee, PhD

www.LaughterRemedy.com

AICPA (American Inst. of Certified Public Acct's)
Apartment Assn. of New Jersey
AT&T
Arkansas Ready-Made Concrete Assn.
BASF Corporation
Bristol-Myers Squibb
Canadian Institute of Chartered Accountants
CIT Group
Community Bankers Assn. of New York State
Farm Credit Services of Iowa
Financial Management Services Users Group
Food Services Assn. of New Jersey
Good Housekeeping Institute
Grey Advertising
Healthcare Marketing & Planning Society
Hoffman-LaRoche
International Facilities Management Assn.
ITT
McNees, Wallace & Nurick (Atty's at Law)
Merrill Lynch
Miller Enterprises, Inc.
New Hampshire Assn. of Counties
New Jersey Natural Gas
New York State Comptrollers Office
NYNEX
Pfizer, Inc.
Public Service, Electricity & Gas (NJ)
Sandoz Pharmaceuticals
Tax Collectors & Treasurers Assn.
United States Dressage Federation
Visions Federal Credit Union
Weavexx Inc.
West Virginia Agricultural Extension Service
Women in Sales Association
Xerox Corporation

American Cyanamid
Assn. of Life Underwriters of New Jersey
Automotive Fleet & Leasing Assn.
Arkansas Workmans Comp. Commission
Blue Cross Blue Shield
Building Owners and Managers Assn.
Chesapeake Area Society of Hosp. Engineers
Commercial Law League of America
Duncan Aviation
Female Executives, New Jersey Assn. of
Food Council of New Jersey
General Motors
Government Finance Offers Assn. of NJ
Health Information Management Assn.
Healthcare Public Relations & Marketing Assn.
International EAP Assn.
International Union of Electrical Workers
John Hancock Insurance
Merck & Co.
MetLife
National Assn. of Home Builders
New Jersey Assn. of Female Executives
New Jersey Personnel Assn.
Novartis
Omaha Public Power District
Prudential Insurance
RE/MAX of Georgia
State Farm Insurance
United States Department of Justice
United States Navy
Warner Lambert Co.
Weil, Gotshal & Manges (Atty's at Law)
Women Business Owners, NJ Assn. of
Worksite Health Promotion Conference

Partial Health Care Client List

Paul McGhee, PhD

www.LaughterRemedy.com

American Academy of Allergy, Asthma
    & Immunology
American Assn. of Office Nurses
American Heart Assn.
American Radiology Nurses Assn. (NJ)
Assn. of Community Mental Health Centers
Assn. of Health Care Facilities
Assn. of Mental Health Administrators
Community Health Care Assn. (NY)
Delaware Valley Clinical Lab Management Assn.
Florida Head Injury Association
Garden State Health Education Council
Health Care Quality Professionals of NJ
Home Health Assembly (NJ)
Keystone Health Promotion Conference (PA)
Licensed Practical Nurse Assn. of NJ
Mental Health Professionals (NJ)
Mid Atlantic Career Counseling Assn.
National Assn. of Health Care Recruitment
    (Mid-Atlantic Reg.)
National Wellness Conference (WI)
NJ Coalition on Disabilities, Alcoholism
    & Drug Abuse
New Jersey Health Care Public Relations
    & Marketing Assn.
Oncology Nursing Society (NJ)
Red Cross
Rutgers School of Alcohol & Drug Studies
North Carolina School of Alcohol & Drug Studies
Visiting Nurses Association (NJ)
Worksite Health Promotion Conference (DE)

American Assn. of Critical Care Nurses

American Cancer Society
American Nephrology Nurses Assn.
Assn. of Community Care Providers (NJ)
Assn. of Diploma Schools of
    Professional Nursing (NJ)
Bays Medical Society (FL)
Critical Care Nursing Assn. (NY)
Desert High Wellness Conference (NM)
Framingham School of Nursing (MA)
Health Care Executives of NJ
Health Promotion Council (NY)
Indiana University Cancer Center
Lakeshore Wellness Conference (IA)
Maine Health Care Assn.
Middle Atlantic Health Congress
Multiple Sclerosis Society
National Assn. for Practical Nurse Education
    & Service
New Jersey Assn. of Public Relations
    & Marketing
New Jersey League of Nursing
Northwest Wellness Conf. for Seniors (OR)
Oncology/Hematology Associates (IL)
Orlando Cancer Center
Rehabilitation Association (NJ)
Seaside Health Promotion Conf. (OR)
Supportive Care (TX)
Women in Health Care Admin. (NJ)

Dr. McGhee has also provided many programs for hospitals across the country.

www.LaughterRemedy.com

If you would like to keep up with the latest developments related to the physical and mental health benefits of humor, and the growing trend to bring your sense of humor to the workplace, check Dr. McGhee's web site every month. He writes two monthly articles on the Internet. Once into his site, click on **"Humor In the Workplace"** to read about issues related to humor on the job. Click on **"Humor Your Tumor"** to read more about humor in connection with cancer and other illnesses. New articles appear each month. You can also read prior months' articles by clicking on the archive listing in the web site.

If you are a corporate or healthcare manager, you can help your staff begin strengthening their ability to reap the many benefits of learning to lighten up on the job by using the content of these monthly articles as a basis for discussion in meetings. If you are a nurse, or other healthcare professional who has regular contact with patients/clients, encouraging them to read the articles at **www.LaughterRemedy.com** will help them realize the importance that humor can have in their lives and learn to use humor to cope with the stress experienced during their current health crisis.

Remember, they who laugh, last.

ORDER FORM
for
Health, Healing and the Amuse System: Humor as Survival Training

# copies ordered	1–10	11–25	26–40	41+
Discount	0	25%	40%	50%
Price per copy	$20	$15	$12	$10

Add $3.00 shipping and handling for the first book and $1 each for additional books. For quantity orders (10 books or more) please call for shipping and handling charges.

# Copies	ISBN #	Price per Copy	Cost

Shipping: _____

Total Enclosed _____

Call 1-800-228-0810 to order by telephone or Fax 1-800-772-9165. Prepayment is required.

☐ Check enclosed
☐ Charge my account:

☐ Master Card   ☐ American Express   ☐ Visa

MC Bank # | | | | Exp. Date ___/___/___

Account # | | | | | | | | | | | | | | | | | | | |

Signature_____

(required for all charges)

Name_____

Phone (_____)_____

Address_____

_____

City/State/Zip _____

Please make check payable to:

Kendall/Hunt Publishing Company
4050 Westmark Drive
Dubuque, Iowa 52004-1840